SEP - 6 2002

Advances in
Clinical Child
Psychology

Advances in

Clinical Child

Psychology

Volume 1

Edited by

Benjamin B. Lahey

University of Georgia, Athens

and

Alan E. Kazdin

Pennsylvania State University, University Park

Plenum Press · New York and London

ISBN 0-306-36281-3

© 1977 Plenum Press, New York
A Division of Plenum Publishing Corporation
227 West 17th Street, New York, N.Y. 10011

Printed in the United States of America

*This series is dedicated to
the children of the world, especially*
MEGAN, EDWARD, ERIN, and NICOLE

Contributors

Teodoro Ayllon — *Georgia State University, Atlanta, Georgia 30303*

Bruce Balow — *Department of Psychoeducational Studies, University of Minnesota, Minneapolis, Minnesota 55455*

Anthony R. Ciminero — *University of Georgia, Athens, Georgia 30601*

Melinda L. Combs — *Children's Orthopedic Hospital and Medical Center and University of Washington, Seattle, Washington. Present address: Children's Behavioral Services, 6171 W. Charleston Blvd., Las Vegas, Nevada 89102*

Ronald S. Drabman — *University of Mississippi School of Medicine, Jackson, Mississippi 38677*

Donna M. Gelfand — *Department of Psychology, University of Utah, Salt Lake City, Utah 87112*

Donald P. Hartmann — *Department of Psychology, University of Utah, Salt Lake City, Utah 87112*

Karen D. Kirkland — *Department of Psychology, University of Missouri at Columbia, Columbia, Missouri 65201*

Robert L. Koegel — *University of California at Santa Barbara and Camarillo Behavior Development and Learning Center, Santa Barbara, California 93106*

Joel F. Lubar   *Department of Psychology, University of Tennessee, Knoxville, Tennessee 37916*

George A. Rekers   *Fuller Theological Seminary, Graduate School of Psychology, Pasadena, California 91101, and University of California at Los Angeles, Los Angeles, California 90032. Present address: Department of Psychiatry, University of Florida, Gainesville, Florida 32610*

Arnold Rincover   *Department of Psychology, University of North Carolina at Greensboro and H. W. Kendall Center, Greensboro, North Carolina 27412*

Brenda L. Roper   *Department of Psychology, University of Utah, Salt Lake City, Utah 87112*

Michael S. Rosenbaum   *Georgia State University, Atlanta, Georgia 30601*

Rosalyn A. Rubin   *Department of Psychoeducational Studies, University of Minnesota, Minneapolis, Minnesota 55455*

Margaret N. Shouse   *School of Medicine, University of California at Los Angeles, Los Angeles, California 90032*

Diana Arezzo Slaby   *Children's Orthopedic Hospital and Medical Center and University of Washington, Seattle, Washington 98105*

Mark H. Thelen   *Department of Psychology, University of Missouri at Columbia, Columbia, Missouri 65201*

Preface

Psychologists have long been interested in the problems of children, but in the last 20 years this interest has increased dramatically. The intensified focus on clinical child psychology reflects an increased belief that many adult problems have their origin in childhood and that early treatment is often more effective than treatment at later ages, but it also seems to reflect an increased feeling that children are inherently important in their own right. As a result of this shift in emphasis, the number of publications on this topic has multiplied to the extent that even full-time specialists have not been able to keep abreast of all new developments. Researchers in the more basic fields of child psychology have a variety of annual publications and journals to integrate research in their areas, but there is a marked need for such an integrative publication in the applied segment of child and developmental psychology.

Advances in Clinical Child Psychology is a serial publication designed to bring together original summaries of the most important developments each year in the field. Each chapter is written by a key figure in an innovative area of research or practice or by an individual who is particularly well qualified to comment on a topic of major contemporary importance. Each author has followed the standard format in which his or her area of research was reviewed and the clinical implications of the studies were made explicit. The authors were encouraged to develop their topics with fewer restrictions than required by most publication outlets, however. As a result, the series allows authors to make "major statements" in their areas of expertise.

We are deeply indebted to our consulting editors and others who freely gave their assistance in the crucial task of choosing authors and topics. Specifically, we are appreciative of the special editorial contributions of Rex Forehand and Walter Isaac. Our greatest gratitude, of course, is extended to the authors, who made what we believe are truly significant contributions to clinical child psychology in this volume.

                                                        Benjamin B. Lahey

Athens, Georgia

                                                        Alan E. Kazdin

Stanford, California

Contents

An Evaluation of Alternative Modes of Child
Psychotherapy
*Donald P. Hartmann, Brenda L. Roper, and
Donna M. Gelfand*

1

Current Developments in the Behavioral
Assessment of Children
Anthony R. Ciminero and Ronald S. Drabman

2

The Behavioral Treatment of Disruption and *3*
Hyperactivity in School Settings
Teodoro Ayllon and Michael S. Rosenbaum

Perinatal Influences on the Behavior and Learning   *4*
Problems of Children
Rosalyn A. Rubin and Bruce Balow

Social-Skills Training with Children   *5*
Melinda L. Combs and Diana Arezzo Slaby

Use of Biofeedback in the Treatment of Seizure Disorders and Hyperactivity   6

Joel F. Lubar and Margaret N. Shouse

Assessment and Treatment of Childhood Gender
Problems
George A. Rekers

7

Uses of Modeling in Child Treatment 8
Karen D. Kirkland and Mark H. Thelen

Research on the Education of Autistic Children: Recent Advances and Future Directions 9
Arnold Rincover and Robert L. Koegel

The Prevention of Childhood Behavior Disorders   **10**
Donna M. Gelfand and Donald P. Hartmann

1 An Evaluation of Alternative Modes of Child Psychotherapy

DONALD P. HARTMANN,
BRENDA L. ROPER,
AND DONNA M. GELFAND

The increasing competition for child mental-health dollars, the related growing concern about accountability to funding agencies, and the demands of science all suggest the need for comprehensive outcome studies in which alternative modes of child psychotherapy are contrasted. Critical reviews of the child-psychotherapy literature indicate that the majority of existing comparative studies suffer from serious methodological flaws that prevent the studies from serving their intended function. The present chapter is therefore directed toward an examination of the major methodological issues in this field, which are organized under the domains of general design strategies, patient and treatment variables, choice of measures, follow-up assessments, and evaluation. Alternative strategies for the solution of methodological difficulties are discussed, and studies illustrating exemplary practices are pointed out. Cost–benefit or effectiveness analysis is discussed as a logical and necessary extension of traditional psychotherapy outcome-research. Finally, special attention is given to political problems associated with the conduct of comparative psychotherapy research in clinical settings.

1. Introduction

In contrast to earlier years, when the mental-health movement had to fight for the respect of society, the more recent situation has

DONALD P. HARTMANN, BRENDA L. ROPER, AND DONNA M. GELFAND • Department of Psychology, University of Utah, Salt Lake City, Utah.

been one of psychological services' "being oversold and unable to deliver" (Cowen & Zax, 1967, p. 12). This situation is in part attributable to the continued reliance on modes of treatment and service delivery of undemonstrated merit. Hobbs (1963) has summed up the situation in no uncertain terms: "Much of the practice of clinical psychology as well as psychiatry is obsolete" (p. 3). In a similar vein, Redl (1966) has maintained that the model of the "holy trinity" (psychiatrist, psychologist, and social worker) as a service delivery team is obsolete (p. 23). Its continuance is perhaps understandable, however, in light of the assertion of the Joint Commission on Mental Health of Children that the child mental-health system has been more concerned with the needs of the professionals providing the services than with the needs of the children being served (Report of the Joint Commission, 1973, p. 97).

The seriousness of the present situation is underscored when one considers several facts. Only a small portion of children thought to be in need of mental-health services are referred for treatment (Report of the Joint Commission, 1969). Of those for whom help has been sought, a significant number do not turn to mental-health professionals (Gurin, Veroff, & Feld, 1960). Of the children who are referred to mental-health professionals for assistance, most obtained no service beyond an evaluation and diagnosis (Rosen, Bahn, Shellow, & Bower, 1965; Norman, Rosen, & Bahn, 1962). The value of diagnosis alone (the most usual service) is especially debatable in light of the repeatedly stressed inadequacies of the classification schemes for childhood disorders (e.g., Clarizio & McCoy, 1976; Robins & O'Neal, 1969). The situation would not be quite so grim if one could at least be assured that the more seriously disturbed children were receiving treatment. However, just the converse is true in that the most disturbed children have typically received the least help (Clarizio & McCoy, 1976; Report of the Joint Commission, 1973). Moreover, those in areas of particularly high risk, such as the nation's poverty pockets, are largely without service facilities (Rosenthal & Levine, 1970).

An even more basic challenge confronts child mental-health workers in the lack of clear-cut empirical support for the two implicit assumptions that have provided much of the justification for treatment intervention with children. These two complementary assumptions have been termed the *continuity hypothesis* and the *intervention hypothesis* (Lewis, 1965). The continuity hypothesis states that behavioral disturbances in children are symptomatic of a continuing psychological process that may lead to adult disturbances. The intervention hypothesis states that therapeutic interventions enhance children's adjustment and thereby reduce the likelihood of adult disturbances. It has been maintained that both of these hypotheses lack convincing support (e.g., Levitt, 1971; Clarizio, 1968; Lewis, 1965; see Cowen, 1973, for a somewhat contrasting view).

Partly as a result of all these factors, traditional psychotherapeutic practices are increasingly being replaced by new technologies, such as the behavior therapies, family therapy, and community consultation (e.g., Kelly, Snowden, & Muñoz, 1977; Bergin & Suinn, 1975). The traditional mental-health deliverers—the psychiatrists, clinical psychologists, and social workers—have recently found themselves competing with paraprofessionals (e.g., Cowen, Trost, Lorion, Dorr, Izzo, & Isaacson, 1975), teachers (e.g., Hall & Copeland, 1972), and parents (e.g., Reisinger, Ora, & Frangia, 1976) as agents of change. No longer is psychotherapy (with children or adults) the exclusive purview of the selected few (see, e.g., Kiesler, 1971; Paul, 1969).

The fervor and conviction of the proponents of new treatment approaches, however, are unlikely to be a reliable guide for the effective allocation of the more than $4.3 billion expended annually for child mental health (Report of the Joint Commission, 1973). Legislatures and health, educational, and welfare agencies are increasingly concerned with hard data and are now frequently mandating "accountability" for child-oriented and other social-action programs (Wortman, 1975). The emphasis on comparative psychotherapy research is not exclusively an outgrowth of the fiscal concerns of funding agencies, however. Scientific considerations dictate a greater concern with the issues of the durability and generalization of treatment changes (e.g., Harris, 1975; Hartmann, 1972). Long-term follow-up studies are necessary to evaluate the self-regulatory and other generalized change-maintaining procedures being advocated (e.g., Gelfand & Hartmann, 1975, Chapter 9). The need for comparative research is particularly acute in the case of those techniques that, having attained a reasonably high level of technological sophistication, are now being prepared for large-scale dissemination (see, e.g., the program described by Patterson, Reid, Jones, & Conger, 1975).

2. The Reviews

Although comparative outcome-studies of child psychotherapy are still infrequent, their number has increased substantially during the past decade (Bergin & Suinn, 1975). Unfortunately, reviews of these more recent studies have not been entirely positive.

In his review of traditional group treatment of children, Kadushin (1974) concluded that "no evaluation studies of any of the family service agency group programs come within respectable range of meeting the requirements of scientific rigor" (p. 112). Segal (1972) reached a similar conclusion after reviewing social-work interventions with children and their families.

Reviews indicate that outcome studies of traditional individual psychotherapy with children fare little better. Heinicke and Strassman (1975) found only two comprehensive studies on long-term treatment of children that incorporated contrast groups in the design. In their commentary on the paucity of well-designed and well-implemented studies, Robins and O'Neal (1969) warned that "casual evaluation may be worse than none at all, since it may falsely confirm us in our habits or falsely overthrow our confidence in perfectly adequate techniques" (p. 803).

Outcome studies of the presumably more scientificially based behavioral programs also have not been noted for their adherence to the canons of science. Gelfand and Hartmann (1968), Pawlicki (1970), and Mash (1975) uniformly expressed disappointment with the methodology used in child behavior-modification treatment studies (for exceptions, see Bijou & Redd, 1975, and MacDonough & McNamara, 1973). Peterson and Hartmann (1975), for example, in their review of 69 comparative group studies of behavior modification with children, found only 6 methodologically adequate studies. In their review of behavior treatment of delinquents, Davidson and Seidman (1974) found only a single sound study.

The conclusions of a number of other critical reviews also provide little ground for optimism. Only 3 of the studies that Johnson and Katz (1973) included in their review of the burgeoning parent-training literature met their criteria of scientific adequacy, and O'Dell (1974), in a slightly more recent review of this same literature, found that only 4 of the 70 studies evaluated were methodologically sound. O'Dell (1974) concluded that "most of the decisions concerning which aspects of the [parent-training] technology to apply in a given situation are often based on value judgments of the experimenter rather than on comparative research" (p. 425). Similar disappointment regarding methodology can be found in reviews of the treatment of psychotic children (Werry, 1972) and of the effectiveness of nonprofessionals working with disturbed adolescents (Karlsruher, 1974).

Thus, it would seem that child-treatment procedures, whether traditional or novel, are not being evaluated in a manner that allows for firm conclusions; consequently mental-health practices with children rest on a rather tenuous empirical base. Lest child-psychotherapy researchers and practitioners find this conclusion too demoralizing, it should be pointed out that such difficulties are not unique to their field. Luborsky, Singer, and Luborsky (1975), in their exhaustive review of 106 comparative psychotherapy studies with adults, found only 5 studies that deserved grade-A status. Going further afield, Klein and Davis (1969) reported that only 11 of 61 semiexperimental studies comparing chlorpromazine to placebos were found to be methodologically sound. When Marholin and Phillips (1976) reanalyzed the eight of Klein and Davis's (1969) adequate studies that they could locate, they found each of the 8 studies to be flawed on the basis of relatively straightforward methodological criteria. Finally, Jones (1950) found that only 0.4% of 2,100 references on employee selection from 1906 to 1948 contained adequately designed and reported experiments.

While it is indeed lamentable that most studies have flaws, this should not detract from the essential pioneering effort made by the investigators who have carried out research in this area. Comparative-outcome research in psychotherapy is undoubtedly one of the most difficult fields of research in the social sciences. Windle (1962), Twain (1975), and Fiske and his associates (Fiske, Hunt, Luborsky, Orne, Parloff, Reiser, & Tuma, 1970) have described the technical problems confronting the applied clinical researcher. These problems include dealing with treatment modalities that are often poorly delineated, that require a substantial period of time to yield any effects, and that necessitate long-term follow-up for their full evaluation. Furthermore, the rates of so-called spontaneous recovery are relatively high, and the means of evaluating recovery are controversial. There is substantial variability among patients in terms of initial complaints, response to treatment, and changes in life situations. Additional problems that face the clinical researcher include the ethical issues and the practical difficulties involved in withholding treatment from control subjects and the threat to the validity of research produced by differential attrition among treatment groups.

To complicate matters further, outcome research with children has its own unique set of problems beyond those experienced in similar research with adults. According to Levitt (1971), these added difficulties arise because (1) many problem behaviors in children are essentially developmental and disappear as a function of time (see also Shepherd, Oppenheim, & Mitchell, 1966); (2) problem behaviors may be transformed as a function of development (i.e., developmental symptom-substitution may occur); and (3) persons other than the child may be a direct focus of treatment, whereas treatment focus is usually not a variable in psychotherapy research with adults.

While these problems pose a serious obstacle to child-psychotherapy researchers, one can only agree with O'Dell (1974, p. 429) that rather than being intimidated or lessening the standards he finds acceptable for research in comparative psychotherapy with children, the applied researcher must try harder.

3. Methodological Considerations

In view of the general design weaknesses in much of the child psychotherapy outcome research literature and the many difficulties and demands confronting those who would do such research, it would seem useful to focus on the major methodological concerns that the comparative treatment researcher must face. This section will focus on six general aspects of comparative treatment methodology: general experimental design, subjects, treatments, choice of measures, follow-up, and evaluation. The discussion of each category will highlight major issues, describe options available to the child psychotherapy outcome researcher, enumerate common pitfalls, and point out methodological procedures worthy of emulation. The discussions are not meant to be exhaustive, and additional references will be presented for the interested reader.

3.1. General Design Strategies

Just as there may be no bad students, merely poor teachers, so it is perhaps also true that there are no bad designs, only researchers who select designs for purposes for which they are ill suited. The choice of design determines the certainty with which causal statements can be asserted—or as Campbell and Stanley (1966) state, the choice of design limits the rival plausible hypotheses that can be rejected.

Kiesler (1971) and Paul (1969) both provide excellent critical analyses of the designs applicable to psychotherapy research. These designs lend themselves to a variety of classification schemes; perhaps the most relevant classification scheme for our purposes is whether the design is most suitable for exploratory or confirmatory purposes. In the former category belong traditional case studies, descriptive investigations, quasi-experimental designs, and other naturalistic correlational designs, such as the comparison of treatment defectors with remainers.

3.1.1. Exploratory Studies

Lazarus and Davison (1971) and Dukes (1965) have described the role of traditional case studies; Kiesler (1971) has pointed out both the advantages and the limitations of naturalistic correlational studies;

and Campbell and his associates (Cook & Campbell, 1976; Campbell & Stanley, 1966) have specified the pros and cons of a variety of quasi-experimental designs. Exploratory designs in general may provide useful circumstantial evidence; however, they are of limited value in comparative psychotherapy research. For example, according to Meltzoff and Kornreich (1970), many exploratory studies, particularly those providing survey results of the effectiveness of a specific program, are neither reproducible nor interpretable and "in the aggregate, form a vast swamp in which the reviewer could easily get lost forever" (p. 65). Similarly, naturalistic correlational studies have been criticized because they tempt investigators to assign powers of proof to them that they do not possess and thus to draw unwarranted conclusions or inferences from the data provided (Shontz, 1965, p. 158). Typically, these exploratory designs do not provide the degree of control for plausible rival hypotheses required for useful comparative treatment studies (Kiesler, 1971; Paul, 1969).

3.1.2. Confirmatory Studies

Two general classes of confirmatory designs are available to the comparative researcher. One class consists of the more recently popularized individual-subject designs, including variants of the multiple-baseline design and the ABAB or reversal design (Hersen & Barlow, 1976; Gelfand & Hartmann, 1975). The second class is composed of the true experimental group-designs. This category includes various multiple-group designs that involve the random assignment of subjects to conditions and is exemplified by the treatment versus no-treatment design, the comparative-treatment design, and designs employing various numbers and combinations of treatment and control groups, sometimes in conjunction with subject (organismic) independent variables (see Kiesler, 1971; Paul, 1969).

The individual-subject designs that have been popularized by behavior-therapy researchers represent an ideal solution to the joint demands of clinical work and science.[1] They were developed for application to units commonly dealt with by the clinician (the individual subject, family, or classroom), and at the same time, they provide safeguards against the common threats to internal validity; that is, they may be used to establish functional relationships between manipulated and dependent variables. In view of the advantages of in-

[1] Despite belief to the contrary, the emphasis on individual-subject experimental designs did not stem entirely from the classic work by Sidman (1960). Intensive individual-subject designs, originating from quite different theoretical positions, have been advocated by Chassan (1960, 1967), Edgington (1969), Shapiro (1963), and Shontz (1965).

dividual-subject designs, it is not surprising that they have been advocated for research in psychotherapy by representatives of quite diverse orientations (e.g., Yates, 1976; Bergin & Strupp, 1972). While these designs have an important role to play in psychotherapy research, they appear to have serious limitations when used in comparative-outcome research of the kind discussed in this chapter (e.g., Kazdin, 1973; O'Leary & Drabman, 1971; Mash, 1975). The first limitation is imposed by the small number of subjects typically treated when one is using an individual-subject design strategy. Unless the treatment has undergone extensive intersubject replication or there are substantial grounds for assuming little between-subject variability in the phenomenon under investigation, the results obtained from individual-subject designs may be seriously limited in generalizability (e.g., Ross, 1974; for a reply, see Edgar & Billingsley, 1974).

A second limitation is that most of these designs entail administering all conditions in some sequence to each subject. Designs sharing this characteristic may be compromised by a number of range (context) effects (e.g., Greenwald, 1976). Range effects such as practice, sensitization, and carry-over resulting from prior treatment may confound specific treatment effects with the particular sequence in which the treatments are administered. Such "multiple-treatment interference" (Campbell & Stanley, 1966) has the effect of limiting the external validity of the results to subjects who receive the same treatment sequence. Finally, most of these designs have the additional disadvantage of restricting long-term follow-up analysis to a single treatment, the last one administered (Kazdin, 1973).

Thorough comparative treatment-outcome studies usually require the use of one of the classic group-experimental designs. Before we proceed to a discussion of some important considerations in employing group confirmatory-designs, some cautions are in order regarding when such designs are appropriate. Bergin and Strupp (1972) wisely warn against the danger of attempting comparative-outcome studies before the requisite treatment, measurement, and analytic techniques have been well established. Various investigators (e.g., Karoly, 1972; Lazarus & Davison, 1971; Paul, 1969) have presented convincing arguments for the importance of maintaining a balance between the various types of exploratory and confirmatory designs in psychotherapy research. Patterson and his colleagues have demonstrated the interplay between design strategies in their programmatic investigations of treatment techniques for aggressive, conduct-problem boys (see, e.g., the discussion by Patterson, 1974a,b).

One of the first considerations in the employment of a confirmatory group-design has to do with the nature of the comparison conditions. The specific purpose of a comparative treatment investigation and the level of knowledge in the field—particularly knowledge concerning various plausible threats to validity—determine the number and kind of comparison and control conditions required (e.g., McNamara & MacDonough, 1972; Campbell, 1969). Naturally defined groups—such as those composed of defectors, terminators, and the like—are unsuitable controls for true experimental investigations (e.g., Lewis, Barnhart, Gosset, & Phillips, 1975; Subotnick, 1972), although they may provide useful circumstantial evidence. The argument that these naturally defined groups can function as adequate controls if they do not differ significantly from treatment groups on any of a set of patient variables (e.g., Levitt, 1963) must be viewed with skepticism. Failure to reject the hypothesis of no difference is *not* equivalent to asserting that no differences exist. Also, the compilation of descriptive data from previous studies of minimally treated children for use as a standard control condition is to be avoided (e.g., Lambert, 1976; Subotnick, 1972). Levitt's (1957) use of such a compilation in his evaluation of the effectiveness of child psychotherapy was criticized as failing to consider problems of comparability and as "grinding disparate reports and surveys into a statistical sausage, concealing more than it reveals" (Subotnick, 1972, p. 33). It is now generally agreed that outcome is not homogeneous (Kiesler, 1966) and may vary with the child's diagnosis, age, and the severity and duration of the disturbance (e.g., Lambert, 1976; Gossett, Lewis, Lewis, & Phillips, 1973; Malan, 1973; Jacob, Magnussen, & Kemler, 1972; Clarizio, 1968). Thus, it would seem that contrast conditions, whether of control or alternative treatment, require comparable, randomly assigned groups of subjects.

3.1.2.1. Untreated Controls. The comparison of treated with untreated subjects, as McNamara and MacDonough (1972) have suggested, is appropriate only for answering the question, "What was the effect of doing something in particular vs. doing nothing in particular?" (p. 363). Even this question assumes that the subjects were initially equivalent and that the untreated subjects were indeed untreated. This latter assumption can be violated in at least two ways. The more serious concern is that subjects assigned to an untreated control-condition may seek treatment services elsewhere, a possibility that requires assessment (e.g., Strupp & Bergin, 1969; see Baker, 1973, for a study that did assess this possibility). It has also been argued that in the process of intake and follow-up, untreated subjects are provided support and reassurance that serves to reduce differences in outcome between treated and untreated subjects (Meltzoff & Kornreich, 1970). While this may be true, if the independent or treatment variable cannot produce changes greater than those produced by assessment, the treatment hardly seems worthwhile.

Wortman (1975) has suggested a number of other possible problems with no-treatment controls. The control subjects may believe that they were placed in the control condition because they have superior prognostic characteristics and thus may work harder at resolving their own problems. Such a reaction could obscure real treatment effects. Alternatively, control subjects could be made bitter or demoralized by not receiving treatment, and this, in turn, may worsen their adjustment. If this were the case, an ineffective treatment could be made to seem effective. The intriguing speculations by Wortman have not yet been supported by child-psychotherapy research data. If, however, these consequences of differential assignment to treatment and control conditions were thought to be important, their effects might be reduced if the random nature of the assignment procedures were explained to the clients or their parents (e.g., Baker, 1973), and if the control subjects were promised that the most effective form of treatment would be administered to them following the conclusion of the study (e.g., Bandura, 1969, p. 188).

Because of these and related problems, such as ethical concerns with withholding treatment and the ever-present possibility of Hawthorne effects, some authors have despaired of ever generating a meaningful untreated-control condition (e.g., Luborsky, Chandler, Auerbach, Cohen, & Bachrach, 1971; Strupp & Bergin, 1969, p. 64) except perhaps when the outcome research is conducted in carefully restricted institutional settings. Even in institutional settings, one must take precautions to ensure that treated and untreated subjects not interact (Meltzoff & Kornreich, 1970), and one must also be alert to the possible confounding effects of differences in treatment location and novelty, particularly if all treated subjects are moved to an experimental ward (Kazdin, 1975).

These conclusions seem unnecessarily pessimistic (see Miller, Barrett, Hampe, & Noble, 1972, for a more optimistic view). For example, in most service agencies, all children for whom treatment is requested cannot be treated immediately and some must be placed on a waiting list. The crucial problem in the use of waiting-list children as untreated control subjects is that those children who are typically placed on a waiting list may have special characteristics (for example, less serious disturbances) not shared by children who receive treatment immediately. Fortunately, however, this problem may be solvable through careful planning. Out of a total pool of applicants for treatment who display a similar target problem, some will be judged to require immediate treatment and must therefore be excluded from the formal design; others will be judged suitable for being placed on a waiting list. It is from this latter subgroup that children can be randomly assigned to treatment and control conditions. A properly executed design of this type provides true experimental comparisons for the children randomly assigned and exploratory (confounded) comparisons between the randomly assigned subjects and those who are judged to be in need of immediate services.

While this design represents a reasonable solution to the problems of generating untreated control conditions, it has two potential drawbacks. First, the length of time during which treatment can be delayed for the waiting-list children is limited, and therefore this procedure may be appropriate only for outcome research investigating brief psychotherapies. Furthermore, it precludes long-term, unconfounded follow-up evaluations for the waiting-list control subjects; that is, after some period of time, these subjects will lose their untreated status (see, e.g., Sloane, Staples, Cristol, Yorkston, & Whipple, 1975). Other procedures for generating no-treatment controls are described by Cook and Campbell (1976) and by Wortman (1975).

3.1.2.2. Active Controls. The presumed ubiquitous therapeutic effects of positive expectancies produced by attention and other nonspecific treatment procedures have resulted in still another type of control condition, the attention placebo or expectancy control (e.g., Goldstein, 1962; Frank, 1959; Rosenthal & Frank, 1956; Thorne, 1952).[2] The use of controls for subject expectancies has been increasingly advocated in psychotherapy research (e.g., Kazdin & Wilcoxon, 1976; Strupp & Bergin, 1969) and recently has been employed in parent-focused child interventions (Walter & Gilmore, 1973). The use of active control conditions in psychotherapy-outcome research may be limited, as may be the use of no-treatment controls, to the investigation of brief psychotherapies. Experimenters are understandably reluctant to withhold treatment for long periods of time, and the long-term use of attention-placebo controls taxes both the creativity of clinical researchers and the credulity of participants (Endicott, 1969). This latter concern would seem to be less a problem in psychotherapy research with children than with adults.

3.1.2.3. Normal Controls. The use of normal controls is occasionally recommended in the child-psychotherapy literature (Walker & Hops, 1976; McNamara, 1975; Patterson, 1974a). Normal control groups who are representatively drawn could provide normative data on the range of acceptable responding and hence aid in the assessment of change.

---

[2] The expectancy construct and its causal status in mediating treatment effects has been challenged in a recent critical review of the literature (Wilkins, 1973).

The use of normal controls, however, should be viewed as supplementary rather than as alternative to more traditional control conditions. As Paul (1969) has indicated, normal controls differ from subjects seeking treatment in both motivation and level of target behavior and would not be expected to show either changes over time or statistical regression.

Psychotherapy researchers now seem to favor the direct comparison of alternative treatment conditions, perhaps with the addition of one or more control conditions (e.g., Erickson, 1975; Meltzoff & Kornreich, 1970; Strupp & Bergin, 1969). The treatment conditions might consist of traditional psychotherapies as they are typically practiced, newly developed techniques, or specific components of existing practices. See Kiesler (1971), for caveats regarding the comparative investigation of established techniques as practices, and Paul (1969), for limitations in the product of studies comparing alternative treatments.

3.1.3. Analogue Studies

Analogue treatment studies can make important contributions to an understanding of behavior change, but there is some danger that the results of these studies may be inapplicable to clinical settings. As Bernstein and Paul (1971) have pointed out, the relevance of analogue research to clinical settings is a function of the extent to which the variables studied share the essential characteristics of the variables employed clinically. Analogue studies become increasingly less generalizable when (1) incentives other than "relief" are promised to the participants; (2) when screening tests used for subject selection result in the inclusion of subjects whose target behaviors differ qualitatively or quantitatively from those found in clinic patients; (3) when measures of dependent variables include irrelevant demand effects or other reactive effects not found in clinical settings; (4) when the treatment techniques are not exact replicas of those used clinically; and (5) when inexperienced or untrained therapists are used to present the treatment procedures (Bernstein, 1973; Bernstein & Paul, 1971; Paul, 1969). Bernstein and Paul have described procedures that may prove useful in increasing the clinical relevance of analogue studies, and they specify the information in the report of analogue studies required to facilitate an assessment of their generalizability.

3.2. Subjects

Early research in psychotherapy employed what Kiesler (1971) describes as naïve generalist designs. In these studies, groups of patients with a wide range of diagnoses and problem behaviors were assigned to "therapy." It is now generally agreed that the contributions of such studies are very likely to be minimal. The myth of patient uniformity (Kiesler, 1966), if it was ever taken seriously, has certainly fallen into disrepute. The general consensus of opinion now appears to be that treatment-outcome studies should focus on a highly limited target behavior, such as enuresis, school phobia, or hyperaggressiveness (e.g., Callner, 1975; Panzetta, 1973; Kiesler, 1971; Paul, 1969; Kellner, 1967). If it is desirable to investigate more than one target behavior in any treatment-outcome study, then groups of children with the same problem behavior should be assigned to separate blocks of a design.

Once patients have been tentatively selected in terms of their general suitability for treatment—that is, when all children have the same target problem-behaviors and treatment goal—what additional data should be gathered? In general, information should be obtained that will aid consumers of the research in assessing the generalizability of the results or that might be used in either subject assignment or exploratory data analysis (Luborsky *et al.*, 1975). The assessment of generality of results requires information on referral sources, socioeconomic status, and any factors used to exclude potential participants from the study, such as the presence of neurological impairment or of multiple serious problems that make immediate treatment mandatory. The subject-assignment procedure might make use of information on the duration or severity of the target behavior (see Section 3.2.1.). Finally, exploratory data analysis might focus on such dimensions as parental cooperativeness, general ability, and the like. A potential pool of supplementary variables that might be useful in fulfilling these functions can be obtained from an examination of those variables that have been shown to affect outcome in related studies (Fiske *et al.*, 1970) or that are typically investigated in pretherapy assessments (e.g., Kanfer & Saslow, 1969).

One must exercise some caution to ensure that requests for supplementary information do not place excessive demands on the child clients, their parents, or their teachers. Whether or not subjects continue to participate in a long treatment study is often the result of a delicate balance of the costs and benefits accruing to them. This balance can be upset if firm control is not exercised over requests by project staff members to add still another variable (e.g., "Wouldn't it be interesting to . . . ?").

3.2.1. Subject Assignment

The *sine qua non* of true experimental design is the random assignment of subjects to conditions. As Campbell (1963) stated, "the magic of randomization is that it attenuates the causal threads of the past as they might co-determine both exposure to the treatment and gain score" (p. 213). The psychotherapy-outcome researcher has a number of random-assignment methods from which to choose. The subjects can be assigned randomly to conditions, without regard to information on problem severity or any other treatment-related variables with the hope that between-condition differences on these variables will be diluted by the random-assignment procedure. As has been suggested by Tversky and Kahneman (1971), this may be a dangerous assumption with the small sample sizes used in many comparative-treatment studies. Certainly, equivalence among conditions on relevant subject variables should be checked by means of appropriate statistical analysis.[3] Alternative random-assignment procedures involve first assigning subjects to homogeneous blocks either on the basis of baseline performance measures obtained on the target behavior or on the basis of scores obtained on some other treatment-related variables. Subjects placed in each block are then randomly assigned to treatment conditions. Feldt (1958) provided a table for determining the optimum number of blocks to employ, given the total sample size; the number of conditions; and the correlation between the variable(s) used in the placement of subjects in blocks and the dependent variable. A popular variant of the blocking procedure involves matching subjects individually on one or more variables and then randomly assigning one member of each matched set of subjects to each treatment condition (for an example of this procedure with children, see Leitenberg & Callahan, 1973). Some caution must be exercised in the use of this procedure because the occurrence of even relatively few non-treatment-related terminators can severely limit the usable sample size, particularly if all subjects matched with each terminator are dropped from the analysis. For example, with 15 subjects in each of three conditions, the loss of only 5 subjects could reduce the sample size from 45 to 30 if each terminator were from a different matched set.

3.2.2. Sample Size

The sample size required for outcome studies can be easily underestimated at the outset. The sample size of concern is the terminal sample size—the portion of the sample that completes all phases of the study, including treatment and all planned follow-up phases. The de-

---

[3] Meltzoff and Kornreich (1970) have suggested that, following random-assignment procedures, "subjects can be dropped later . . . to improve the match, providing that it is done without knowledge of the patient's progress" (p. 27). This recommendation violates the requirements of random assignment and should be avoided. Adjustment procedures employing analysis-of-covariance techniques seem preferable to eliminating subjects in order to achieve equivalent groups.

sired terminal sample size should be sufficiently large to provide adequate power to detect differences in outcome that would have practical or theoretical relevance (see, e.g., Cook & Campbell, 1976; Cohen, 1965, 1969). The determination of the required initial sample size, then, requires some estimate of the likely attrition rate. In their review of the factors associated with dropping out of treatment, Baekeland and Lundwall (1975) reported that the typical psychotherapy patient is a terminator; the dropout rate in child-focused psychotherapy has ranged as high as 91% (Bernal, 1975). Recommendations by Bernal (1975) and Baekeland and Lundwall (1975) for reducing patient attrition include emphasizing to prospective patients the preventive, treatment, and evaluative aspects of the program, as opposed to highlighting its research nature, and offering incentives for patients who complete the final follow-up evaluations. Heitler (1976) has emphasized the importance of employing explicit preparatory techniques so that the expectations of therapists and clients are congruent and attrition is reduced (see Holmes & Urie, 1975, for an example of the use of preparatory techniques with child clients).

3.3. Treatments

The treatments employed in psychotherapy research may vary (1) in terms of their breadth as well as (2) in the degree of control that is exercised over their implementation. One extreme on both dimensions is represented by comparisons of existing practices such as "psychoanalytic therapy" and "behavior therapy"—treatments involving broad variables over which poor control is exercised. Such studies essentially represent what Kiesler (1971) has termed a comparison of "artisan" practices. (See, however, the recent impressive study by Sloane et al., 1975, in which idealized versions of psychoanalytic and behavior therapy were compared and in which reasonably stringent control was exercised over implementation of the independent variables.) At the other extreme are studies that compare treatments differing in only a single, highly controlled, quantitative or qualitative characteristic. The former comparisons have some advantages with regard to external validity and can certainly aid in funding decisions; studies of the latter type are far more likely to produce scientific gains (e.g., Goldstein, Heller, & Sechrest, 1966). According to Strupp and Bergin (1969), "the isolation and manipulation of single variables is essential for advancing knowledge concerning the process of therapeutic change" (p. 25). When tight control is required over treatment variables, the uniform application of treatments may be difficult to achieve. Paul (1966), in his classic outcome study of public-speaking phobias, sought to ensure the uniform application of the desensitization treatment (but not the insight treatment) by employing a specially prepared therapist manual. Sloane *et al.* (1975), in their comparison of psychoanalytic and behavior therapy, generated a list of acceptable and unacceptable therapist practices that were agreed upon by the participating therapists. For example, role playing was sanctioned for behavior therapists but not for psychoanalytic therapists; transference interpretations were proscribed for behavior therapists but allowed for psychoanalytic therapists (p. 377). Paul (1969) recommended the use of role playing and prompts to therapists to ensure a homogeneous application of the independent variable.

Regardless of which research tactic is pursued and which independent variables are compared, it is critically important to describe the specific operations and procedures included in the treatment manipulations. Unfortunately, failure to specify the independent variable is frequently mentioned in the litany of criticisms found in recent reviews of child-psychotherapy research (e.g., Heinicke & Strassman, 1975; Karlsruher, 1974; Johnson & Katz, 1973; Pawlicki, 1970; Peterson & Hartmann, 1975). Inadequate independent-variable description limits intelligent evaluation of the study, leaves the reader uncertain as to the limits of generality of the results, precludes replication, does not allow for an orderly development of a data base for the science of behavior change (e.g., McLean & Miles, 1974; Paul, 1969), and seems unlikely to lead to the development of a treatment technology, which London (1972) has recommended as our primary objective.

Systematic and complete description of the independent variable requires attention to at least two quite different aspects of treatment. The first concerns the specific procedures employed in treatment; the second concerns the characteristics of the persons who deliver the treatment.

3.3.1. Description of Treatment Procedures

The treatment techniques employed, their frequency of use, and their temporal distribution all require careful description. Bernstein and Paul (1971) have also emphasized the importance of describing the initiation ritual used, including the explicit expectations given to subjects regarding behavior change. Twain (1975) and Fiske *et al.* (1970) have suggested that attention also be given to the dimension of service exposure, which includes the number and the duration of contacts, as well as the type of contact (e.g., clinical and home visits and telephone contacts).

Therapy researchers might adopt as a model for treatment description the procedural descriptions used in experimental studies. When standard procedures are followed, reference is made to a *specific* description of these procedures. When standard procedures are revised, these revisions are described in detail. All procedures relevant to the conduct of treatment require description, whether they are affective qualities of the therapeutic interaction, specialized equipment used (such as the Mower bed-wetting sensors), fee schedules, or special characteristics of the physical-social environment in which treatment occurs (Paul, 1969).

In those treatment studies in which treatment techniques are described in some detail, the description typically is based either on therapist self-reports or on a list of prescribed procedures. These sources of information might not be adequate, however, as demonstrated in Murray's (1956) analysis of a case treated by Carl Rogers. In contrast to the ideal of a completely accepting, nonjudgmental, nondirective therapist, Rogers tended to approve and disapprove of his patient's statements in systematic ways. Thus, it would seem that systematic and independent assessment is required to determine the degree to which the independent variables in psychotherapy research are successfully implemented. Some evaluators have provided ratings of actual therapist behavior during treatment (e.g., Sloane *et al.*, 1975; Wodarski, Feldman, & Pedi, 1974). The research of Stallings (1975) on the effectiveness of various Project Follow-Through teaching models provides an example of independent-variable assessment worthy of emulation.

3.3.2. Therapist Characteristics

Techniques cannot be regarded as operating in a vacuum but may interact with various therapist factors. Fiedler (1950), for example, has shown that such therapist attributes as amount of therapy experience can produce greater uniformity of results across therapists than does shared formal allegiance to one or another technique. Recognition of the importance of therapist variables has come belatedly to the most technique-dominated camp of all, behavior therapy (e.g., Stuart & Lott, 1974; Hartmann, 1972). Luborsky *et al.* (1975) have recommended that in addition to ensuring that the therapists employed are not inexperienced, therapist competency and valuation of treatment should be equated across conditions. This implies that information should be provided on these therapist qualities and, ideally, that objective measures of these factors should be obtained (for an example, see Tavormina, 1975). Recommendations for a more extensive assessment of a variety of other therapist variables—including empathy, warmth, and genuineness—have been made by Fiske *et al.* (1970).

3.4. Choice of Measures

Discussions of measurement in psychotherapy-outcome research typically emphasize measurement of the dependent variable. However, as previous sections of this chapter have suggested, important measurement issues also confront the comparative-psychotherapy researcher in the assessment of independent or treatment variables, as well as in the assessment of therapist and patient variables. While the emphasis in this section is on the dependent variable, much of the material is directly relevant to the various classes of independent variables as well.

Various early commentators despaired of sufficient consensus' ever evolving regarding the dependent variable to allow for meaningful comparative research (e.g., Rubinstein & Parloff, 1959). Although current attitudes are far less pessimistic, selection of the dependent variable(s) remains perhaps the most controversial topic in psychotherapy-outcome research.

The selection of dependent measures requires the investigator to define treatment goals, at least implicitly. In addition, the researcher must choose between global and specific measures, single or multiple measures, newly devised or traditional measures, etc. Because measures can be applied at any point in the treatment process, the investigator must also decide just when to evaluate therapy effects: during, at the close of, or following therapy. In this section, we will consider the various options available concerning the type and timing of the dependent measures.

3.4.1. Definition of Goals

The matter of goal setting is often not as straightforward a matter as it seems, partly because the goals could be reasonably defined by various persons. Krause (1969) and Hiebert (1974) have discussed goal setting from four perspectives: the person receiving the treatment; the persons whose complaints are to be remedied by the treatment (this may be the patient, but in much of child psychotherapy it is a parent, a teacher, or a judge); the treatment sponsor (either an institution or, in the area of private therapy, the patient or complainant); and the person who performs the treatment. A researcher could even have goals independent of those of the other interested parties. In many cases, the goals of the respective parties coincide. In others, they do not, and the researcher must decide which perspectives to consider.

3.4.2. Global versus Specific Measures

Therapist improvement-ratings are perhaps the most often used and the most global of dependent measures. Therapist improvement-ratings have a long, but checkered history in psychotherapy research. They are supposed to avoid some of the problems associated with raw change scores, they avoid the ceiling or floor effects found with other measures, and they can be applied to any patient with any problem (Mintz, 1972; Luborsky, 1971). They have the obvious advantages of simplicity on the one hand and face validity on the other—the therapist is presumably a sensitive and informed observer of the patient's progress. Unfortunately, simplicity can be a minor consideration, and face validity is neither necessary nor sufficient as an indicator of a measure's adequacy. Therapist improvement-ratings are susceptible to retrospective falsification and selective recall (Luborsky et al., 1971). In addition, they may show spurious relationships with either pre- or posttreatment measures. For example, Mintz (1972) found that omnibus ratings of improvement were positively correlated with initial prognostic ratings even in simulation studies in which the relationship of initial status to improvement was held at zero. In other studies in which outcome was varied, improvement was rated greater for those patients who were better adjusted at the end of therapy, regardless of the amount of change actually involved. Finally, therapist improvement-ratings tell us nothing in operational terms about the basis for the clinician's judgment and hence do not provide the information necessary for a replication (Meltzoff & Kornreich, 1970). If therapist judgments are to be used to assess treatment effects, they should involve ratings on specific dimensions obtained at the beginning and at the end of treatment and at the follow-up evaluations.

Other global measures, although perhaps more objective than omnibus therapist ratings of client improvement, may have the problem of being somewhat insensitive to the specific changes that may have been produced. General problem checklists and measures of achievement—such as standardized tests, grade-point averages, and high-school rank—may not enable one to track changes in specific problem areas. Other criteria, such as recidivism, are vague and fail to distinguish between children reinstitutionalized for multiple versus single offenses (Sarri & Selo, 1974). Case-disposition variables, such as "discharge rate," may be more highly influenced by economic and institutional policy changes and by the availability of supportive relatives in the posttreatment environment than by treatment effectiveness.

Although there is a role for general or somewhat global dependent measures in psychotherapy research, priority should be given to obtaining specific measures of the target behavior (e.g., Kazdin, 1973). Paul (1969) summed up the argument for specific measurement of the target complaint very nicely: "Since the purpose of treatment—in fact, the basis for existence of the field—is to help with the problems for which help was asked, the real question of effectiveness is whether or not the distressing behaviors which brought the client to treatment have changed in the desired direction without producing new problems" (p. 41).

The role, then, of more general measures of adequate functioning would be to help assess any positive generalized effect of treatment (Kazdin, 1973), as well as to assess possible detrimental side effects of treatment (Fiske et al., 1970). Marholin and Phillips (1976) have emphasized the importance of assessing general functioning in addition to changes in the target response. This approach is particularly appropriate when interventions, such as drug treatment, are thought on *a priori* grounds to produce symptomatic improvements at the risk of undesirable side effects.

3.4.3 Single versus Multiple Measures

As suggested in the previous section, investigators may decide to include more than one dependent variable so that assessments can be conducted both on the target response and on more generalized changes in the child-patient's functioning. It may also be necessary to include more than one dependent variable in comparative-treatment studies to ensure that the dependent variables adequately probe the changes expected by each of the techniques (Goldstein, Heller, & Sechrest, 1966).

Once the dependent variables have been selected, investigators must decide whether single or multiple indexing should be employed for each variable. For example, should general functioning be assessed with just an observational measure of deviant behavior, or should it be assessed with both an observational measure and parents' verbal report? When multiple measures have been employed, the consistent finding in both the psychotherapy literature and the child experimental-psychology literature is that the measures display far less than perfect correspondence (e.g., Tavorminia, 1974; O'Leary, Turkewitz, & Taffel, 1973; Lytton, 1971; Yarrow, Campbell, & Burton, 1970). This ought not to be surprising when one considers that these measures often:

1. Come from different domains (e.g., cognitive, physiological, and behavioral).
2. Differ in their specificity (see Section 3.4.2).
3. Differ in method of data collection (e.g., direct behavior observations, achievement tests, self-reports, and physiological measures).
4. Differ in their sources or vantage points (therapist, parent, and teacher).

5. Differ in their setting (home, school, and clinic).
6. Differ in the times at which they are obtained.

In addition to these systematic sources of variability, there are the inevitable sources of random error in measurements of this kind (e.g., Mintz, Auerbach, Luborsky, & Johnson, 1973).[4] Thus, in view of the inconsistencies resulting from both error and measurement factors (e.g., method, source, locus, and time), multiple indexing for each dependent variable is certainly desirable whenever possible.

3.4.4 Standardized versus Unique Measures

It is generally agreed that whenever possible, standardized evaluation procedures should be used (e.g., McNamara, 1975; Fiske et al., 1970; Nunnally, 1967). Standardized procedures facilitate interstudy comparisons and also have known psychometric properties. This position is not meant to provide support, however, for the indiscriminate use of standardized measures. All too often the choice of dependent measures is based on their convenience and availability rather than on the relevance of the measures to the study at hand. As Yarrow, Campbell, and Burton (1970) have suggested, "Methods originally judged expedient for temporary use may become progressively established and uncritically accepted as legitimate approaches to given research questions" (p. 60).

3.4.5. Timing

In addition to the general issues involved in the selection of dependent variables, there are a number of considerations involved in the selection of the appropriate times for administering the measures. (Issues involved in follow-up assessments are dealt with in the next section.) If one of the purposes of measurement is to allow for the meaningful adjustment of ongoing treatment procedures, then indices of the target behavior should be obtained continuously throughout treatment (e.g., Walker, 1972; Baer, Wolf, & Risley, 1968). On the other hand, if one's primary purpose is to evaluate the relative effectiveness of predefined and unadjusted treatment procedures, then measures are necessary only to assess the target behavior at certain selected points, most often immediately preceding and following treatment.

Few would dispute the appropriateness of including at least pre-

---

[4] This lack of correspondence has repeatedly provoked the suggestion that change is multidimensional. While this is probably true, as behavior is often under the control of a wide range of changing environmental stimuli, this assumption has typically been made without proper recognition of measurement and other technique-related sources of error (e.g., Clum, 1975; Campbell & Fiske, 1959).

tests and posttests on the dependent variables. Pretest measures are necessary to evaluate both the amount and the direction of change produced by treatment. In addition, a number of useful statistical analyses necessitate pretest scores. The need for posttreatment measures seems obvious. What is perhaps not so obvious, however, is the need to obtain such measures as soon as possible after termination of the intervention procedure. Otherwise the measurements may well reflect the program impact plus subsequent nontreatment events rather than just the program impact (Twain, 1975).

The necessity of such endpoint measurements thus seems well-established, but their exclusive use is unwise. Chassan (1962) argued against placing sole reliance on posttests as follows:

> It becomes apparent that mere end-point observations for the purpose of estimating change in the patient-state after, say the intervention of some form of treatment, places generally severe limitations on the precision of the estimation of change. For random fluctuation in the patient state can then easily be mistaken for systematic change. To overcome this difficulty, frequent repeated observations must be made of each patient in the study. (p. 615)

3.4.6. Bias, Reliability, and Validity

A series of technical considerations face the psychotherapy researcher once he has made the initial decisions regarding dependent measures: the issues concern bias, reliability, and validity.

3.4.6.1 Bias. Meltzoff and Kornreich (1970, p. 28ff.) have discussed four sources of bias that relate directly to the dependent variable. *Patient-response bias* refers to the variety of biases involved in the patient's responding to obtrusive measurement devices (Webb, Campbell, Schwartz, & Sechrest, 1966). These include the typical response biases that may occur on psychological tests, attitude scales, and interviews (e.g., Wiggins, 1973; Fiske, 1971; Kleinmuntz, 1967). There are also special biases particularly prominent in psychotherapy-outcome research such as the "hello–goodbye" effect (Hathaway, 1948), which consists of the client's thanking the therapist for help received regardless of the actual success of the therapy.

Criterion bias refers to the unfair selection of measurement devices so that either the measure is unrepresentative of the measurement domain of interest or the criterion measure is not equally fair to the treatments under comparison. *Interviewer and therapist biases* refer to the consistent errors in measurement produced by the failure to employ blind arrangements. Judges, raters, and interviewers who are knowledgeable about the project and who have definite expectations concerning the study's outcome can, as is well known, produce errors favoring their expectations (e.g., Rosenthal, 1969). The optimum conditions for avoiding this bias involve the use of personnel who are independent of the project and the treatment and who have neither knowledge of, nor a stake in the hypothesis. One should employ blind procedures in the scoring of test responses, video tapes, and the like by using unlabeled products that have been randomly ordered with regard to treatment condition and measurement occasion (e.g., pretreatment, posttreatment, and follow-up). Because blind procedures are sometimes difficult to maintain, data gatherers should be assessed regarding the degree to which they have remained unaware of the treatment conditions or the phase of the study. Beatty (1972) has described a simple procedure for assessing blindness, and Johnson and Christensen (1975) have employed a sophisticated version of this technique to test for naïveté in observers who gather observational data in the homes of treated children. If the assessment data indicate that the observers are not blind as to the treatment conditions, then the dependent variable should be checked for the presence of bias.

Reviews of the outcome literature suggest that the procedures for checking for rater bias are not well understood. The assumption seems to be that if some measure of interobserver reliability is adequate, then the data are unbiased. Unfortunately, this is not entirely correct, as a distinction must be made between reliability and accuracy (Mischel, 1968, p. 65; also see the discussion by Johnson & Bolstad, 1973, of consensual observer drift). For example, a rater or judge may share the biases of a second observer (reliability checker), and the two may show impressive reliability but poor accuracy. Detection of bias in this case requires the use of a third observer, who is a calibration observer (e.g., Jones, Reid, & Patterson, 1975). Even comparisons with a calibration observer may not disclose bias in this example if typical correlational measures are employed to describe the reliability of the ratings because the correlation coefficient is insensitive to consistent errors shared by all observers. An additional analysis is required to examine the differences between means of the observers' ratings in the compared conditions (Hartmann, 1977).

3.4.6.2. Reliability. Two aspects of reliability are of particular concern to psychotherapy-outcome researchers. The first has already been alluded to in the previous section and concerns the consistency with which raters or judges score the same protocols (interobserver reliability). The second concerns the adequacy of the sample of behavior that constitutes the dependent variable (internal or temporal consistency). Weaknesses in either of these two aspects can jeopardize the statistical

validity of the study (Cook & Campbell, 1976) and result in no differences between procedures that in reality are differentially effective.
The procedures required to demonstrate interobserver reliability are
described in Cronbach, Gleser, Nanda, and Rajaratnan (1972), in Hartmann (1977), in McNemar (1969), and in Wiggins (1973) and are not
elaborated upon here.

Unfortunately interobserver reliability checks themselves are potentially reactive (e.g., O'Leary & Kent, 1973; Reid, 1970; but see
Whelan, 1974). Reliability estimates obtained during overt checks may
be overestimates of the reliability obtained under a different set of
surveillance conditions, thus suggesting the need for random covert
checks of reliability as well as periodic observer retraining.

The second aspect of reliability involves the adequacy of the data
sample and seems to be less often considered. Unless the data show
some consistency, there is no basis for supposing that they will be
sensitive to the effects of treatment (see Cronbach *et al.,* 1972, for
methods of assessing consistency). Lack of consistency in the sample
of behavior obtained may suggest that the behavior is inherently
unreliable and hence represents a poor choice in the selection of the
dependent variable. Alternatively, poor consistency may suggest that
the behavioral sample was too small and that larger samples of data
are required.

In general, when one is considering reliability, it is important to
keep in mind that there is no such thing as *the* reliability: "a reliability
coefficient is not an intrinsic property of the scale for which it may
have been reported" (Lyerly & Abbott, 1965, p. 7). Each unique application of a test, a scale, or an observation procedure requires assessment of the relevant types of reliability for that particular application.

3.4.6.3. Validity. While the topic of validity is familiar to most
clinical researchers, two validity issues seem deserving of brief mention. The first concerns the use of indirect measures as exemplified by
projective tests (e.g., the Children's Apperception Test and the Ror-
schach) and other theoretically derived but largely untested measures
of constructs that are purported to change as the result of treatment.
All too often these measures are employed before their relationship to
direct measures is established (O'Leary, 1972). Studies that combine
outcome research and test-validity research on the dependent variable
in a single project severely challenge the credibility of the reader and
run the risk of doing an injustice to the test and the treatment or both.
The second concern relates to the warning mentioned in the discussion of reliability. No measurement technique is inherently valid, not
even direct behavioral observation (see Johnson & Bolstad, 1973, for a
discussion of validity issues in direct behavior observation).

3.5. Follow-up Assessments

The need for long-term follow-up data has been emphasized with such consistency that it has taken on the characteristics of dogma (Paul, 1969). Follow-up assessments may alert investigators to aspects of the environment that deserve support or require change and may allow those children whose performance is deteriorating to receive booster treatments (e.g., Bijou & Redd, 1975; Atthowe, 1973; Johnson & Katz, 1973). Of course, the booster treatments administered preclude unambiguous interpretation of the results of subsequent follow-up evaluations. The most important function of follow-up measurements, however, is to assess the effectiveness of treatment (e.g., Bergin & Suinn, 1975). Ross (1974), for example, has indicated that no treatment procedure can be said to have demonstrated its effectiveness until stability of improvement has been analyzed over time, and Patterson, Ray, and Shaw (1968) have stated that "interventions which do not persist . . . have little utility" (p. 54). Unfortunately, the call for follow-up assessments in child-psychotherapy studies has seldom been answered; and when follow-up assessments are included, they are typically brief and unsystematic (Mash, 1975). This lack of adequate follow-up is perhaps not surprising in view of the inherent methodological problems associated with follow-up studies, such as differential loss of subjects and various instrument errors (e.g., Paul, 1969). Nor is lack of follow-up lamented by those who believe that treatment effects become so intrinsically confounded with the changes in the posttreatment environment that follow-up data are relatively meaningless (e.g., Bijou & Peterson, 1971). As Mash (1975) correctly points out, the traitlike expectations for treatment persistence run contrary to the vast assemblage of data indicating the importance of situational control over behavior (see also Mischel, 1968, 1973).

Sargent (1960, p. 495) has suggested that the importance of follow-up is equaled only by the magnitude of the methodological problems it presents. In psychotherapy research with children, these problems fall into three general classes: comparability of measurements, timing of follow-up assessments, and sample attrition (e.g., McNamara & MacDonough, 1972; Windle, 1962; Sargent, 1960).

3.5.1. Measurement Issues

Two general types of follow-up data might be obtained: data that allow both longitudinal and cross-sectional (treatment) comparisons and data that allow only comparisons among treatment conditions. For example, home observations taken on the rate of failure to comply with instructions and obtained over the entire course of a study allow for both types of comparisons. However, school-expulsion data obtained at the end of a two-year follow-up allow only for treatment comparisons.

Whenever longitudinal comparisons are planned, the measurement points to be contrasted must yield comparable data (see McNamara & MacDonough, 1972, for a general discussion of this issue). Data suitable for comparison purposes may be difficult to obtain whenever the duration of a study can be expected to span adjacent developmental periods, as the types of problem behaviors may shift considerably with development (e.g., Subotnik, 1972, p. 38). For example, tantruming at age 6 might be functionally equivalent to vandalism at age 8. One possible solution to this problem is the use of broad categorical measurement scales. For example, Patterson, Ray, and Shaw (1968) have developed observational procedures that classify behavior into the two broad categories of *deviant* and *nondeviant*. However, unless such scales also include separate subscales for the targeted response, they may sacrifice sensitivity in exchange for breadth.

Problems of data comparability also occur when institutional indicators employed as dependent variables change either in availability or nature. For example, school grades are not typically available during summer months, and grading policies may change between elementary school and junior high school. The nonequivalent measurement scales may be resolvable through the use of traditional scaling procedures (see, e.g., discussions of scaling issues in Harris, 1963, and Nunnally, 1967). Problems associated with the developmental nature of target behaviors and discontinuities in the occasions for measurement are unlikely to have general solutions applicable to all psychotherapy studies, but it is critical that they be considered at the initial planning stage.

3.5.2. Timing of Follow-up Assessments

The proper timing of follow-up assessments is particularly important in child-psychotherapy research (e.g., Heinicke & Strassman, 1975). Unfortunately, follow-up assessments are usually conducted at arbitrarily determined times dictated by practical exigencies rather than by some predetermined rationale (Mash, 1975). The interval between treatment and follow-up assessments can, on the one hand, be too brief to allow an assessment of the stability of treatment effects, or on the other hand, it may be so long that the specific effects of treatment are overwhelmed by intervening life experiences (e.g., Kellner, 1967).

In addition to the measurement and developmental issues previously discussed, the choice of number and timing of follow-up assessments also involves the following issues:

1. *The nature of the treatments compared.* Luborsky et al. (1975) implied the need for multiple follow-ups and long temporal delays in their observation that some forms of treatment—such as behavior therapy, pharmacological therapy, time-limited therapy, and directive therapy—exert their effects early, whereas other treatments, such as long-term analytic therapy, take a slower course.

2. *The rate of the target behavior.* Lower-rate target behaviors that are cumulatively indexed, such as fire setting and auto theft, may require longer follow-up periods, whereas higher-rate responses, such as compliance to parental requests and thumb sucking, can usually be assessed in briefer follow-up periods (Mash, 1975).

3. *The client's developmental phase.* Lewis et al. (1975), for example, have suggested that the use of a single follow-up assessment shortly following treatment might be undesirable with adolescents because of the substantial fluctuations in their immediate posttreatment behavior.

Whichever decisions are made regarding the timing of follow-up assessments, it is important to ensure that treatment groups are assessed during comparable time periods and that they do not differ with respect to the duration between assessment periods (see Windle, 1962, p. 30, for a discussion of problems that can arise when temporal factors are confounded with treatment conditions).

3.5.2.1. Sample Attrition. A frequent cost incurred in the use of long-term follow-up assessment intervals is increased sample attrition (e.g., Erickson, 1975). With longer follow-up intervals, factors such as subject mobility, family instability, and name changes by female subjects make it increasingly difficult to contact former patients and their families for assessment purposes. Unfortunately for the psychotherapy researcher, the availability of patients for follow-up assessments may be related to outcome (e.g., O'Leary, Turkewitz, & Taffel, 1973; Robins & O'Neal, 1969). Techniques that have been found useful in the location of errant patients are described in Lewis et al. (1975), Mumford and Linburn (1969), and Robins and O'Neal (1969).

Even patients who are located may be unwilling to participate in follow-up assessments. Sometimes their reluctance can be overcome by financial incentives for continued cooperation (e.g., Robins, 1972). At other times, requests for follow-up information may be perceived as an infringement on the patient's and his family's right to privacy. These issues must be handled with sensitivity, and would seem less likely to provide impediments to successful completion of the study if the need and the specific plan for obtaining follow-up data are explained to the patient and his family at the time of their admission to treatment (e.g., Lewis *et al.*, 1975).

3.6. Evaluation

Evaluation of results should be planned at the time that decisions are made regarding general design strategy and the independent and dependent variables are chosen. Even with proper planning, expert statistical advice may be required if investigators are to avoid major pitfalls (Fiske *et al.*, 1970). Typically, analyses are required on three classes of variables: independent variables (treatment variables); control variables, such as age and socioeconomic status; and dependent variables. Because the form of analysis employed for these three classes is often quite similar, this section focuses exclusively on the dependent variable.

Prior to engaging in a formal analysis of psychotherapy-outcome data, the investigator typically must decide how to deal with subjects who have terminated before completion of the study. Unless terminators are appropriately dealt with, the findings can be seriously compromised (Lasky, 1962). The first step in dealing with terminators requires ascertaining which of the patients defected from treatment because of treatment-related reasons and which were lost because of factors unrelated to treatment (see Meltzoff & Kornreich, 1970, for a discussion of this issue). Typically, subjects who terminate for reasons unrelated to treatment, such as a change of residence, are simply dropped from the analysis. Treatment-related terminators, however, cannot be dismissed lightly and should be either analyzed separately or given an estimated score for the missing measurement occasions. For subjects who begin treatment but terminate between baseline and posttreatment assessment periods, the baseline-assessment scores may appropriately be substituted for subsequent measurement occasions. Lasky (1962) and May, Yale, and Dixon (1972) have suggested techniques that may be useful in the estimation of scores for subjects who terminate after the end of treatment and before follow-up evaluations.

3.6.1. Assessment of Treatment Effectiveness

The most crucial analyses in treatment-outcome studies concern the differential effectiveness of the treatment conditions. The assessment of treatment effectiveness is highly complex, requiring consideration of the degree, the generality, and the persistence of change (e.g., Baer, Wolf, & Risley, 1968). In general, this assessment will be facilitated through the use of a variety of judgmental aids, including careful visual inspection as well as statistical analyses of the data. Because many of our intervention techniques produce only weak effects, most group-comparison studies require statistical analyses. There is still some debate over the utility of statistical analyses for the data produced by individual-subject designs (e.g., Society for the Experimental Analysis of Behavior, 1975). Even here, however, we recommend statistical procedures such as those described by Kazdin (1976) and Jones and his colleagues (Jones, Vaught, & Weinrott, 1977) when visual inspection fails to reveal clear trends and when the assumptions of the statistical test can be met. However, psychology researchers must be alert to the dangers resulting from reliance on probability values to determine the effectiveness of treatment interventions. (See discussions by Michael, 1974, and by Cohen, 1965, on the important distinction between statistical significance and applied significance.) These dangers can, in large part, be avoided if one compares the performance of treated subjects with treatment goals or with the behavior of normal subjects. Only if the goals are fairly closely approximated, or if the behavior of the treated clients resembles that of ordinary people, can truly meaningful change be claimed.

Typically, statistical analysis involves some form of either univariate or multivariate analysis of variance procedures. The latter procedures are recommended for studies that employ multiple dependent variables and that can meet the assumptions of the specific multivariate technique employed; for example, the number of subjects per condition must exceed the number of variables (Davidson, 1972). In general, multivariate procedures have the advantage of being based on less restrictive assumptions and of providing some protection against the troublesome problem of grossly inflated Type I error rates that occur when separate analyses are conducted on each of many dependent variables.

Other investigators may choose to employ more traditional univariate techniques, such as the analysis of covariance, split-plot (conditions by measurements) techniques, or other related procedures (see Huck & McLean, 1975, and Feldt, 1958, for discussions of the advantages and disadvantages of these designs). Because these procedures are frequently applied incorrectly in psychotherapy-outcome studies, the most commonly occurring errors are listed here. When appropriate, citations are made of works in which these problems are discussed.

1. On occasion, continuous variables—either dependent or independent—are artificially dichotomized, presumably for the sake of convenience. The degrading of variables in this matter is essentially

equivalent to throwing out subjects, as it typically decreases the power of the analysis (Cohen, 1968, p. 441).

2. Some behavioral coding systems and objective tests produce ipsative scales, the scores from which are necessarily nonindependent; for example, receiving a high score on one scale requires that lower scores be obtained on other scales. Ipsative data can pose serious interpretive problems, are unsuitable for many traditional statistical procedures, and in general are inferior to normatively derived data (see Jones, 1973, and Hicks, 1970, for discussions of these problems).

3. In simple two-group designs, investigators sometimes evaluate change by performing two separate t tests either on the pre- and then the postmeasures for the two groups or on the change scores for each group. In either case, if one comparison is statistically significant and the other is not, an argument is made for differential change for the two groups. Unfortunately, neither of these procedures accurately tests differences in net change between the two groups (e.g., McNemar, 1969, pp. 96–98).

4. It is not uncommon for investigators to use a matching procedure in assigning subjects to conditions and then to fail to take the matching into account when selecting a statistical model for data analysis. This is not unlike using an independent t test when a correlated t test is required, and can lead to serious bias.

5. Still more common is the failure to take into account more elusive nesting procedures. For example, when subjects are treated or assessed in groups, their performances may become correlated. When such correlation occurs, each group's score and not each subject's score should be considered the unit of analysis (e.g., Myers, 1966, Chapter 9).

6. Investigators frequently fail to test the assumptions required by the statistical model they employ. Unlike simpler analysis of variance models, those involving repeated measures make stringent assumptions about the structure of the matrix of correlations between the repeated measures. These assumptions require testing because their violation can produce serious overestimations of statistical significance (e.g., McCall & Appelbaum, 1973).

7. The selection of error terms (and degrees of freedom when some subjects have missing data) seems to be a continual source of confusion. Most standard statistical texts (e.g., Kirk, 1968) provide rules for determining appropriate error terms and degrees of freedom.

8. The inclusion of multiple groups and multiple-measurement occasions in psychotherapy research tempts even otherwise conscientious investigators to perform numerous *post hoc* analyses in search of some significant results. These "fishing expeditions" can seriously

inflate Type I error rates. When multiple comparisons are made, appropriate protection methods should be employed (e.g., Kirk, 1968, Chapter 3; see also Cook & Campbell, 1976, for a discussion of this and other threats to statistical validity).

3.6.2. Correlates of Change

A common procedure followed in outcome studies, especially in those studies that fail to find treatment differences, is to search for variables that are correlated with change. Favorite targets in the search for prognostic indicators include a wide variety of demographic and organismic variables that are typically obtained at intake. The problems associated with the search for treatment-outcome predictors are at best serious and at worst insurmountable (Luborsky et al., 1971; Windle, 1962). The typical criterion measure used in these investigations—raw change scores—often suffers from poor reliability (McNemar, 1969, pp. 173–176) and is seriously confounded with regression effects (e.g., Lord, 1963). The problems involved in the development of adequate baseline-free measures are sufficiently complex (O'Connor, 1972; Cronbach & Furby, 1970) to defeat all but the most persistent investigators.

The search for useful prognostic indicators is further limited by the small sample sizes employed in most treatment-outcome studies. Small samples place serious limitations on the ability to detect effective predictors (power), and when combined with large sets of potential predictor variables, they make multiple prediction a dubious enterprise (McNemar, 1969, pp. 203–211). A final caveat concerns the interpretation of predictors of change or improvement that are derived solely from an analysis of the performance of treated subjects. Unless these variables show significantly *different* predictive validities for subjects in untreated conditions, they may help little in decisions about which patients are likely to benefit most from treatment. Similar predictive validities for both treated and untreated subjects may simply indicate that patients with particular characteristics, whether treated or untreated, exhibit greater positive change than do patients without these characteristics (see Cronbach & Gleser, 1965, for a discussion of related issues).

The problems addressed in this section concern the assessment of the relative effectiveness of treatment interventions. Investigations of this kind are difficult to conduct, as is clear from the number of problems raised. Section 4 deals with a still more difficult problem: the assessment of the relative costs and benefits associated with various treatment procedures. As Panzetta (1973) has described the situation, having failed to adequately subdue an alligator, we are now going to try a lion (p. 454).

4. Cost–Benefit Analysis

Psychotherapy investigators are increasingly being asked to address broader issues of evaluation than those of relative treatment effectiveness (Panzetta, 1973). These issues concern treatment efficiency as well as other cost-related aspects of treatment, ranging from the training of staff and the use of consultants to reinforcer expenses (e.g., Sherman & Bushell, 1975; Davidson & Seidman, 1974; O'Dell, 1974; Tavormina, 1974; Johnson & Katz, 1973; O'Leary & Drabman, 1971; Marks, 1969; Patterson, 1971).

Yates (1975) and Panzetta (1973), among others (e.g., Perloff, Perloff, & Sussna, 1976) have recently distinguished among the various evaluation strategies that address the issue of the costs of psychotherapy. At the most elementary level is cost accounting, which is simply a listing of costs per unit of service without consideration of effectiveness. Cost–efficiency, a somewhat more sophisticated procedure, is essentially comparative cost-accounting (Panzetta, 1973), again without consideration of relative effectiveness. Even when assessed in terms of these rudimentary evaluation strategies, most psychotherapy-outcome studies with children are deficient in cost–effectiveness evaluation. For example, Peterson and Hartmann (1975) found that only 19% of the comparative child-psychotherapy–outcome studies reviewed contained any cost data, and in most cases this information was limited to "a brief description of either therapist time or reinforcer costs" (p. 12).

The next level of assessment, cost–benefit analysis, compares the costs incurred in treatment with the monetary benefits generated by that treatment (Yates, 1975). This procedure is limited to situations in which the effects of treatment are amenable to monetary quantification. Snider, Sullivan, and Manning (1974) described a cost–benefit analysis of the Regional Intervention Program (Ora & Reisinger, 1971) that supplemented evaluations involving specifically defined organizational and client objectives, data-based assessments of child progress, and accountability to a consumer-based evaluation committee.

The most relevant level of evaluation for most child-psychotherapy–outcome studies is cost-effectiveness analysis, which contrasts nonmonetary measures of treatment effectiveness with treatment costs. Yates (1975) has described in some detail the steps required in a cost-effectiveness analysis of treatments, and has illustrated this material with examples from a treatment program for behaviorally disturbed preadolescents. Many of the steps described by Yates are familiar to investigators of treatment effectiveness (e.g., specifying variables and goals, choosing alternative treatments, and generating effectiveness indices that allow outcome comparisons for patients with different problems or with similar problems but different baseline rates). Less familiar steps are those involved in:

1. Specifying cost variables (e.g., the cost of time expended by professionals, paraprofessionals, volunteers, and supportive staff; transportation costs; and the costs for equipment, material, and space).
2. Generating cost indices (the analogue of effectiveness indices).
3. Developing cost–effectiveness indices.

Unfortunately, we are years away from the routine inclusion of sophisticated cost–efficiency analyses in evaluations of child-treatment techniques. Thus, funding and implementation decisions for child mental-health services will continue to be based on inadequate information. More promising, however, is the increasing attention directed to both treatment costs and treatment benefits in training manuals for child therapists (Gelfand & Hartmann, 1975, Chapter 3) and in the evaluations of behaviorally based treatment programs (see Davidson, Clark, & Hamerlynck, 1974).

5. *The Social Context of Outcome Research*

Outcome research in child psychotherapy can be conducted only in settings that provide a number of children requiring treatment. Thus, most psychotherapy-outcome studies are conducted in existing service centers, such as university clinics, schools, community mental-health agencies, or residential treatment programs. As Twain (1975) has suggested, there are problems unique to the conduct of research in these human-service agencies, whether the investigator is a part of the in-house staff, is an external evaluator, or is simply seeking to use the agency's resources. Some of these problems may be generated by ideological differences between research and practice; by the difficulties inherent in the application of research techniques to social-service settings; by conflicts in perceived goals, priorities, or professional obligations; and by obstacles that may arise from agency structure that affect the conduct of research (Twain, 1975, p. 28).

The agency staff, even if only indirectly involved in the project, may resent any intrusion into their setting. They may perceive research as irrelevant to their activities and find the skeptical attitude of the researcher incongruous with their own ideological commitment (Twain, 1975). They may express hesitancy over the ethics of some of the research procedures, such as the use of random techniques to determine who is treated and how they are treated (Wortman, 1975).

If agency staff are more directly tied to the project, they may resent their role as research assistants and the restrictions that the requirements of the design impose on their freedom of action (Brody, 1957). If traditional institutional practices are under study, the clinical staff may, in addition, see the research project as a challenge to their own sense of worth (Lewis et al., 1975). These sources of conflict between the researcher and the agency staff have consequences for what kind of study is done, how well it is done, and what reception it gets when completed (Weiss, 1973). Twain (1975) and Glaser and Taylor (1973) have provided a number of suggestions that the applied researcher might follow to ensure the successful completion of a study:

1. Be aware of the structural characteristics of the agency in terms of its receptiveness to effective research involvement, and be aware of the style and power of its administrator(s).

2. Understand and respect the individual roles and functions of agency personnel.

3. Actively work at establishing rapport with agency staff. Invite their opinions and reactions, and avoid adopting an us-versus-them attitude.

4. Develop some form of negotiated contract with the agency. Particular items appropriate for inclusion in the contract concern the nature of the data to be gathered, the procedures to be used in subject selection, and any standardization of procedures that may be required.

5. Provide feedback to agency staff in a form that is perceived as promoting professional effectiveness and not as casting blame for poor performance (Krumboltz, 1974).

One can only agree with the conclusions of Glaser and Taylor (1973) that researchers must understand and use appropriate organizational-management theory and practices in their relations with participating agencies if they wish to carry out research successfully in applied clinical settings.

6. Summary and Conclusions

As with many other worthwhile pursuits, effective outcome research in child psychotherapy requires extensive planning and a broad range of interpersonal and technical skills. To aid investigators and consumers of child-psychotherapy–outcome research in finding their way through the thicket of technical problems, we have summarized the primary methodological issues in Table 1. This summary includes the issues discussed in this chapter as well as criteria previously employed in evaluating psychotherapy-outcome studies (e.g., Luborsky et al., 1975; Davidson & Seidman, 1974; O'Dell, 1974).

In preparing this chapter, we examined hundreds of monographs,

TABLE 1
*Methodological Criteria for Evaluating Outcome Research
in Child Psychotherapy*

General Design
    Design guards against all major threats to internal validity.
    Suitable comparison groups included; active control conditions (if used) are equivalent in credibility to treatment conditions.
    Subjects are randomly assigned.
    Absence of differential drop-outs between conditions.
    Subjects in untreated conditions are in fact untreated; concurrent unprogrammed treatment is not unequal in the compared groups.
Subjects
    Actual patients were employed.
    Subjects are homogeneous with regard to problem behavior and treatment goal.
    Subjects are adequately described; criteria for exclusion are made explicit.
Treatments
    Independent evaluation indicates that treatments are of the designated type.
    Treatments are given in reasonable amounts and, if applicable, in equal amounts.
    Therapists are experienced, and therapists for compared groups are equally competent.
Measures
    Outcome variables include specific measures of the target behavior as well as measures of general functioning.
    Evidence presented that outcome measures are unbiased, sensitive, reliable, and valid.
Follow-up Assessments
    Follow-up assessments are included, and are obtained at appropriate time periods.
    Comparable measures are used during follow-up and previous assessments.
Evaluation
    The terminal sample size is adequate for formal evaluation.
    Terminators are handled correctly.
    Appropriate analyses are conducted on the data, and the analyses correctly performed.
    Distinction made between statistical and applied significance.
    Cost as well as effectiveness information is included.

articles, and reports. As a result of our reading, we formed some impressions that seem sufficiently well founded to sustain the test of replicability. The first is that although we have not yet arrived at the golden age of outcome research in child psychotherapy, the technical quality of recent studies has markedly improved over those performed a decade or more ago. The comment made by Heinicke and Goldman (1960) that terminator controls were the only ones available as of 1957 (p. 487) seems truly to come out of a different and less sophisticated era. We found the work by Stallings (1975) on Project Follow-Through to be an exemplary model for evaluation research with child programs. We have also been particularly impressed by the applied-research programs conducted by Patterson and his colleagues at the University of Oregon (e.g., Patterson, 1976; Patterson et al., 1975; Jones et al., 1975) and by Wolf, Fixsen, Phillips, and their colleagues at the University of Kansas (e.g., Braukmann & Fixsen, 1975). Continuing projects such as these seem most likely to produce advances in our fund of knowledge as well as in our treatment technology.

We also noted a reduction in the ideological and propagandistic warfare of an earlier age. The optimism over monolithic comparative studies seems to have cooled, and what controversy remains over designs is largely concerned with the role of analogue and individual-subject studies and with the role of studies of existing practices. Though there are still unresolved technical problems, it is our impression that an adequate technology for outcome studies in child psychotherapy is now available. More work is required, for example, in the development of measurement systems that are sensitive, relatively nonreactive, and at the same time economical. Indices of improvement are still not entirely satisfactory, despite at least 15 years of attention to the problem of change scores (see, e.g., Harris, 1963).

Finally, while we have developed an adequate outcome-assessment technology, new demands now are being placed on investigators, particularly for cost–efficiency information. Fortunately, the therapy-outcome researcher will increasingly have available the technology and information that appears to be developing rapidly in the general field of program evaluation (e.g., Struening & Guttentag, 1975).

In this chapter, we have attempted to highlight the primary issues in the conduct of outcome research in child psychotherapy. Our justification for this emphasis is simple: there is a need for outcome studies, and those studies that have attempted to fill this need are typically flawed and hence theoretically and practically ambiguous. Just as reliability forces a ceiling on validity, so does methodology force a ceiling on knowledge in science (MacDonald & Tobias, 1976, p. 448). As we sharpen our evaluation skills and apply these skills to child-treatment programs, we may find ourselves with practices that are effective and are maintained for better reasons than simply that they are there. It is through the use of carefully planned and executed evaluation research that we may break the cycle of initial enthusiasm followed by disenchantment that has characterized the history of psychotherapy (Hersch, 1968).

References

Atthowe, J. M. Behavior innovation and persistence. *American Psychologist*, 1973, *28*, 34–41.

Baekeland, F., & Lundwall, L. Dropping out of treatment: A critical view. *Psychological Bulletin*, 1975, *82*, 738–783.

Baer, D. M., Wolf, M. M., & Risley, T. R. Some current dimensions of applied behavior analysis. *Journal of Applied Behavior Analysis*, 1968, *1*, 91–97.

Baker, B. L. Camp Freedom: Behavior modification for retarded children in a therapeutic camp setting. *American Journal of Orthopsychiatry*, 1973, *43*, 418–427.

Bandura, A. *Principles of behavior modification*. New York: Holt, Rinehart & Winston, 1969.

Beatty, W. W. How blind is blind? A simple procedure for estimating observer naïveté. *Psychological Bulletin*, 1972, *78*, 70–71.

Bergin, A. E., & Strupp, H. H. *Changing frontiers in the science of psychotherapy*. Chicago: Aldine-Atherton, 1972.

Bergin, A. E., & Suinn, R. M. Individual psychotherapy and behavior therapy. In M. R. Rosenzweig & L. W. Porter (Eds.), *Annual review of psychology*, Vol. 26. Palo Alto, Calif.: Annual Reviews, 1975.

Bernal, M. E. Comparison of behavioral and nondirective parent counseling. Paper presented at the annual meeting of the American Association of Behavior Therapists, San Francisco, December 1975.

Bernstein, D. A. Behavioral fear assessment: Anxiety or artifact? In H. E. Adams & I. P. Unikel (Eds.), *Issues and trends in behavior therapy*. Springfield, Ill.: Charles C Thomas, 1973.

Bernstein, D. A., & Paul, G. L. Some comments on therapy analogue research with small animal "phobias." *Journal of Behavior Therapy and Experimental Psychiatry*, 1971, *2*, 225–237.

Bijou, S. W., & Peterson, R. F. Functional analysis in the assessment of children. In P. McReynolds (Ed.), *Advances in psychological assessment*, Vol. 2. Palo Alto, Calif.: Science & Behavior Books, Inc., 1971.

Bijou, S. W., & Redd, W. H. Child behavior therapy. In S. Arieti (Ed.), *American handbook of psychiatry*, 2nd ed., Vol. 5. New York: Basic Books, 1975.

Braukmann, C. J., & Fixsen, D. L. Behavior modification with delinquents. In M. Hersen, R. M. Eisler, & P. M. Miller (Eds.), *Progress in behavior modification*, Vol. 1. New York: Academic Press, 1975.

Brody, E. B. Discussions of "Anxieties associated with the conduct of research in clinical settings." *American Journal of Orthopsychiatry*, 1957, *27*, 327–330.

Callner, D. A. Behavioral treatment of drug abuse. *Psychological Bulletin*, 1975, *82*, 143–164.

Campbell, D. T. From description to experimentation: Interpreting trends as quasi-experiments. *In* C. W. Harris (Ed.), *Problems in measuring change*. Madison: University of Wisconsin Press, 1963.

Campbell, D. T. Prospective: Artifact and control. *In* R. Rosenthal and R. L. Rosnow (Eds.), *Artifact in behavioral research*. New York: Academic Press, 1969.

Campbell, D. T., & Fiske, D. Convergent and discriminant validation by the multi-trait, multi-method matrix. *Psychological Bulletin*, 1959, *56*, 81–105.

Campbell, D. T., & Stanley, J. C. *Experimental and quasi-experimental designs for research*. Chicago: Rand McNally, 1966.

Chassan, J. B. Statistical inference and the single case in clinical design. *Psychiatry*, 1960, *23*, 173–185.

Chassan, J. B. Probability processes in psychoanalytic psychiatry. *In* J. Scher (Ed.), *Theories of the mind*. New York: Free Press, 1962.

Chassan, J. B. *Research design in clinical psychology and psychiatry*. New York: Appleton-Century-Crofts, 1967.

Clarizio, H. F. Stability of deviant behavior through time. *Mental Hygiene*, 1968, *52*, 288–293.

Clarizio, H. F., & McCoy, G. F. *Behavior disorders in children*, 2nd ed. New York: Thomas Y. Crowell, 1976.

Clum, B. A. Intrapsychic variables and the patient's environment as factors in prognosis. *Psychological Bulletin*, 1975, *82*, 413–431.

Cohen, J. Some statistical issues in psychological research. *In* B. B. Wolman (Ed.), *Handbook of clinical psychology*. New York: McGraw-Hill, 1965.

Cohen, J. Multiple regression as a general data-analytic system. *Psychological Bulletin*, 1968, *70*, 426–443.

Cohen, J. *Statistical power analysis for the behavioral sciences*. New York: Academic Press, 1969.

Cook, T. D., & Campbell, D. T. The design and conduct of quasi-experiments and true experiments in field settings. *In* M. D. Dunnette (Ed.), *Handbook of industrial and organizational research*. Chicago: Rand McNally, 1976.

Cowen, E. L. Social and community interventions. *In* P. H. Mussen & M. R. Rosenzweig (Eds.), *Annual review of psychology*, Vol. 24. Palo Alto, Calif.: Annual Reviews, 1973.

Cowen, E. L., Trost, M. A., Lorion, R. P., Dorr, D., Izzo, L. D., & Isaacson, R. V. *New ways in school mental health: Early detection and prevention of school maladaptation*. New York: Human Sciences, 1975.

Cowen, E. L., & Zax, M. The mental health fields today: Issues and problems. *In* E. L. Cowen, E. A. Gardner, & M. Zax (Eds.), *Emergent approaches to mental health problems*. New York: Appleton-Century-Crofts, 1967.

Cronbach, L. J., & Furby, L. How should we measure change—or should we? *Psychological Bulletin*, 1970, *74*, 68–80. (See also errata, 1970, *74*, 218.)

Cronbach, L. J., & Gleser, G. C. *Psychological tests and personnel decisions*. Urbana: University of Illinois Press, 1965.

Cronbach, L. J., Gleser, G. C., Nanda, H., & Rajarathan, N. *The dependability of behavioral measurements: Theory of generalizability for scores and profiles*. New York: Wiley, 1972.

Davidson, M. L. Univariate versus multivariate tests in repeated-measures experiments. *Psychological Bulletin*, 1972, *77*, 446–452.

Davidson, P. O., Clark, F. W., & Hamerlynck, L. A. *Evaluation of behavioral programs*. Champaign, Ill.: Research Press, 1974.

Davidson, W. S., II, & Seidman, E. Studies of behavior modification and juvenile delinquency: A review, methodological critique, and social perspective. *Psychological Bulletin*, 1974, *81*, 998–1011.

Dukes, W. F. *N* = 1. *Psychological Bulletin*, 1965, *74*, 74–80.

Edgar, E., & Billingsley, F. Believability when *N* = 1. *Psychological Record*, 1974, *24*, 147–160.

Edgington, E. S. *Statistical inference: The distribution-free approach.* New York: McGraw-Hill, 1969.

Endicott, N. A. Standard methods needed. *International Journal of Psychiatry*, 1969, *7*, 118–121.

Erickson, R. C. Outcome studies in mental hospitals: A review. *Psychological Bulletin*, 1975, *82*, 519–540.

Feldt, L. S. A comparison of the precision of three experimental designs employing a concomitant variable. *Psychometrica*, 1958, *23*, 335–354.

Fiedler, F. E. The concept of an ideal therapeutic relationship. *Journal of Consulting Psychology*, 1950, *14*, 239–245.

Fiske, D. W. *Measuring the concepts of personality.* Chicago: Aldine, 1971.

Fiske, D. W., Hunt, H. F., Luborsky, L., Orne, M. T., Parloff, M. B., Reiser, M. F., & Tuma, A. H. Planning of research on effectiveness of psychotherapy. *Archives of General Psychiatry*, 1970, *22*, 22–32.

Frank, J. D. Problems of control in psychotherapy as exemplified by the psychotherapy research project of the Phipps Psychiatric Clinic. *In* E. A. Rubinstein & M. B. Parloff (Eds.), *Research in psychotherapy.* Washington, D.C.: American Psychological Association, 1959.

Gelfand, D. M., & Hartmann, D. P. Behavior therapy with children. A review and evaluation of research methodology. *Psychological Bulletin*, 1968, *69*, 204–215.

Gelfand, D. M., & Hartmann, D. P. *Child behavior analysis and therapy.* New York: Pergamon Press, 1975.

Glaser, E. M., & Taylor, S. H. Factors influencing the success of applied research. *American Psychologist*, 1973, *28*, 140–146.

Goldstein, A. P. *Therapist–patient expectancies in psychotherapy.* New York: Pergamon Press, 1962.

Goldstein, A. P., Heller, K., & Sechrest, L. B. *Psychotherapy and the psychology of behavior change.* New York: Wiley, 1966.

Gossett, J. T., Lewis, S. B., Lewis, J. M., & Phillips, V. A. Follow-up of adolescents treated in a psychiatric hospital: I. A review of studies. *American Journal of Orthopsychiatry*, 1973, *43*, 602–610.

Greenwald, A. G. Within-subjects designs: To use or not to use. *Psychological Bulletin*, 1976, *83*, 314–320.

Gurin, G., Veroff, J., & Feld, S. *Americans view their mental health: A nationwide interview survey.* New York: Basic Books, 1960.

Hall, R. V., & Copeland, R. E. The responsive teaching model: A first step in shaping school personnel as behavior modification specialists. *In* F. W. Clark, D. R. Evans, & L. A. Hamerlynck (Eds.), *Implementing behavior programs for schools and clinics.* Champaign, Ill.: Research Press, 1972.

Harris, C. W. (Ed.). *Problems in measuring change.* Madison: University of Wisconsin Press, 1963.

Harris, S. L. Teaching language to nonverbal children—with emphasis on problems of generalization. *Psychological Bulletin*, 1975, *82*, 565–580.

Hartmann, D. P. *Some neglected issues in behavior modification with children.* Paper presented at the Sixth Annual Meeting of the American Association of Behavior Therapy, New York, October 1972.

Hartmann, D. P. Considerations in the choice of interobserver reliability estimates. *Journal of Applied Behavior Analysis*, 1977, *10*, 103–116.

Hathaway, S. R. Some considerations relative to nondirective counseling as therapy. *Journal of Clinical Psychology*, 1948, *4*, 226–231.

Heinicke, C. M., & Goldman, A. Research on psychotherapy with children: A review and suggestions for further study. *American Journal of Orthopsychiatry*, 1960, *30*, 483–494.

Heinicke, C. M., & Strassman, L. H. Toward more effective research on child psychotherapy. *American Academy of Child Psychiatry*, 1975, *14*, 561–588.

Heitler, J. B. Preparatory techniques in initiating expressive psychotherapy with lower-class, unsophisticated patients. *Psychological Bulletin*, 1976, *83*, 339–352.

Hersch, C. The discontent explosion in mental health. *American Psychologist*, 1968, *23*, 497–506.

Hersen, M., & Barlow, D. H. *Single case experimental designs: Strategies for studying behavior change*. Oxford: Pergamon Press, 1976.

Hicks, L. E. Some properties of ipsative, normative, and forced-choice normative measures. *Psychological Bulletin*, 1970, *74*, 167–184.

Hiebert, S. Who benefits from the program? Criteria selection. *In* P. O. Davidson, F. W. Clark, & L. A. Hamerlynck (Eds.), *Evaluation of behavioral programs*. Champaign, Ill.: Research Press, 1974.

Hobbs, N. Strategies for the development of clinical psychology. *American Psychological Association Division of Clinical Psychology Newsletter*, 1963, *16*, 3–5.

Holmes, D. S., & Urie, R. G. Effects of preparing children for psychotherapy. *Journal of Consulting and Clinical Psychology*, 1975, *43*, 311–318.

Huck, S. W., & McLean, R. A. Using a repeated measures ANOVA to analyze the data from a pretest–posttest design: A potentially confusing task. *Psychological Bulletin*, 1975, *82*, 511–518.

Jacob, T., Magnussen, M. G., & Kemler, W. M. A follow-up of treatment terminators and remainers with long-term and short-term symptom duration. *Psychotherapy: Theory, Research and Practice*, 1972, *9*, 139–142.

Johnson, C. A., & Katz, R. C. Using parents as change agents for their children: A review. *Journal of Child Psychology and Psychiatry*, 1973, *14*, 181–200.

Johnson, S. M., & Bolstad, O. D. Methodological issues in naturalistic observations: Some problems and solutions for field research. *In* L. A. Hamerlynck, L. C. Handy, & R. J. Mash (Eds.), *Behavior change: Methodology, concepts, and practice*. Champaign, Ill.: Research Press, 1973.

Johnson, S. M., & Christensen, A. Multiple criteria follow-up of behavior modification with families. *Journal of Abnormal Child Psychology*, 1975, *3*, 135–154.

Jones, M. The adequacy of employee selection reports. *Journal of Applied Psychology*, 1950, *34*, 219–224.

Jones, R. R. Behavioral observation and frequency data: Problems in scoring, analysis, and interpretation. *In* L. A. Hamerlynck, L. C. Handy, & E. J. Mash (Eds.), *Behavior change: Methodology, concepts, and practices*. Champaign, Ill.: Research Press, 1973.

Jones, R. R., Reid, R. B., & Patterson, G. R. Naturalistic observation in clinical assessment. *In* P. McReynolds (Ed.), *Advances in psychological assessment*, Vol. 3. San Francisco: Jossey-Bass, 1975.

Jones, R. R., Vaught, R. S., & Weinrott, M. Time series analysis in operant research. *Journal of Applied Behavior Analysis*, 1977, *10*, 151–166.

Kadushin, A. *Child welfare services*, 2nd ed. New York: Macmillan, 1974.

Kanfer, F. H., & Saslow, G. Behavioral diagnosis. In C. M. Franks (Ed.), Behavior therapy: Appraisal and status. New York: McGraw-Hill, 1969.

Karlsruher, A. E. The nonprofessional as a psychotherapeutic agent: A review of the empirical evidence pertaining to his effectiveness. American Journal of Community Psychology, 1974, 2, 61–77.

Karoly, P. On controls in psychotherapy research: A plea for innocence. Psychotherapy: Theory, Research and Practice, 1972, 9, 11–12.

Kazdin, A. E. Methodological and assessment considerations in evaluating reinforcement programs in applied settings. Journal of Applied Behavior Analysis, 1973, 6, 517–531.

Kazdin, A. E. Recent advances in token economy research. In M. Hersen, R. M. Eisler, & P. M. Miller (Eds.), Progress in behavior modification, Vol. 1. New York: Academic Press, 1975.

Kazdin, A. E. Statistical analyses for single-case experimental designs. In M. Hersen & D. H. Barlow (Eds.), Single case experimental designs: Strategies for studying behavior change. Oxford: Pergamon Press, 1976.

Kazdin, A. E., & Wilcoxon, L. A. Systematic desensitization and nonspecific treatment effects: A methodological evaluation. Psychological Bulletin, 1976, 83, 729–758.

Kellner, R. The evidence in favor of psychotherapy. British Journal of Medical Psychology, 1967, 40, 341–358.

Kelly, J. G., Snowden, L. R., & Muñoz, R. F. Social and community intervention. In M. R. Rosenzweig & L. W. Porter (Eds.), Annual Review of Psychology, Vol. 28 Palo Alto, Calif.: Annual Reviews, 1977.

Kiesler, D. J. Some myths of psychotherapy research and the search for a paradigm. Psychological Bulletin, 1966, 65, 110–136.

Kiesler, D. J. Experimental designs in psychotherapy research. In A. E. Bergin & S. L. Garfield (Eds.), Handbook of psychotherapy and behavior change: An empirical analysis. New York: Wiley, 1971.

Kirk, R. E. Experimental design: Procedures for the behavioral sciences. Monterey, Calif.: Brooks/Cole, 1968.

Klein, D., & Davis, J. Diagnosis and drug treatment of psychiatric disorders. Baltimore: Williams & Wilkins, 1969.

Kleinmuntz, B. Personality measurement: An introduction. Homewood, Ill.: Dorsey Press, 1967.

Krause, M. S. Construct validity for the evaluation of therapy outcomes. Journal of Abnormal Psychology, 1969, 74, 524–530.

Krumboltz, J. D. An accountability model for counselors. Personnel and Guidance Journal, 1974, 52, 639–646.

Lambert, M. J. Spontaneous remission in adult neurotic disorders: A revision and summary. Psychological Bulletin, 1976, 83, 107–119.

Lasky, L. J. The problem of sample attrition in controlled treatment trials. Journal of Nervous and Mental Disease, 1962, 135, 332–337.

Lazarus, A. A., & Davison, G. C. Clinical innovation in research and practice. In A. E. Bergin & S. L. Garfield (Eds.), Handbook of psychotherapy and behavior change. New York: Wiley, 1971.

Leitenberg, H., & Callahan, E. J. Reinforced practice and reduction of different kinds of fears in adults and children. Behaviour Research and Therapy, 1973, 11, 19–30.

Levitt, E. E. The results of psychotherapy with children: An evaluation. Journal of Consulting Psychology, 1957, 21, 189–196.

Levitt, E. E. Psychotherapy with children: A further evaluation. Behaviour Research and Therapy, 1963, 1, 45–51.

Levitt, E. E. Research on psychotherapy with children. In A. E. Bergin & S. L. Garfield (Eds.), Handbook of psychotherapy and behavior change. New York: Wiley, 1971.

Lewis, S. B., Barnhart, F. D., Gossett, J. T., & Phillips, V. A. Follow-up of adolescents treated in a psychiatric hospital-operational solution to some methodological problems of clinical research. American Journal of Orthopsychiatry, 1975, 45, 813–824.

Lewis, W. Continuity and intervention in emotional disturbance: A review. Exceptional Children, 1965, 31, 465–475.

London, P. The end of ideology in behavior modification. American Psychologist, 1972, 27, 913–920.

Lord, F. M. Elementary models for measuring change. In C. W. Harris (Ed.), Problems in measuring change. Madison: University of Wisconsin Press, 1963.

Luborsky, L. Perennial mystery of poor agreement among criteria for psychotherapy outcome. Journal of Consulting and Clinical Psychology, 1971, 37, 316–319.

Luborsky, L., Chandler, M., Auerbach, A. H., Cohen, J., & Bachrach, H. M. Factors influencing the outcome of psychotherapy: A review of quantitative research. Psychological Bulletin, 1971, 75, 145–185.

Luborsky, L., Singer, B., & Luborsky, L. Comparative studies of psychotherapy. Archives of General Psychiatry, 1975, 32, 995–1008.

Lyerly, S. B., & Abbott, P. S. Handbook of psychiatric rating scales (1950–1964) (Public Health Service Publication No. 1495). Washington, D.C.: U.S. Government Printing Office, 1965.

Lytton, H. Observation studies of parent-child interaction: A methodological review. Child Development, 1971, 42, 651–684.

MacDonald, M. L., & Tobias, L. L. Withdrawal causes relapse? Our response. Psychological Bulletin, 1976, 83, 448–451.

MacDonough, T. S., & McNamara, J. R. Design-criteria relationships in behavior therapy research with children. Journal of Child Psychology and Psychiatry and Allied Disciplines, 1973, 14, 271–282.

Malan, D. The outcome problem in psychotherapy research. Archives of General Psychiatry, 1973, 29, 719–729.

Marholin, D., and Phillips, D. Methodological issues in psychopharmacological research: Chlorpromazine—A case in point. American Journal of Orthopsychiatry, 1976, 46, 477–495.

Marks, I. M. Empiricism is accepted. International Journal of Psychiatry, 1969, 7, 141–148.

Mash, E. J. Behavior modification and methodology: A developmental perspective. Unpublished manuscript, University of Calgary, 1975.

May, P. R. A., Yale, C., & Dixon, W. J. Assessment of psychiatric outcome. I. Cross-section analysis. Journal of Psychiatric Research, 1972, 9, 271–284.

McCall, R. B., & Appelbaum, M. I. Bias in the analysis of repeated-measures designs: Some alternative approaches. Child Development, 1973, 44, 401–415.

McLean, P. D., & Miles, J. E. Evaluation and the problem-oriented record in psychiatry. Archives of General Psychiatry, 1974, 31, 622–625.

McNamara, J. R. Ways by which outcome measures influence outcomes in classroom behavior modification research. Journal of School Psychology, 1975, 13, 104–113.

McNamara, J. R., & MacDonough, T. S. Some methodological considerations in the design and implementation of behavior therapy research. Behavior Therapy, 1972, 3, 361–379.

McNemar, Q. Psychological statistics, 4th ed. New York: Wiley, 1969.

Meltzoff, J., & Kornreich, M. Research in psychotherapy. New York: Atherton Press, 1970.

Michael, J. Statistical inference for individual organism research: Mixed blessing or curse. *Journal of Applied Behavior Analysis,* 1974, 7, 647–653.

Miller, L. C., Barrett, C. L., Hampe, E., & Noble, H. Comparison of reciprocal inhibition, psychotherapy, and waiting list control for phobic children. *Journal of Abnormal Psychology,* 1972, 79, 269–279.

Mintz, J. What is "success" in psychotherapy? *Journal of Abnormal Psychology,* 1972, 80, 11–19.

Mintz, J., Auerbach, A. H., Luborsky, L., & Johnson, M. Patient's, therapist's, and observer's views of psychotherapy: A "Rashoman" experience or a reasonable concensus. *British Journal of Medical Psychology,* 1973, 46, 83–89.

Mischel, W. *Personality and assessment.* New York: Wiley, 1968.

Mischel, W. Towards a cognitive social learning reconceptualization of personality. *Psychological Review,* 1973, 80, 252–283.

Mumford, E., & Linburn, E. Overcoming difficulties in follow-up studies of adolescent psychiatric patients. *Hospitals, Journal of American Hospitals Association,* 1969, 43, 58–62.

Murray, E. J. A content-analysis method for studying psychotherapy. *Psychological Monographs,* 1956, 70, No. 420.

Myers, J. L. *Fundamentals of experimental designs.* Boston: Allyn & Bacon, 1966.

Norman, V. B., Rosen, B. M., & Bahn, A. K. Psychiatric clinic outpatients in the United States, 1959. *Mental Hygiene,* 1962, 46, 321–343.

Nunnally, J. *Psychometric theory.* New York: McGraw-Hill, 1967.

O'Connor, E. F. Extending classical test theory to the measurement of change. *Review of Educational Research,* 1972, 42, 73–97.

O'Dell, S. Training parents in behavior modification: A review. *Psychological Bulletin,* 1974, 81, 418–433.

O'Leary, K. D. The assessment of psychopathology in children. *In* H. C. Quay & J. S. Werry (Eds.), *Psychopathological disorders of childhood.* New York: Wiley, 1972.

O'Leary, K. D., & Drabman, R. Token reinforcement programs in the classroom: A review. *Psychological Bulletin,* 1971, 75, 379–398.

O'Leary, K. D., & Kent, R. Behavior modification for social action: Research tactics and problems. *In* L. A. Hamerlynck, L. C. Handy, & E. J. Mash (Eds.), *Behavior change: Methodology, concepts, and practice.* Champaign, Ill.: Research Press, 1973.

O'Leary, K. D., Turkewitz, H., & Taffel, S. J. Patient and therapist evaluation of behavior therapy in a child psychological clinic. *Journal of Consulting and Clinical Psychology,* 1973, 41, 279–283.

Ora, J. P., & Reisinger, J. J. Preschool intervention: A behavioral service delivery system. Paper presented at the meeting of the American Psychological Association, Washington, D.C., September, 1971.

Panzetta, A. F. Cost–benefit studies in psychiatry. *Comprehensive Psychiatry,* 1973, 14, 451–455.

Patterson, G. R. Intervention in the homes of predelinquent boys: Steps toward stage two. Paper presented at the workshop entitled Delinquent behavior: Some psychological research and applications, at the annual meetings of the American Psychological Association, Washington, D.C., 1971.

Patterson, G. R. Interventions for boys with conduct problems: Multiple settings, treatment, and criteria. *Journal of Consulting and Clinical Psychology,* 1974a, 42, 471–481.

Patterson, G. R. Retraining of aggressive boys by their parents: Review of recent literature and follow-up evaluation. *Canadian Psychiatric Association Journal,* 1974b, 19, 142–158.

Patterson, G. R. A three-stage functional analysis for children's coercive behaviors: A tactic for developing a performance theory. *In* B. C. Etzel, J. M. LeBlanc, & D. M. Baer (Eds.), *New developments in behavioral research: Theory, methods, and applications*. Hillsdale, N.J.: Lawrence Erlbaum, 1976.

Patterson, G. R., Ray, R. S., & Shaw, D. A. Direct intervention in families of deviant children. *Oregon Research Institute Research Bulletin*, 1968, *8*, No. 9.

Patterson, G. R., Reid, J. B., Jones, R. R., & Conger, R. E. *A social learning approach to family intervention*, Vol. 1. Eugene, Ore.: Castalia, 1975.

Paul, G. L. *Insight versus desensitization in psychotherapy: An experiment in anxiety reduction*. Stanford, Calif.: Stanford University Press, 1966.

Paul, G. L. Behavior modification research: Design and tactics. *In* C. M. Franks (Ed.), *Behavior therapy: Appraisal and status*. New York: McGraw-Hill, 1969.

Pawlicki, R. Behaviour-therapy research with children: A critical review. *Canadian Journal of Behavioural Science*, 1970, *2*, 163–173.

Perloff, R., Perloff, E., & Sussna, E. Program evaluation. *In* M. R. Rosenzweig & L. W. Porter (Eds.), *Annual review of psychology*, Vol. 27. Palo Alto, Calif.: Annual Reviews, 1976.

Peterson, L., & Hartmann, D. P. Some treatment-methodological problems in current child behavior therapy. Paper presented at the annual convention of the American Association of Behavior Therapists, San Francisco, 1975.

Redl, F. *When we deal with children*. New York: Free Press, 1966.

Reid, J. B. Reliability assessment of observational data: A possible methodological problem. *Child Development*, 1970, *41*, 1143–1150.

Reisinger, J. J., Ora, J. P., & Frangia, G. W. Parents as change agents for their children: A review. *Journal of Community Psychology*, 1976, *4*, 103–123.

Report of the Joint Commission. *Crisis in child mental health: Challenge for the 1970's*. New York: Harper & Row, 1969.

Report of the Joint Commission. *The mental health of children: Services, research, and manpower*. New York: Harper & Row, 1973.

Robins, L. N. Follow-up studies of behavior disorders in children. *In* H. C. Quay & J. S. Werry (Eds.), *Psychopathological disorders of childhood*. New York: Wiley, 1972.

Robins, L. N., & O'Neal, P. The strategy of follow-up studies with special reference to children. *In* J. G. Howell (Ed.), *Modern perspectives in international child psychiatry*. New York: Brunner/Mazel, 1969.

Rosen, B. M., Bahn, A. K., Shellow, R., & Bower, E. Adolescent patients served in outpatient psychiatric clinics. *American Journal of Public Health*, 1965, *55*, 1563–1577.

Rosenthal, A. J., & Levine, S. V. Brief psychotherapy with children. *American Journal of Psychiatry*, 1970, *127*, 646–651.

Rosenthal, D., & Frank, J. D. Psychotherapy and the placebo effect. *Psychological Bulletin*, 1956, *53*, 294–302.

Rosenthal, R. Interpersonal expectations: Effects of the experimenter's hypothesis. *In* R. Rosenthal & R. L. Rosnow (Eds.), *Artifact in behavioral research*. New York: Academic Press, 1969.

Ross, A. O. *Psychological disorders of children*. New York: McGraw-Hill, 1974.

Rubinstein, E. A., & Parloff, M. B. (Eds.). *Research in psychotherapy*, Vol. 1. Washington, D.C.: National Publishing Co., 1959.

Sargent, H. D. Methodological problems of follow-up studies in psychotherapy research. *American Journal of Orthopsychiatry*, 1960, *30*, 495–506.

Sarri, R. C., & Selo, E. Evaluation process and outcome in juvenile corrections: Musings on a grim tale. *In* P. O. Davidson, F. W. Clark, & L. A. Hamerlynck (Eds.), *Evaluation of behavorial programs*. Champaign, Ill.: Research Press, 1974.

Segal, S. P. Research on the outcome of social work therapeutic interventions: A review of the literature. *Journal of Health and Social Behavior,* 1972, *13,* 3–17.

Shapiro, M. B. Clinical approach to fundamental research with special reference to the study of the single patient. *In* P. Sainsbury & N. Kreitman (Eds.), *Methods of psychiatric research.* London: Oxford University Press, 1963.

Shepherd, M., Oppenheim, A. N., & Mitchell, S. Childhood behavior disorders and the child-guidance clinic. *Journal of Child Psychology and Psychiatry and Allied Disciplines,* 1966, *7,* 39–52.

Sherman, J. A., & Bushell, D., Jr. Behavior modification as an educational technique. *In* F. D. Horowitz (Ed.), *Review of child development research,* Vol. 4. Chicago: University of Chicago Press, 1975.

Shontz, F. C. *Research methods in personality.* New York: Appleton-Century-Crofts, 1965.

Sidman, M. *Tactics of scientific research.* New York: Basic Books, 1960.

Sloane, R. B., Staples, F. R., Cristol, A. H., Yorkston, N. J., & Whipple, K. Short-term analytically oriented psychotherapy versus behavior therapy. *American Journal of Psychiatry,* 1975, *132,* 373–377.

Snider, T., Sullivan, W., & Manning, D. Industrial engineering participation in a special education program. *Tennessee Engineer,* 1974, *1,* 367–373.

Society for the Experimental Analysis of Behavior. Statistical inference for individual organism research. *Journal of Applied Behavior Analysis Monograph,* 1975, No. 4.

Stallings, J. Implementation and child effects of teaching practices in Follow Through classrooms. *Monographs of the Society for Research in Child Development,* 1975, *40,* Nos. 7–8.

Struening, E. L., & Guttentag, M. *Handbook of evaluation research,* Vol. 1–2. Beverly Hills, Calif.: Sage, 1975.

Strupp, H. H., & Bergin, A. E. Some empirical and conceptual bases for coordinated research in psychotherapy: A critical review of issues, trends, and evidence. *International Journal of Psychiatry,* 1969, *7,* 18–90.

Stuart, R. B., & Lott, L. A., Jr. Behavioral contracting with delinquents: A cautionary note. *In* C. M. Franks & G. I. Wilson (Eds.), *Annual review of behavior therapy and practice: 1974.* New York: Brunner/Mazel, 1974.

Subotnik, L. Spontaneous remission: Fact or artifact. *Psychological Bulletin,* 1972, *77,* 32–48.

Tavormina, J. B. Basic models of parent counseling: A critical review. *Psychological Bulletin,* 1974, *81,* 827–835.

Tavormina, J. B. Relative effectiveness of behavioral and reflective group counseling with parents of mentally retarded children. *Journal of Consulting and Clinical Psychology,* 1975, *43,* 22–31.

Thorne, F. C. Rules of evidence in the evaluation of psychotherapy. *Journal of Clinical Psychology,* 1952, *8,* 38–41.

Tversky, A., & Kahneman, D. Belief in the law of small numbers. *Psychological Bulletin,* 1971, *76,* 105–110.

Twain, D. Developing and implementing a research strategy. *In* E. L. Struening & M. Guttentag (Eds.), *Handbook of evaluation research.* Beverly Hills, Calif.: Sage, 1975.

Walker, H. M., & Hops, H. Use of normative peer data as a standard for evaluating classroom treatment effects. *Journal of Applied Behavior Analysis,* 1976, *9,* 159–168.

Walker, R. A. The ninth panacea: Program evaluation. *Evaluation,* 1972, *1,* 45–53.

Walter, H. I., & Gilmore, S. K. Placebo versus social learning effects in parent training procedures designed to alter the behavior of aggressive boys. *Behavior Therapy,* 1973, *4,* 361–377.

Webb, E. J., Campbell, D. T., Schwartz, R. D., & Sechrest, L. *Unobtrusive measures: Nonreactive research in the social sciences.* Chicago: Rand McNally, 1966.

Weiss, C. H. Evaluation research in the political context. Paper presented at the annual meeting of the American Psychological Association, Montreal, August 1973.

Werry, J. S. Childhood psychosis. *In* H. C. Quay & J. S. Werry (Eds.), *Psychopathological disorders of childhood.* New York: Wiley, 1972.

Whelan, P. *Reliability of human observers.* Unpublished doctoral dissertation, University of Utah, 1974.

Wiggins, J. S. *Personality and prediction: Principles of personality assessment.* Reading, Mass.: Addison-Wesley, 1973.

Wilkins, W. Expectancy of therapeutic gain: An empirical and conceptual critique. *Journal of Consulting and Clinical Psychology,* 1973, *40,* 69–77.

Windle, C. Prognosis of mental subnormals. *American Journal of Mental Deficiency,* 1962, *66* (5, Monograph Supplement).

Wodarsky, J. S., Feldman, R. A., & Pedi, S. J. Objective measurement of the independent variable: A neglected methodological aspect in community-based behavioral research. *Journal of Abnormal Child Psychology,* 1974, *2,* 239–244.

Wortman, P. M. Evaluation research: A psychological perspective. *American Psychologist,* 1975, *30,* 562–575.

Yarrow, M. R., Campbell, J. D., & Burton, R. V. Recollections of childhood: A study of the retrospective method. *Monographs for the Society for Research in Child Development,* 1970, *35,* No. 5.

Yates, A. J. Research methods in behavior modification. *In* M. Hersen, R. M. Eisler, & P. M. Miller (Eds.), *Progress in behavior modification,* Vol. 2. New York: Academic Press, 1976.

Yates, B. T. Toward cost-effectiveness analysis of psychological treatments. Unpublished manuscript, Stanford University, Stanford, Calif., 1975.

2 Current Developments in the Behavioral Assessment of Children

Anthony R. Ciminero
and Ronald S. Drabman

Within recent years, there has been a phenomenal growth in the interest in behavior therapy with children. The advances in behavioral approaches is evidenced by the fact that in the 1950s, behavior modification was not even considered a major treatment technique for children (Buxbaum, 1954), and now there are several books devoted exclusively to this topic (e.g., Graziano, 1975; Mash, Hamerlynck, & Handy, 1976; Ross, 1974).

Behavioral-assessment strategies, however, have not kept pace with these developments in behavior therapy. Although there has been a long-standing interest in the evaluation, classification, and diagnosis of children, most of the work has been carried out within a traditional medical/disease model. This type of assessment strategy has not yielded data that are particularly useful to behavior therapists, who have had to adopt a different philosophy and approach to assessment. The interest in *behavioral assessment* has generated considerable research and some new strategies for evaluating child-behavior problems. This chapter reviews and evaluates these recent developments in the behavioral assessment of children.

1. Behavioral Assessment

It is not within the scope of this chapter to provide a detailed comparison of traditional and behavioral approaches to assessment,

Anthony R. Ciminero • University of Georgia, Athens, Georgia. Ronald S. Drabman • University of Mississippi School of Medicine, Jackson, Mississippi.

especially since there are several discussions of this topic elsewhere (e.g., Goldfried & Kent, 1972; Goldfried & Sprafkin, 1974; Mischel, 1968; Wolff & Merrens, 1974). However, it should be noted that the authors agree with Evans and Nelson (1977) that some "traditional" methods of child assessment (e.g., intelligence and achievement tests, interviews, and other self-report measures) can be useful in a comprehensive assessment. The same techniques can be considered traditional or behavioral methods, depending on the assumptions about the data and how the data are used in relationship to treatment.

There are several features that are characteristic of the behavioral-assessment strategy. The behavioral approach views the child's responses as a sample of his or her behavioral repertoire in a specific stimulus situation. Since a child's behavior is largely a function of environmental events (i.e., both antecedents and consequences), and since behavior can change from setting to setting (Mischel, 1968), it is important to measure the behavior in a variety of settings, especially those in which the problem behaviors occur naturally.

Not only are multiple settings sampled, but the ideal behavioral assessment also collects measures from various response channels (i.e., verbal–cognitive, overt motor, and psychophysiological). Since there is not a perfect correlation among the three response modalities (Hersen & Bellack, 1977), there may be treatment implications that are dependent on how each response channel is affected for a given child (e.g., Borkovec, 1973). Another feature of behavioral assessment is that collected data are related directly to treatment decisions in several ways (Cautela, 1968; Ciminero, 1977; Goldfried & Pomeranz, 1968; Stuart, 1970). First, the assessment data initially provide an accurate and relatively complete *description* of the problem behavior and the conditions maintaining the responses. Second, the data help in the *selection* of the target behavior and the selection of the most appropriate treatment strategy. This function of assessment will become even more crucial as the variety of effective treatment techniques increases. Third, the continued collection of data provides an *evaluation* of treatment effects. This ongoing objective evaluation helps one decide whether treatment is effective and when to change or terminate the treatment strategy.

1.1. Behavior-Analytic Models for Assessment

As was mentioned above, two of the primary functions of assessment are description of the child's behavior and evaluation of the effects of any attempt to modify problem behaviors. Different behavior-analytic models seem to be quite useful in meeting these functions.

Several models varying in comprehensiveness have been suggested to describe the major factors that influence a given individual's behavior. At the extremes are the simple A-B-C (antecedents–behaviors–consequences) model of Stuart (1970) and the complex BASIC–ID (behavior–affect–sensations–imagery–cognitions—interpersonal factors–drugs) model suggested by Lazarus (1973) for use in multimodal behavior therapy. Between these extremes is the comprehensive and flexible model of Kanfer and Saslow (1969). Their S-O-R-K-C model includes a description of antecedent stimulus conditions (S), organismic variables (O), target responses (R), contingencies (K), and reinforcing consequences (C). If it is assumed that the responses can occur in several channels (i.e., motor, cognitive, or psychophysiological), the S-O-R-K-C model seems to be adequate in providing a thorough description of the child's behavior.

Several other characteristics of Kanfer and Saslow's approach should be briefly summarized. First, no variable (e.g., biological, social–cultural, reinforcement history, developmental) is ignored as an unimportant factor in the analysis. Second, the assessment is individualized, with each client's unique analysis having important implications for the design of treatment plans. Third, the assessment does not focus solely on problematic behaviors but also attempts to identify behavioral strengths or assets.

Although the S-O-R-K-C model seems well suited to the initial description of a child and may lead to some form of treatment, another model—the *functional analysis of behavior*—is needed for the *evaluation* of the outcome of treatment (Bijou & Peterson, 1971; Gardner, 1971). Peterson (1968) summarized the major features of a functional analysis, which involves four steps. First, the problem behavior must be specified so that observational techniques can be used to *obtain a baseline measure* for that behavior. Second, there must also be some *specification of controlling variables* (antecedents or consequences) that possibly exert some control over the behavior. Third, a *manipulation of one of the variables* that seems to exert control over the behavior is made so that it can be ascertained whether that variable is functionally related to the target behavior. The fourth step involves the *continued observation* of the behavior so that any changes that do occur can be measured.

A functional analysis is a very active method of assessment in that ongoing measures of behavior are obtained before and during some "experimental manipulation." If treatment intervention is viewed as an experimental manipulation, the functional analysis can be used to evaluate the effectiveness of treatment. The functional analysis is essentially a variant of an A-B single-case experimental design, with *A* representing the baseline phase and B representing the treatment phase (Ciminero, 1977; Hersen & Barlow, 1976). It should also be noted that later follow-up measures help complete the evaluation function of assessment (Cautela, 1968).

The descriptive and evaluative functions of assessment seem to be adequately served by the S-O-R-K-C and functional-analysis models. However, there is no general model that has been developed and accepted for aiding in the *selection* of target behaviors and treatment strategies. This selection is especially important for a behavioral approach with children, since there are many behaviors that could be modified and a growing number of therapeutic strategies that could be selected. In the past, most of these selection decisions have been based on clinical impressions. This method may have been fairly efficient for a specific target behavior, since a parent or teacher complaint frequently determined which behavior was to be modified. However, as the options for therapeutic techniques increase, the selection of specific therapeutic strategies will become a more complicated decision.

A model that aids in treatment selection would be extremely useful in behavioral assessment, but no such model is now available. One question that is raised is whether the absence of an accepted behavioral classification system for children is impeding effective therapy selection. Is classification a clinically useful function in behavioral assessment? Will classification aid in the differential selection of treatment? Although these are empirical questions, they cannot be answered at this time simply because the research has not been conducted. However, the issue of behavioral classification is an important one that needs to be addressed.

2. Classification of Children's Behavior

For several years, behaviorally oriented clinicians have eschewed diagnostic methods and classification systems that were based upon a medical model of abnormal behavior. This rejection was partially due to the lack of reliability, validity, and utility of traditional classification systems. However, there was also considerable concern about the potential negative effects that the labeling process would have on children (Hobbs, 1975a). Unfortunately, this avoidance behavior generalized to any form of diagnosis or classification, which consequently has hindered the development of behavioral-assessment strategies. If one considers diagnosis as a process of collecting *relevant* information about the client and his behavior (Achenbach, 1974), then it is obvious that behavior therapists have not been arguing against diagnosis *per se* but instead have been criticizing the actual methods used to collect data (e.g., projective tests), the types of data collected, and the interpretations of those data in terms of underlying causes of the behavior. Perhaps the title of Kanfer and Saslow's (1969) chapter ("Behavioral Diagnosis") was a reminder that we should not avoid an important activity such as diagnosis simply because of the association of the term with the medical model. Since the publication of Kanfer and Saslow's work, there has been considerable progress in the development of procedures for behavioral diagnosis, although they are labeled behavioral-*assessment* strategies (e.g., Ciminero, Calhoun, & Adams, 1977) to avoid the connotation of a disease or a medical model (Achenbach, 1974). However, a widely accepted behavioral classification system that could be used to organize the data collected during assessment has not been developed, although some systems have been suggested (e.g., Adams, Doster, & Calhoun, 1977; Bandura, 1968; Ferster, 1965). As Achenbach (1974) has stated, "The basic question is not *whether* to classify, but *how* to classify" (p. 543).

There have been numerous attempts to develop other classification systems (see reviews by the Group for Advancement of Psychiatry [GAP], 1966), but none of these is essentially behavioral in nature. The more commonly used systems (e.g., Diagnostic and Statistical Manual-II, 1968; GAP, 1966) have been criticized severely for a variety of problems, including their reliability, coverage, predictive validity, utility, and basic disease-oriented conceptualization (see reviews by Achenbach, 1974; Hobbs, 1975a,b,c; Ross, 1974).

The closest approximation to behavioral classification systems for children are those that were developed from a dimensional approach using multivariate statistical methods (i.e., factor analysis and cluster analysis). As reviewed by Quay (1972), this approach assumes that there are a number of independent dimensions of behavior and that each individual exhibits the behavior to a greater or lesser extent. Basically, the approach attempts to isolate clusters of behaviors that occur together. Although it is possible to view a "cluster of behaviors" in a "trait" conceptualization or as a syndrome of some underlying disorder (Mischel, 1968), it is just as easy to interpret the cluster in terms of response–response relationships. As such, response clusters become a legitimate concern in behavioral assessment with tremendous implications for treatment (O'Leary, 1972; Wahler, 1975).

Although there is no currently accepted behavioral classification system, there have been a number of attempts to identify the essential clusters of child-behavior problems (see reviews by Achenbach, 1974; Quay, 1972; Ross, 1974). An overview of this research indicates that two factors are identified with relatively good consistency. The first factor (labeled as *conduct disorder, aggressive, unsocialized psychopathic,* or *externalizing*) can be viewed simply as excessive acting out or aggressive behavior. This factor has been found in schools, clinics, and other institutions from teacher and parent ratings, case-history data, and children's self-report. The second factor (variously labeled as *over-inhibited, personality disorder, withdrawn,* or *internalizing*) can be viewed as excessive withdrawal. This factor also has been found with different types of data in several settings. As Ross (1974) has suggested, both of these can be conceptualized from a behavioral framework as behavioral excesses: "These categories differentiate excess approach behavior (aggression) and excess avoidance behavior (withdrawal)" (p. 28).

Excessive approach and avoidance behavior is not a comprehensive classification system. The frequency with which these behavior patterns are found is probably due to the sample of children studied and the type of data selected. For example, it would be difficult to identify the behavioral deficits that might be found in a retarded population simply because data from this group are frequently not included in factor-analytic studies (Ross, 1974). It appears that factor analyses using different measures, samples of behavior, populations, and settings might very well identify other clusters of behavior as was done with adaptive behavior (see study by Kohn, described in Ross, 1974), learning disabilities (Miller, 1967), socialized delinquency and inadequacy–immaturity (Quay, 1972). Such findings might initially identify existing clusters of behavior that would then serve as the basic elements of a behavior-classification scheme.

Obviously, there are many problems and issues related to classification (see Eron, 1966; Hobbs, 1974a,b,c; Kessler, 1971; Mahrer, 1970), and it is unlikely that such a classification will be available for several years. In the interim, we could collect more extensive behavioral assessment data to maximize our chances of relating these data to treatment outcome. This procedure would be especially helpful whenever a large group study comparing treatment techniques is conducted. This type of data has been examined in adults (e.g., Sloane, Staples, Cristol, Yorkston, & Whipple, 1976; Luborsky, Chandler, Auerbach, Cohen, & Bachrach, 1971), but very little is available for predicting a child's response to treatment.

3. Other Problems Related to Child-Behavior Assessment

In addition to the absence of a well-accepted behavioral classification system, there are other problems associated with child assessment. First, it has frequently been noted (e.g., Evans & Nelson, 1977) that children are invariably referred for assessment and /or treatment by some significant adult (usually a parent or a teacher). Thus, the behavior is of some concern or bother to the adults but not necessarily distressful to the child; the adult plays the crucial role in determining whether the child is evaluated. Since this pattern is not likely to change, even with the increased interest in children's rights, some problems are encountered because of this practice. One problem is that the behavior identified by the adults may not be the most relevant behavior that needs modification. For example, the authors recently had a boy referred by his mother because her 5-year-old child had resumed wetting his bed. Assessment via behavioral observations indicated that the child was extremely noncompliant, which would probably interfere with a program aimed at treating the bed-wetting. Thus, we were faced with increasing the child's compliance (something the parent was not initially concerned about changing) before dealing with his bed-wetting. Fortunately, the child's bed-wetting was easily modified once his compliance was increased. Here, there was not much of a problem since the original concern of the parent was successfully handled. However, the issue is more significant when the target behavior identified by the adult is not "deviant" by some normative standard. This is likely to happen rather frequently since the parent's perceptions and not the child's behaviors seem to be more important in determining whether a child is referred (Lobitz & Johnson, 1975).

A second and related problem for child-behavior assessment is that a comprehensive behavior analysis requires assessing a relevant adult's behavior as well as the child's behavior. Only by observing the parents, teachers, etc., can we determine how their behavior may contribute to the child's problem behavior. Since there is considerable data demonstrating the important relationship between parental behavior and child behavior (Hetherington & Martin, 1972), assessment of the significant adults as well as other aspects of the child's environment seems essential.

Third, there is a practical problem associated with the ethological and ecological assessment of children (Evans & Nelson, 1977). Observing children in naturalistic settings, such as the home or the school, is rather costly and may not be readily accepted by all parents or school officials. A fourth problem revolves around the rapid developmental changes observed in children. The assessment must take into consideration the possibility that some developmental lag may account for the behavior problem. Although there is a limit to how much can be attributed to developmental factors, they cannot be overlooked. Developmental norms may be of some help here, but most of the norms are based on infants and very young children (e.g., Gesell & Amatruda, 1947; Bayley, 1969) and may not be directly relevant to many behavior problems. What is needed are norms based on direct observations of child behaviors (both appropriate and inappropriate) in a variety of settings, including homes and schools (Nelson & Bowles, 1975).

Despite the long-standing interest in the assessment of children, many problems must still be solved. In spite of the problems of classification and the related issues mentioned above, considerable progress is being made in the actual methods used in the gathering of assessment data. Some of these, such as the interview and intelligence and achievement tests, have been used for many years, while other methods such as self-recording and direct-observation procedures are more contemporary. Section 4 summarizes these methods as they are used in behavioral assessment. It should become clear that no one method is sufficient and that a multifaceted approach to assessment is the most productive.

4. Methods of Behavioral Assessment

4.1 Behavioral Interviews

The clinical/behavioral interview is a popular method of assessment from both a traditional and a behavioral approach. Although the content of the behavioral interview may be different from that of a traditional interview, the problems of reliability, validity, and utility are shared by both aproaches. For the behavioral assessor, the interview is a necessary starting point, but it is certainly not sufficient for the entire assessment; the interview is seen as a procedure that must be used in conjunction with other strategies. Although the primary function of the interview is to obtain descriptive information about the child's problem behavior and the conditions maintaining it, the interview can be used for other purposes. For example, establishing rapport with the parent and/or the child during interviews may be extremely helpful for later treatment purposes. Also, the interview affords the clinician the opportunity to observe directly how the parent and child behave during the interview. How the child reacts to parental commands and therapist's questions provides an important sample of the child's behavior. Finally, the interview gives the clinician a direct opportunity to evaluate the cooperation of the parents or the other significant adults who will most likely be involved with the treatment program. Will the parents carry out therapeutic assignments? Will they record the child's behavior when necessary? Will they cooperate with home or school observations by coders? These and other questions relevant to further treatment and assessment can easily be obtained during an interview. Unfortunately, space does not permit an extensive discussion of the appropriate content of the interview or the many practical issues associated with interviews. For such material, one should review a number of other articles (e.g., Bersoff & Grieger, 1971; Kanfer & Saslow, 1969; Wahler & Cormier, 1970; Yarrow, 1960).

Interviews for child assessment can be conducted with a number of individuals including the child, the parents, teachers, and even peers. Although there have been a number of studies evaluating parental interviews, very few empirical investigations have been reported on the reliability and validity of child, teacher, and peer interviews. With children, especially those younger than 6 years of age, it is relatively safe to assume that very little *content* will be obtained that will aid in specifying the target behavior or its maintaining conditions. However, it is possible to get reliable and valid ratings of disturbance from half-hour interviews with children 7–12 years of age (Rutter & Graham, 1968). These ratings were more reliable when the behavior pattern was global rather than specific. However, it should be noted that Rutter and Graham's study examined the reliability of psychiatrists who rated the children based on an interview. Thus, it is still quite possible that the actual *reports* from the child were unreliable while the ratings of their behavior (e.g., tearfulness, overactivity, anxiety) by coders were reliable.

Herjanic, Herjanic, Brown, and Wheatt (1975) also found with a *structured* interview that children were reliable reporters when their responses were compared to those of their parents. An average agreement of 80% was found with a slightly higher agreement (84%) on factual information and lower agreement (69%) on mental-status types of questions. In general, girls were more reliable than boys. In spite of the limited data on the reliability and validity of children's reports, an interview with the child seems to be useful, especially when used in conjunction with other behavior-assessment strategies.

Interviews with parents have not fared much better in producing reliable and valid data. Yarrow, Campbell, and Burton (1970) found considerable bias in parental interviews. In retrospective accounts, mothers generally reported more positive behavior in their children. In a similar fashion, Graham and Rutter (1968) reported that over a third of the parents of children independently rated as having a "definite psychiatric disorder" rated their children as having average difficulties or no problems at all. In contrast with this positive bias, Graham and Rutter also found a small percentage (14%) of parents who rated "normal" children as definitely disturbed. It must still be noted that these general ratings by parents were accurate in the majority of cases. Graham and Rutter reported that test–retest reliability for parents interviewed twice were rather low (0.43).

It appears that accuracy depends significantly on the type of information gathered from parents. For example, parents are more accurate on specific data such as the height and weight of their children and less accurate on personality factors (Haggard, Brekstad, & Skard, 1960; Yarrow *et al.*, 1970). These data might suggest that the more specific one is during an interview, the more accurate the data will be. However, Schnelle (1974) found that even when parents based their evaluations on a specific behavior (school attendance), parental reports were invalid. As is true of child interviews, parent reports are necessary, but they cannot be accepted as sufficient data for describing a child's behavior or evaluating a treatment procedure (Cox, 1974; Lytton, 1973).

The primary setting outside the home in which a child is likely to be treated is the school. There, the teacher is a vital person in the assessment process, and indeed, teachers have been the best predictors of which children will have school problems (Ferinden, Jacobson, & Linden, 1970). Surprisingly, we were unable to find any direct attempts to assess the reliability or validity of teacher interviews. This gap in the literature may result because most behavioral research in the school has relied on direct-observation procedures and may not have had to check with the reliability of a prior teacher interview.

As an assessment strategy, the interview has had a lengthy history and it will certainly have a longer future. However, the data available at this time suggest that we must be very cautious, if not skeptical, of interview data from children and parents. Again, this caution does not mean that the interview has no useful function. It certainly appears to be a necessary starting point in any assessment that will eventually result in treatment. The parent's and the child's cooperation are necessary, and the potential for cooperation can be globally assessed and possibly reinforced in the interview. Eventually, we may be able to learn which variables can be manipulated to produce the most reliable and valid data from an interview. Until that time, it will be necessary to use, in addition to the interview, one or more of the procedures described in Sections 4.2–4.6.

4.2. Problem Checklists and Rating Scales

Behavior-problem checklists have become a popular assessment technique for gathering data on children. This method has become a frequently used strategy for a number of reasons. First, the checklists are very economical in cost, effort, and therapist time (Wolff & Merrens, 1974). In addition, the checklists are structured so that a rather comprehensive survey of problem areas can be obtained. Thus, the checklist may identify target behaviors that were missed in an interview (Novick, Rosenfeld, Bloch, & Dawson, 1966). A third reason for the popularity of checklists is that they provide data that are easily quantified. These data, in turn, allow for factor-analytic studies that can identify the dimensions or response clusters that were described in Section 1. The fourth reason for their popularity is that the checklists provide a convenient measure that can be used for evaluating therapy outcome throughout a treatment program or simply as pre- and postmeasures. Finally, if populations of clients can be accurately described in terms of their response to the checklist items, this information helps to indicate the "type" of clients that were treated and how they responded to a specific treatment program (e.g., Kent & O'Leary, 1976).

A number of criteria must be considered in the use of a rating scale as an assessment method. In addition to many practical issues, such as whether the items are specific and easy to read and whether the test is not too long, there are major theoretical concerns. There are obvious criteria in the reliability and validity of the obtained scores. Although many scales report reliability data in terms of test–retest, internal consistency, or interjudge agreements, most reports use a very liberal estimate of reliability. For example, instead of a measure of reliability computed item by item, total scores or factor scores may be correlated. Although the reliability of these composite scores may be quite high, the actual agreement on individual items may be extremely low. For example, Lahey, Johnson, Stempniak, Resick, and Giddings, (1976) found that reliability could be as high as 95% for total scores but drop to 10% when individual items are compared. Thus, many checklists may give a reliable estimate of total deviance but may not accurately identify specific target behaviors.

Validity is also a crucial factor. Many studies have obtained data indicating validity by comparing deviant populations with normal populations and showing that these groups differ on their checklist scores (e.g., Speer, 1971). Although this approach does provide an indication of validity, the most important demonstrations are needed in the area of predictive validity. If scores can help predict the response to various forms of treatment or no treatment at all, then the scores will increase dramatically in their utility.

Another criterion of a useful rating scale is whether or not normative data are provided for adequate samples (i.e., both males and

females over several age groups). Some authors have collected normative data, whereas a number of checklists have no established norms
(see Spivack & Swift, 1973).

The final criterion for a checklist is that it should provide data not
only on deviant or problem behavior but also on appropriate behavior. This idea is in line with the argument that appropriate behavior is
more than simply the absence of deviant behavior (Ross, 1963).

There are numerous checklists available for parents and teachers
to complete (Spivack & Swift, 1973), and the choice of one should be
based on the four criteria listed above. Although some of the checklists come close to meeting all of the criteria, all of these still seem to
need further evaluation of their psychometric properties and clinical
utility. Although there are numerous checklist available, only a few of
the more popular and promising rating scales are discussed here.

The Behavior Problem Checklist by Quay and Peterson (1967) is
based on the items used in a factor-analytic study (Peterson, 1961) of
child-behavior problems rated by teachers. The checklist consists of 55
items; some are fairly specific (e.g., crying, thumb-sucking), some
require considerable inference (e.g., lack of self-confidence, jealousy),
and some relate to physical condition (e.g., skin allergy, hay fever or
asthma). Each item is rated by a teacher or parent on a three-point
scale that indicates the severity of the problem. Peterson's original
analysis of kindergarten through sixth grade indicated two factors
(conduct and personality problems).

The reliability of the Behavior Problem Checklist seems adequate
for young children but decreases for older children or adolescents. Peterson (1961) found interjudge reliabilities of 0.75 and 0.77 for per-
sonality- and conduct-factor scores for kindergarten children. However, Quay and Quay (1965) found interjudge reliabilities ranging
from 0.58 to 0.71 for conduct problems and 0.22–0.31 for personality
problems in seventh- and eighth-grade students.

Data relating to the validity of the checklist have also been reported. For example, McCarthy and Paraskevopoulos (1969) and Speer
(1971) found significant differences between "deviant" and "control"
subjects on the basis of the checklist. More recent attempts indicate
that the scales may also have predictive validity (e.g., Proger, Mann,
Green, Bayuk, & Burger, 1975). Normative data are also available for
young children and indicate that boys generally exhibit more behavior
problems than girls (Werry & Quay, 1971).

Although the Behavior Problem Checklist appears to be an adequate instrument, one must be cautious about its reliability with older
children. Norms are available, and at least some studies have looked at

the predictive validity of the scale. One major deficiency in the scale is that it does not have a sample of positive or appropriate behaviors.

Most of the other rating scales that were reviewed have not been as extensively evaluated as the Quay and Peterson checklist. However, some of these have been sufficiently examined to suggest that they are potentially useful assessment devices. For example, Ross, Lacey, and Parton (1965) designed the Pittsburgh Adjustment Survey Scale for 6-year-old to 12-year-old boys. In addition to items that identify conduct and personality problems, items that tap prosocial behaviors are included. Miller (1972) expanded the scale and collected normative data on males and females. Although test–retest reliability is quite acceptable (0.71–0.96), few data are available at this time relating to the validity of the instrument.

The Louisville Behavior Checklist (Miller, 1967a,b) is another scale that includes both problem and prosocial items. There are eight scales contained within three larger broad-band factors (aggression, inhibition, and learning disabilities). Most of the scales are reliable (split-half reliabilities), and norms are available for children 7–12 years old (Miller, Hampe, Barrett, & Noble, 1971).

Another promising checklist is the Conners Teacher Rating Scale (Conners, 1969, 1973), for which norms are available (Werry, Sprague, & Cohen, 1975). The scale was designed to provide a measure of change due to treatment and has proved to be sensitive in drug studies (Conners, 1972).

Several other checklists with various advantages and disadvantages are available (see Spivak & Swift, 1973). However, none of the available checklists has adequately met all of the criteria listed above (i.e., reliability, predictive validity, norms, and positive behavior items). In addition, most of the studies that do report interjudge or test–retest reliability are probably obtaining an inflated measure by comparing factor scores or total scores rather than individual items. Validity is typically assumed when a scale can differentiate normal and deviant groups rather than predicting response to treatment. Considerable research appears to be needed to establish the validity of the scales and to obtain more appropriate reliability estimates.

As with the interview, the problem-oriented checklist cannot be considered sufficient in meeting all assessment functions. However, the checklists that result in reliable and stable factor structures have the potential of describing client characteristics that may be useful in predicting treatment outcome. In addition to the comprehensive, survey-type checklists described above, there have been attempts to develop fear surveys (Scherer & Nakamura, 1968) and reinforcement surveys (Clement & Richard, 1971) for children. However, these have not been thoroughly evaluated with regard to reliability, validity, and utility.

4.3. Direct-Observation Procedures

The most accepted behavioral assessment strategy is to observe and record target behaviors in naturalistic or contrived analogue settings. This acceptance of direct behavioral observations is undoubtedly related to its face validity and the problems inherent in the other methods of assessment. However, direct-observation methods have their own problems, which are discussed below.

The earliest attempts at direct behavioral observations were aimed at providing continuous observations and narration of the child's behavior. These *diary descriptions* and *specimen records* were deliberately nonselective and included everything that happened to be observed (Wright, 1960). From this tradition, the early attempts at an assessment of target behaviors adopted a very selective approach by which a limited number of specific behaviors were pinpointed so that two coders could reliably record these responses (Bijou, Peterson, Harris, Allen, & Johnston, 1969). Although this focus on a very limited number of target behaviors is still very popular, there has been a recent trend toward developing more comprehensive behavioral coding sytems that are capable of measuring many specific responses (e.g., O'Leary, Romanczyk, Kass, Dietz, & Santagrossi, 1971; Patterson, Ray, Shaw, & Cobb, 1969; Wahler, House, & Stambaugh, 1976).

Although direct-observation procedures differ in many ways (Boyd & DeVault, 1966), they share many common features and problems. Jones, Reid, and Patterson (1975) summarized three major defining characteristics of a "naturalistic observational system." These included "recording of behavioral events in their natural settings at the time they occur, not retrospectively; the use of trained impartial observer–coders; and descriptions of behaviors which require little if any inference by observers to code the events" (p. 46). These systems have generally been designed specifically for use in the home or school, although the Wahler *et al.* (1976) system can be used in either setting as well as in the laboratory.

There are three well-recognized coding systems in use today, each having certain advantages and disadvantages. These include systems developed by Patterson and his colleagues at the Oregon Research Institute, by O'Leary and his colleagues at the State University of New York at Stony Brook, and by Wahler and his colleagues at the University of Tennessee. None of the codes has been widely accepted throughout the country; each one is used primarily in the area in which it was developed. Although each one was designed for research purposes, there is an implicit and sometimes explicit assumption that the coding system may be adopted more widely for behavioral assessment purposes. Each system uses precoded data sheets on which recordings of behavior can be made through a time-sampling or continuous-recording procedure. A timing device (or tape recorder) is used to signal observational intervals for the coders.

The Behavioral Coding System (BCS) developed at Oregon (Patterson, Ray, Shaw, & Cobb, 1969) has been the most widely researched instrument (see Jones, Reid, & Patterson, 1975). Although designed primarily for home observations (Patterson, Reid, Jones, & Conger, 1975), the BCS has been extended to school use (Patterson, Cobb, & Ray, 1973). As described by Jones *et al.* (1975), there are 28 behavioral categories identified by individual symbols. Numbers are used to identify the subject and the significant others in his environment so that sequences of behavioral interactions can be coded. Thus, the BCS records not only the child's behavior but the reactions of others. Originally, 30-second observation intervals were used, but these were later dropped in favor of 6-second intervals, which appeared to be easier for coders, who observed each family member for 5-minute periods. Jones *et al.* (1975) summarized the reliability and validity of the BCS. Both test–retest and interobserver agreement are satisfactory, and several studies support the validity of the coding system.

Among the advantages of the BCS are that it does record interactions of family members and is capable of producing reliable and valid data. Its disadvantages lie in its complexity and the time and cost required to train coders and to maintain good reliabilities, as well as the impossibility of determining whether behaviors coded in successive intervals were actually continuous or not. In general, the BCS seems to be a very promising instrument for the behavioral assessment of family interactions in home settings. Because of the cost of trained observers, the system will most likely be used as a research instrument rather than as an assessment device in routine clinical practice.

The O'Leary code (O'Leary *et al.*, 1971) was designed for research in classroom settings. This code also uses a time-sampling procedure in which coders circle a behavior symbol on a precoded data sheet. There are nine disruptive child behaviors (e.g., out of chair, inappropriate verbalization). Unlike the BCS, the O'Leary code does not record specific interactions between the teacher and the child. Although there are only limited data relating to the reliability and validity of this coding system (see Kent & Foster, 1977), the code is relatively easy to use and certainly warrants further investigation as an assessment device.

Both the BCS and the O'Leary code are somewhat limited since they were primarily designed for use in specific settings. Wahler *et al.* (1976) developed a system that can be used in the home, the school, or the laboratory setting, thus allowing for cross-situational comparisons of data. This code contains 19 response categories that cover 5 general classes of behavior: compliance–opposition, autistic, play, work, and social behaviors. Also included in the code are 6 stimulus categories that cover both aversive and nonaversive instances of adult instructions, adult attention, and child attention. Thus, like the Patterson code, the Wahler code is also capable of recording interactions between the child and his teachers, parents, or peers.

Data reported by Wahler *et al.* (1976) indicate that high observer agreement (generally above 80%) can be obtained even when conservative estimates are calculated. Aside from its apparent face and content validity and aside from some case studies that are reported as evidence for the validity of the coding system, very little data are currently available to support the validity of this relatively new system. Because of its high reliability and the possibility of using this system across several settings, it is a very promising coding procedure. However, there is a definite need for validity studies similar to those reported on the BCS.

There are many problems common to direct behavioral observations. The material below is only an overview of these problems. For a more detailed discussion, several excellent papers are available (e.g., Johnson & Bolstad, 1973; Kent & Foster, 1977; Lipinski & Nelson, 1974; Wright, 1960). Although some problems (e.g., reliability) are more difficult for the inclusive coding systems than for the assessment of a very limited number of target behaviors, the problems need to be considered with any direct-observation procedure.

As with all other assessment strategies, the reliability (i.e., interobserver agreement) of an observational system is a crucial factor. Kent and Foster (1977) reviewed many factors that influence the reliability estimate. In addition to the influence of the different formulae used to calculate interobserver agreement, factors such as the complexity of the coding system, the knowledge that reliability is being checked, biased observers, and cheating among observers can all influence reliability. A more subtle problem in the obtaining of accurate reliability estimates is the phenomenon of consensual observer drift, in which a pair or a subgroup of coders develop their own idiosyncratic definitions of the coded behaviors, thereby providing inflated reliability measures within this group of coders. When reliability is checked with the use of another group of coders, the reliability estimates are decreased. A final factor that may influence reliability is "instrument decay," in which the accuracy simply decreases over time. Johnson and Bolstad (1973) pointed out that decay may be due to many factors, including fatigue, forgetting, or the different reactions coders may have after an extensive training program is completed. Most of these problems are directly relevant when one is using interobserver agreement as the estimate of reliability. Johnson and Bolstad also emphasized that other more traditional reliability measures of observational data need to be examined.

Reactivity, whereby the behavior of the subjects changes simply as a function of being observed, is another major problem in direct-observation procedures (Webb, Campbell, Schwartz, & Sechrest, 1966). Johnson and Bolstad (1973) reviewed several studies that demonstrated different degrees of reactivity in the observed behavior. Several factors—including the conspicuousness of the observer, subject characteristics, observer characteristics, and the rationale for observations—may affect reactivity. The characteristics of the observational environment and the observed behavior as well as the method of recording are other potential factors in reactivity (Kent & Foster, 1977).

The generality of observational data across different settings is also a problem. Although the results are not in perfect agreement, several studies suggest that the behavior of children or parents in one setting may not be comparable to their behavior in other settings (Forehand & Atkeson, in press). Serious questions have been raised about generalization from clinic or laboratory settings to naturalistic settings (Moore & Bailey, 1973) as well as generalization across naturalistic settings (Bernal, Delfini, North, & Kreutzer, 1976; Wahler, 1969). In their review, Forehand and Atkeson noted that obtaining cross-situational generality depends on the type of data collected. Direct observational data might not indicate generalization even though parental verbal reports do. The more stringent the research methodology, the lower the probability of finding generalization across settings. This situational specificity suggests that whenever possible, direct observations should take place in the setting in which the behavior is the largest problem.

Another problem for direct-observation systems has been the absence of normative data. There may have been little need for such norms in the early behavior-modification studies, in which a single behavior in one individual was targeted for assessment. However, the increased use of more comprehensive behavior-coding systems will necessitate the establishment of norms. Nelson and Bowles (1975) have argued that normative data from direct observations would help in an objective identification of the behavioral excesses and deficits a given child was exhibiting. Since it is likely to be many years before normative data are available on an accepted coding system, Nelson and Bowles have recommended that behavioral assessors record the behaviors of both the target child and nonproblem children from the same setting in order to compare their behavior. This procedure would help identify the specific behaviors that defined a given child as a problem to a teacher. Although Nelson and Bowles were primarily concerned with collecting normative data in schools, normative data are also needed in home and laboratory settings.

The validity of data collected through direct behavioral observations is the final issue directly related to the previously discussed problems. As indicated above, the face validity of these data is quite acceptable, especially when a very specific behavior is recorded. Behavior codes have by design included a wide range of behaviors and thus improved the content validity (e.g., Jones *et al.*, 1975). There have also been investigations that indicate the concurrent validity (Patterson & Reid, 1973) and the predictive validity (Meyers, Attwell, & Orpet, 1968) of observational data (i.e., the BCS). However, the data on predictive validity are rather meager at this time, and much more research is needed to establishing predictive validity. Construct validity has also been demonstrated (at least for the BCS at Oregon) and shows that scores differentiate normal and deviant children (Lobitz & Johnson, 1975) and that scores on deviant behaviors change after treatment (see Jones *et al.*, 1975).

Direct behavioral observations will remain a very important method of assessment, especially in evaluations of the progress of treatment. However, it should be noted that the comprehensive behavioral codes will be of primary use in research and will have limited utility in clinical practice. The cost of extended behavioral observation by trained coders in naturalistic settings is very high. Thus, it is quite understandable that gathering direct behavioral recording from observers already present in the naturalistic setting (i.e., parents, teachers, or the children themselves) will continue to be popular in clinical practice. However, these methods share most of the problems listed above. For example, self-recording by children is likely to be unreliable, reactive, and subject to bias, just as observations by an independent coder would be (see Ciminero, Nelson, & Lipinski, 1977). However, the convenience of gathering self-recorded data cannot be overlooked. As methods are developed to improve the reliability and decrease the reactivity of self-recording, these techniques will become even more useful with children. Obviously, this would also be true of parent and/or teacher recordings.

4.4. Psychophysiological Data

The use of psychophysiological measures in child assessment has increased considerably in recent years. This interest is undoubtedly related to several general trends, including the advances in instrumentation (Rugh & Schwitzgebel, 1977) and the increased utilization of biofeedback and other behavioral procedures to treat psychophysiological disorders (Katz & Zlutnick, 1975). Additionally, it has been found that physiological measures are not perfectly correlated with verbal reports and measures of overt behavior (Borkovec, Weerts, & Bernstein, 1977). This evidence makes it imperative that whenever psychophysiological data are needed for the assessment, they must be measured directly and must not be inferred from other behavioral data.

Thus far, most psychophysiological assessments of children have been used for diagnostic purposes. For example, it is quite common to see the electroencephalogram (EEG) used as a criterion for diagnosing epileptic-seizure disorders (e.g., Zlutnick, Mayville, & Moffat, 1975). Numerous other studies have tried to identify psychophysiological differences between "normal" children and those who are "deviant" in some way. As examples, children with reading disabilities differ from normals in the amplitude of visual-evoked responses (Preston, Guthrie, & Childs, 1974); compared to normals, hyperactive children have lower basal skin resistance and take longer to habituate to a stimulus (Spring, Greenberg, Scott, & Hopwood, 1974); and learning-disabled children differ in their habituation of cortical arousal to auditory stimuli (Rourke, 1975). Although this research will be important in establishing the validity of various psychophysiological measures, it is unfortunate that this type of data has seldom been used in any direct relationship with treatment. One early exception was the work of Lang and Melamed (1969), who identified various electromyograph (EMG) patterns that correlated with sucking and vomiting in a 9-month-old infant with chronic rumination. Having a detailed description of the entire response chain, Lang and Melamed used the EMG to help distinguish vomiting from the sucking that immediately preceded the initial stages of vomiting. They were then able to punish the vomiting response with peripheral electric shock and to avoid punishing the sucking behavior. With this precise description of the topography of the response, they were able to eliminate vomiting quickly.

It is clear that psychophysiological assessment of children is in its very early stages of development. Considerable research is needed to establish the validity of specific psychophysiological responses (e.g., skin resistance, EMG, EEG, heart rate, blood pressure) when used as a measure for various problem behaviors. Although there are few validity studies available, psychophysiological measures appear to be very promising in behavioral assessment, particularly when applied to psychophysiological disorders.

Various problems prevent the routine use of psychophysiological measures for behavioral assessments of children. In addition to problems such as the high cost of equipment and its limited availability in most facilities, there are pragmatic issues that must be confronted (Wolff & Merrens, 1974). The ultimate aim in most treatment programs is change in the behavior and not necessarily in the physiological response. Decreases in hyperactive behaviors, in the number of seizures, or in asthmatic attacks are probably more relevant than changes in skin resistance or EEG. Consequently, psychophysiological measures have to be combined with other behavioral assessment strategies.

4.5. Intelligence and Achievement Testing

Although assessments of intellectual functioning and school achievement are generally considered traditional assessment strategies, they can be used within a behavioral strategy (Kanfer & Saslow, 1969; Staats, 1971). Although there are many reasons why testing should be avoided (e.g., Bersoff, 1973; McNemar, 1964), there also appear to be valid reasons for using such tests. As with the interview, it is not the method itself but the way in which the data are used that defines a technique as behavioral or traditional.

It is not within the scope of this section to review the reliability, validity, standardization, stability, and factor structure of the various intelligence tests used with children. Suffice it to say that the most commonly used tests (i.e., the Wechsler scales and the Stanford–Binet) are relatively reliable instruments (Anastasi, 1976) and that their scores account for a considerable portion of the variance in the prediction of school achievement (Vernon, 1958). From a behavioral perspective, the intelligence test measures a sample of general behavioral skills that have been acquired through learning (Staats, 1971). In this sense, the intelligence tests measure various behaviors that have been defined as "intelligent behaviors" and not some underlying mentalistic construct (intelligence *per se*) that accounts for the child's performance on the tasks. With this as a basic assumption, the intelligence test can help identify certain treatable behavioral deficits. For example, Engelmann (1970) has shown that a structured training program can be used to develop the behaviors that are necessary to improve performance on the IQ test. One group that received such training over a two-year period increased their mean IQ scores from 95.33 to 121.08, whereas the control group had only a slight increase (94.50 to 99.61). Similar improvements were found on achievement-test scores.

Certainly, intelligence tests provide only limited amounts of the type of information for which behavior therapists are looking. Nevertheless, the IQ test is part of the behavioral assessment package for three additional practical reasons. First, in many states, municipalities, and school districts, it is required by law for school or institutional diagnosis. Second, it does provide a sample of many school-related activities. Third, taking standardized tests is a skill that may be important in the child's life. If a child shows a deficit in that area, then test-taking skills may need to be directly taught. For example, a child who is doing well in school but who does poorly on an IQ test because of "anxiety" may be taught to relax while taking tests. Successful treatment of this kind may prevent problems later, when employment or college-admission examinations must be passed.

In addition to identifying the general behavioral deficits, the data from IQ tests may be even more useful when they are compared with a child's performance on an achievement test that is designed to measure more specific academic skills (see Anastasi, 1976). For example, when an achievement-test score is significantly lower than the IQ score, the child may need help with specific academic skills, general classroom behavior, or study skills at home and at school (Evans & Nelson, 1977). However, if both scores are low, the child may need help with both general and specific skills (Engelmann, 1970). For these reasons, it may be useful to include an achievement-test battery (which may include some informal measures, such as samples of reading and writing from the child's text) when the treatment decisions warrant the collection of such data.

Standardized intelligence and achievement tests are primarily used when one wants to gain a complete description of the child's assets and deficits. Tests should probably not be used routinely but should be given when the problem behavior may be related to the child's academic performance or when supplementary material is needed in a neuropsychological evaluation. In addition to their use for the descriptive functions of assessment, repeated measures on specific academic tasks can be used for evaluation when such behaviors are targeted for change. However, there is little data indicating that IQ level is useful when one is selecting specific behavioral treatment strategies for a given child.

4.6. Multifaceted Assessment

It should be clear that there is no single procedure or type of data that constitutes a behavioral assessment. Instead, a number of procedures are necessary to gather a variety of data from the three response channels (overt motor, verbal–cognitive, and psychophysiological) for a number of purposes (description, selection, and evaluation). Not only must there be multiple methods of assessment, a given technique may need to be used in more than one setting because of the situational specificity of many behaviors. At the present time, some types of data seem to be more useful in meeting the different functions of assessment. For example, interview and questionnaire data are more useful in contributing to a general description of the behavior problems but because of bias may not be very useful in evaluations of the effects of treatment. In contrast, direct observations of behavior may provide a more complete description of the behavior and a relatively unbiased evaluation of treatment outcome. All of the measures discussed thus far can contribute to a complete description of the child and his problem behavior. However, direct-observation data and performance on specific academic tasks appear to be the most valid methods for evaluating the effects of treatment. Although all of the methods are capable of providing data that might be useful in the selection functions of assessment, at this time very few advances have been made in prediction of the differential responsiveness of individuals to the various treatments.

The above discussion is not meant to imply that every behavioral assessment of every child must include each of the methods discussed in this chapter. This procedure would be very costly and inefficient in clinical practice. In research, it would be ideal to gather as many data as possible, but this approach would be unrealistic for anyone who does not have a team of assessors/therapists for every referred child. Thus, we are forced to be selective in the assessment strategies we use. Obviously, there are many practical issues that help us in selecting our methods of assessment. At one extreme, the interview is inexpensive, easy to conduct, and important in any assessment (O'Leary, 1972). However, psychophysiological measures are used in a limited number of cases. We should avoid the routine use of a strategy simply because it is available (e.g., the IQ test), but we should collect the data needed to make various therapeutic decisions.

5. The Psychological Evaluation from a Behavioral Viewpoint

The following case illustrates the "psychological" evaluation that resulted when a behavioral assessment approach was followed in clinical practice. The report is based on an actual case, but the data have been modified to protect the identity of the child and his family. It is obvious that for practical reasons, the use of behavioral assessment strategies in clinical practice is not as rigorous as in many research investigations. For example, in the collection of direct observations of the child at home and in school, a formal coding procedure was not used. In addition, the evaluations are only the beginning of the assessment process if treatment is to follow. In this sense, the behavioral psychological evaluation presents the initial descriptive information. If the effectiveness of treatment is to be evaluated, various problem behaviors must be pinpointed and measured during baseline and treatment conditions.

The format of this initial evaluation has been strongly influenced by the consumers of psychological reports. Other than the therapist, the chief consumers of a psychological evaluation are the school and the residential-facility staff. The complaint is frequently heard that psychological evaluations do not provide these consumers with realistic guidance in terms of suggestions for dealing with the problem child. It is too often the case that a completed psychological report is read by the referring adult and then filed in the child's cumulative folder to gather dust.

To deal with some of these criticisms, the formal behavioral psychological evaluation is divided into five parts. In the first section, the results of the testing are described in terms of the scores and inter and intratest scatter. Additionally, the particular behavioral deficits and abilities that enter into the scores are detailed. An effort is made to answer the consumer's question of "What can and can't this child currently do?"

The second section of the report contains behavioral assessment data gathered from the interviews with the child, his parents, and his teacher, as well as the results of the problem checklists and behavioral observations of the child in home and school settings. Its purpose is to give the consumer a picture of how the child relates to his environment.

The third section describes recommendations for the placement of this child. These would include suggestions as to whether the child should be placed in a school, a hospital, or an employment setting, along with the specific details regarding the type of settings within those broader categories that would most benefit the child. For example, a special class versus a regular class and resource room or a male versus a female teacher might be recommended.

The fourth section is labeled "Educational Prescription" and describes specific educational techniques that would be helpful to the child. It also includes behavioral techniques that the teacher and/or the parent can use to improve both the academic and the discipline problems of the child. This section is written as a didactic educational prescription that a teacher or a parent can follow without unreasonable difficulty.

The final section of the write-up outlines the therapeutic recommendations—if any—for the particular child. Based upon the results of all the testing, interviews, and observation, a behavioral program may be suggested and continued therapy recommended.

The completed psychological evaluation provides the clinician with the information needed to initiate a broadly based behavioral therapeutic regimen with that particular child. Additionally, it provides the baseline against which the success of treatment can be measured.

6. Case Report

6.1. Preliminary Evaluation

Name: Bob
Age: 5 years, 4 months
Grade: Preschool
Tests Administered:
  WISC (Scaled scores):
    Information   : 7
    Comprehension   : 4
    Arithmetic   : 6
    Similarities   : 4
    Vocabulary   : 4
    Digit span   : 8
    Picture completion   : 7
    Picture arrangement   : 5
    Block designs   : 9
    Object assembly   : 8
    Coding   : 4

VIQ = 69
PIQ = 76
FSIQ = 70

Other assessment strategies:

Behavioral interviews

Conners's parent and teacher questionnaires

Behavioral observations at home and at school

Bob is a 5-year, 4-month-old Caucasian male referred for intellectual and psychological evaluation by his preschool teacher. He was brought to the testing center by his mother. At the time of testing, he was neatly dressed and well groomed. He is the appropriate weight and height for his age and appears to be healthy. His mother expressed concern that his behavior would interfere with attempts to test Bob and remarked that previous testing generally proved inconclusive because of his behavior problem.

The testing session took place at a university clinic. Initially, Bob eagerly accompanied the examiner to the small testing room. The first test administered was the Wechsler Intelligence Scale for Children (WISC). During the first 30 minutes of the WISC administration, Bob was alert and cooperative. He maintained good eye contact and tried to answer the questions presented, although he seemed to have trouble understanding what was required on some of the verbal tasks. He was very friendly and struck up conversations with the examiner between items. However, after approximately 35 minutes of testing, his behavior began to change dramatically (the change started about midway through the vocabulary subtest). He became easily distracted by the metal shelves in the room, he constantly traced his finger along the walls, and he was frequently out of his seat, wandering about the room. Eye contact and on-task behavior began to disappear, and the examiner had to command him to sit down and pay attention. After Bob answered a question, he would ask, "Is that all?" and stand up, ready to leave. During the last four performance subtests, Bob's behavior was such that the examiner had to coax him continuously to do the items.

Bob's full-scale IQ score on the WISC of 70 falls within the borderline range of intellectual functioning. There is no significant inter-test scatter between the verbal and the performance portions of this test.

Individual interpretation of the subtests would not be valuable since his test scores when he appeared cooperative did not deviate significantly from his uncooperative performances. It is difficult to gauge how much the scores reflect an inability to do the task versus distractability or an unwillingness to do the task.

6.2. Behavioral Assessment

Bob was observed for approximately two hours in the home/family environment. It was noted that Bob frequently argued with his siblings and would not comply with their requests to leave their toys and other belongings alone. On occasion, he played cooperatively but only as long as he seemed to be getting his own way. Also, interactions between Bob and his mother revealed his tendency to defy her commands. For example, when his mother asked him to pick up the pieces of a game with which he had finished playing, he motioned as though to throw the box into the television screen. When his mother reprimanded him, he stared at her and continued to act as though he would break the screen. Bob's mother reports that he consistently "stares at her" defiantly when she tells him not to do something. The father interacted little with his son; however, on one occasion, Bob obeyed his father's command to stop misbehaving, and he did not "stare" at his father as he did at his mother. Most of his misbehavior in the home during the observation period consisted of non-compliance with the commands of others, especially his siblings. His parents reported that he does not go to bed until late at night (approximately 11:00), even though his siblings go to bed earlier.

Bob was observed at school in his morning classroom for approximately two and a half hours. During this time, his behavior significantly disrupted classroom functioning. He made loud noises during the pledge of allegiance and the prayer and refused to stand or to say either one. His frequent silliness was apparently reinforced by the laughter of others in his class. He generally did not comply with his teacher's commands and threw tantrums whenever physically forced to participate in a task or denied freedom to do as he pleased. His teacher constantly pleaded with him to behave and frequently threatened him with spankings and not being able to earn tokens. However, she seldom followed through on her threats and spent much of her time explaining the consequences instead of actually administering them. Twice during the observation period, she spanked Bob with a paddle. This involved her asking another teacher (a witness) to step into her room to watch while she spanked Bob. Her paddling consisted of two quick swats of questionable impact. As soon as the witness left the room, Bob openly defied his teacher and engaged in other disruptive behavior. The teacher expressed doubt that her spankings were effective in correcting his disruptive behavior. She reported that "nothing seemed to work." She said that she had tried spanking, time out, tokens for appropriate behavior, and even, on occasion, sending him home, but none of these procedures seemed effective.

During classroom activities, Bob constantly demanded his teacher's undivided attention. With the teacher's complete attention and a task that he seemed to like, he behaved appropriately. However, when the teacher turned to attend to the two other children at the table, Bob repeatedly asked her to look at his work or pulled on her arm to try to get her attention. The teacher attempted to ignore him, and Bob got out of his seat and began to play with other objects in the room. When the teacher asked him to continue his work, he refused. She then physically returned him to the table, and he threw a tantrum.

In general, Bob does what he wants, when he wants, in the classroom situation. Most of the time, if his teacher tries to force him to attend to tasks, she meets with strong resistance. Because of his extremely disruptive behavior in the classroom, it seems that the amount of material Bob is learning is limited. The teacher spends much of the school day dealing with his behavior problem, which might account for some of his low scores on the standardized tests. Not only has he learned how to avoid putting effort into something he does not like, but he may also have deficits in many preacademic areas as a result of his avoidance tactics.

The behaviors marked as problems on the Conners checklists corroborate the interview and observational data. Most of the items checked as problems revolve around issues of noncompliance and disruptive behavior (e.g., picks on other children, throws or breaks things, will not obey school rules). No other general category of problems seems to be of major concern to Bob's parents and teacher.

6.3. Recommendations for Placement

At this time, it is difficult to assess Bob's intellectual functioning because of his problem behaviors. The WISC seems to be an accurate indicator of his current functioning. However, it was difficult to distinguish what he could do from what he did not want to do. At this time, it does not appear that placement away from home is necessary. However, if Bob's parents and teacher cannot carry out the necessary behavioral programs needed to improve his behavior, special academic placement may have to be considered.

6.4. Educational Prescription

Two programs designed to control Bob's disruptive behavior in the home and the school are discussed here. It is important that these programs be carried out under the supervision of a behavior therapist.

6.4.1. Home

It is recommended that the mother initiate a "time-out" procedure in the home. This would entail sending Bob to an unstimulating portion of the house for a preset period of time contingent upon noncompliance with her requests. The details of this procedure can be worked out in conjunction with the behavior therapist. In addition to instruction in this system for dealing with disruptive or inappropriate behavior, the mother should be alerted to when Bob is "good" and "on-task" and should immediately and generously reinforce him for such behavior. Reinforcements may consist of praise or simple treats.

Efforts should be made to enlist Bob's father in the program. Also, Bob's siblings should be alerted to the procedure and prevented from interfering in the time-out procedure.

6.4.2. School

Any behavioral system in the classroom should be consistent and also carefully monitored by a behavior therapist. For example, if the spanking punishment is to be made effective, several changes should occur in its administration. It appears that Bob can discriminate situations in which the witness is or is not present. Therefore, arrangements should be made either to drop the witness procedure (in agreement with the parents) or to have an aide readily available just outside the door. The paddling should come after only one warning. Thus, the teacher should be able to summon the aide quickly and deliver the punishment immediately. Whatever the target behavior, the punishment for transgression should be quick and consistent (every time it occurs). The teacher should not allow Bob to cajole her into letting him off, nor should she allow his attempts at "good" behavior after transgression to keep her from paddling him. Initially, she can expect his tantrum behavior to increase significantly, but if she is consistent, Bob will learn the consequences for his disruptive behaviors, and the rate should decline.

An immediate token/reward system should also be initiated for Bob in the classroom. Currently, the students in his class are allowed to exchange their tokens only once a week. Shaping appropriate behaviors in Bob will require immediate verbal praise and material reinforcement. In addition, he should be given tokens that can be exchanged for small trinkets or prizes from a grab bag at the end of each hour. Later, the schedule can be thinned, so that he exchanges his tokens at the end of three hours, four hours, daily, twice a week, etc.

The behaviors desired and the reinforcement system should be explained to Bob. Each time he is reinforced for appropriate behavior, the behavior should be mentioned as the reinforcers are distributed. This procedure will allow him to become quickly acquainted with what is required of him and the consequences of performing the desired behaviors.

To help increase Bob's general verbal skills, his teacher should have him do some "magazine training." This involves having Bob thumb through children's and popular magazines, naming the objects he sees in the pictures and making up little stories about them. The reinforcement system can even be set up so that Bob can earn the opportunity to tell the stories to his classmates. This activity should be made pleasant for him, so that verbal conversation becomes fun as well as instructive.

Currently, Bob's disruptive behavior in the classroom not only interferes with classroom functioning but also seems to be preventing him from benefiting from what his teacher is attempting to teach him. In addition, his disruptive and resistive behavior at home is taxing on his mother and family. Behavioral programs in both situations should be initiated immediately. It is also recommended that after his disruptive behavior has been brought under control, he be retested in about a year to provide a more accurate estimate of his intellectual functioning and abilities.

6.5. Therapeutic Recommendations

Behavioral programs in the home and in the classroom are needed. Currently, his disruptive behavior interferes with classroom functioning, and he is probably not benefiting from what his teacher is attempting to teach him. Intervention should occur as soon as possible, since it is important that his behavior improve to ensure advancement in his present school.

1. The witness rule for punishment should be discontinued in the classroom for this particular child. The punishment should be administered immediately—after one (and only one) warning.
2. The teacher should initiate magazine training as described in the educational prescription.
3. An immediate-reward system should be established in the school for Bob.
4. Bob's mother should be supervised in the use of the time-out procedure.
5. The phenomena of response burst should be explained.
6. Bob's mother should dramatically increase her praise of her

son. She should work at "catching him being good" in the behavioral sense.

7. Bob's father should be enlisted to aid in the program.
8. Bob's mother should be taught to extinguish Bob's staring behavior.
9. Bob should be referred to a child psychiatrist for possible pharmacological intervention. If medications are currently appropriate, they could be used temporarily and phased out after behavior controls are established.

7. Conclusion

There are many problems, issues, and questions related to the behavioral assessment of children. At this time, many of the problems have not been solved and relatively few questions have been answered. Some of the questions that remain to be answered center on more general theoretical issues: Will classification eventually lead to the successful selection of appropriate treatment techniques? Can a behavioral classification scheme avoid the detrimental effect of labeling? How important are differences in the three channels of assessment? How much of the traditional approach should be retained by behavioral assessors and how much should be abandoned?

Other questions relate to more specific practical issues: Will it be possible to assess the child's environment accurately, including the reaction of other individuals such as parents, teachers, siblings, and peers? Since behavior is situationally specific, how many subenvironments in which the child behaves need to be assessed? How much assessment information (from interview, checklists, coding procedures, etc.) is sufficient? There are many more questions that need to be and hopefully will be answered through empirical investigation.

It is difficult to imagine an assessment situation in which clinical judgment plays no role. Assessment techniques and the resulting data are simply tools used in a decision-making process. For the behavioral assessor, the decisions to be made are related to various aspects of treatment. First, a decision must be made about whether a child should be treated. If the clinician decides to treat the child, several other decisions based on assessment data must be made. Which behaviors will be treated and in what order will they be treated? The specific treatment strategies must also be selected and implemented in the appropriate environments. Once the treatment program is started, further decisions must be made about the ongoing effectiveness of the intervention. Thus, some decision may be required to change or terminate a given form of treatment. Finally, the therapist must decide when the child is no longer in need of treatment. All of these treatment-related decisions should be based on the most objective criteria available. At this time, however, there are very few clearly established criteria for making treatment decisions, and considerable clinical judgment is required. As more and more data become available, we will be able to rely more on empirically derived "rules" and less on clinical impression for making treatment decisions. However, some clinical judgment will always be required.

Since there are many unanswered questions about the types of data that aid in making good decisions and accurate predictions, we have taken a somewhat liberal view on what are appropriate behavioral assessment strategies. For example, some behaviorists might completely disavow intelligence tests. However, we believe that it is too early to rule out any procedure simply because it sounds too traditional. Again, it is not the technique that defines a given procedure as behavioral or traditional; the defining characteristics are the assumptions about what is being sampled with that technique and how the data are used. In making the many treatment-related decisions that are required of all therapists, we cannot close our eyes to any reliable and valid data that could be useful.

References

Achenbach, T. M. *Developmental psychopathology*. New York: Ronald, 1974.

Adams, H. E., Doster, J. A., & Calhoun, K. S. A psychologically based system of response classification. *In* A. R. Ciminero, K. S. Calhoun, & H. E. Adams (Eds.), *Handbook of behavioral assessment*. New York: Wiley-Interscience, 1977.

Anastasi, A. *Psychological Testing*, 4th ed. New York: MacMillan, 1976.

Bandura, A. A social learning interpretation of psychological dysfunctions. *In* P. London & D. Rosenhan (Eds.), *Foundations of abnormal psychology*. New York: Holt, Rinehart, & Winston, 1968.

Bayley, N. *Bayley Scales of Infant Development: Birth to two years*. New York: Psychological Corporation, 1969.

Bernal, M. E., Delfini, L. F., North, J. A., & Kreutzer, S. L. Comparison of boys' behaviors in homes and schools. *In* E. J. Mash, L. A. Hamerlynck, & L. C. Handy (Eds.), *Behavior modification and families*. New York: Brunner/Mazel, 1976.

Bersoff, D. N. Silk purses into sows' ears: The decline of psychological testing and a suggestion for its redemption. *American Psychologist*, 1973, *28*, 892–899.

Bersoff, D. N., & Grieger, R. M. An interview model for the psychosituational assessment of children's behavior. *American Journal of Orthopsychiatry*, 1971, *41*, 483–493.

Bijou, S. W., & Peterson, R. F. Functional analysis in the assessment of children. *In* P. McReynolds (Ed.), *Advances in psychological assessment*, Vol. 2. Palo Alto, Calif.: Science and Behavior Books, 1971.

Bijou, S. W., Peterson, R. F., Harris, F. R., Allen, K. E., & Johnston, M. S. Methodology for experimental studies of young children in natural settings. *The Psychological Record*, 1969, *19*, 177–210.

Borkovec, T. D. The effects of instructional suggestion and psychological cues on analogue fear. *Behavior Therapy*, 1973, *4*, 185–192.

Borkovec, T. D., Weerts, T. C., & Bernstein, D. A. Assessment of anxiety. In A. R. Ciminero, K. S. Calhoun, & H. E. Adams (Eds.), *Handbook of behavioral assessment*. New York: Wiley-Interscience, 1977.

Boyd, R. D., & DeVault, M. V. The observation and recording of behavior. *Review of Educational Research*, 1966, *36*, 529–551.

Buxbaum, E. Techniques of child therapy: A critical evaluation. *Psychoanalytic Study of the Child*, 1954, *9*, 297–333.

Cautela, J. R. Behavior therapy and the need for behavioral assessment. *Psychotherapy: Theory, Research, and Practice*, 1968, *5*, 175–179.

Ciminero, A. R. Behavioral assessment: An overview. In A. R. Ciminero, K. S. Calhoun, & H. E. Adams (Eds.), *Handbook of behavioral assessment*. New York: Wiley-Interscience, 1977.

Ciminero, A. R., Calhoun, K. S., & Adams, H. E. (Eds.). *Handbook of behavioral assessment*. New York: Wiley-Interscience, 1977.

Ciminero, A. R., Nelson, R. O., & Lipinski, D. P. Self-monitoring procedures. In A. R. Ciminero, K. S. Calhoun, & H. E. Adams (Eds.), *Handbook of behavioral assessment*. New York: Wiley-Interscience, 1977.

Clement, P. W., & Richard, R. C. *Childrens Reinforcement Survey*. Pasadena, Calif.: Fuller Theological Seminary (Graduate School of Psychology), 1971.

Conners, C. K. A teacher rating scale for use in drug studies with children. *American Journal of Psychiatry*, 1969, *126*, 884–888.

Conners, C. K. Pharmacotherapy of psychopathology in children. In H. C. Quay & J. S. Werry (Eds.), *Psychopathological disorders of childhood*. New York: Wiley, 1972.

Conners, C. K. Rating scales for use in drug studies with children. *Psychopharmacology Bulletin*, 1973, Special Issue, 24–84.

Cox, A. The assessment of parental behaviour. *Journal of Child Psychology, Child Psychiatry, and Allied Disciplines*, 1975, *16*, 255–259.

Diagnostic and statistical manual of mental disorders (II). Washington, D.C.: American Psychiatric Association (2d ed.), 1968.

Engelmann, S. The effectiveness of direct verbal instruction on IQ performance and achievement in reading and arithmetic. In J. Hullmuth (Ed.) *Disadvantaged child: Vol. 3. Compensatory education: A national debate*. New York: Brunner/Mazel, 1970.

Eron, L. D. (Ed.). *The classification of behavior disorders*. Chicago: Aldine, 1966.

Evans, I. M., & Nelson, R. O. Assessment of child behavior problems. In A. R. Ciminero, K. S. Calhoun, & H. E. Adams (Eds.), *Handbook of behavioral assessment*. New York: Wiley-Interscience, 1977.

Ferinden, W. E., Jacobson, S., & Linden, N. J. early identification of learning disabilities. *Journal of Learning Disabilities*, 1970, *3*, 589–593.

Ferster, C. B. Classification of behavior pathology. In L. Krasner & L. P. Ullmann (Eds.), *Research in behavior modification*. New York: Holt, Rinehart, & Winston, 1965.

Forehand, R., & Atkeson, B. M. Generality of treatment effects with parents as therapists: A review of assessment and implementation procedures. *Behavior Therapy*, in press.

Gardner, W. M. *Behavior modification in mental retardation*. Chicago: Aldine-Atherton, 1971.

Gesell, A., & Amatruda, C. S. *Developmental diagnosis*, 2nd ed. New York: Harper, 1947.

Goldfried, M. R., & Kent, R. N. Traditional versus behavioral assessment: A comparison of methodological and theoretical assumptions. *Psychological Bulletin*, 1972, *77*, 409–420.

Goldfried, M. R., & Pomeranz, D. M. Role of assessment in behavior modification. *Psychological Reports*, 1968, *23*, 75–87.

Goldfried, M. R., & Sprafkin, J. N. *Behavioral personality assessment*. Morristown, N.J.: General Learning Press, 1974.

Graham, P., & Rutter, M. The reliability and validity of the psychiatric assessment of the child: II. Interview with the parent. *British Journal of Psychiatry*, 1968, *114*, 581–592.

Group for the Advancement of Psychiatry. *Psychopathological disorders in childhood: Theoretical considerations and a proposed classification*. GAP Report 62, 1966.

Graziano, A. M. (Ed.) *Behavior therapy with children*, Vol. 2. Chicago: Aldine, 1975.

Haggard, E. A., Brekstad, A., & Skard, A. G. On the reliability of the anamnestic interview. *Journal of Abnormal and Social Psychology*, 1960, *61*, 311–313.

Herjanic, B., Herjanic, M., Brown, F., & Wheatt, T. Are children reliable reporters? *Journal of Abnormal Child Psychology*, 1975, *3*, 41–48.

Hersen, M., & Barlow, D. H. *Single case experimental designs: Strategies for studying behavior change*. New York: Pergamon Press, 1976.

Hersen, M., & Bellack, A. S. Assessment of social behavior. *In* A. R. Ciminero, K. S. Calhoun, & H. E. Adams (Eds.), *Handbook of behavioral assessment*. New York: Wiley-Interscience, 1977.

Hetherington, E. M., & Martin, B. Family interaction and psychopathology in children. *In* H. C. Quay & J. S. Werry (Eds.), *Psychopathological disorders of childhood*. New York: Wiley, 1972.

Hobbs, N. *The futures of children: Categories, labels, and their consequences*. San Francisco: Jossey-Bass, 1975a.

Hobbs, N. (Ed.). *Issues in the classification of children*, Vol. 1. San Francisco: Jossey-Bass, 1975b.

Hobbs, N. (Ed.). *Issues in the classification of children*, Vol. 2. San Francisco: Jossey-Bass, 1975c.

Johnson, S. M., & Bolstad, O. D. Methodological issues in naturalistic observation: Some problems and solutions for field research. *In* L. A. Hamerlynck, L. C. Handy, & E. J. Mash (Eds.), *Behavior change: Methodology, concepts, and practice*. Champaign, Illinois: Research Press, 1973.

Jones, R. R., Reid, J. B., & Patterson, G. R. Naturalistic observation in clinical assessment. *In* P. McReynolds (Ed.), *Advances in psychological assessment*, Vol. 3. San Francisco: Jossey-Bass, 1975.

Kanfer, F. H., & Saslow, G. Behavioral diagnosis. *In* C. M. Franks (Ed.), *Behavior therapy: Appraisal and status*. New York: McGraw-Hill, 1969.

Katz, R. C., & Zlutnick, S. (Eds.). *Behavior therapy and health care*. New York: Pergamon Press, 1975.

Kent, R. N., & Foster, S. L. Direct observation procedures: Methodological issues in naturalistic settings. *In* A. R. Ciminero, K. S. Calhoun, & H. E. Adams (Eds.), *Handbook of behavioral assessment*. New York: Wiley-Interscience, 1977.

Kent, R. N., & O'Leary, K. D. A controlled evaluation of behavior modification with conduct problem children. *Journal of Consulting and Clinical Psychology*, 1976, *44*, 586–596.

Kessler, J. W. Nosology in child psychopathology. *In* H. E. Rie (Ed.), *Perspectives in child psychopathology*. Chicago: Aldine-Atherton, 1971.

Lahey, B. B., Johnson, V. S., Stempniak, M., Resick, P. A., & Giddings, C. W. The clinical and experimental usefulness of behavior rating scales for children: Interrater reliability. Manuscript submitted for publication, 1976.

Lang, P. J., & Melamed, B. G. Case report: Avoidance conditioning therapy of an infant with chronic ruminative vomiting. *Journal of Abnormal Psychology*, 1969, 74, 1–8.

Lazarus, A. A. Multimodal behavior therapy: Treating the "BASIC ID." *Journal of Nervous and Mental Disease*, 1973, 156, 404–411.

Lipinski, D. P., & Nelson, R. O. Problems in the use of naturalistic observation as a means of behavioral assessment. *Behavior Therapy*, 1974, 5, 341–351.

Lobitz, G. K., & Johnson, S. M. Normal versus deviant children: A multimethod comparison. *Journal of Abnormal Child Psychology*, 1975, 3, 353–374.

Luborsky, L., Chandler, M., Auerbach, A. H., Cohen, J., & Bachrach, H. M. Factors influencing the outcome of psychotherapy: A review of quantitative research. *Psychological Bulletin*, 1971, 75, 145–185.

Lytton, H. Three approaches to the study of parent–child interaction: Ethological, interview, and experimental. *Journal of Child Psychology, Child Psychiatry, and Allied Disciplines*, 1973, 14, 1–17.

Mahrer, A. R. (Ed.). *New approaches to personality classification*. New York: Columbia University Press, 1970.

Mash, E. J., Hamerlynck, L. A., & Handy, L. C. (Eds.). *Behavior modification and families*. New York: Brunner/Mazel, 1976.

Mash, E. J., Handy, L. C., & Hamerlynck, L. A. (Eds.). *Behavior modification approaches to parenting*. New York: Brunner/Mazel, 1976.

McCarthy, J. McR., & Paraskevopoulos, J. Behavior pattern of learning disabled, emotionally disturbed, and average children. *Exceptional Children*, 1969, 36, 69–74.

McNemar, Q. Lost our intelligence? Why? *American Psychologist*, 1964, 19, 874–879.

Meyers, C. E., Attwell, A. A., & Orpet, R. E. Prediction of fifth grade achievement from kindergarten test and rating data. *Educational and Psychological Measurement*, 1968, 28, 457–463.

Miller, L. C. Dimensions of psychopathology in middle childhood. *Psychological Reports*, 1967a, 21, 897–903.

Miller, L. C. Louisville Behavior Checklist for males 6–12 years of age. *Psychological Reports*, 1967b, 21, 885–896.

Miller, L. C. School behavior checklist: An inventory of deviant behavior for elementary school children. *Journal of Consulting and Clinical Psychology*, 1972, 38, 134–144.

Miller, L. C., Hampe, E., Barrett, C., & Noble, H. Children's deviant behavior within the general population. *Journal of Consulting and Clinical Psychology*, 1971, 37, 16–22.

Mischel, W. *Personality and assessment*. New York: Wiley, 1968.

Moore, B. L., & Bailey, J. S. Social punishment in the modification of a preschool child's "autistic like" behavior with mother as therapist. *Journal of Applied Behavior Analysis*, 1973, 6, 497–507.

Nelson, R. O., & Bowles, P. E. The best of two worlds—Observation with norms. *Journal of School Psychology*, 1975, 13, 3–9.

Novick, J., Rosenfeld, E., Bloch, D. A., & Dawson, D. Ascertaining deviant behavior in children. *Journal of Consulting Psychology*, 1966, 30, 230–238.

O'Leary, K. D. The assessment of psychopathology in children. In H. C. Quay & J. S. Werry (Eds.), *Psychopathological disorders of childhood*. New York: Wiley, 1972.

O'Leary, K. D., Romanczyk, R. G., Kass, R. E., Dietz, A., & Santagrossi, D. Procedures for classroom observations of teachers and children. Unpublished manuscript, 1971.

Patterson, G. R., Cobb, J. A., & Ray, R. S. A social engineering technology for retraining the families of aggressive boys. In H. E. Adams & I. P. Unikel (Eds.), *Issues and trends in behavior therapy*. Springfield, Ill.: Charles C Thomas, 1973.

Patterson, G. R., Ray, R. S., Shaw, D. A., & Cobb, J. A. *Manual for coding family interac-*

tions, sixth revision, 1969. Available from ASIS National Auxiliary Publications Service, in care of CCM Information Services, Inc., 909 Third Ave., New York, N.Y. 10022. Document #01234.

Patterson, G. R., & Reid, J. B. Intervention for families of aggressive boys: a replication study. *Behaviour Research and Therapy*, 1973, *11*, 383–394.

Patterson, G. R., Reid, J. B., Jones, R. R., & Conger, R. E. *A social learning approach to family intervention: Vol. 1. Families with aggressive children.* Eugene, Ore.: Castalia, 1975.

Peterson, D. R. Behavior problems of middle childhood. *Journal of Consulting Psychology*, 1961, *25*, 205–209.

Peterson, D. R. *The clinical study of social behavior*. New York: Appleton-Century-Crofts, 1968.

Preston, M. S., Guthrie, J. T., & Childs, B. Visual evoked responses (VERs) in normal and disabled readers. *Psychophysiology*, 1974, *4*, 452–457.

Proger, B. B., Mann, L., Green, P. A., Bayuk, R. J., & Burger, R. M. Discriminators of clinically defined emotional maladjustment: Predictive validity of the Behavior Problem Checklist and the Devereux scales. *Journal of Abnormal Child Psychology*, 1975, *3*, 71–82.

Quay, H. C. Patterns of aggression, withdrawal, and immaturity. *In* H. C. Quay & J. S. Werry (Eds.), *Psychopathological disorders of childhood*. New York: Wiley, 1972.

Quay, H. C., & Peterson, D. R. *Manual for the behavior problem checklist.* Champaign: University of Illinois, Child Research Center, 1967.

Quay, H. C., & Quay, L. C. Behavior problems in early adolescence. *Child Development*, 1965, *36*, 215–220.

Ross, A. O. The issue of normality in clinical child psychology. *Mental Hygiene*, 1963, *47*, 267–272.

Ross, A. O. *Psychological disorders of children: A behavioral approach to theory, research, and therapy*. New York: McGraw-Hill, 1974.

Ross, A. O., Lacey, H. M., & Parton, D. A. The development of a behavior checklist for boys. *Child Development*, 1965, *36*, 1013–1027.

Rourke, B. P. Brain behavior relationships in children with learning disabilities: A research program. *American Psychologist*, 1975, *30*, 911–920.

Rugh, J. D. & Schwitzgebel, R. L. Instrumentation for behavioral assessment. *In* A. R. Ciminero, K. S. Calhoun, & H. E. Adams (Eds.), *Handbook of behavioral assessment*. New York: Wiley-Interscience, 1977.

Rutter, M., & Graham, P. The reliability and validity of the psychiatric assessment of the child: I. Interview with the child. *British Journal of Psychiatry*, 1968, *114*, 563–579.

Scherer, M. W., & Nakamura, C. Y. A fear survey schedule for children (FSS–FC): A factor analytic comparison with manifest anxiety (CMAS). *Behaviour Research and Therapy*, 1968, *6*, 173–182.

Schnelle, J. F. A brief report on invalidity of parent evaluations of behavior change. *Journal of Applied Behavior Analysis*, 1974, *7*, 341–343.

Sloane, R. B., Staples, F. R., Cristol, A. H., Yorkston, N. J., & Whipple, K. Patient characteristics and outcome in psychotherapy and behavior therapy. *Journal of Consulting and Clinical Psychology*, 1976, *44*, 330–339.

Speer, D. C. The behavior problem checklist (Peterson–Quay): Baseline data from parents of child guidance and nonclinic children. *Journal of Consulting and Clinical Psychology*, 1971, *36*, 221–228.

Spivack, G., & Swift, M. The classroom behavior of children: A critical review of teacher-administered rating scales. *Journal of Special Education*, 1973, *7*, 55–89.

Spring, C., Greenberg, L., Scott, J., & Hopwood, J. Electrodermal activity in hyperactive boys who are methylphenidate responders. *Psychophysiology*, 1974, *4*, 436–442.

Staats, A. W. *Child learning, intelligence, and personality*. New York: Harper & Row, 1971.

Stuart, R. B. *Trick or treatment: How and when psychotherapy fails*. Champaign, Ill.: Research Press, 1970.

Vernon, P. E. Education and the psychology of individual differences. *Harvard Educational Review*, 1958, *28*, 91–104.

Wahler, R. G. Setting generality: Some specific and general effects of child behavior therapy. *Journal of Applied Behavior Analysis*, 1969, *2*, 239–246.

Wahler, R. G. Some structural aspects of deviant child behavior. *Journal of Applied Behavior Analysis*, 1975, *8*, 27–42.

Wahler, R. G., & Cormier, W. H. The ecological interview: A first step in out-patient child behavior therapy. *Journal of Behavior Therapy and Experimental Psychiatry*, 1970, *1*, 279–289.

Wahler, R. G., House, A. E., & Stambaugh, E. E. *Ecological assessment of child problem behavior: A clinical package for home, school, and institutional settings*. New York: Pergamon Press, 1976.

Webb, E. J., Campbell, D. T., Schwartz, R. D., & Sechrest, L. *Unobtrusive measures: Nonreactive research in social sciences*. Chicago: Rand McNally, 1966.

Werry, J. S., & Quay, H. C. The prevalence of behavior symptoms in younger elementary school children. *American Journal of Orthopsychiatry*, 1971, *41*, 136–143.

Werry, J. S., Sprague, R. L., & Cohen, M. N. Conners' Teacher Rating Scale for use in drug studies with children—An empirical study. *Journal of Abnormal Child Psychology*, 1975, *3*, 217–229.

Wolff, W. T., & Merrens, M. R., Behavioral assessment: A review of clinical methods. *Journal of Personality Assessment*, 1974, *38*, 3–16.

Wright, H. F. Observational child study. *In* P. H. Mussen (Ed.), *Handbook of research methods in child development*. New York: Wiley, 1960.

Yarrow, L. J. Interviewing children. *In* P. H. Mussen (Ed.), *Handbook of research methods in child development*. New York: Wiley, 1960.

Yarrow, M. R., Campbell, J. D., & Burton, R. V. Recollections of childhood: A study of the retrospective method. *Monographs of the Society for Research in Child Development*, 1970, *35*, No. 5.

Zlutnick, S., Mayville, W. J., & Moffat, S. Modification of seizure disorders: The interruption of behavioral chains. *Journal of Applied Behavior Analysis*, 1975, *8*, 1–12.

3 The Behavioral Treatment of Disruption and Hyperactivity in School Settings

TEODORO AYLLON
AND MICHAEL S. ROSENBAUM

Mrs. Gates: (In a moderately firm voice) All right class, go to your seats.

(The talking and the jostling behavior continue)

Mrs. Gates: (Focusing her attention on one child) Rosalyn!

Rosalyn has been standing in the doorway talking to several boys in the hall. She turns her head momentarily in Mrs. Gates' direction, ignores the admonition to sit down, and then calmly resumes her discussion. Mrs. Gates appears nonplussed by Rosalyn's behavior and she turns to a child in the back of the room.

Mrs. Gates: Carlos, please sit down. (Carlos is seated in the windowsill)

Carlos: (mockingly) But I am sitting down, teacher!

Mrs. Gates: (With some frustration) Carlos, you know what I mean. (Firmly) In a chair, this minute! (Then, to the rest of the class) Get to your seats!

The noise and the movement in the room continue to mount as the teacher attempts futilely to direct students to their assigned seats. Rosalyn finishes her conversation with the boys in the hallway and slowly takes a seat.

Mrs. Gates: Adam, now I'm going to ask you one more time to move.

Adam makes a face, picks up a chair, puts it noisily into the corner, and stands, shouting at Rosalyn who is laughing at him.

TEODORO AYLLON AND MICHAEL S. ROSENBAUM • Georgia State University, Atlanta, Georgia.

Mrs. Gates: Adam, sit down! (Adam sits, continuing his discourse with Rosalyn across the room)

John: (Yelling across the room to Chester) Hey, Chester! (Chester is watching Rosalyn and Adam; he looks up but does not respond)

Mrs. Gates: Jeanne, will you come over to the seat where you belong?

Jeanne: I don't know where I sit. (Laughter in the class)

John: Sit next to me.

Mrs. Gates walks over to Jeanne's seat and puts her hand on the desk. Jeanne works her way over to the desk, throws her books on the desk, and drops into the seat, smiling. The noise in the room continues. Mrs. Gates goes to the piano.

Mrs. Gates: (Screaming) All right! Whoever continues to talk will be assigned to detention hall! (Pause) Get into the seats you've been assigned to! (Two students come in and slam the door)

Mrs. Gates: (Turning to them) I've told you two for the last time to come in on time. Report to the principal's office, both of you.

(Greenwood, Good, & Siegel, 1971, pp. 87–88)

Chronic behavior problems such as these constitute a major concern in schools today. While there are various theories as to the factors responsible for such discipline problems, these views may be subsumed under two major conceptualizations. The most prevalent one regards disruptive behavior and related discipline problems as reflections of other, more fundamental conflicts in the life of the child (Berkowitz & Rothman, 1967). This view maintains that the misbehavior of the child in school either represents a reenactment of his problems with authority figures or symbolizes his hostility (Grossman, 1965). The premise here is that the origins of such acting-out behavior stem from childhood problems. This conceptualization has resulted in extremely provocative speculations regarding the effects of broken, fatherless, and disadvantaged homes on the classroom behavior of children (Long, Morse, & Newman, 1965). Based on this conceptualization, the present "mental-health" approach to remediating such problems relies for the most part on child-guidance clinics and private psychological and psychiatric practitioners to provide therapeutic assistance to schoolchildren. The major therapeutic premise of this mental-health approach is that when the child engages in play therapy or a discussion of his feelings toward authority figures in particular, he experiences relief from anxiety or hostility, and that this experience is facilitated by a protective clinical environment. In this view, only a sophisticated clinical practitioner would be able to guide the child into resolving the mental conflicts responsible for the child's school problems.

While the above approach is widespread, an alternative to dealing with behavior problems in school is based on the premise that behavior is largely governed by its environmental consequences (Ferster & Skinner, 1957; Skinner, 1938). Since the environmental consequences of classroom behavior are provided primarily by the teacher, this approach suggests that the child's misbehavior may be linked to the teacher's reaction to such misbehavior. If so, the child's misconduct may be amenable to modification if the teacher's reaction to it is changed. Thus, the classroom, rather than the clinic, becomes the locale of therapeutic behavioral intervention, and the teacher, rather than the therapist, becomes the major agent of behavior change.

Based on this behavioral conceptualization, several procedures have been employed to reduce the disruptive behavior of children in the classroom. All of these techniques focus on pinpointing and manipulating the consequences that follow classroom misbehavior.

1. The Role of Teachers in Controlling Misbehavior

One of the earliest and most influential approaches involved the use of teacher attention (e.g., close physical proximity to the student, a pat on the student's shoulder) and verbal praise as reinforcing stimuli contingent upon the task-relevant behaviors of students (e.g., orientation toward the teacher, working with pencil and paper, answering questions posed by the teacher). Inappropriate behaviors (e.g., being out of the seat, talking without permission, fighting) were followed by the teacher's either ignoring them or expressing disapproval. In achieving great success with these procedures in controlling classroom misbehavior, Becker, Madsen, Arnold, and Thomas (1967) and Madsen, Becker, and Thomas (1968) pointed out that rules specifying appropriate classroom behavior, used alone or in conjunction with the teacher's ignoring disruptive behavior, were ineffective in controlling misbehavior. The combination of ignoring inappropriate behaviors and simultaneously reinforcing task-relevant behaviors, however, was found to be quite successful. Hall, Lund, and Jackson (1968) stressed that in the typical classroom, misbehaving children received considerable attention for their misbehavior in the form of teacher reprimands. It was found that shifting teacher attention from misbehavior to appropriate behaviors produced increases in task-relevant and decreases in disruptive behaviors. Thomas, Becker, and Armstrong (1968) demonstrated that it was the contingent application of teacher approval, as opposed to noncontingent approval, that was critical in producing desirable results. McAllister, Stachowiak, Baer, and Conderman (1969) suggested that praise might function as positive reinforcement, increasing task-relevant behaviors, and that disapproval might function as punishment, decreasing misbehavior. Other researchers were also able to control classroom misbehavior through teacher attention and praise for task-relevant behavior, combined with ignoring or disapproving disruptive behavior (Hall, Fox, Willard, Goldsmith, Emerson, Owen, Davis, & Porcia, 1971; Hall, Panyan, Rabon, & Broden, 1968; Ward & Baker, 1968; Wasik, Senn, Welch, & Cooper, 1969). The major conclusions to be derived from this research are:

1. The emergence of discipline problems or disruptive behavior is largely linked to the teacher's reaction to them.
2. Attention in the form of reprimands may be as effective in maintaining the child's troublesome conduct as if he were being praised for such conduct.
3. Involving the child in alternative conduct to the disruptive behavior, while selectively "ignoring" disruption, appears to aid in reducing classroom problems in general.

2. The Role of Peers in Controlling Misbehavior

The teacher is not the only person who provides attention for misbehavior in the classroom. Indeed, guffaws, laughter, etc., from peers often follow the antics of a specific child, possibly providing an additional source of maintenance of misbehavior. Broden, Bruce, Mitchell, Carter, and Hall (1970) showed that increasing the attending behavior of one child through reinforcement led to a parallel increase in the attending behavior of a second child seated nearby. Further, a decrease in their disruptive behavior was also noted. The authors suggested that this procedure was effective because the absence of peer attention for misbehavior for the student not being reinforced. This general tactic for influencing the misbehavior of children received experimental support from Solomon and Wahler (1973), who demonstrated that peer attention and praise could be used to decrease disruptive classroom behavior. Initially, these authors showed that peers were almost exclusively attentive to the misbehavior of "problem" children, while ignoring prosocial behaviors. Through a training procedure, it was shown that these social contingencies could be shifted, so that peers ignored misbehavior and attended to prosocial behaviors, resulting in an increase in desirable behaviors and a decrease in problem behaviors.

A variation of this procedure, involving the removal of peer attention to the misconduct of a classmate, includes reinforcing the class as a whole when the disruption is minimal. This means that it is to the peer group's advantage to keep the disruption below a level specified by the teacher. Using this technique, sometimes referred to as a *group contingency*, Sulzbacher and Houser (1968) and Schmidt and Ulrich (1969) found that nondisruptive students ignored the disruptive behaviors of others, whereas prior to the group contingency, misbehaving students were receiving considerable peer attention. Barrish, Saunders, and Wolf (1969), Medland and Stachnik (1972), and Harris and Sherman (1973) were successful in controlling disruptive behavior by dividing their classes into two teams and having each team compete against the other for the least number of disruptions. The disruptive behavior of an individual child increased the probability of the entire groups' losing reinforcing privileges. In this way, a contingency was arranged for the disruptive behavior of each individual child, while the consequences of each child's behavior was shared by the members of the group as a whole. If both teams did not exceed a stated level of disruption, both were declared winners and were entitled to reinforcement. Results from group contingencies point to the following conclusions:

1. Peer reinforcement is an important factor in the maintenance of disruptive classroom behavior.
2. Peer reinforcement for misbehavior can be effectively removed by the institution of a group contingency, in which the behavior of an individual student affects the consequences for the entire group.

3. The Role of a Token System in Controlling Misbehavior

The above research showed that the social consequences controlled by teachers and peers can be systematically manipulated to minimize misbehavior in the classroom. Such social control may not be sufficiently effective with some children (Kazdin & Bootzin, 1972), who require additional procedures to control their misbehavior. Indeed, empirical support for this notion has been provided by O'Leary, Becker, Evans, and Saudargas (1969). After successively introducing rules, classroom structure, and social control in the form of praise for appropriate behaviors combined with ignoring disruption, they found these procedures to be generally ineffective in decreasing disruption. When tokens were introduced for on-task behavior, however, disruptive behavior immediately decreased. The implementation of token economies has provided teachers with another effective technique for controlling disruptive classroom behavior. Typically, points are provided for desirable behaviors; these points, or tokens, are exchangeable for back-up reinforcers in the classroom. O'Leary and Becker (1967) pointed out that token reinforcement offers an excellent means of providing immediate feedback to students regarding their behavior, without the disruption often caused by the continuous delivery of the back-up reinforcers.

What exactly do tokens do? Kazdin (1973), in attempting to analyze the separate effects of instructions and token reinforcement, found that contingent token reinforcement, irrespective of instructions for appropriate behavior, was effective in increasing on-task and decreasing deviant behavior. Further, Herman and Tramontana (1971) found that reinforcement alone, prior to instructions for appropriate behavior, did not produce any substantial effect on disruption. Yet, when instructions were paired with token reinforcement, disruptive behavior decreased markedly. Following a return to baseline conditions, the presentation of instructions alone did not affect disruption. These authors, therefore, concluded that the consistent presentation of token reinforcement with instructions was necessary to maintain appropriate behaviors prompted by the instructions. Up to this point, the assumption underlying behavioral research in the classroom was that once children were quiet and attentive, academic learning would ensue. This notion was challenged by Ferritor, Buckholdt, Hamblin, and Smith (1975), who found that when tokens were contingent upon attending behavior, disruptive behavior decreased, but surprisingly academic achievement did not change appreciably from baseline. When they made tokens contingent upon academic performance, not only did this class of behaviors increase, but so did disruption! Only when tokens were made contingent upon attending and academic achievement did they produce increases in both and a decrease in disruptive behavior. This study demonstrated that a contingency that increases attending and decreases disruptive behavior does not necessarily result in an increase in academic performance, unless the contingency is also applied to this latter class of behaviors.

Token procedures have not been limited to dispensing tokens for appropriate behavior. Indeed, taking tokens away for disruption has been found effective in reducing it. For example, in a variation of the token-reinforcement procedure, Kaufman and O'Leary (1972) investigated the differential effects on disruptive behavior of the application of reward versus response-cost procedures. Tokens were delivered to the reward group contingent upon appropriate classroom behavior. Tokens were given to the response-cost group on a noncontingent basis and were taken away contingent upon inappropriate classroom behavior. The results showed that reward and response-cost procedures were equally effective in reducing misbehavior, that no detrimental side effects were produced by the response-cost procedures, and that students did not show any preference for one procedure or the other. These findings were further corroborated by Iwata and Bailey (1974). In summary, one may conclude that:

1. Token-reinforcement procedures may be more effective in those situations in which rules, instructions, and teacher praise are ineffective in producing desirable behavioral changes.
2. It may be necessary to reinforce both attending behavior and academic achievement in order to increase both classes of behavior and decrease disruptive behavior.
3. Token-reward or token-cost procedures appear equally effective in reducing misbehavior in the classroom.

4. Additional Procedures for Controlling Classroom Misbehavior

4.1. Feedback

Informing the target child of his behavior according to a rating along a continuum from very good to very poor was the approach taken by Drabman and Lahey (1974). This procedure resulted in a decrease in disruptive behavior for this child, and the authors concluded that feedback alone may be both necessary and sufficient for behavioral change in some classrooms.

4.2. Reinforcement Schedule

A stated level of disruption as the criterion for reinforcement versus no reinforcement characterized the research of Dietz and Repp (1973, 1974). These authors found that differentially reinforcing low rates of misbehavior in the classroom (drl schedule of reinforcement) with reinforcers such as free time, candy, and nonexchangeable tokens resulted in rates of misbehavior below a level specified by the teacher.

4.3. Free Time as a Reinforcer

Osborne (1969) successfully employed free time as a reinforcer to increase on-task behavior and indirectly decrease disruptive behavior. He pointed out two possible functions of free time: (1) if the regular classroom was aversive, free time provided the opportunity for an escape response; and (2) free time might have represented a period during which the student could engage in reinforcing activities.

4.4. Self-Regulation

A more recent procedure for managing classroom disruption is one in which the student evaluates his own behavior and delivers his own reinforcement relative to a specified criterion for that evaluation. Bolstad and Johnson (1972) and Kaufman and O'Leary (1972) found that following a period of external regulation, in which the teacher's evaluation and reinforcement of students' behavior produced decreases in disruption, the evaluative and reinforcement systems could be transferred to the students themselves, with a low level of disruption being maintained. In both studies, it was reported that self-evaluation permitted periods of noncontingent reinforcement, during which the students could reinforce themselves independently of their behavior. Yet, the results showed that the students continued to display low rates of misbehavior and high ratings during self-evaluation. Santogrossi, O'Leary, Romanczyck, and Kaufman (1973) reported that although rates of disruptive behavior increased during self-evaluation, students still gave themselves high ratings and received maximum reinforcement. These researchers mentioned the necessity of being careful in implementing self-evaluation and self-reinforcement systems, especially with clinical populations. It appears, then, that while self-evaluation and self-reinforcement represent an alternative to external regulation of students' behavior by the teacher, thereby freeing the teacher to do more "teaching," such procedures may have severe limitations because they depend upon the students' reporting their own behavior.

4.5. Time-Out

Surprisingly, punishment, in the form of time-out, has not been frequently used to deal with disruptive behavior in the classroom. Ramp, Ulrich, and Dulaney (1971) used a delayed time-out procedure, in which each instance of disruptive behavior during the school day resulted in a loss of gym time or recess. While instructions for appropriate behavior were ineffective in increasing such behavior, the delayed time-out was effective in reducing misbehavior and increasing desirable behavior.

4.6. Home-Based Reinforcement

One final procedure that has been used to control misbehavior in the classroom is based on the finding that reinforcers for some disruptive children may not be found in the classroom. In an attempt to solve this problem, a tactic has been developed whereby behavior is evaluated in the classroom but is reinforced in the home. Bailey, Wolf, and Phillips (1970) and Todd, Scott, Bostow, and Alexander (1976) used a daily report card on which the teacher evaluated the students' behavior. This report card was then taken home, where the appropriate reinforcer or punishment was delivered, typically being the earning or losing of privileges, respectively. In both studies, significant reductions in disruption in the classroom were obtained. Bailey *et al.* mentioned that in order for such home-based or remote consequences to be effective, it was necessary to have a teacher who could differentiate between appropriate and inappropriate behavior, in addition to having effective reinforcers in the home.

5. A Direct versus an Indirect Approach to Controlling Classroom Misbehavior

The research reviewed so far represents a direct approach to eliminating misbehavior in the classroom, in which reinforcement is contingent upon refraining from engaging in such misbehavior. Why did behavioral research in the classroom take this direction? It must be remembered that the individuals most affected by discipline problems in the classroom are the teachers. Not surprisingly, their cooperation in extending behavioral principles to the classroom was based on their receiving help for their problems as they viewed them. The request for assistance was not based on the need for teaching methods, since that was the teachers' expertise. Rather, their need was to have help in managing the discipline problems in the classroom. Specifically, their perspective was that once the disrupting child had learned to pay attention, to mind the teacher's directions, and to concentrate on and show interest in the subject matter at hand, he would cease being disruptive and would derive the academic benefits of being in the classroom. Unfortunately, such expectations turned out to be at variance with experimental evidence indicating that merely increasing "attending" behaviors does not produce academic achievement (Ferritor *et al.*, 1972). Furthermore, this direct approach has received a good deal of criticism, especially from Winett and Winkler (1972). These authors suggested that behavior modifiers, most notably the ones in the research reviewed, have contributed to strengthening the *status quo*, which maintains that the effectiveness of the educational system is measured not necessarily by increases in academic performance but by the maintenance of classrooms in which students are orderly, docile, and obedient. Winett and Winkler have characterized this "direct-approach" research tactic as follows:

> Taken as a fairly accurate indicator of what public schools deemed as the "model" child, these studies described this pupil as one who stays glued to his seat and desk all day, continually looks at his teacher or his text-book/workbook, does not talk to or in fact look at other children, does not talk unless asked to by the teacher, hopefully does not laugh or sing (or at the wrong time), and assuredly passes silently in the halls. (p. 501)

It is their contention that these goals are contrary to effective learning. Indeed, according to Winett and Winkler, behaviors that behavior modifiers consider inappropriate—such as walking around, laughing, and talking to other students—may contribute to more effective learning, especially in settings such as the "open" classroom. The notion of eliminating such "inappropriate" behavior is, in their view, at best unwise and at worst a disservice to effective learning.

It appears, then, that behavioral research in the classroom, encouraged and abetted by teachers, has focused upon eliminating misbehavior by strengthening attention, obedience, concentration, and interest in academic work. This strategy attempts to develop response topographies that compete with disruption. For example, reinforcing a student when he is "oriented toward the teacher" or appears to be "concentrating on his work" or "shows interest in his work" may lead to a reduction in disruption but does not necessarily result in his achieving academically.

Consistent with developing responses that compete with misbehavior, an alternative to selecting response topographies is to select responses that are both topographically and, more importantly, functionally academic. Here the focus would be on increasing academic skills by reinforcement, thereby indirectly reducing disruption through response competition. Indeed, to the extent that a child is performing well academically, it can safely be assumed that he is paying attention, concentrating, and showing interest in the appropriate academic skills. The converse of this should also be true: to the extent that the child's academic performance is low or nonexistent, it can be safely assumed that he is not interested, is not paying attention, is away from his desk, or possibly may be disturbing others with his misbehavior. If this reasoning is correct, then the major behavioral targets for measurement and modification are not concentration, interest, or attention *per se* but the academic performances that require these components for their successful completion. In summary, then, it would be desirable to develop a system to influence the child's classroom behavior by having the teacher implement behavioral procedures to indirectly eliminate classroom misbehavior by reinforcing academic performance that competes with it.

The following research deals with decreasing disruptive classroom behavior through response competition by focusing on academic performance.[1] This research can be typified by two general approaches: (1) the manipulation of antecedent events involving the systematic introduction of stimuli that precede and set the occasion for academic performance; and (2) the manipulation of consequent events involving the systematic application of stimuli that follow academic performance.

6. Controlling Misbehavior through Events That Precede Academic Performance

6.1. Classroom Structure

Ayllon, Layman, and Burke (1972) worked with four educable mentally retarded children who presented the greatest problems in classroom management. Disruptive behavior was defined in three major categories: (1) gross motor (out of seat, running without permission); (2) verbalization (talking out loud to self or others, calling out to teacher); and (3) noise (tapping, pounding objects, dropping objects). During a two-day baseline, in which the class was observed under normal conditions, disruption averaged 98%. In addition, the teacher made several attempts to instruct the children. Although her assignments were quite unsystematic, the discipline problems were so overwhelming that additional efforts on her part were precluded. The opportunity to measure academic performance, therefore, was absent by definition, and the teacher even considered it a waste of time.

In order to provide a systematic basis for assessing academic performance, the following structure for the class was introduced on the third day. Academic performance was defined in the areas of reading and arithmetic. For reading, a 2-min story was to be read silently, followed by a 2-min written multiple-choice test of five items. For arithmetic, which involved the addition of whole numbers, the teacher

[1] These studies were conducted with the cooperation of teachers from the Atlanta public schools. We wish to thank Dr. Jarvis Barnes, the assistant superintendent for research and development, for his kindness and support.

provided 5 min of instruction, followed by a 1½-min test of five problems. The class time was divided into two consecutive periods of 30 min each. During the first period, four teaching–testing math sessions were presented, and during the second period four reading–testing sessions were presented. Papers were collected at the end of each test and were graded and returned later in the day. This meant that 46 min out of a total of 60 min (or 67% of the time), the teacher systematically exposed the children to academic instruction and materials that set the occasion for academic performance. The introduction of this procedure *alone* produced a marked decrease in disruption from 98% to 17% (see Figure 1). It can be seen that subsequent token reinforcement of academic performance could do no better than maintain the low level of disruption achieved with classroom structure. Academic performance,

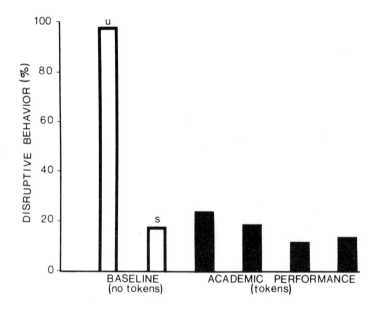

FIGURE 1. Percentage of disruptive behavior for four children. The first baseline bar, designated with a *U*, shows the level of disruptive behavior under unstructured conditions. The second baseline bar, designated with an *S*, shows the level of disruptive behavior under structured conditions. The remaining bars show the level of disruptive behavior during procedures of reinforcement for academic performance. Notice that the reduction in disruption achieved with classroom structure alone could not be improved upon by token-reinforcement procedures. Each bar is based on 144 minutes of 10-second intervals. $N = 4$. (From Ayllon, Layman, & Burke, 1972. Copyright © 1972 by Denison University, Granville, Ohio. Reprinted by permission.)

however, was consistently low across children prior to reinforcement procedures. During reinforcement, the reinforced academic behavior (i.e., either reading or arithmetic) was high relative to the academic behavior under extinction. How does one explain the drastic drop in disruption in the absence of systematic consequences for either on-task behavior or nondisruption? One interpretation emerging from these results is that the academic materials functioned as a cue to engage in academic behaviors that competed with disruption.

6.2. Instructions and Modeling

It has been well established that instructions as well as modeling may serve as discriminative stimuli to generate behavior. Instructions can prompt behavior in the absence of reinforcement, but they become progressively less effective if reinforcement is not instituted (Ayllon & Azrin, 1964; Findley, 1966; Herman & Tramontana, 1971; Hopkins, 1968; Schutte & Hopkins, 1970; Zimmerman, Zimmerman, & Russell, 1969). Studies of modeling approaches under controlled laboratory conditions with a wide variety of behaviors indicate:

1. Arranging behavioral consequences may not be necessary in the use of modeling techniques (Bandura, 1969; Lahey, 1971).
2. Modeling is more efficient than differential reinforcement in producing behavioral changes (Bandura & McDonald, 1963; Craig, 1967; Masters & Branch, 1969).
3. Exposure to modeling cues can produce enduring effects (Bandura & McDonald, 1963; Bandura & Mischel, 1965; Thelen, 1970; Zimmerman & Pike, 1972).

Instructions and modeling, therefore, are effective in producing behavior, and their effectiveness does not necessarily depend upon the manipulation of differential reinforcement.

There has been a paucity of research involving the control of classroom misbehavior through the modeling of task-relevant behaviors. Allison (unpublished) investigated the following issues:

1. Whether appropriate classroom behavior could be learned through modeling.
2. Whether instructions alone (without modeling or extrinsic reinforcement) are as effective as modeling in changing behavior.
3. Whether the effects of either instructions or modeling would be temporary or enduring.
4. Whether extrinsic reinforcement would be needed to maintain

any new behavior patterns initiated by instructions or modeling.

Three children were chosen from a middle-elementary-school class. These target children were ranked by their teacher as being the most disruptive children and the poorest academic achievers in the class. Disruptive behaviors fell within three categories: (1) gross motor (out of seat without permission, running, leaving the classroom without permission); (2) verbalization (conversing with peers without permission, screaming, yelling out remarks); and (3) other inappropriate behavior (ignoring the teacher's questions, doing something different from what they had been directed to do). Academic performance was measured as performance in the following areas: (1) math (percentage correct of individualized assignments); (2) reading (percentage correct of individualized reading activities, such as workbooks or worksheets); and (3) spelling (percentage correct on each daily lesson emphasizing spelling accuracy and word meaning).

The effects of the various experimental manipulations were evaluated in a multiple-baseline-across-subjects design. During baseline, disruptive behavior and academic performance were measured under usual classroom conditions. The teacher met with the target children and instructed them in appropriate behavior during the next phase (instructions). In addition, these instructions were written on the board, and the children were reminded of them at least twice a day. In the third phase (instructions plus modeling of appropriate behavior), the teacher individually instructed each target child to observe the behavior of a "model" child in the classroom (e.g., sitting quietly while working, raising one's hand for help and for permission to engage in various activities). At least twice a day, the target children were reminded to observe the model. Similar instructions to those of phase three—but with emphasis on the importance of the model child's behavior for academic performance (e.g., workbook is open and student is actively writing, keeps eyes on own paper, keeps writing even if help is not available immediately when hand is raised for it)—comprised the fourth phase (instructions plus modeling of academic performance). In the fifth phase, each of the target children was able to earn points, exchangeable for back-up reinforcers, contingent upon the percentage of completion of each academic subject (instructions and modeling of academic performance plus reinforcement for meeting minimum academic criteria). For each of the three subject matters 50–79% correct, 5 points were awarded, and 50 points were awarded for each subject matter 80–100% correct. Although this phase produced an increased academic output, the children's daily percentage correct for each subject matter was unstable. To stabilize this academic parameter, the reinforcement schedule was adjusted in the final phase of the study (instructions and modeling of academic performance plus reinforcement for meeting maximum academic criteria). The difference between the two levels of academic requirements was that during minimum academic criteria, the completion of each subject resulted in points independently of the other subjects. During maximum academic criteria, only completion of the first subject resulted in points, while the other two subjects were linked to one another so that success in one allowed access to the other. Then, success in the third and final subject resulted in points. During maximum academic criteria, the same amount of work as that during minimum academic criteria now produced two-thirds the amount of reinforcement. In the first subject period during maximum academic criteria, the child could choose between math and reading and receive 5 points for 50% correct and 50 points for 80% correct. In the second subject period, the child was required to complete spelling at a satisfactory level without points in order to proceed to the third subject period. In this final period, the child completed either math or reading, whichever was not done in the first subject period, and he received 5 points for 50% correct or 50 points for 80% correct.

The results of this study show that although instructions initially reduced disruptive behavior from its baseline level for each boy, disruption eventually returned to a high level (see Figure 2). Disruption averaged 70% during baseline and 52% during the instructions phase. Modeling of appropriate behavior initially reduced disruptive behavior, and the effects appeared more stable than under instructions alone, with disruptive behavior averaging 31%. Yet, for one child (Wendell), disruption gradually returned to a high level. Modeling of academic performance initially maintained disruptive behavior at the level attained under the previous condition. Over the sessions of this phase, however, disruption increased for all children. Reinforcement at minimum academic criteria produced a marked decrease in disruptive behavior for two children and a more gradual decrease for the third child. Under this condition, disruption averaged 27%. The final condition, reinforcement at maximum academic criteria, did not produce any more of an effect than the previous phase. Academic performance for the children averaged 7% during baseline and increased to an average of 16% during the instructions phase.

Modeling of appropriate behavior increased average academic performance to 23%, where it remained during the modeling-of-academic-performance phase. During reinforcement at the minimum criteria, academic performance averaged 44% and almost doubled to

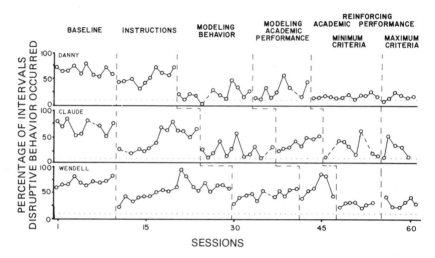

Figure 2. Percentage of disruptive behavior for the three target children as a function of the different experimental conditions. Each session consisted of 72 intervals, each of 10-sec duration. (From Allison, unpublished.)

83% during the final phase, reinforcement at maximum criteria. In summary, the general findings indicated that instructions were partially effective in reducing disruptive behavior and increasing academic performance, but across time these gains were lost. Instructions combined with modeling had a similar effect but seemed to have more stability across time. When consequences were added to a history of modeling behavior and academic performance, the effects were rapid and, in contrast to the previous conditions, enduring on both dimensions for all three of the children.

Allison concluded that while both instructions and modeling were immediately effective in reducing disruptive behavior and increasing academic performance, they were limited in their enduring effects. A combination of instructions and modeling, however, maintained behavioral changes more effectively than instructions alone. Although reinforcement was only as effective as these other procedures in generating behavior, it had the singular advantage of producing effects that endured over time.

6.3. Time Limits

Increasing the academic performance of retarded, learning-disabled, and culturally deprived children through reinforcement procedures has been well documented (O'Leary & O'Leary, 1972). Yet, most of these studies have included only continuous-reinforcement schedules. One of the schedules of reinforcement described by Ferster and Skinner (1957), which produces much higher rates of performance than continuous reinforcement, is the "limited hold." This particular schedule limits the period of time during which reinforcement is available. Hopkins, Schutte, and Garton (1971), using time limits similar to the limited hold, gradually decreased the amount of time available for students to complete their work and participate in a reinforcing activity. Their results showed that the rate of correct performance increased as the time limits decreased. Yet, several methodological problems precluded determining whether the availability of reinforcement or the opportunity for the response to occur was responsible for the rate increase. This question prompted a study by Garber (unpublished) that investigated the issue of whether decreasing temporal limits for completion of academic assignments would maximize response competition with disruptive behaviors.

Three second-graders diagnosed as hyperactive with perceptual problems and enrolled in a class for children with learning disabilities served as subjects for this study. Academic performance was measured in terms of the total number of math problems completed out of 10 in a specific amount of time. These problems were at one of two levels of difficulty: level 1 consisted of two-digit addition with carrying, and level 2 consisted of three-digit addition with carrying. Disruption included behaviors such as talking without permission, throwing objects, kicking feet against the desk, humming, singing, and being out of the seat without permission. When the study began, a token-reinforcement system was already in operation, and the amount of reinforcement available to the children remained constant throughout the study. Under this system, students earned one token for each problem completed correctly, and bonuses were awarded for each problem beyond five done correctly.

The effects of the experimental manipulations on disruptive behaviors were evaluated in a design of combined reversal within a multiple-baseline-across-subjects. During the baseline phase, both academic performance and disruptive behavior were measured under usual classroom conditions, with students being allowed as much time as they needed to complete their work with level-1 problems. Based upon the average amount of time taken by each child during baseline, each child was given half as long to complete his work during the second phase (8–10 min, level 1). In the next phase, the time limits were halved again (4–5 min, level 1). With the introduction of level-2 problems, the time was reversed to 8–10 min. The following phases were conducted in succession: 4–5 min, 8–10 min, and 4–5 min, all with level-2 problems.

The results of this study are presented in Figure 3 and show that as the time limits were decreased, the frequency of disruptive behaviors decreased. The largest reduction occurred when the time limits were initially halved from their baseline length. The average number of disruptions across all three children decreased from 13.8 during baseline to 4.8 in the first 8–10 min phase. In the following 4–5 min phase, a further reduction in disruptions from 4.8 to 0.86 per session occurred. The return to an 8–10 min phase produced an increase in disruptions to 4.1. Reinstatement of the 4–5 min phase resulted in

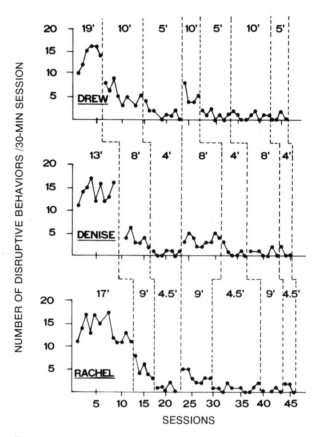

FIGURE 3. Frequency of disruptive behaviors for the three target children as a function of the different changes in time limits. (From Garber, unpublished.)

disruptions averaging less than 1 per session, a level at which they remained for the duration of the study. Academic performance doubled in rate when the time limits were initially halved from their baseline length. A further increase in rate of academic performance from 1.1 to 2.1 resulted when the time limits were further reduced from 8–10 min to 4–5 min. Returning to 8–10 min produced a decrease in the rate of academic performance from 2.1 to 1.1, which increased during the shift to 4–5 min from 1.1 to 2.1 and remained at this level for the next 8–10 min phase. During the final 4–5 min phase, the rate of academic performance increased even further for two of the three children. These results led Garber to conclude that disruptive behavior decreases in relationship to increases in competing behaviors, facilitated by a reduction in the amount of time in which academic performance is to be completed.

The results of the studies by Ayllon *et al.* (1972), Allison, and Garber demonstrate that manipulating antecedent stimuli to academic behavior can be an effective approach for reducing disruptive classroom behavior, at least initially. Although all of the studies reviewed in Sections 1–5 concentrated on manipulating consequent events (e.g., teacher attention and praise, peer attention, token-reinforcement systems, group contingencies, self-determination of reinforcement), several of them included manipulations of antecedent stimuli prior to the manipulation of consequences. For example, Becker *et al.* (1967), Madsen *et al.* (1968), O'Leary *et al.* (1969), Kazdin (1973), Herman and Tramontana (1971), and Ramp, Ulrich, and Dulaney (1971) found that instructions for appropriate classroom behavior presented alone were ineffective in reducing disruptive behavior. These results differ somewhat from those of Allison, who found that instructions were initially effective in reducing disruption but that disruption soon returned to a high level.

The effects of classroom structure on disruptive behavior obtained by Ayllon *et al.* (1972) appear to conflict with those of O'Leary *et al* (1969). In the O'Leary *et al.* study, classroom structure was introduced after rules, and this manipulation also produced no effect on disruptive behavior. The students in the class in this study were achieving academically during baseline, with disruptive behavior averaging 55%. Classroom structure involved reorganizing the program into four successive 30-min periods with the entire class participating in each period. Four different subject matters were taught, one in each of the four periods.

In the Ayllon *et al.* study, the children were so disruptive during baseline—averaging 98% disruptions—that academic behavior was not even observed. The marked decrease in disruptive behavior produced during the initial session of classroom structure may have been due to the short time required for each assignment (2 min for reading test, 1½ min for math test). An interesting point concerns the fact that in the O'Leary *et al.* study, contingent reinforcement produced a marked decrease in disruptive behavior after structure had been imposed, whereas in the Ayllon *et al.* study, reinforcement was no more effective than structure in reducing disruptive behavior and may have served only to maintain the low level achieved with structure.

It appears, then, that classroom structure involving the systematic use of antecedent stimuli—such as academic materials, instructions for appropriate classroom behavior, and modeling of appropriate classroom behavior—prompt academic behaviors that compete with disruptive behavior and lead to its decrease. Finally, Garber (unpublished) showed that manipulating temporal limits, while maintaining reinforcement at a constant level, also sets the occasion for academic behaviors that effectively compete with disruptive behavior.

7. Controlling Misbehavior through Events That Follow Academic Performance

7.1. Strengthening Academic Performance in Normal Children

In a study by Ayllon and Roberts (1974), the authors attempted to decrease disruptive behavior indirectly by strengthening academic skills. Five fifth-graders were the target children in this study and were ranked by their teachers as being the most disruptive in the class. Disruptive behavior included being out of their seats without permission, talking out, and engaging in any motor behavior that interfered with another student's studying. Academic behavior was measured in reading and was defined in terms of the percentage of correct answers in daily performance sessions in which written answers to test materials based on reading activities were required.

Following baseline, during which disruptive and academic behaviors were measured under prevailing classroom conditions, a token economy was instituted to strengthen work completion and accuracy. Each child could earn points for his academic performance and could exchange the points for a variety of activities, privileges, and priorities on a daily (e.g., access to the game room, having the lowest test grade removed, becoming an assistant teacher) or weekly (e.g., seeing a movie, doing the bulletin board, having a good-work letter sent home) basis. Points were awarded on the basis of two points for a minimum of 80% correct and five points for 100% correct work. The token economy was removed and reinstated in the final two phases of the study. The effectiveness of this intervention was evaluated in a reversal design.

The results showed that disruptive behavior decreased as academic performance (reading accuracy) increased during token reinforcement (see Figure 4). During the initial baseline, the mean academic performance and disruptive behavior ranged from 40 to 50%. Reinforcement for reading resulted in 70% reading accuracy and a decrease in disruption from about 40% to 15%. When the baseline conditions were reinstated, disruptive behavior increased and reading accuracy decreased. Reinstatement of the token system for reading once again indirectly decreased disruption from 40% to about 5% and directly increased reading accuracy to about 85%.

The authors pointed out that these results suggested a reciprocal relationship between academic performance and disruptive behavior, in which a systematic increase in one will produce a decrease in the other. Although such a relationship provides the basis for an indirect approach to decreasing disruptive behavior, in some instances it may be necessary to use a combination of both direct and indirect methods. For example, severe behavior problems may necessitate a direct approach in which reinforcement is available for sitting quietly or appearing to be on-task. Later on, it may be possible to add or substitute reinforcement for academic performance to further minimize disruptive behavior or maintain it at a low level.

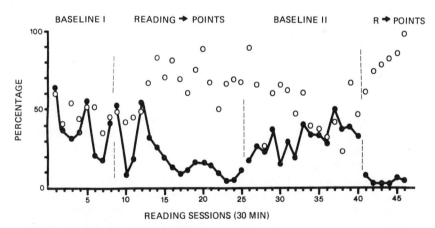

FIGURE 4. Mean percentage of disruption and mean percentage of correct work on reading assignments for the five target students. Each point represents 24 observations per child for each 30-min session. ●━━● Disruption, ○ ○ reading. N = 5. (From Ayllon & Roberts, 1974. Copyright © 1974 by the Society for the Experimental Analysis of Behavior, Inc. Reprinted by permission.)

7.2. Strengthening Academic Performance of Hyperactive Children

A study by Ayllon, Layman, and Kandel (1975) investigated the effectiveness of behavioral techniques compared with drugs in controlling hyperactivity in the classroom. In addition, the authors were concerned with whether or not such behavioral techniques could help the hyperactive child improve academically. The subjects of the study were three children clinically diagnosed as chronically hyperactive. Each child was taking drugs (methylphenidate) to control his hyperactivity. The children were enrolled in a self-contained learning-disability class of 10 children. Academic performance was measured in terms of math (percentage correct out of 10 problems dealing with the addition of whole numbers under 10) and reading (percentage correct in workbook responses to previously read stories). Hyperactivity was defined in terms of the following behaviors: (1) gross motor (running around the room, rocking in the chair, jumping); (2) disruptive noise (constant turning of book pages); (3) disturbing others (constant moving of arms causing destruction to objects and hitting others); and (4) blurting out (screaming).

The experimental design of the study, a multiple-baseline-across-subject matters, included four phases. In the first phase, (on medication), the children were simply observed, and an effort was made to evaluate hyperactivity and academic performance. Following a three-day "wash-out" period, during which the drug was removed, the second phase began. This phase (off medication) was the same as the first phase except that the children were not receiving any medication. This phase provided a basis against which the effects of reinforcemnt could be compared. The third phase (reinforcement of math and no medication) involved the introduction of a token-reinforcement system for math performance. Tokens in the form of checkpoints exchangeable for back-up reinforcers later in the day were awarded for each correct academic response. The final phase (no medication and reinforcement of math and reading) involved introducing the token-reinforcement system for reading.

The results showed that when the drug was removed, the level of hyperactivity doubled or tripled from its initial level. When reinforcement was introduced for academic performance, however, hyperactivity decreased to a level comparable to that under drug control of hyperactivity. The results for a representative child are presented in Figure 5. During the drug phase, in math hyperactivity averaged about 20%, while academic performance was zero. Removal of the

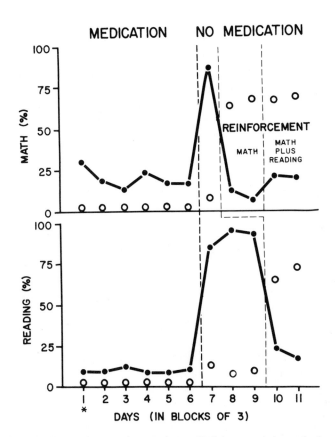

FIGURE 5. Crystal. The percentage of intervals in which hyperactivity took place and the percentage of correct math and reading performance. Each data point for hyperactivity is based on 150 observations per 3-day block. The first and second segments, respectively, show the effects of medication and its subsequent withdrawal on hyperactivity and academic performance. A multiple-baseline analysis of the effects of reinforcement across math and reading and concurrent hyperactivity is shown starting on the third top segment. The last segment shows the effects of reinforcement on math plus reading and its concurrent effect on hyperactivity. (The asterisk indicates one data point averaged over two rather than three days). ●—● Hyperactivity, ○ ○ academic performance. (From Ayllon, Layman, & Kandel, 1975. Copyright © 1975 by the Society for the Experimental Analysis of Behavior, Inc. Reprinted by permission.)

drug resulted in an increase in hyperactivity to an average of 87%, whereas math performance increased slightly to an average of 8%. Reinforcement of math without drugs produced a decrease in hyperactivity from 87% to about 9% and an increase in math performance to 65%. Simultaneous measures were taken for reading, during which hyperactivity averaged 10% and academic performance was zero under medication. Removal of drugs resulted in an increase in hyperactivity to 91% and a slight increase in reading performance to about 10%. Reinforcement for reading produced a decrease in hyperactivity from 91% to 20% and an increase in reading performance from 10% to an average of 69%. Reinforcement only for math did not produce any effects whatsoever for reading; only when reinforcement was initiated for reading did hyperactivity decrease and reading performance increase in that academic area.

Pre- and postmeasures for hyperactivity and academic performance for the three children are presented in Figure 6. The presence of drugs effectively controlled hyperactivity at an average of about 24%. Academic performance, however, only averaged 12%. The removal of medication and establishment of reinforcement procedures to strengthen academic performance resulted in hyperactivity at an average level of 20%, whereas academic performance averaged 85%.

These results with clinically diagnosed hyperactive children extend those obtained with normal school children by Ayllon and Roberts (1974). Once again, by reinforcing competing academic behaviors it was possible to drastically reduce such an extreme form of disruption as hyperactivity. These results strongly support the tactic of eliminating behavior by focusing on other behaviors that compete with it.

7.3. Strengthening Reinforcers by Including the Child's Home

Ayllon, Garber, and Pisor (1975) suggested that with chronically disruptive children, effective reinforcers may not always be available in the classroom. Their study investigated the effects of school-based procedures and a combination of school- and home-based procedures for eliminating discipline problems. Twenty-three children, one year behind in reading and math skills and extremely disruptive, served as subjects in this study. Disruptive behavior was defined as being out of their seats, talking out, and any motor behavior that interfered with another student's studying.

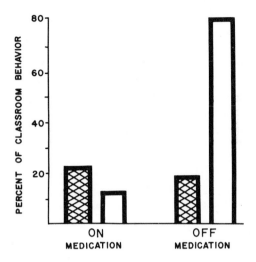

FIGURE 6. Average percentage of hyperactivity and academic performance in math and reading for three children. The first two bars summarize findings from the 17-day baseline under drug therapy. The last two bars show results for the final 6-day period without drug therapy but with a reinforcement program for both math and reading performance. ▩ Hyperactivity, □ academic performance. N = 3. (From Ayllon, Layman, & Kandel, 1975. Copyright © 1975 by the Society for the Experimental Analysis of Behavior, Inc. Reprinted by permission.)

During the baseline phase, disruption measured 85% under normal classroom conditions. Following baseline, the tactic whereby disruptive behavior would be eliminated by indirect means was adopted. Specifically, a token-reinforcement system was introduced in which students could earn one point for each page of work completed with at least 70% accuracy. On the basis of previous results, it was expected that reinforcement for academics would lead to a reduction in disruption. Surprisingly, the effects of this manipulation were transient. Disruptive behavior was drastically reduced for one day but rapidly returned to its baseline level. A direct approach, therefore, was added: in addition to reinforcement for academics, students could earn one point for each 15-min period free from disruptive behavior. Engaging in disruptive behavior resulted in losing the point for that 15-min period, and two or more disruptions during any single 15-min period resulted in a loss of all quiet points earned to that point in the day. Reinforcement, therefore, was being delivered for both academic performance and good conduct.

Figure 7 depicts the results of this part of the study. During base-line, disruptive behavior averaged 85%. Reinforcement for academics produced an initial decrease in disruption to 20%, but disruption increased to about 90% within two days. The combined effect of rein-forcement for academics and good conduct produced an initial de-crease in disruption, which lasted about 7 days. At the end of this period, however, disruptive behavior increased to 95%. Although this combination of indirect and direct procedures for the reduction of disruption was slightly more effective in terms of duration, it was clearly another failure.

In the analysis of these results, several features of the procedures used were carefully considered. First, was the measurement of disrup-tive behavior reliable? Indeed, not only was it reliable, it was high and stable; hence, it provided a substantive test of the procedures thought to be sufficient to overcome disruption. Second, was the academic requirement too high to ensure frequent contact with reinforcement? To explore this possibility, the investigators also made reinforcement

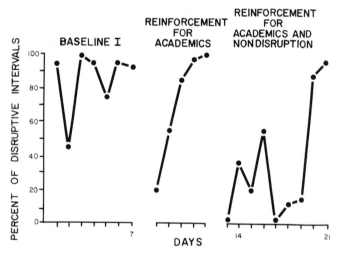

FIGURE 7. Percentage of 10-sec intervals scored as disruptive for 23 students. The first phase, "Baseline I," designates the period of standard teaching procedures. During the second phase, "Reinforcement for Academics," the teacher initiated a period of rewards contingent on meeting academic criteria. The third phase added a procedure to reinforce good conduct. Each data point represents approximately 540 observation intervals taken within a period of 90 min each day. $N = 23$. (From Ayllon, Garber, & Pisor, 1975. Copyright © 1975 by Academic Press, Inc. Reprinted by permission.)

available for good conduct; yet, the results obtained did not differ appreciably from those found with reinforcement for academic performance alone. Third, were such reinforcers as dolls, comics, recess, and admittance to a game room too weak to maintain the change in behavior over time? Fourth, was the novelty of the contingency possibly responsible for the rapid change in disruption? Indeed, support for these final two issues was found in a careful analysis of the results. When the original contingency was introduced and the children received points for academics, disruption immediately decreased. Yet, it returned to its baseline levels within 3 days. The next contingency, with the only new feature being the addition of points for good conduct, also produced a decrease in disruption. Within 8 days, however, disruption returned to its baseline levels, despite the fact that contingencies were being applied to the two relevant dimensions of behavior in the classroom, academics and conduct. It appeared, therefore, that the novelty of the contingency may have been sufficient to generate a behavior change in each case, but that the back-up reinforcers may have been too weak to maintain such a change.

Methodologically, to enhance a weak reinforcer, one should increase its magnitude or frequency. In the context of school, such a tactic presented severe practical problems. For example, to strengthen free time as a reinforcer would require allowing children to leave their classrooms frequently or for long periods of time. This, however, would require administrative arrangements that were impossible to implement. Therefore, another tactic was explored, based on previous research by Bailey *et al.* (1970), who found that the children's own homes could be effective sources of reinforcement. Parents, therefore, were informed about the discipline problems in school during a 2-hour meeting, and their aid in eliminating these problems was sought. Direct contacts by phone were made with those parents unable to attend this meeting. Parents were coached in the management of a home-based reinforcement system, which included the receipt of a "good-behavior" letter. If their child came home with such a letter, addressed to the parents, it indicated that he had been well-behaved in school that day, and the parents were instructed to provide rewards of their choice. If the child came home without the letter, indicative of his being disruptive that day, the parents were to express their displeasure and disapproval. Parents were encouraged to use their own style of rewarding and sanctioning their children rather than adopting some idealized or book-derived form of disciplining. In the course of this study, parents reported using praise, movies, special treats, allowances, and extended TV privileges as rewards. Among the sanctions reported by parents were the withholding of allowances, loss of TV or outdoor privileges, an earlier bedtime hour, and even a hit with a belt!

Following a second baseline of disruptive behavior, the combined school–home motivational system began. The only addition to the previous school-based system was the contingency for earning the letter. Any student who did not exceed two disruptions in any single 15-min period earned the letter, whereas three or more disruptions during any single 15-min period resulted in losing the letter for that day.

The addition of the contingent letter resulted in a marked decrease in disruptive behavior (see Figure 8). Disruptive behavior averaged 90% during baseline and was reduced to a mean of 10% during implementation of the contingent letter. This time, disruption did not return to baseline levels even after 13 days of following this new procedure. To determine whether or not this latest procedure was responsible for the drastic reduction in the disruptive behavior—rather than the novelty of the procedure itself—a period was initiated during which all children received the letter independent of their behavior. This took the form of giving children the letter as they came into the classroom and obviously prior to their displaying any behavior in the classroom. Noncontingent presentation of the letter resulted in an increase in disruption from about 10% to an average of 50%. Reinstatement of the contingent presentation of the letter produced an immediate decrease in disruption to zero, underscoring the relationship between misbehavior and its consequences. Briefly, then, it was neither the novelty of this procedure nor classroom points that produced the results obtained; instead, it was demonstrated that the contingent use of the "good-behavior" letter, which resulted in either rewards or sanctions in the home, was responsible for decreasing disruptive behavior.

The results of the studies by Ayllon and Roberts (1974), Ayllon, Layman, and Kandel (1975), and Ayllon, Garber, and Pisor (1975) clearly demonstrated that if the consequences that follow academic behavior are manipulated, disruptive behavior can be reduced. Although previous studies in the literature reviewed in Sections 1–5 concentrated on the manipulation of consequent events to control classroom misbehavior, that research attempted to eliminate disruption directly through reinforcement contingnent upon refraining from engaging in such disruption. The behaviors that were strengthened, therefore, were largely response topographies as opposed to functional academic bahaviors. The present research, however, has considered

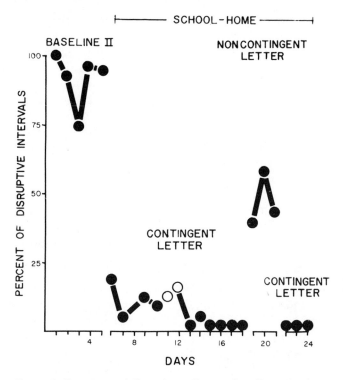

FIGURE 8. Percentage of 10-sec intervals scored as disruptive for 23 students. "Baseline II" represents a return to the standard teaching procedures used in this class. During the next phase, "School–Home Contingent Letter," the "good-behavior" letter was sent home with the child upon his meeting criteria for good conduct. The third phase, "School–Home Noncontingent Letter," consisted of presenting the "good-behavior" letter immediately upon the child's entering the classroom. The fourth phase indicates the reinstatement of the contingent presentation of the letter. Each data point represents approximately 540 observation intervals taken within a period of 90 min each day. ○, substitute teacher. $N = 23$. (From Ayllon, Garber, & Pisor, 1975. Copyright © 1975 by Academic Press, Inc. Reprinted by permission.)

the maintenance of good conduct (refraining from disruption) as secondary to the teaching and learning of academic skills. Even in the one case in which a direct approach was used (Ayllon, Garber, & Pisor, 1975), this approach was included only after attempts at strengthening academic performance alone had failed.

The results of the Ayllon, Layman, and Kandel study led the authors to conclude not only that reinforcement of academic performance suppressed hyperactivity as well as drugs, but also that the academic gains resulting for each child contrasted with their lack of academic performance under medication. The use of drugs, therefore, to control hyperactivity may result in obedient students who are incompetent academically. The authors suggested the possibility that in some instances, the combination of a drug and a behavioral program may also control hyperactivity without sacrificing academic progress.

Disruption may be approached differently, depending on the presence or the absence of severe academic deficits. When basic academic components are present, the reinforcement of academic behavior alone may be sufficient to decrease disruption. Shaping procedures, however, may be necessary to establish requisite academic skills when these are relatively weak or absent. Because shaping by its very nature takes time as new bits of behavior are required, concurrent strong behaviors such as disruption continue to compete with the newly emerging ones. For this reason, adding a direct approach involving reinforcement for good conduct minimizes the competing disruption and allows the shaping of requisite academic skills to proceed smoothly. When the basic academic components are finally established, the probability that the reinforcement of academics alone (indirect approach) will control disruption is markedly increased. Of course, in the use of either an indirect or a direct approach to control disruption, an effective reinforcer is necessary, and it may not always be found in the school or the classroom (Ayllon, Garber, & Pisor, 1975). The child's home appears to provide an excellent source of reinforcement for the remote control of classroom disruptive behavior.

8. Summary and Conclusions

It has been demonstrated that an indirect approach, focusing on academic performance by manipulating its antecedent and consequent stimuli, can effectively reduce disruptive behavior in the classroom. Much of the literature reviewed in Sections 1–5 employed this tactic where the alternative response selected was "on-task" behavior or "good-conduct" behaviors. The methodological advantage of selecting these behaviors is that they compete with disruption, although their functional value to academic performance has not been conclusively demonstrated. A variation on the same tactic is offered by the present research, with a distinctive educational advantage. Instead of selecting responses that competed with disruption but bore only component relationships to academic performance, the investigators in the present research selected responses that not only competed with disruption but whose functional value to academic learning was demonstrated. These findings taken together suggest a "package" of procedures designed to control disruptive behavior effectively while enhancing academic learning. The three major components included in this package are structure, instructions and modeling, and reinforcement of academic performance.

1. *Structure*. The presence of some type of structure involving the systematic use of academic materials at a level at which students are capable of performing is necessary. This structure by itself will either generate behaviors that compete with disruption or simplify the implementation of other procedures designed to deal with disruption. For example, Ayllon, Layman, and Burke (1972) devised an academic structure; Allison (unpublished) administered individual assignments; Garber (unpub.) imposed time limits on the students based on their individual baseline performance; Ayllon and Roberts (1974) assured a consistent assignment length in addition to carefully planning performance sessions of 15-min duration; and Ayllon, Layman, and Kandel (1975) included a design in which students were given a standard amount of time in which to complete a standard amount of work.

2. *Instructions and modeling*. Instructions concerning appropriate academic behaviors and modeling of these behaviors are effective in generating behaviors that compete with disruption. In addition, instructions have the advantage of maximizing the child's repertoire by using verbal behavior, thereby avoiding time-consuming shaping procedures.

3. *Reinforcement of academic performance*. Strengthening the completion and accuracy of academic performance generated by the two preceding procedures with reinforcement can effectively maintain a high level of academic behaviors that compete with disruption, thereby reducing disruption and maintaining it at a low level. Emphasis must also be placed on the sumultaneous extinction of disruptive behaviors when academic behaviors are being reinforced. Specifically, two alternatives are available with the contingency on academic performance. First, an academic response can be reinforced both socially (verbal praise and attention) and with tokens. Second, disruptive behavior (in addition to nonacademic responses) must not be reinforced either socially or with tokens. Reinforcement here includes not just praise but also other forms of attention, such as verbal reprimands.

It should also be noted that the absence of academic performance does not imply that requisite academic skills are missing. Instead, academic performance may not be displayed because of stronger competing behaviors. For example, in the Ayllon, Layman, and Kandel (1975) study on hyperactivity, two of the children displayed a near-zero level of academic performance under medication. When reinforcement was introduced contingent upon reading and math, academic performance immediately increased, even though no formal instruction in requisite skills was being provided. It appeared that these skills were present but were not displayed because of the stronger hyperactive behaviors. Yet once reinforcement was instituted for academic performance that competed with and weakened hyperactivity, these academic skills (math and reading) readily emerged.

9. Special Conditions Requiring Further Behavioral Analysis

In the event that a system employing the three procedures described above fails to control disruptive behavior, two reasons for such failure must be considered. First, the students may have severe academic deficits that may well contribute to their being chronically disruptive. This situation requires a direct approach to the control of disruption, in which reinforcement is contingent upon good conduct. Once the requisite academic skills can be established, indirect methods involving the reinforcement of academic performance should be added to maintain these academic behaviors that compete with disruption.

The second reason for the failure of the initial three-procedure system may be the use of relatively weak reinforcers. It may, therefore, be necessary to seek additional sources of reinforcement outside the school, such as in the home environment. A combination school–home motivational system may effectively control disruption in the classroom through reinforcement at home.

Once fairly stable levels of disruption and academic performance have been achieved, a gradual reduction in the amount of time given to students to complete their work, while maintaining a constant level of reinforcement, may result in maximum levels of academic behaviors that compete with and minimize or virtually eliminate disruption.

One final point deserving of mention concerns the prevention of disruption through a structuring of the entire school day rather than just specific periods of the day. Lack of such total structure may easily result in "free" time, during which the student does not know what to do. In this instance, previous disruptive behavior may emerge, since it has occurred in past situations without structure (i.e., without antecedent stimuli paired with reinforcement, thus occasioning specific activities). Teachers should, therefore, avoid having periods of the day that are void of specific antecedent stimuli paired with specific activities. Structuring, in turn, will ensure that there are always some specific stimuli, preferably academic, for behaviors that compete with disruption.

References

Allison, M. G. The effects of modeling on disruptive behavior and academic performance. Unpublished master's thesis, Georgia State University, 1974.

Ayllon, T., & Azrin, N. H. Reinforcement and instructions with mental patients. *Journal of Experimental Analysis of Behavior*, 1964, 7, 327–331.

Ayllon, T., Garber, S., & Pisor, K. The elimination of discipline problems through a combined school–home motivational system. *Behavior Therapy*, 1975, 6, 616–626.

Ayllon, T., Layman, D., & Burke, S. Disruptive behavior and reinforcement of academic performance. *The Psychological Record*, 1972, 22, 315–323.

Ayllon, T., Layman, D., & Kandel, H. J. A behavioral–educational alternative to drug control of hyperactive children. *Journal of Applied Behavior Analysis*, 1975, 8, 137–146.

Ayllon, T., & Roberts, M. D. Eliminating discipline problems by strengthening academic performance. *Journal of Applied Behavior Analysis*, 1974, 7, 71–76.

Bailey, J. S., Wolf, M. M., & Phillips, E. L. Home-based reinforcement and the modification of pre-delinquents' classroom behavior. *Journal of Applied Behavior Analysis*, 1970, 3, 223–233.

Bandura, A. (Ed.). *Principles of behavior modification*. New York: Holt, Rinehart and Winston, 1969, Chapter 3, pp. 118–216.

Bandura, A., & McDonald, F. J. The influence of social reinforcement and the behavior of models in shaping children's moral judgements. *Journal of Abnormal and Social Psychology*, 1963, 67, 274–281.

Bandura, A., & Mischel, W. The influence of models in modifying delay of gratification patterns. *Journal of Personality and Social Psychology*, 1965, 2, 698–705.

Barrish, H. H., Saunders, M., & Wolf, M. M. Good behavior game: Effects of individual contingencies for group consequences on disruptive behavior in a classroom. *Journal of Applied Behavior Analysis*, 1969, 2, 119–124.

Becker, W. C., Madsen, C. H., Arnold, C. R., & Thomas, D. R. The contingent use of teacher attention and praise in reducing classroom behavior problems. *Journal of Special Education*, 1967, 1, 287–307.

Berkowitz, P., & Rothman, E. *The disturbed child: Recognition and psycho-educational therapy in the classroom*. New York: New York University Press, 1967.

Bolstad, O. D., & Johnson, S. M. Self-regulation in the modification of disruptive classroom behavior. *Journal of Applied Behavior Analysis*, 1972, 5, 443–454.

Broden, M., Bruce, C., Mitchell, M. A., Carter, V., & Hall, R. V. Effects of teacher attention on attending behavior of two boys at adjacent desks. *Journal of Applied Behavior Analysis*, 1970, 3, 199–203.

Craig, K. D. Vicarious reinforcement and noninstrumental punishment in observational learning. *Journal of Personality and Social Psychology*, 1967, 7, 172–176.

Dietz, S. M., & Repp, A. C. Decreasing classroom misbehavior through the use of drl schedules of reinforcement. *Journal of Applied Behavior Analysis*, 1973, 6, 457–463.

Dietz, S. M., & Repp, A. C. Differentially reinforcing low rates of misbehavior with normal elementary school children. *Journal of Applied Behavior Analysis*, 1974, 7, 622.

Drabman, R. S., & Lahey, B. B. Feedback in classroom behavior modification: Effects on the target and her classmates. *Journal of Applied Behavior Analysis*, 1974, 7, 591–598.

Ferritor, D. E., Buckholdt, D., Hamblin, R. L., & Smith, L. The noneffects of contingent reinforcement for attending behavior on work accomplished. *Journal of Applied Behavior Analysis*, 1972, 5, 7–17.

Ferster, C. B., & Skinner, B. F. *Schedules of reinforcement.* New York: Appleton-Century-Crofts, Century-Crofts, 1957.

Findley, J. D. Programmed environments for the experimental analysis of human behavior. *In* W. K. Honig (Ed.), *Operant behavior: Areas of research and application.* New York: Appleton-Century-Crofts, 1966.

Garber, S. W. The effects of time limits on academic performance. Unpublished doctoral dissertation, Georgia State University, 1974.

Greenwood, G. E., Good, T. L., & Siegel, B. L. *Problem situations in teaching.* New York: Harper & Row, 1971.

Grossman, H. *Teaching the emotionally disturbed child.* New York: Holt, Rinehart, and Winston, 1965.

Hall, R. V., Fox, R., Willard, D., Goldsmith, L., Emerson, M., Owen, M., Davis, F., & Porcia, E. The teacher as observer and experimenter in the modification of disputing and talking-out behaviors. *Journal of Applied Behavior Analysis*, 1971, 4, 141–149.

Hall, R. V., Lund, D., & Jackson, D. Effects of teacher attention on study behavior. *Journal of Applied Behavior Analysis*, 1968, 1, 1–12.

Hall, R. V., Panyan, M., Rabon, D., & Broden, M. Instructing beginning teachers in reinforcement procedures which improve classroom control. *Journal of Applied Behavior Analysis*, 1968, 1, 315–322.

Harris, V. W., & Sherman, J. A. Use and analysis of the "good behavior game" to reduce disruptive classroom behavior. *Journal of Applied Behavior Analysis*, 1973, 6, 405–417.

Herman, S. H., & Tramontana, J. Instructions and group versus individual reinforcement in modifying disruptive group behavior. *Journal of Applied Behavior Analysis*, 1971, 4, 113–119.

Hopkins, B. L. Effects of candy and social reinforcement, instructions, and reinforcement schedule leaning on the modification and maintenance of smiling. *Journal of Applied Behavior Analysis*, 1968, 1, 121–129.

Hopkins, B. L., Schutte, R. C., & Garton, K. L. The effects of access to a playroom on the rate and quality of printing and writing of first and second-grade students. *Journal of Applied Behavior Analysis*, 1971, 4, 77–88.

Iwata, B. A., & Bailey, J. S. Reward versus cost token systems: An analysis of the effects on students and teacher. *Journal of Applied Behavior Analysis*, 1974, 7, 567–576.

Kaufman, K. F., & O'Leary, K. D. Reward, cost, and self-evaluation procedures for disruptive adolescents in a psychiatric hospital school. *Journal of Applied Behavior Analysis*, 1972, 5, 293–309.

Kazdin, A. E. Role of instructions and reinforcement in behavioral changes in token reinforcement programs. *Journal of Educational Psychology*, 1973, 64, 63–71.

Kazdin, A. E., & Bootzin, R. R. The token economy: An evaluative review. *Journal of Applied Behavior Analysis*, 1972, 5, 343–372.

Lahey, B. B. Modification of the frequency of descriptive adjectives in the speech of Head Start children through modeling without reinforcement. *Journal of Applied Behavior Analysis*, 1971, 4, 19–22.

Long, N. J., Morse, W. C., & Newman, R. G. *Conflict in the classroom: The education of emotionally disturbed children.* Belmont, Calif. Wadsworth, 1965.

Madsen, C. H., Becker, W. C., & Thomas, D. R. Rules, praise, and ignoring: Elements of elementary classroom control. *Journal of Applied Behavior Analysis*, 1968, 1, 139–150.

Masters, J. C., & Branch, M. N. Comparison of the relative effectiveness of instructions, modeling, and reinforcement procedures for inducing behavior change. *Journal of Experimental Psychology*, 1969, *80*, 364–368.

McAllister, L. W., Stachowiak, J. G., Baer, D. M., & Conderman, L. The application of operant conditioning techniques in a secondary school classroom. *Journal of Applied Behavior Analysis*, 1969, *2*, 277–285.

Medland, M. B., & Stachnik, T. J. Good-behavior game: A replication and systematic analysis. *Journal of Applied Behavior Analysis*, 1972, *5*, 45–51.

O'Leary, K. D., & Becker, W. C. Behavior modification of an adjustment class: A token reinforcement program. *Exceptional Children*, 1967, *33*, 637–642.

O'Leary, K. D., Becker, W. C., Evans, M. B., & Saudargas, R. A. A token reinforcement program in a public school: A replication and systematic analysis. *Journal of Applied Behavior Analysis*, 1969, *2*, 3–13.

O'Leary, K. D., & O'Leary, S. G. *Classroom management: The successful use of behavior modification*. New York: Pergamon Press, 1972.

Osborne, J. G. Free-time as a reinforcer in the management of classroom behavior. *Journal of Applied Behavior Analysis*, 1969, *2*, 113–118.

Ramp, E., Ulrich, R., & Dulaney, S. Delayed timeout as a procedure for reducing disruptive classroom behavior: A case study. *Journal of Applied Behavior Analysis*, 1971, *4*, 235–239.

Santogrossi, D. A., O'Leary, K. D., Romanczyck, R. G., & Kaufman, K. F. Self-evaluation by adolescents in a psychiatric hospital school token program. *Journal of Applied Behavior Analysis*, 1973, *6*, 277–287.

Schmidt, G. W., & Ulrich, R. E. Effects of group contingent events upon classroom noise. *Journal of Applied Behavior Analysis*, 1969, *2*, 171–179.

Schutte, R. C., & Hopkins, B. L. The effects of teacher attention on following instructions in a kindergarten class. *Journal of Applied Behavior Analysis*, 1970, *3*, 117–122.

Skinner, B. F. *The behavior of organisms*. New York: Appleton-Century-Crofts, 1938.

Solomon, R. W., & Wahler, R. G. Peer reinforcement control of classroom problem behavior. *Journal of Applied Behavior Analysis*, 1973, *6*, 49–56.

Sulzbacher, S. I., & Houser, J. E. A tactic to eliminate disruptive behavior in the classroom: Group contingent consequences. *American Journal of Mental Deficiency*, 1968, *73*, 88–90.

Thelen, M. H. Long-term retention of verbal imitation. *Developmental Psychology*, 1970, *2*, 29–31.

Thomas, D. R., Becker, W. C., & Armstrong, M. Production and elimination of disruptive classroom behavior by systematically varying teacher's behavior. *Journal of Applied Behavior Analysis*, 1968, *1*, 35–45.

Todd, D. D., Scott, R. B., Bostow, D. E., & Alexander, S. B. Modification of the excessive inappropriate classroom behavior of two elementary school students using home-based consequences and daily report-card procedures. *Journal of Applied Behavior Analysis*, 1976, *9*, 106.

Ward, M. H., & Baker, B. L. Reinforcement therapy in the classroom. *Journal of Applied Behavior Analysis*, 1968, *1*, 323–328.

Wasik, B. H., Senn, K., Welch, R. H., & Cooper, B. R. Behavior modification with culturally deprived school children: Two case studies. *Journal of Applied Behavior Analysis*, 1969, *2*, 181–194.

Winett, R. A., & Winkler, R. C. Current behavior modification in the classroom: Be still, be quiet, be docile. *Journal of Applied Behavior Analysis*, 1972, *5*, 499–504.

Zimmerman, B. J., & Pike, E. O. Effects of modeling and reinforcement on the acquisition and generalization of question-asking behavior. *Child Development*, 1972, *43*, 892–907.

Zimmerman, E. H., Zimmerman, B. J., & Russell, C. D. Differential effects of token re-inforcement on instruction-following behavior in retarded students instructed as a group. *Journal of Applied Behavior Analysis*, 1969, *2*, 101–112.

4 Perinatal Influences on the Behavior and Learning Problems of Children

ROSALYN A. RUBIN
AND BRUCE BALOW

1. Introduction

For more than a century there has been speculation that the antecedents of mental retardation, learning disabilities, personality disorders, and similar educational and behavioral problems may be associated with anomalies of pregnancy, birth, and infancy. While most of the substantive research in this area has taken place during the past 25 years, its antecedents can be directly traced to the late 19th century. Systematic observation appears to have begun in 1862 with Little, who maintained that birth difficulties—specifically asphyxia, prematurity, and abnormal labor—were directly related to mental deficiency and cerebral palsy.

Early in the 20th century, the possibility of a relationship between reading disability and perinatal events began to interest investigators. In a review of published reports of specific reading disability, McCready (1910, summarized by Bronner, 1921) suggested that intrauterine and delivery factors were probable causes of "congenital

ROSALYN A. RUBIN AND BRUCE BALOW • Department of Psychoeducational Studies, University of Minnesota, Minneapolis, Minnesota. The research reported herein was performed pursuant to a grant (OEG-32-33-0402-6021) from the National Institute of Education, U.S. Department of Health, Education and Welfare. Data were also made available through the cooperation of the Minnesota section of the Collaborative Project, directed by Dr. Robert O. Fisch, supported by the National Institute of Neurological Diseases and Stroke (Public Health Service grant Ph-43-68-9).

alexia." Within a decade of McCready's paper, Hinshelwood (1917), an English ophthalmologist, proposed the theory that reading failure could be caused by an underdevelopment of, or injury to, the dominant hemisphere of the brain and that varying degrees of brain abnormality would account for varying degrees of reading deficiency. Two decades later, Orton (1937) described incomplete cerebral dominance as the cause of reading and other learning disabilities. Shortly thereafter, Gesell and Armatruda (1941) postulated that perinatal events can cause brain damage.

Since that time, an increasing amount of research has explored the relationships among perinatal events, neurological injury, and behavior and learning difficulties. A substantial research effort undertaken by Pasamanick and his co-workers at Ohio State University found maternal and fetal factors to be related to a variety of subsequent disorders. Out of this work, they developed the concept of a "continuum of reproductive casualty" extending from fetal death through a descending gradient of neurological impairment manifested by cerebral palsy, epilepsy, mental deficiency, behavior disorders, and reading disability (Pasamanick & Lilienfeld, 1955; Kawi & Pasamanick, 1959). Recent research in psychology and medicine (reviewed by Balow, Rubin, & Rosen, 1975–1976; Caputo & Mandell, 1970; Gottfried, 1973; Sameroff & Chandler, 1975) supports the hypothesis that behavioral and school-achievement difficulties are among the outcomes related to factors occurring in pregnancy, birth, and infancy. However, the precise nature of these relationships has not yet been specified.

The establishment of the National Institute of Neurological Diseases and Blindness (NINDB) in the 1950s had major research implications; it both reflected and encouraged increased interest in the study of the neural system. The Perinatal Research Branch of the Institute, in particular, was concerned with the investigation of neurological and sensory disorders of childhood as well as the behavioral outcomes of prenatal and perinatal stress. In the pursuit of this investigation, an unparalleled data bank of perinatal predictor and developmental outcome variables was developed under the auspices of the Collaborative Perinatal Research Project.

The Educational Follow-up Study (EFS) was initiated at the University of Minnesota as an outgrowth of the Collaborative Project sponsored by the NINDB. This study is designed to extend the investigation of subjects originally enrolled in the Minnesota branch of the Collaborative Project through their elementary- and secondary-school careers in order to determine possible influences of prenatal, perinatal, and early-childhood conditions and events on school learning and behavior outcomes. While previous research has tended to concentrate on measures of intelligence and reading achievement as outcome variables, the EFS has, from the time of school entrance, collected data in a number of academic areas, including reading, arithmetic, spelling, and written language, as well as indicators of classroom behavior and general school progress. The combined Collaborative Project and EFS data pool for a sample of over 1,500 children, the youngest of whom are now completing elementary school, makes possible the most extensive long-term prospective analysis of perinatal influences on school-related outcomes that has yet been done. A review of the activities and selected findings of the EFS is presented here following more detailed examination of other research in this area.

2. Major Research Issues

In explorations of the possibility that perinatal characteristics may be predisposing factors in the occurrence of certain types of behavioral problem outcomes, there are important issues of research design and theory to be considered.

2.1. Methodology

In terms of the time of data collection, the three types of research design used to study the influence of perinatal factors are generally referred to as *retrospective, retrospective follow-up,* and *prospective.*

When a retrospective design is followed, samples are selected on the basis of established handicaps or behavioral characteristics, and a search follows for possible predisposing variables in the records of sample subjects. The sources of error inherent in such retrospective investigations are unavoidable and serious. The sampling process introduces unknown biases; human memory is fallible even after brief time intervals and is highly suspect over a period of years (see, for example, Bernstein, 1955; Wenar & Coulter, 1962). Maternal recall may also be biased by knowledge of the child's present problems and by fashions in child rearing (Wenar, 1963). Written records contain measurements and observations obtained under widely varying conditions with little uniformity even in the types of observations made. Also, the retrospective study yields backward-contingency probabilities when forward contingencies may be of primary interest. For example, it may be more useful to know the probability that a perinatally stressed infant will have reading difficulty (a forward contingency) than to know the probability that a child with reading difficulties has had perinatal stress (a backward contingency). In addition, previous evidence strongly indicates that retrospective studies limited to identified handicapped populations yield a distorted picture of the origins and development of handicapping conditions.

In a retrospective follow-up design, the sample is established through a retrospective examination of birth records for indicators of specified perinatal conditions or anomalies. Subjects are then assessed on the basis of their current functioning in designated areas. The method yields forward-contingency probabilities, but the reliance on old clinical records maintained for the delivery of service rather than for research purposes introduces the same data problems associated with the retrospective method.

A prospective design calls for the systematic recording of events as they occur within an overall plan for the analysis of relationships between early characteristics and later development. This type of study avoids the data and sampling problems of retrospective designs and permits the statement of forward-contingency probabilities. Its problems are practical rather than methodological. It is expensive, time-consuming, and slow to produce results, and it presents the difficult problem of sample retention. However, for definitive research on the questions of interest it would seem to be a minimum design requirement.

Investigations of the influence of perinatal factors also differ in the number of predictor and criterion variables that they consider. Some studies seek to determine the relationship between a single predictor and a single criterion, for example, the relationship between cigarette smoking during pregnancy and the birth weight of the infant. Others examine a range of outcome criteria thought to be associated with a single perinatal predictor, such as premature birth or anoxia. Conversely, a single criterion is often specified and the influence of a number of predictors is traced; for example, the antecedents of reading disability may be sought among a variety of perinatal events. Finally, interrelationships among a broad range of both predictor and criterion variables may be explored concurrently.

It appears that studies of single rather than multiple predictor or criterion variables are too simple in design to account for the complexity of the phenomena they investigate. Such studies cannot reveal possible interactions among perinatal complications, among outcome measures, or among combinations of perinatal, environmental, and behavioral outcome variables.

The statistical model on which an analysis is predicated may also determine the types of relationships it can reveal. An assumption inherent in many research designs is that the relationship of perinatal complications to later problems is linear; small complications create small effects, and progressively larger complications produce increasingly larger effects, always in a straight-line relationship. The data presented in support of this assumption are usually quite weak and, to complicate matters, may support equally well an interpretation in terms of threshold effect. That is, a factor may be of little consequence so long as it is above some critical minimum level or below some critical maximum level.

2.2. Developmental Models

Sameroff and Chandler (1975) have discussed the importance of the developmental model used to analyze the effects of perinatal complications. The main-effect model, used by much of the research described here, assumes that constitution and environment exert independent effects on development, so that predictions may be made about certain constitutions regardless of environment and about certain environments regardless of constitution. The interactional model creates a more two-dimensional picture, with constitutional factors balanced against the environmental factors. The transactional model, which Sameroff and Chandler believe best fits the data, describes the environment as ever-changing and the child as an active participant in shaping it; therefore, both constitution and environment are seen as actively adapting to and changing each other.

Obviously, medical problems, where they do exert an influence, are not the sole contributors to educational and behavior handicaps. Many children with serious reading disabilities, for example, come from home environments that are not conducive to academic learning. Others are in educational settings that do not adequately provide for their needs. Sameroff and Chandler described environmental hazards as causing a "continuum of caretaking casualty" analogous to Pasamanick and Lilienfeld's (1955) continuum of reproductive casualty. If one is to understand learning and behavior problems from a developmental perspective, both types of casualty—reproductive and caretaking—must be considered. That many studies do not consider them is attested to by Gottfried (1973), who found that studies of perinatal anoxia and intellectual development that used intelligence as a criterion measure failed to control for known correlates of IQ, such as socioeconomic status (SES).

The effects of perinatal factors may be sought immediately, during infancy, or at any time thereafter. In some instances, events that have strong immediate effects upon the infant may nonetheless be transient in nature, so that they contribute little to long-term predictions of behavior, while other events, more subtle in their original impact, may have a lasting effect on developmental outcomes.

Predictors may also show different relationships to outcome variables at different ages, partly because of the nature of the criterion measures. If, for example, severe anoxia has an influence upon language development, the effects would not be discernible until the age at which normal language functions would ordinarily be observed. Similarly, impairment in the manipulation of abstract symbols would not be manifested until the child was called upon to perform tasks that require this type of cognitive ability. Such demands may not be made upon the majority of children until they reach the age of formal schooling.

Measures obtained at a single point in time or on single measures of behavior may totally miss the age or the dimension at which the perinatal influence is manifested. Only continuous long-term monitoring of a wide range of possible outcomes so that discontinuities and modifications of effects of perinatal anomalies may be detected are apt to contribute significantly to our understanding of these relationships.

2.3. Assessment

One problem in the interpretation of available research data is the unknown validity and reliability of many of the instruments employed in their collection. To the extent that measures fail to assess accurately underlying dimensions of perinatal damage, cognitive development, academic skills, and deviancy of behavior, any relationships that do exist among these characteristics will be obscured. An examination of the consistency of one of the criterion measures from the EFS may serve to illustrate this problem. Recent analyses show that teacher ratings of behavior problems vary considerably from teacher to teacher, so that the majority of children are identified as behavior problems by some of their teachers but not by others during the course of their elementary-school careers. Thus, to differentiate between problem and no-problem children on the basis of teacher identification at any given point in time may result in spurious classifications that, of course, could not be accurately predicted.

There also exists a problem in the use of terminology. Definitions often lack uniformity across research studies, making it difficult to equate findings. It is not unusual for subjects to be described by catch-all terms or phrases within which wide variation is possible, for example, all children admitted to mental hospitals, all clinic outpatients over a certain time period, all children referred to counselors by teachers for any of a wide variety of problems. Such loose aggregates are not comparable from study to study—and possibly not from subject to subject in the same study. Without operational definitions, assessments of reading disability, hyperactivity, and other problems are often subjective and nonreplicable.

Additionally, a large number of studies measure rates of behavior in perinatally stressed children without using a control group or other means of obtaining base rates for a normal population. Our own research (Rubin & Balow, 1971), like that of others (Huessy, Marshall, & Gendron, 1973), has shown that the incidence of a reported behavior may be relatively stable across the elementary-school years; however, the particular children to whom it is ascribed shift from year to year. Therefore, a study using repeated measures is likely to obtain elevated rates of deviant behavior. Whether these high rates necessarily indicate a population at greater risk than average is unknown unless appropriate base rates are used for comparison.

Optimally, studies of the relationship of perinatal complications to learning and behavior problems should be longitudinal and prospective. If the probable chain of relationship is from perinatal complications to neurologic damage, which in turn causes learning and behavior problems, neurologic damage should be assessed. Children who experience perinatal complications should be compared with appropriate controls. Finally, statistical methods capable of indicating the strength of multivariate relationships and patterns of interaction should be used.

3. Review of the Literature

Hundreds of studies have collected data on the perinatal antecedents of a variety of problem conditions. A description of all findings relating to these factors is beyond the scope of this paper. It may interest the reader, however, to have some idea of the range of variables that have been thought to be possibly relevant to the identification or prediction of behavior and learning problems. They include:

1. Prenatal variables: factors suggestive of an abnormal fetus, prenatal strain, or accident.
2. The general birth process: abnormal delivery, delivery procedures, instrumental delivery, baby held back, unusual presentation, premature separation of placenta, cord around neck, induced labor.
3. The neonate: serum bilirubin levels, minimal brain damage

(organic damage), convulsions, absent cry or sucking, fractures, intracranial hemorrhage, head misshapen or marked, jaundice, paralysis, pupillary abnormalities, sleeping and feeding difficulties, abnormal reflexes, projectile vomiting, incubator use, comatose state, convulsions.
4. The mother: illness, weight gain, blood pressure, smoking, severe effects of delivery, personal tensions in pregnancy, weight loss, history of rubella, virus infection during pregnancy, influenza, abnormal or contracted pelvis.
5. Other pregnancies: previous fetal loss, abnormalities, miscarriages, months since last pregnancy.

It is apparent that research in this field is extremely heterogeneous in terms both of characteristics studied and of methodologies employed. Therefore, any classification for purposes of review necessitates the arbitrary grouping of studies whose differences may well equal their similarities. In Section 3.1, studies are organized primarily according to the behavioral outcomes investigated, since it is these behaviors that are of primary significance to practitioners in the fields of psychology and education.

3.1. Reading Disability

Although the possibility that perinatal complications may have some relationship to reading disabilities has been considered for some years, most of the research done in this area prior to 1950 is primarily of historical interest (Beskow, 1949; Bronner, 1921; Eames, 1945; Hinshelwood, 1917; McCready, 1910) because of the ambiguity of definitions and a shortage of experimental evidence. In the first major study in this area, Kawi and Pasamanick (1959), using a retrospective design, reported that significantly more poor readers than controls were of low birth weight (under 2500 g) or had pregnancy and birth complications, particularly maternal preeclampsia, hypertensive disease, and placental abnormalities. Malmquist (1958) found that shorter gestation periods and low birth weight occurred more often in poor readers than in controls but found no differences in the incidence of difficult births.
Versacci (1966) found that low birth weight in combination with a shortened period of gestation differentiated between high- and low-achieving readers, while birth weight or gestation period alone, delivery complications, operative procedures, and frequency of previous miscarriage or stillbirth did not. Doehring (1968) reported that poor and normal readers were not differentiated by complications of pregnancy, type of delivery, and general condition at birth; however, a

somewhat higher incidence of prematurity, low birth weight, and short or prolonged labor (under 3 or over 24 hr) was found for the poor readers.

Kappelman, Rosenstein, and Ganter (1972), comparing an index group of children with behavior and learning problems to controls found that the index group had a higher incidence of breech extraction, low birth weight, preeclampsia, and neonatal respiratory distress, although not more total neonatal problems. The authors suggested that since the index group came from more socially disorganized families than did the control group, family environment may have aggravated the effects of perinatal complications. This is one of the few studies to make the step from a simple to an interactive interpretation of findings.

Using a multiple-regression technique, Lyle (1970) found that symptoms of brain injury at birth were correlated with perceptual-motor difficulties and academic-learning difficulties; birth weight was correlated with perceptual-motor difficulties; and birth variables as a group correlated with early speech defects. Toxemia, complications *in utero*, birth complications, and long and short labor were not related to reading problems.

Abnormalities of birth (Black, 1972) and unusual birth histories (Galante, Flye, & Stephens, 1972) were also found to be more common among retarded than among normal readers. Other studies (Bakwin, 1973; Hunter & Johnson, 1971; Richardson, 1958) have failed to find any links between perinatal problems and reading disability.

The results of the above studies must be interpreted cautiously, since all were retrospective in design. Other things being equal, more credence may be assigned results from the following three studies, which used a retrospective follow-up design in which the birth records of the children were examined retrospectively in order to establish a perinatal-problems group and a nonproblem cohort, both of which were then followed to establish outcome data.

Jordon (1964) found that children who suffered from one or more complications of pregnancy or birth had significantly more reading and learning problems than controls without complications. Caplan, Bibace, and Rabinovitch (1963) found that subjects who had been born prematurely did not differ in reading ability from a control group at ages 7–8 but that the control group read significantly better at ages 11–12. Uddenberg (1955) found that former prematures showed no difference from controls in their ability to reach a criterion reading score but that significantly more achieved only a "poor pass."

A final group of studies in this area were prospective in design. Douglas (1960) found that British prematures (birth weight ≤ 2500 g) scored lower on measures of reading than did controls. Another study using the same definition of prematurity but with a sample from the United States showed that prematures had poorer reading ability and lower IQs than did controls (DeHirsch, Jansky, & Langford, 1966). Studies done in Baltimore found that premature children at 8–10 years of age scored lower on the Wide Range Achievement Test (WRAT) than did controls and also showed more neurological abnormalities (Wiener, Rider, Oppel, & Harper, 1968). When neurological status was statistically controlled, differences in reading were no longer significant. The authors concluded that low birth weight may be associated with reduced achievement scores to the extent that neurological disturbance accompanies the prematurity. Further work with the same subjects at ages 12–13 revealed a low but significant correlation ($r = 0.14$) between birth weight and reading level (Wiener, 1968); at this age, prematures showed a reading deficit compared with controls even after neurological effects were partialed out, raising some question regarding the validity of the earlier conclusion that neurological disturbance was the factor of primary importance.

Two studies failed to find a significant relationship between neonatal anoxia and achievement in reading (Corah, Anthony, Painter, Stern, & Thurston, 1965; Fraser & Wilks, 1959). Robinson and Robinson (1965) found no relationship between reading skills and birth weight. However, birth weight and social class were confounded in this study, with subjects of lower birth weight tending to come from more disadvantaged homes. The finding that subjects who were both lower in SES and lower in birth weight did as well as subjects of higher SES and higher birth weight is, on the face of it, without explanation.

The British National Child Development Study, a large-scale prospective investigation of an unselected sample of children, found that reading performance at age seven was correlated with maternal age at pregnancy, maternal smoking during pregnancy, and birth weight (Davie, Butler, & Goldstein, 1972).

The Collaborative Perinatal Research Project has produced several studies relevant to this topic. Denhoff, Hainsworth, and Hainsworth (1972), using the Brown University sample, found that neurological signs present at birth and during the first year of life were associated with poor learning skills and school performance at age 7. Subjects were from predominantly low-SES families.

Conflicting results were reported in a study by Colligan (1974), based on the Minnesota sample, which found no significant relationship between WRAT performance and perinatal stress. Two methodological problems may have contributed to this finding. First, subjects identified as neurologically abnormal or suspicious had previously been removed from the sample group. Second, the method of rating perinatal stress may have been inadequate. In reassessing his data, Colligan found that the perinatal-stress score did not increase systematically with evidence of neurologic impairment.

3.2. Hyperactivity

Hyperactivity is referred to in the research literature as a major symptom of the syndrome of minimal brain dysfunction (MBD) in children. It is considered one of the "soft signs" thought to be present in perhaps half of all MBD children (Wender, 1973). The debates concerning the usage of the term *minimal brain dysfunction* cannot be discussed in adequate detail here. However, it should be noted that serious questions have been raised about the use of terminology implying a known etiology that cannot in fact be demonstrated and that disagreement exists as to the behavioral indicators of MBD, their significance, and their categorization (for useful discussions of these issues, see Benton, 1962; Cohn, 1964; Ingram, 1973; Rutter, Graham, & Yule, 1970; Wender, 1973). It is important to recognize that behaviors observed under the rubric *hyperactivity* may not be the same from study to study.

Estimates of the prevalence of hyperactive behaviors in the general population range from approximately 5% (Gorin & Kramer, 1973; Miller, Palkes & Stewart, 1973) to approximately 30% for boys (Werry & Quay, 1971). Prevalence rates are affected by both methodological and definitional differences, with smaller estimates reported by studies that attempted to identify a combination of behaviors rather than a single behavior.

Retrospective data about hyperactive children indicate that from 9.5% to 73% show perinatal problems (Anderson, 1963; Bandera & Churchill, 1961; Millichap, Aymat, Sturgis, Larsen, & Egan, 1968; Paine, 1962; Prechtl & Stemmer, 1962; Safer, 1973). The enormous range of incidence figures in all likelihood reflects the unreliability of the data. Definitions of hyperactivity were varied and subjective and all the problems of retrospective data collection were present.

Studies using control groups provide far less support for the belief that perinatal complications contribute to hyperactivity. Brandon's (1971) prospective study found no significant differences in the incidence of perinatal insults experienced by overactive, disturbed but not overactive, and normal control children. However, mothers of overactive children more frequently reported feeling ill during pregnancy compared with the mothers of disturbed children and reported more emotional distress in pregnancy than mothers of controls. Such reports, of course, are highly subjective.

Several other studies using control groups are retrospective in design. Rogers, Lilienfeld, and Pasamanick (1955) found significantly more prematurity, abnormal neonatal conditions, maternal toxemia of pregnancy, and complications in the history of white children labeled "hyperactive and/or confused disorganized" than in their controls, and they found a similar but nonsignificant difference for black children. Burks (1960) found more pregnancy and birth problems and five times as much prematurity among hyperactive children as among their classmates. Although Burks stated that his findings "appear significant," he included no data in his report. Fowler (1965) found "soft neurological signs" including hyperactivity in 23% of children whose mothers had had difficult pregnancies and in 2% of children with no perinatal difficulties. Minde, Webb, and Sykes (1968) found that forceps delivery was more common for hyperactive children and that mothers of hyperactive children more frequently had had unusually long or short labors. No significant differences were found between hyperactive and control children in studies by Stewart, Pitts, Craig, and Dieruf (1966) and by Werry, Weiss, and Douglas (1964).

Several prospective studies have been reported. Bailey (1966) reported that the children of toxemic pregnancies living in nonconsistent environments were rated significantly higher than other subjects on hyperactivity, distractibility, restlessness, and confusion. On a test of cognitive style, toxemic subjects from both consistent and nonconsistent environments appeared more impulsive than nontoxemic subjects. This type of investigative approach, which takes into account a possible interaction between perinatal events and child-rearing style, seems one more likely to prove fruitful than an approach that does not.

Anoxic subjects, studied prospectively, were significantly more distractible than controls at ages 3 and 7 (Corah, Anthony, Painter, Stern, & Thurston, 1965; Graham, Ernhart, Thurston, & Craft, 1962). Low birth weight was a nonsignificant factor in hyperactivity in two studies (Abrams, 1969; DeHirsch, Jansky, & Langford, 1966) and was significantly related to restlessness and overactivity in another (Drillien, 1964). Drillien, like Bailey, attempted to measure environmental as well as perinatal factors. In general, she found that environmental stress interacted with low birth weight, particularly in the case of subjects of extremely low birth weight (under 1350 g), to increase the likelihood of restless, hyperactive behavior.

In contrast, a large study of perinatal stress, which followed 1,102 subjects on the Hawaiian island of Kauai over a three-year period, found that children who suffered severe or moderate perinatal complications did not show significantly more hyperkinetic symptoms than children who suffered mild or no stress (Werner, Bierman, & French, 1971). This study was also unusual in finding no relationship between hyperkinetic symptoms and SES. However, virtually all subjects had access to prenatal care, hospital delivery, and postnatal medical services, which may have eliminated the effects usually associated with socioeconomic level.

Over the past few years, Waldrop and her colleagues have reported significant relationships between minor congenital anomalies and hyperactivity, freneticism, inability to delay, congenital speech and hearing difficulties, and, in girls, overcontrolled, inhibited, perseverative behavior (Waldrop & Halverson, 1971). In general, high-anomaly children tended to have problems with control, usually undercontrol but sometimes overcontrol. In similar studies (Quinn & Rapoport, 1974; Rosenberg & Weller, 1973), high anomaly scores were associated with high activity level, parental report of early hyperactive symptoms, and maternal report of serious prenatal and perinatal complications, but they did not relate to impulsivity and instability. A significant relationship was found between anomaly score and failing grade and between anomalies and Peabody Picture Vocabulary Test IQ, although not performance on other IQ tests.

The anomalies investigated in these studies are those often associated with Down's syndrome and other chromosomal irregularities, rubella, and the effects of noxious agents during pregnancy. A likely interpretation is that some genetic or traumatic insult early in pregnancy produces both the anomalies and the central-nervous-system (CNS) abnormalities that are expressed in behavioral symptoms and a variety of developmental deviations. Though most studies of congenital anomalies have looked at hyperactivity, other developmental deviations that have been correlated significantly with such anomalies are schizophrenia (Goldfarb, 1967), mental retardation, learning disabilities, nonachieving, juvenile delinquency, and emotional disturbance (Durfee, 1974). Further research in this area would seem to have promise of demonstrating a relationship between perinatal insults and later behavior disorders.

3.3. School Maladjustment

The major flaw in research that has studied perinatal complications in children who are considered problems by their teachers is the nature of the criterion variable: teacher referral is among the loosest of all descriptors. Consequently, all such samples comprise a mixture of deviant behaviors.

Rogers, Lilienfeld, and Pasamanick (1955) examined perinatal complications in children whom teachers in the Baltimore public schools had referred for special services as showing abnormal behavior. These deviant subjects were grouped into 15 categories. They found that significantly more children in the category "disorganized and confused behavior" had birth weights under 2500 g or had more than one perinatal abnormality when compared with matched controls. Among whites only, there was more toxemia of pregnancy among the group of subjects referred by teachers than among controls. For both white and nonwhite children, there were no significant differences between the entire group of deviant children and controls in the incidence of prematurity alone or in the incidence of pregnancy and birth complications other than maternal complications of pregnancy. These findings suggest that some relationship does exist between perinatal stress and teacher referral, but one must take into account the retrospectively gathered data, the mixed behaviors shown by the subjects, and the possible variability of criteria for referral. Certainly, perinatal stress cannot be linked to specific behavioral outcomes on the basis of these data.

Two British studies (Davie, Butler, & Goldstein, 1972; Drillien, 1964), both of which were well-designed prospective studies based on sizable samples, obtained teacher ratings of the frequency of behaviors considered symptomatic of maladjustment. Their findings supported the hypothesis that premature children show significantly more maladjustment than do children of normal birth weight. However, a study by Chazan (1965) that used the same teacher rating system found no relationship between maladjustment in educationally subnormal Welsh children and perinatal complications.

In the National Child Development Study (Davie et al., 1972), factors affecting teacher ratings, in order from most to least influential, include social class, sex, birth order, maternal smoking during pregnancy, length of pregnancy, number of younger children in the family, maternal age, birth weight, and height. Drillien (1964), in an extensive follow-up of premature Scottish children, found that the proportion of children considered unsettled or maladjusted increased as birth weight declined and that environmental stress accentuated the differences between prematures and controls. Also, difficult delivery and perinatal conditions associated with anoxia were related to maladjustment and seemed to lower resistance to environmental stress.

3.4. Emotional Disturbance

Prechtl and Dijkstra (1960) reported higher rates of neurological abnormality in children born with perinatal complications than in

controls. In a follow-up at ages 2–4, emotional problems (sleep disturbance, restlessness, lability of mood, angry behavior, and weakness of
concentration) appeared in 70% of children born with complications
who showed neurological abnormalities at birth, 39% of children born
with complications who appeared normal at birth, and 12% of the
control group, who were born without complications. A relationship
between deviant-behavior scores and neurological abnormality associated with low birth weight was also reported by Wortis, Braine,
Cutler, and Freedman (1964).

Schacter and Apgar (1959) did not find significant differences on
ratings of attention, emotional control, and activity between children
with and without perinatal complications either when the children
were rated by their mothers or when they were rated by a psychologist. Tapia (1968) found abnormal obstetric factors to be slightly, but
not significantly, more common in girls with behavior problems than
in controls.

One group of studies deals with perinatal factors in the back-
grounds of children with mixed or unstated psychiatric diagnoses.
Mura (1974) found that children hospitalized for psychiatric reasons
had more pregnancy and delivery complications and more severe total
complications than did their siblings; one item, condition judged poor
at birth, by itself significantly differentiated patients from controls.
Mura noted that maternal recall may have been biased. Similarly,
studies by Hinton (1963), and Whittam, Simon, and Mittler (1966),
which depended on maternal recall, reported more pregnancy difficulties among psychotic children than among controls.

Zitrin, Ferber, and Cohen (1964) found more prematurity among
children hospitalized for psychiatric reasons, but found no differences
in the prevalence of previous fetal loss, toxemia, or premature separation of the placenta.

Baker and Holzworth (1961) found no differences between adolescents hospitalized with psychiatric problems and controls on pregnancy and delivery factors, except for subjective factors such as maternal feeling that the pregnancy was characterized by ill health and
unpleasantness.

3.5. Psychoses

The evidence thus far suggests that perinatal problems may play a
role in the etiology of the psychoses, particularly childhood schizophrenia and infantile autism. Most work in this area is unavoidably
retrospective because of the relative rarity of childhood psychoses, the
prevalence of which in the United States and England is most com-

monly estimated to be 4 cases per 10,000. Another difficulty is the
problem of diagnosis. Several different diagnostic systems for each
syndrome exist. For example, a comparison of five different systems of
diagnosing autism and childhood schizophrenia found the overlap to
be no more than 35% (DeMyer, Churchill, Pontius, & Gilkey, 1971). It
is difficult to compare findings, given the confusion of diagnoses and
labels.

3.5.1. Autism

Nonsignificant differences in the prevalence of pregnancy and
birth complications in the histories of autistic children, their siblings,
and nonautistic, disturbed children were reported by Lotter (1967). An
Australian study (Lobasher, Kingerlee, & Gubbay, 1970) found that
autistic children, compared with matched controls, had significantly
more labor complications, forceps used and assisted deliveries, abnormal conditions at birth, neonatal complications, and gestation periods
over 287 days. Another Australian study compared autistic children,
emotionally disturbed but not psychotic children, and children hospitalized for medical conditions (Harper & Williams, 1974). The autistic
group differed significantly from the other two groups on a number of
medical factors, including virus infection during pregnancy, induced
labor, and cord around neck.

Knobloch and Pasamanick (1975) reported that autistic children
differed significantly from children with organic central nervous dysfunction and children without neuropsychiatric disorder in the
frequency of toxemia and/or bleeding during pregnancy and in neonatal complications, but not in the frequency of low birth weight.

Chess, Korn, and Fernandez (1971), Harper and Williams (1974),
and Pinsky, Mendelson, and Lajoie (1973) have all found evidence
linking maternal gestational rubella to autism and autistic-like syndromes.

3.5.2. Schizophrenic Children

Rutt and Offord (1971), Taft and Goldfarb (1964), and Vorster
(1960) found more prenatal and perinatal complications in the histories
of child schizophrenics than in those of their siblings or controls. Patterson, Block, Block, and Jackson (1960), however, found no relationship between symptoms surrounding pregnancy and diagnosis as
schizophrenic, as mild behavior disorder, as neurotic, or as undis-
turbed. Similarly, a study by Terris, Lapouse, and Monk (1964) found
no differences between schizophrenics and controls in prenatal and
perinatal complications, although it did find that in multiparous mothers, previous stillbirth or spontaneous abortion was significantly more

common among the mothers of schizophrenics than among the mothers of controls.

In another study, neither birth difficulties nor breast feeding alone differentiated schizophrenics from neurotics, but schizophrenics were significantly more likely to have had both birth difficulties and a short period of breast feeding (Osterkamp & Sands, 1962). The authors interpreted these findings as reflecting the mothers' rejection of their children. Another possible interpretation, offered by Pasamanick and Knobloch (1963), is that shortened breast feeding is often due to neonatal sucking difficulties, which may be related to neurological abnormalities.

3.6. Summary of Research Outcomes

The general impression created by the research literature is that of diffusion of effort and nonadditivity. Later research tends not to build on earlier studies, and no clear picture of perinatal influence emerges from these 25 years of disparate investigations. It should also be noted that the studies reviewed here were conducted in five different countries (United States, Great Britain, Denmark, Sweden, and Australia); the extent to which cross-cultural comparisons are valid is not known.

The majority of studies support the hypothesis that perinatal complications are related to school learning and behavior problems; however, these relationships are generally not strong and their nature is unclear. In the numerous studies of reading, prematurity appears to be the most frequently identified negative predictor; but prematurity, as well as other anomalies, may be of consequence only to the extent that it results in neurological abnormality.

In the realm of behavioral and emotional disorders, the more careful studies of better design, with the exception of the Kauai Island study of Werner, Bierman, and French (1971), suggest a limited relationship between perinatal complications and behavioral outcomes (Bailey, 1966; Corah et al., 1965; Drillien, 1964; Graham et al., 1962). The few studies of minor congenital anomalies seem consistent in reporting an association with hyperactivity. For the most severe disorders—autism and childhood schizophrenia—the major findings suggest a more definite connection, but studies differ greatly in their details.

Conclusions drawn from available findings must, too often, be qualified by serious concern with the quality of research on which they are based. With few exceptions, the existing studies have serious limitations: they tend to be retrospective rather than prospective; they focus on single rather than multiple predictor and criterion variables;

and they fail to examine the interrelationships among perinatal factors and the interactions of perinatal factors with a range of subsequent environmental influences. Good research has, of course, been done in this area. It is lengthy, complicated, and expensive. The results from such research are quite complex and, if anything, even less indicative of simple solutions than are the studies of lesser quality.

4. Background of the Educational Follow-up Study

4.1. Collaborative Project

By far the most extensive prospective study of perinatal complications conducted in the United States was the Collaborative Perinatal Project for the Study of Cerebral Palsy, Mental Retardation, and Other Neurological and Sensory Disorders of Childhood—most commonly referred to as the Collaborative Project. It represented the joint efforts of 14 medical centers together with the National Institute of Neurological Diseases and Blindness, since renamed the National Institute of Neurological Diseases and Stroke. The purpose of the project was to investigate the antecedents of pregnancy wastage, which was broadly defined so as to include not only fetal and infant loss but the occurrence and course of abnormalities such as prematurity, cerebral palsy, mental retardation, speech and language disorders, sensory disorders, and minimal brain syndromes (Berendes, 1966). Following five years of planning activity, the collection of data began in January 1959 and continued until January 1966. To provide a large enough sample of abnormal, and therefore infrequent, outcomes, over 60,000 pregnant women were enrolled in the project, which ensured a long-term follow-up of approximately 50,000 children.

Standardized protocols were developed by panels of experts from appropriate fields for use in each of the interview and examination settings. The study of the mother included a vast amount of detail on medical history, physical examination and laboratory tests, examination at labor and delivery, observations of the progress and complications of labor and delivery, and recording of anesthesia and other medications administered.

Studies of the child included observation of the immediate neonatal period, pediatric and neurological examination in the nursery, laboratory studies during the neonatal period, and regular physical and neurological examinations at specified periods throughout the years of infancy. At 3 and 4 years of age, representative psychological and speech, language, and hearing information were gathered on the child. Final examinations were made at 7 and 8 years of age to provide an ending checkpoint in neurology, pediatrics, psychology, speech, and audiology.

The Collaborative Project was basically a medical project with special attention directed to sensory and neurological disorders. Although socioeconomic data, psychological information, and extensive speech, language, and hearing data were gathered, the major concerns were medically oriented. The majority of publications thus far derived from the project reflect this focus (e.g., Niswander & Gordon, 1972), albeit with a number of contributions to the psychological literature as well (e.g., Broman, Nichols, & Kennedy, 1975). Relatively little recognition was given to the possible educational implications of the project data.

4.2. Educational Follow-up Study

The Educational Follow-up Study (EFS) was begun in the early 1960s with the full cooperation of the Perinatal Research Branch of NINDB and the Minnesota branch of the Collaborative Project (Balow, Anderson, Reynolds, & Rubin, 1969). All available subjects from the Collaborative Project born at the University of Minnesota Hospitals from 1960 through 1964 were enrolled in the EFS when they reached age 5 and have been followed up to the present time. Financial support originally came from the Bureau of Education for the Handicapped, U.S. Office of Education, and since 1972 has come from the National Institute of Education.

The EFS is a continuing longitudinal investigation of the educational and behavioral consequences of prenatal, perinatal, and early-childhood conditions and events. It draws its unique identity and value from the unequaled perinatal medical data that serve as the basis for comparative and normative analyses of later educational and behavioral observations.

The major objectives of the EFS are to: (1) assess the relationship of prenatal and perinatal conditions to later school achievement and behavior; (2) determine the limiting effects, if any, of early physical anomalies on readiness for the learning of school skills at preschool levels and on the later acquisition of these skills; and (3) identify the antecedents of such gross problems as mental deficiency, learning disability, speech handicap, behavior disorders, and other categories of handicap.

While the primary focus of the EFS is upon relationships between perinatal data and educational and behavioral outcomes, the extensive data base makes possible the exploration of additional significant educational, psychological, and child-development concerns, such as the establishment of prevalence rates for disorders of school learning and behavior; the development of normative data for measures of pre-school readiness, school behavior, speech articulation, and written-language skills; and the assessment of the influence of socioeconomic and family conditions interacting with all of these and a variety of other major influences in child development.

Published study results to date include the prediction of school readiness and achievement from perinatal data (Rubin, Balow, & Dorle, 1975; Rubin & Balow, 1975a,b), the assessment of the long-term correlates of premature birth (Rubin, Rosenblatt, & Balow, 1973) the identification of factors associated with special class placement (Rubin, Krus, & Balow, 1973), and the prevalence rates for special school problems in the elementary grades (Rubin & Balow, 1971, 1977).

4.2.1. Educational Follow-up Study Sample

The EFS population consists of 1,613 subjects, born at the University of Minnesota Hospitals between 1960 and 1964, who were participants in the Collaborative Project. The EFS population is 96.5% white, with 2.5% American Indian, 0.5% black, and 0.5% Oriental children. The distribution of Socioeconomic Index scores closely approximates the distribution of these scores within the urban population of the North Central states (Myrianthopoulos & French, 1968).

Although the Minnesota study sample was not initially drawn in a random fashion from the general population, sample characteristics along the dimensions of IQ, neonatal neurological abnormalities, proportion of birth anomalies, preschool language development, school readiness, and school achievement all attest to the essential normality of the study sample on these variables (Ireton, Thwing, & Gravem, 1970; Rubin, 1972, 1974).

Additional evidence regarding the representativeness of the EFS sample is provided by results of the National Health Examination Survey (Roberts & Baird, 1972) based upon a probability sample of 7,119 children drawn from the nation's 24 million noninstitutionalized children aged 6 through 11. Findings of this survey regarding the proportion of children in specific school-related problem areas such as school retention (15% of the study sample by age 11) and recommendations for special educational resources (30%) were comparable to the prevalence rates for these same categories of problems within the EFS population (Rubin & Balow, 1971).

The normality of the total EFS population provides a basis for the exploration of problems of significance to general education as well as to education of the handicapped. Most importantly, these factors make possible the generalization of study findings—with suitable caution— to broad populations of school-age children, more so than in the case of any other similar studies:

4.2.2. Educational Follow-up Study Data

To the basic pool of Collaborative Project medical and psychological information the EFS has added measures of school readiness, language development, speech articulation, academic achievement, and school behavior as well as data regarding school progress, special school services, and special placements.

During the summer immediately preceding kindergarten entrance, at age 5 each study child was individually administered a battery of tests, which included the Metropolitan Readiness Tests (MRT), the Illinois Test of Psycholinguistic Abilities (ITPA), the Templin speech-articulation test, and a rating of test behavior. The same battery of tests was administered again one year later, prior to entry into first grade, with the exception of the Templin test, which was replaced by a measure of laterality.

The mothers of the study children were interviewed at the time of the preschool testing so that the type of learning environment provided by the home could be determined. Parental attitudes toward various child-rearing practices were explored, and information was obtained regarding the amount and types of reading material in the home, the use of television, and the child's interests and favored play activities. Information was also obtained regarding the reading skills of the parents and the other children, and the reading section of the WRAT was administered to the mother.

Each year, the classroom teachers of the study children are asked to report on their progress in the basic subject-matter areas and are asked to rate the subjects on the School Behavior Profile (Balow & Rubin, 1973), a descriptive checklist covering such areas as developmental immaturity and acting-out behavior. Additional data on school progress are also obtained through a review of the cumulative records to determine patterns of school attendance, involvement of special services such as psychological evaluation or treatment, tutoring or speech therapy, and possible retention or special placement. Reading-achievement tests are administered at the conclusion of each elementary-school year to aid in a determination of the amount of academic progress being made.

At age 9 and again at ages 12 and 15, the subjects are tested individually. The word-meaning, spelling, and arithmetic-computation subtests of the Stanford Achievement Tests (SAT) are administered at age 9, the word-meaning section of the SAT plus the reading, spelling, and arithmetic sections of the WRAT are administered at age 12, and at age 15 the three sections of the WRAT are readministered along with the reading section of the SAT. At all three ages, measures of written language and ratings of test behavior are obtained.

5. Analysis of Educational Follow-up Study Data

Major analyses of EFS data thus far have used (1) multiple-regression analyses to determine the strength of predictive relationships between sets of perinatal variables and relevant outcome behaviors for the total study population and (2) analysis-of-variance procedures to compare groups of subjects selected either prospectively on the basis of perinatal complications or retrospectively on the basis of identified educational or behavioral problems. Additional analyses have been addressed to developing base-rate data for specified learning and behavior problems among unselected study children.

5.1. Multiple-Regression Analysis

The present analysis illustrates the type of predictive outcomes that have been derived from EFS data thus far. All EFS subjects ($N = 734$) for whom complete data were available on each of the perinatal and school-outcome variables listed in Tables 1 and 2 were included in the present set of analyses.

5.1.1. Perinatal Measures [1]

As described above, a very large and complex pool of data on study subjects has been established under the auspices of the Collaborative Project. The major perinatal medical, psychological, and demographic variables currently included in EFS analyses are listed in Table 1. These 76 maternal and infant variables were selected from the extensive pool of available data as having possible relevance for later educational and behavioral outcomes through a process of preliminary statistical analyses, review of previously reported research evidence, and clinical judgments.

5.1.2. Outcome Measures

Stanford–Binet (L–M, Short Form)—administered at age 4.
Wechsler Intelligence Scale for Children (WISC)—administered at age 7.

---

[1] Perinatal measures, IQ tests, and the reading section of the WRAT were administered at the University of Minnesota Hospitals and made available through the cooperation of the Collaborative Project.

Metropolitan Readiness Tests (MRT)—administered at ages 5 and 6.

Illinois Test of Psycholinguistic Abilities (ITPA)—administered at ages 5 and 6.

Wide Range Achievement Test (WRAT)—word-recognition section administered at age 7.

Stanford Achievement Test (SAT)—word-meaning, spelling, and arithmetic-computation sections administered at age 9.

Behavior problems—response of fifth-grade teacher to items on a mail questionnaire asking whether or not the study child shows behavior problems in the classroom.

School Behavior Profile (SBP)—a 58-item checklist on which the classroom teacher is asked to indicate the frequency of occurrence of specified behaviors (Balow & Rubin, 1973). Ratings used in the present analysis were obtained during the latter part of the sixth-grade year.

Retentions—total number of times retained in grade through age 12.

Receipt of special school services—total number of special services, including psychological examinations, social-work assistance, and remedial tutoring received through age 12.

Mean scores and standard deviations on measures of IQ, school readiness, language development, school behavior, and the number of special services received are reported in Table 2 for subjects included in the present analysis. IQ scores are normally distributed about a mean of 105 on the Stanford–Binet and a mean of 104 on the WISC, with standard deviations of 15.9 and 13.7, respectively. For the ITPA the means reported in Table 2 are based on language-age scores, while the means for the MRT, WRAT, SAT, and SBP are based on raw scores. The ITPA mean scores of 59.9 and 74.8 months closely approximate the respective chronological ages of 60 and 73 months at which they were administered.

5.1.3. Analysis

Product–moment correlations between each of the 76 selected perinatal variables and performance on later outcome or criterion measures were of relatively low magnitude with the exception of SES, which consistently yielded predictive correlations in the range from 0.20 to 0.35. Therefore, it was judged that analyses based on combinations of perinatal variables rather than on single measures of characteristics would be more likely to yield useful predictive information.

TABLE 1
Measures of Maternal and Infant Characteristics

A. Demographic characteristics of the pregnant woman
  1. Maternal age
  2. Marital status
  3. SES (NAM index)
  4. Highest grade completed

B. Maternal reproductive history
  5. Total live born
  6. Number of abortions—ectopic pregnancies
  7. Previous pregnancies—motor defect
  8. Previous pregnancies—sensory defect
  9. Previous pregnancies—retardation
  10. Total children now living

C. Maternal medical history
  11. History of hypertension
  12. Gravida—congenital malformations
  13. Gravida—other physical defects
  14. Gravida—sensory defects
  15. Gravida—diabetes
  16. Gravida—seizures
  17. Gravida—motor defect
  18. Gravida—mental retardation
  19. Gravida—mental illness

D. Variables of this pregnancy
  20. Complications of this pregnancy
  21. Infectious diseases of this pregnancy
  22. Total number of diseases and/or complications
  23. Blood pressure up to labor
  24. Blood-pressure rise up to labor
  25. Blood-pressure rise intrapartum
  26. Proteinuria 24th week to labor
  27. Persistent edema above waist to labor
  28. Persistent edema above waist intrapartum
  29. Weight gain to labor
  30. Toxemia screen
  31. Length of gestation
  32. Toxemia
  33. Toxemia recode

E. Delivery variables
  34. Duration of labor—third stage
  35. Duration of labor—total
  36. Duration of labor—sum of first and second stages
  37. Special procedures at birth

Table 1 (*continued*)

E. Delivery Variables (*continued*)
   38. Type of delivery
   39. Forceps
   40. Cord pathology

F. Neonatal variables
   41. 48-hr serum bilirubin
   42. Cord clamped before/after delivery
   43. Cord-clamp time in minutes
   44. First-breath time
   45. First cry before/after delivery
   46. First-cry time
   47. Moro reflex
   48. Cry
   49. Normal skin
   50. Cyanosis skin
   51. Stained skin
   52. Combination of codes on skin
   53. Dysmaturity
   54. 1-min Apgar total
   55. 5-min Apgar total
   56. Direct Coombs
   57. First bilirubin
   58. Highest bilirubin, total
   59. Clinical impressions of CNS defect or injury
   60. Report of CNS from last exam
   61. Congenital other than CNS
   62. Other clinical impressions
   63. Jaundice
   64. Head circumference
   65. Total number of abnormalities reported
   66. Neurological abnormalities
   67. CNS malformation
   68. Birth weight
   69. Percentage of birth weight lost at 48 hr

G. Infant developmental measures/exams
   70. Neonatal neurological diagnosis
   71. 4-month neurological abnormalities
   72. 4-month nonneurological abnormalities
   73. 1-year neurological abnormalities
   74. 1-year nonneurological abnormalities

H. Examinations during first year
   75. 8-month Bayley Mental Scale
   76. 8-month Bayley Motor Scale

TABLE 2

Mean Scores on Measures of IQ, School Readiness, Language Development, School Achievement, School Behavior, Number of Retentions, and Number of Special Services Received (N = 734)

Measure	Age administered	$\overline{X}$	SD
1. Stanford–Binet IQ	4	104.96	15.88
2. WISC—FS IQ	7	103.94	13.51
3. MRT[a]	5	30.52	14.35
4. ITPA[b]	5	59.92	11.40
5. MRT	6	57.40	17.06
6. ITPA	6	74.80	12.15
7. WRAT[c]—reading	7	36.51	12.71
8. SAT[d]—word meaning	9	23.13	8.65
9. SAT—spelling	9	16.51	8.86
10. SAT—arithmetic	9	26.02	11.97
11. Behavior problems	10	0.29	0.54
12. School Behavior Profile	11	194.86	25.14
13. Retentions	12[e]	0.15	0.38
14. Receipt of special services	12[e]	0.86	1.18

[a]Metropolitan Readiness Tests raw scores.
[b]Illinois Test of Psycholinguistic Abilities language-age score.
[c]Wide Range Achievement Test raw scores.
[d]Stanford Achievement Test raw scores.
[e]Cumulative to age 12.

5.1.4. Results

For the purposes of regression analyses, the 76 variables listed in Table 1 were grouped into the following eight subsets on the basis of the chronological availability of the different types of data as well as the logical interrelatedness of the variables included within each group. Four of the eight sets of variables (A–D) reflect maternal characteristics, one set (E) includes both maternal and infant variables, and three sets (F–H) consist of infant characteristics.

A. Maternal age, education, and SES
B. Maternal reproductive history
C. Maternal medical history
D. Variables of this pregnancy
E. Delivery variables
F. Neonatal variables
G. Examinations during first year
H. Infant developmental measures

Tables 3 and 4 present multiple-correlation coefficients between each of these sets of predictor variables and a series of criterion variables obtained at ages 4 through 12, which are representative of the

TABLE 3

Multiple-Regression Correlation Coefficients Predicting Performance on Measures of IQ, School Readiness, Language Development, and School Achievement from Perinatal Maternal and Infant Characteristics

Variable Group	Binet IQ 4 yr	WISC IQ 7 yr	MRT 5 yr	ITPA 5 yr	MRT 6 yr	ITPA 6 yr	WRAT reading 7 yr	SAT word meaning 9 yr	SAT spelling 9 yr	SAT arithmetic 9 yr
A. Maternal age, education, and SES	.41	.47	.40	.40	.44	.37	.40	.43	.36	.34
B. Maternal reproductive history	.23	.28	.22	.20	.25	.17	.22	.25	.19	.14
C. Maternal medical history	.14	.14	.11	.11	.15	.09	.16	.11	.09	.15
D. Variables of this pregnancy	.23	.23	.26	.23	.20	.13	.28	.29	.26	.26
E. Delivery variables	.13	.14	.08	.13	.15	.12	.11	.11	.10	.12
F. Neonatal variables	.23	.23	.25	.26	.25	.29	.23	.25	.25	.25
G. Examinations during first year	.22	.19	.14	.17	.18	.22	.17	.22	.18	.18
H. Infant developmental exams	.25	.21	.15	.18	.22	.22	.17	.17	.16	.16
Total	.57	.58	.53	.55	.57	.53	.55	.57	.52	.51

TABLE 4

Multiple-Regression Correlation Coefficients Predicting School Behavior, Retentions, and Receipt of Special School Services from Perinatal Maternal and Infant Characteristics

Variable group	Teacher-identified beh. prob. 10 yr	School behavior profile 11 yr	Retention[a]	Receipt of special services[b]
A. Maternal age, education, and SES	.28	.31	.15	.31
B. Maternal reproductive history	.25	.18	.06	.18
C. Maternal medical history	.13	.11	.07	.11
D. Variables of the pregnancy	.18	.17	.17	.17
E. Delivery variables	.18	.12	.10	.11
F. Neonatal variables	.22	.22	.17	.24
G. Examinations during first year	.11	.18	.06	.17
H. Infant developmental exams	.04	.01	.07	.12
Total	.46	.49	.33	.45

[a] Based on cumulative number of retentions for each subject through end of sixth grade.
[b] Based on cumulative number of special services received by each subject through end of sixth grade.

types of educational and behavioral outcomes upon which the EFS has focused. At the time these data were analyzed, results of tests administered at age 13 and over were available only for the oldest groups of subjects and therefore were not included. Each of the eight variable groups was independently entered in multiple-regression equations to predict each of the specified outcome variables. All eight variable groups were then combined in total multiple-regression equations to predict these same outcomes.

The outcome variables in Table 3 consist of scores on standardized measures of IQ, school readiness, language development, and academic achievement. The outcome variables in Table 4 are more direct indications of actual classroom functioning, consisting of teacher-identified behavior problems, scores on a teacher-administered behavior-rating scale, and evidence of difficulty in making satisfactory school progress as shown by retention in grade or by receipt of special school services.

In all instances reported in Table 3, variable Group A, consisting primarily of SES and related factors, yielded the highest predictive correlations with multiple Rs ranging from 0.34 with 9-year SAT arithmetic to 0.45 with 6-year MRT scores. Variable Groups F (neonatal) and D (variables of this pregnancy) most frequently yielded the next highest correlations, ranging from 0.13 to 0.29. Variable Groups C (maternal medical history) and E (delivery) consistently yielded the lowest predictive correlations. Multiple correlations based on the total series of 76 variables were in the 0.50s for all outcome variables, ranging from 0.51 with 9-year SAT arithmetic scores to 0.58 with 7-year WISC IQ scores, thus accounting for 26–34% of the total outcome variance.

Variable Group A (SES and related factors) was also the best predictor of three out of the four outcome variables in Table 4; however, the absolute magnitude of the multiple correlations yielded by Group A was considerably lower—ranging from 0.15 to 0.31—than it was for the measures reported in Table 3. In almost all instances, variable groups showed the same relative strength in predicting classroom-functioning variables as they did in predicting standardized-test performance, although most were reduced in absolute magnitude. When all 76 perinatal variables were combined in the regression equations, the resulting predictions of school-functioning outcomes were less accurate (Rs from 0.33 to 0.49) than the corresponding predictions of scores on standardized tests (Rs from 0.51 to 0.58).

The eight sets of variables used in the above analyses are grouped, in part, on a chronological basis, so that variables in Groups A through C consist of data available prior to the mother's pregnancy, Group D variables concern events occurring during pregnancy, and each of the subsequent sets of data become available at progressively later points in time. This chronological sequence enables a stepwise multiple-regression analysis of the cumulative effects of adding data gathered at each subsequent point in time on the magnitude of the predictive correlations.

Table 5 presents the results of combining successive sets of variables in the prediction of Binet IQ, 5-year MRT scores, and teacher-identified behavior problems in grade 5. The correlations between Group A and the outcome variables were 0.41, 0.20, and 0.28, respectively, while the correlations between Group B and the same outcomes were 0.23, 0.22, and 0.25, respectively. When Groups A and B were combined, the resulting multiple correlations were 0.42 with Binet IQ, 0.41 with MRT, and 0.34 with behavior problems, representing increases of 0.01, 0.01, and 0.05 over the predictions based on Group A alone. Each subsequent set of data was then added to the preceding combination of variables, one group at a time. New multiple correlations were computed as each set of variables was added, each combination including a progressively larger number of variables.

The largest increases in multiple Rs in the prediction of all three outcome variables occurred with the addition of Group F (neonatal). The magnitude of the increases indicates the extent to which each new set of variables made a contribution to the total multiple R, which was independent of all preceding sets of variables.

TABLE 5

Multiple-Regression Correlation Coefficients Predicting IQ, School Readiness, and School Behavior Problems from Perinatal Maternal and Infant Characteristics Grouped Separately and in Sequential Combination

Variable Group	Binet IQ 4 yr	MRT 5 yr	Teacher-identified behavior problems 10 yr		Binet IQ 4 yr	MRT 5 yr	Teacher-identified behavior problems 10 yr
A. Maternal age, education, and SES	.41	.40	.28	A	.41	.40	.28
B. Maternal reproductive history	.23	.22	.25	A+B	.42	.41	.34
C. Maternal medical history	.14	.11	.13	A+B+C	.43	.42	.37
D. Variables of this pregnancy	.23	.26	.18	A+B+C+D	.46	.45	.39
E. Delivery variables	.13	.08	.18	A+B+C+D+E	.46	.45	.41
F. Neonatal variables	.23	.25	.22	A+B+C+D+E+F	.52	.51	.46
G. Examinations during first year	.22	.14	.11	A+B+C+D+E+F+G	.54	.52	.46
H. Infant developmental exams	.25	.15	.04	A+B+C+D+E+F+G+H	.57	.53	.46
Total	.57	.53	.46	(Total)			

5.1.5. Summary of Regression Analysis

The moderate but statistically significant multiple correlations between perinatal and school-related outcome variables reported in Tables 3 and 4 are consistent with the earlier research findings reviewed above. None of the multiple correlations yielded by any of the variable groups separately or by all groups combined were of sufficient magnitude to warrant individual predictions.

The interrelatedness of the different sets of maternal and infant variables is apparent from the data reported in Table 5. Variable set A, consisting of SES and related characteristics, is the strongest predictor of the outcome variables. When succeeding sets of variables were added to the regression equations, the resulting increases in the size of the multiple correlations were low, indicating that their contributions to the regression equations were not for the most part independent of the contributions already made by SES and other preceding variables. For example, variable Group G (examinations during first year) correlated 0.25 with Binet IQ but added only 0.02 to the multiple correlation based on variable Groups A through E. Most of the variance in outcome measures accounted for by multiple correlations based on the entire set of 76 perinatal variables has already been accounted for by variables that were available by the end of the neonatal period.

5.2. Selected Group Comparisons

5.2.1. Perinatal Problem versus Control Groups

While multiple-regression analyses yield information regarding relationships between predictor and criterion variables over the full range of scores for the total sample, this statistical model is not appropriate for the examination of all relationships among EFS variables. Multiple-regression analysis assumes linearity of relationships between predictor and criterion variables. To the extent that this assumption is not met, the predictive correlations may be spuriously attenuated.

Available evidence suggests that for a number of maternal and infant variables, the relationship between predictor and outcome variables is curvilinear rather than linear in nature, so that changes in predictor measures may be of little consequence as long as they occur above some critical minimum level and below some critical maximum. Comparisons between subjects categorized on the basis of the presence or absence of certain types of perinatal problem are particularly

useful where there is reason to hypothesize the existence of curvilinear rather than linear relationships.

Birth weight is one such variable. Available evidence strongly
suggests that there is an inverse relationship between birth weight
and extent of impairment for children of premature birth weight
($\leq$2500 g); increasing developmental and psychological impairment is
associated with decreasing birth weight for infants whose birth
weight is below 2500 g (Parmalee & Schulte, 1970; Wiener, Rider,
Oppel, & Harper, 1968). However, differences in birth weight above
the level of 2500 g have not been found to be associated with differences in developmental outcomes except for infants of extremely
high birth weight who are the offspring of diabetic mothers. For this
reason, one of the EFS analyses focused on comparisons between subjects of low birth weight ($\leq$2500 g) and subjects of full birth weight
(>2500 g) (Rubin, Rosenblatt, & Balow, 1973). Low birth weight was
found to be associated with reduced performance on measures of intelligence and school achievement, even though product–moment correlations between birth weight and these same outcome variables for
the total study population were not significantly different from zero.

Similarly, previous research evidence suggests the likelihood that
any relationship between serum bilirubin level in the neonate and developmental outcomes is curvilinear in nature. It is generally accepted
(Diamond, Allen, Vann, & Powers, 1952) that bilirubin levels of 0–10
mg% fall within the "normal" range, while Boggs, Hardy, and Frazier
(1967) determined a critical threshold of 16–19 mg%, beyond which
impaired mental and motor development become more likely. Therefore, groups of EFS subjects with high (16–23 mg%), moderate (11–15
mg%), and low (0–10 mg%) neonatal bilirubin levels were compared
on a series of developmental and school variables through analysis-of-
variance procedures. This analysis indicated that high bilirubin levels
were associated with impaired mental and motor performance at 8
months of age but failed to show any long-term association with impaired performance beyond the first year of life (Rubin, Balow, &
Hara, 1975).

Another illustration of curvilinear relationships among EFS variables was found through analysis of outcomes associated with scores
on the Bayley Scales of Mental and Motor Development (Rubin &
Balow, 1975b). Groups of subjects with high (upper 5%), middle (5th
to 95th percentile), and low (lower 5%) Bayley scores were compared
on later IQ and school-achievement outcomes. Analysis-of-variance
procedures indicated significant differences among the three groups
on all outcome measures. However, further analysis with Newman–

Keuls tests (Winer, 1962) revealed that the overall differences found across groups were the result of highly significant differences between the low and the middle Bayley groups ($p < 0.001$), while the middle and high groups differed significantly on only one of the nine variables under investigation. These findings suggest that very low Bayley scores may be predictive of later reduced performance but that Bayley scores along the continuum from average to high do not differentially predict criterion variables.

5.2.2. Socioeconomic Level

An examination of EFS data indicates that the single best predictor of all developmental, educational, and behavioral outcomes is the SES of the child's family. This finding supports previously reported results based on white subjects from Collaborative Project data (Broman, Nichols, & Kennedy, 1975; Drage, Berendes, & Fisher, 1969; Ireton, Thwing, & Gravem, 1970; Smith, Flick, Ferriss, & Sellmann, 1972) as well as other similar investigations (Davie, Butler, & Goldstein, 1972). Correlations between SES-related measures and EFS educational and behavioral measures consistently fall between 0.24 and 0.42, accounting for 5.8% to 17.6% of the outcome variance. However, the specific factors associated with SES that most directly account for this relationship with performance in many socially important areas have yet to be clearly identified.

A detailed analysis was made of the interaction between SES and scores on the Bayley Scale of Mental Development in relation to educational outcome variables at ages 4 through 7 (Rubin & Balow, 1975b). Comparisons between EFS subjects scoring in the upper and lower 5% on the Bayley scale showed significant differences favoring the high Bayley group on all outcome variables. When subjects within the two Bayley groups were classified according to SES level, there were significant differences on a number of these outcome variables that favored high-SES subjects within each Bayley group. The influence of SES was such that high-SES subjects who were in the bottom Bayley group scored higher than low-SES subjects who were in the top Bayley group on the 6-year MRT and ITPA and on the reading sections of the 7-year WRAT.

Findings from this study suggest that upper-SES subjects who show signs of impairment in their early development may indeed be handicapped in comparison with subjects of similar SES at a later time; however, their absolute level of performance on later measures may still be higher than that of low-SES subjects who show no early signs of impairment.

6. Clinical Implications

In most studies using perinatal data, the attempt has been to directly link complications of pregnancy and birth with cognitive,
school-achievement, and behavioral outcomes in childhood years. The
results of these investigations show significant but low correlations
between independent and dependent variables whether predictions
are from perinatal variables to school disability or from school disabilities back to perinatal anomalies. Direct progression from perinatal
anomalies to later childhood disorders seems not to exist, with the exception of that rare gross insult that leads to serious brain damage or
similar disability. Instead, there is evidence that argues for a more
complex model of development involving interaction among perinatal
and subsequent environmental variables.

Data from the Educational Follow-up Study and similar studies,
such as that of Drillien (1964), support the view that environmental
variables interact with and greatly influence the impact of complications of pregnancy and birth. The variables most reflective of environment—for example, socioeconomic class and mother's education—
influence school-related outcomes much more strongly than any cluster of perinatal variables. It would be difficult to conclude from the
regression analyses of EFS data that any of the major clusters of variables, other than that based primarily on SES, is of practical importance for the selection of high-risk children. The clusters reflecting maternal reproductive history, conditions of the specific pregnancy, and
neonatal variables show definite relationships to these cognitive and
behavioral outcomes, but at magnitudes appropriate primarily for
heuristic purposes.

Drillien's (1964) data indicate that developmental quotient scores
decline as socioeconomic status declines and, within each status
group, developmental quotient scores decline as birth weight declines.
Children of very low birth weight (3 lb., 8 oz. and under) from
the highest social classes outperformed children in the heaviest
weight-grouping (5 lb., 9 oz. and over) of the lowest class, with mean
scores at 4 years of 97.1 and 95.3 respectively, but showed a deficit relative to the heaviest weight-group of their own social grade, whose
mean IQ at 4 years was 110.2. The Werner, Bierman, and French (1971)
report on the children born and raised on the Hawaiian island of
Kauai appears also to support an interpretation of greater influence on
school-related outcomes from the family–social–environmental conditions than from any but the most severe perinatal anomalies.

From such evidence, it seems appropriate to consider that the
concept of the vulnerable child, as discussed by Garmezy (1971) in

relation to research on the etiology of severe psychopathology, is equally relevant to the exploration of the consequences of perinatal complications. Thus, when measured for school achievement, the child of low birth weight reared in a low-SES family and attending a poverty-area school, is likely to perform significantly below average for his age. However, when similarly measured, a child of equally low birth weight reared in a high-SES family and attending an upper-middle-class suburban school will quite likely perform within the average range. In neither instance can it be said that the perinatal insult was directly causal, on the one hand, or unimportant, on the other. The relationship has been, in each instance, altered by the environment.

Findings that show lower-SES children with perinatal complications to have more serious impairment than upper-SES children with similar complications have led to the conclusion that "high socioeconomic status dissipates the effects of such perinatal complications as anoxia or low birth weight" (Sameroff & Chandler, 1975, p. 236). However, findings by Drillien and the EFS study both suggest that factors such as SES tend to mask rather than dissipate the effects of perinatal complications. Since upper-SES children suffering no perinatal damage would be expected, all other things being equal, to score well above average on educational-outcome measures, the effects of the perinatal complications may have been to impair their functioning to the extent that they perform in the average rather than the above-average range. It is more relevant to consider appropriate expectations for the individual rather than the population average in order to determine the existence and the extent of possible impairment.

Within the framework of interactions between perinatal anomalies and subsequent environmental influences, and with a recognition of the low magnitude of the correlations typically found, certain clinical suggestions and implications can be offered based on research findings to date.

1. Medical history, except in extreme instances, does not provide an adequate basis for predictions of school achievement. The data strongly suggest that groups of children who have had perinatal complications tend to have more learning problems than children without such complications. However, one cannot predict that a particular perinatal complication will have a specific effect on the generality of children or any effect at all on a particular child. While certain early conditions or events clearly increase the likelihood of later impaired performance, one cannot make accurate individual predictions.

2. Predictions or explanations of the emotional status of children seem no more directly linked to perinatal anomalies than school-

achievement results. Perinatal factors are more clearly implicated in the case of hyperactivity, but the above observations regarding vulnerability and interactions with the environment hold true. The evidence does not support any easy explanation for hyperactive behavior based on neurological insults or maldevelopment related to complications of pregnancy, birth, or infancy.

3. Perhaps the clearest implication for practice is the strong weight of evidence that negates the validity of current professional beliefs and actions based on the assumption that a linear relationship of importance exists between perinatal anomalies and school performance. The current press for the early screening of potentially handicapped children, to the extent that it is based on such assumptions, is not supportable. Similarly, the notion that children with special learning disabilities suffer from some defect in underlying psychological processes that is in turn related to neurological insult gets no encouragement from these findings.

Although current knowledge in this area does not permit identification or explanation of potential school-learning and behavior problems solely on the basis of perinatal complications, further research into the interactions among perinatal and subsequent environmental factors (e.g., investigations of the influence of perinatal complications within SES levels) may make possible a clearer specification of the extent of "risk" associated with perinatal complications under varying environmental conditions. This outcome is particularly likely if carefully designed prospective research is pursued with detailed attention to the environmental influences and with a proper regard for the dynamic interaction between different elements of the problem.

ACKNOWLEDGMENT

The authors wish to thank Ruoh-Yun Hsieh Lai for her contribution in the computer analysis of study data and Susanne Sandidge for her assistance in the preparation of the manuscript.

References

Abrams, S. The upper weight level premature child. *Diseases of the Nervous System,* 1969, *30,* 414–417.
Anderson, W. W. The hyperkinetic child: A neurological appraisal. *Neurology,* 1963, *13,* 968–973.
Bailey, M. Toxemia of pregnancy: Cognitive and emotional effects in children from consistent and non-consistent environments. Paper presented at the annual meeting of the American Psychological Association, New York, 1966.

Baker, J. W., & Holzworth, A. Social histories of successful and unsuccessful children. *Child Development*, 1961, *32*, 135–149.

Bakwin, H. Reading disability in twins. *Developmental Medicine and Child Neurology*, 1973, *15*, 184–187.

Balow, B., Anderson, J., Reynolds, M., & Rubin, R. *Educational and behavioral sequelae of prenatal and perinatal conditions*. (USOE, BEH, Project No. 6-1176, Interim Report No. 3) Department of Special Education, University of Minnesota, September 1969.

Balow, B., & Rubin, R. *School Behavior Profile*. Minneapolis: Department of Special Education, University of Minnesota, 1973.

Balow, B., Rubin, R., & Rosen, M. Perinatal events as precursors of reading disability. *Reading Research Quarterly*, 1975–1976, *11*(1), 36–71.

Bandera, E. A., & Churchill, J. A. Prematurity and neurological disorders. *Henry Ford Hospital Medical Bulletin*, 1961, *9*, 414–418.

Benton, A. L. Behavioral indices of brain injury in school children. *Child Development*, 1962, *33*, 199–208.

Berendes, H. W. The structure and scope of the Collaborative Project on Cerebral Palsy, Mental Retardation, and Other Neurological and Sensory Disorders of Infancy and Childhood. *In* S. S. Chipman, A. M. Lilienfeld, B. G. Greenberg, & J. F. Donnelly (Eds.), *Research methodology and needs in perinatal studies*. Springfield, Ill.: Charles C Thomas, 1966.

Bernstein, A. Some relations between techniques of feeding and training during infancy and certain behavior in childhood. *Genetic Psychology Monographs*, 1955, *51*, 3–44.

Beskow, B. Mental disturbances in premature children at school age. *Acta Paediatrica Scandinavica*, 1949, *37*, 125–149.

Black, F. W. EEG and birth abnormalities in high- and low-perceiving reading-retarded children. *Journal of Genetic Psychology*, 1972, *121*, 327–328.

Boggs, T., Hardy, J., & Frazier, T. Correlation of neonatal serum total bilirubin concentrations and developmental status at age eight months. *Journal of Pediatrics*, 1967, *71*, 553–560.

Brandon, S. Overactivity in childhood. *Journal of Psychosomatic Research*, 1971, *15*, 411–415.

Broman, S. H., Nichols, P. L., & Kennedy, W. A. *Preschool IQ*. New York: Halsted, 1975.

Bronner, A. F. *The psychology of special abilities and disabilities*. Boston: Little, Brown, 1921.

Burks, H. F. The hyperkinetic child. *Exceptional Children*, 1960, *27*, 18–26.

Caplan, H., Bibace, R., & Rabinovitch, M. S. Paranatal stress, cognitive organization and ego function: A controlled follow-up study of children born prematurely. *Journal of American Academy of Child Psychiatry*, 1963, *2*, 434–450.

Caputo, D., & Mandell, W. Consequences of low birth weight. *Developmental Psychology*, 1970, *3*, 363.

Chazan, M. Factors associated with maladjustment in educationally subnormal children. *British Journal of Educational Psychology*, 1965, *35*, 277–285.

Chess, S., Korn, S. J., & Fernandez, P. B. *Psychiatric disorders of children with congenital rubella*. New York: Brunner/Mazel, 1971.

Cohn, R. The neurological study of children with learning disabilities. *Exceptional Children*, 1964, *31*, 179–185.

Colligan, R. C. Psychometric deficits related to perinatal stress. *Journal of Learning Disabilities*, 1974, *7*, 154–160.

Corah, N. L., Anthony, E. J., Painter, P., Stern, J. A., & Thurston, D. Effects of perinatal anoxia after seven years. *Psychological Monographs*, 1965, *79*(3, Whole No. 596).

Davie, R., Butler, N., & Goldstein, H. *From birth to seven: The second report of the National Child Development Study*. London: Longman Group, 1972.

DeHirsch, K., Jansky, J., & Langford, W. S. Comparisons between prematurely and maturely born children at three age levels. *American Journal of Orthopsychiatry*, 1966, *36*, 616–628.

DeMyer, M. K., Churchill, D. W., Pontius, W., & Gilkey, K. M. A comparison of five diagnostic systems for childhood schizophrenia and infantile autism. *Journal of Autism and Childhood Schizophrenia*, 1971, *1*, 175–189.

Denhoff, E., Hainsworth, P. K., & Hainsworth, M. L. The child at risk for learning disorders: Can he be identified during the first year of life? *Clinical Pediatrics*, 1972, *11*, 164–170.

Diamond, L. K., Allen, F. H., Vann, P. D., & Powers, J. R. Erythroblastosis fetalis. *Pediatrics*, 1952, *10*, 337–347.

Doehring, D. G. *Patterns of impairment in specific reading disability: A neuropsychological investigation*. Bloomington: Indiana University Press, 1968.

Douglas, J. W. B. "Premature" children at primary schools. *British Medical Journal*, 1960, *1*, 1008–1013.

Drage, J., Berendes, H., & Fisher, P. The Apgar scores and four-year psychological examination performance. *Perinatal Factors Affecting Human Development*, 1969, *185*, 222–227.

Drillien, C. M. *The growth and development of the prematurely born infant*. Baltimore: Williams & Wilkins, 1964.

Durfee, K. E. Crooked ears and the bad boy syndrome: Asymmetry as an indicator of minimal brain dysfunction. *Bulletin of the Menninger Clinic*, 1974, *38*, 305–316.

Eames, T. H. Comparison of children of premature and full term birth who fail in reading. *Journal of Educational Research*, 1945, *38*, 506–508.

Edwards, N. The relationship between physical condition immediately after birth and mental and motor performance at age four. *Genetic Psychology Monographs*, 1968, *78*, 257–289.

Fowler, I. The relationship of certain perinatal factors to behavior, speech, or learning problems in children. *Southern Medical Journal*, 1965, *58*, 1245–1248.

Fraser, M. S., & Wilks, J. The residual effects of neonatal asphyxia. *Journal of Obstetrics and Gynaecology of the British Empire*, 1959, *66*, 748–752.

Galante, M. B., Flye, M. E., & Stephens, L. S. Cumulative minor deficits: A longitudinal study of the relationship of physical factors to school achievement. *Journal of Learning Disabilities*, 1972, *5*, 75–80.

Garmezy, N. Vulnerability research and the issue of primary prevention. *American Journal of Orthopsychiatry*, 1971, *41*(1), 101–116.

Gesell, A., & Armatruda, C. *Developmental diagnosis*. New York: Hoeber, 1941.

Goldfarb, W. Factors in the development of schizophrenic children: An approach to subclassification. Proceedings of the First Rochester International Conference on the Origins of Schizophrenia, March 1967. *Excerpta Medica*, International Congress Series No. 151, 70–91.

Gorin, T., & Kramer, R. A. The hyperkinetic behavior syndrome. *Connecticut Medicine*, 1973, *37*, 559–563.

Gottfried, A. W. Intellectual consequences of perinatal anoxia. *Psychological Bulletin*, 1973, *80*, 231–242.

Graham, F. K., Ernhart, C. B., Thurston, D., & Craft, M. Development three years after perinatal anoxia and other potentially damaging newborn experiences. *Psychological Monographs*, 1962, *76*(3, Whole No. 522).

Harper, J., & Williams, S. Early environmental stress and infantile autism. *Medical Journal of Australia*, 1974, *1*, 341–346.

Hinshelwood, J. *Congenital word blindness*. London: H. K. Lewis, 1917.

Hinton, G. G. Childhood psychosis or mental retardation: A diagnostic dilemma: II. Pediatric and neurological aspects. *Canadian Medical Association Journal*, 1963, *89*, 1020–1024.

Huessy, H. R., Marshall, C. D., & Gendron, R. Five hundred children followed from grade 2 through grade 5 for the prevalence of behavior disorder. *Acta Paedopsychiatrica*, 1973, *39*, 301–309.

Hunter, E. J., & Johnson, L. C. Developmental and psychological differences between readers and nonreaders. *Journal of Learning Disabilities*, 1971, *4*, 572–577.

Ingram, T. T. S. Soft signs. *Developmental Medicine and Child Neurology*, 1973, *15*, 527–529.

Ireton, H., Thwing, E., & Gravem, H. Relationships between infant mental development, infant medical data, socio-economic data, and intelligence at age four. *Child Development*, 1970, *41*, 937–945.

Jordan,T. E. Early developmental adversity and classroom learning: A prospective inquiry. *American Journal of Mental Deficiency*, 1964, *69*, 360–371.

Kappelman, M. M., Rosenstein, A. B., & Ganter, R. L. Comparison of disadvantaged children with learning disabilities and their successful peer group. *American Journal of Diseases of Children*, 1972, *124*, 875–879.

Kawi, A. A., & Pasamanick, B. Prenatal and paranatal factors in the development of childhood reading disorders. *Monographs of the Society for Research in Child Development*, 1959, *24* (4, Serial No. 73).

Knobloch, H., & Pasamanick, B. Some etiological and prognostic factors in early infantile autism and psychosis. *Pediatrics*, 1975, *55*, 182–191.

Little, W. J. On the influence of abnormal partuition, difficult labor, premature birth, and asphyxia neonatorum on the mental and physical condition of the child, especially in relation to deformities. *Transaction of the Obstetric Society of London*, 1862, *3*, 293–344.

Lobasher, M. E., Kingerlee, P. E., & Gubbay, S. S. Childhood autism: An investigation of aetiological factors in twenty-five cases. *British Journal of Psychiatry*, 1970, *117*, 525–529.

Lotter, V. Epidemiology of autism conditions in young children: II. Some characteristics of the parents and children. *Social Psychiatry*, 1967, *1*, 163–173.

Lyle, J. G. Certain antenatal, perinatal, and developmental variables and reading retardation in middle-class boys. *Child Development*, 1970, *41*, 481–491.

Malmquist, E. Factors related to reading disabilities in the first grade of elementary school. *Acta Universitatis Stockholmiensis: Stockholm Studies in Educational Psychology* 2. Stockholm: Almqvist & Wiksell, 1958.

McCready, E. B. Congenital word-blindness as a cause of backwardness in school children: Report of a case associated with stuttering. *Pennsylvania Medical Journal*, 1910, *13*, 278–284.

Miller, R. G., Palkes, H. S., & Stewart, M. A. Hyperactive children in suburban elementary schools. *Child Psychiatry and Human Development*, 1973, *4*, 121–127.

Millichap, J. G., Aymat, F., Sturgis, L. H., Larsen, K. W., & Egan, R. A. Hyperkinetic behavior and learning disorders: III. Battery of neuropsychological tests in controlled trial of methylphenidate. *American Journal of Diseases of Children*, 1968, *116*, 235–244.

Minde, K., Webb, G., & Sykes, D. Studies on the hyperactive child: VI. Prenatal and paranatal factors associated with hyperactivity. *Developmental Medicine and Child Neurology*, 1968, *10*, 355–363.

Mura, E. L. Perinatal differences: A comparison of child psychiatric patients and their siblings. *Psychiatric Quarterly*, 1974, *48*, 239–255.

Myrianthopoulos, N. C., & French, K. S. An application of the U.S. Bureau of the Census socioeconomic index to a large diversified patient population. *Social Science and Medicine*, 1968, *2*, 283.

Niswander, K. R., & Gordon, M. *The women and their pregnancies.* Philadelphia: Saunders 1972.

Orton, S. T. *Reading, writing, and speech problems in children.* New York: W. W. Norton, 1937.

Osterkamp, A., & Sands, D. J. Early feeding and birth difficulties in childhood schizophrenia: A brief study. *Journal of Genetic Psychology*, 1962, *101*, 363–366.

Paine, R. S. Minimal chronic brain syndromes in children. *Developmental Medicine and Child Neurology*, 1962, *4*, 21–27.

Parmalee, A., & Schulte, F. Developmental testing of preterm and small-for-date infants. *Pediatrics*, 1970, *45*, 21.

Pasamanick, B., & Knobloch, H. Early feeding and birth difficulties in childhood schizophrenia: An explanatory note. *Journal of Psychology*, 1963, *56*, 73–77.

Pasamanick, B., & Lilienfeld, A. Association of maternal and fetal factors with development of mental deficiency: I. Abnormalities in the prenatal and paranatal periods. *Journal of the American Medical Association*, 1955, *159*(3), 155–160.

Patterson, V., Block, J., Block, J., & Jackson, D. D. The relation between intention to conceive and symptoms during pregnancy. *Psychosomatic Medicine*, 1960, *22*, 373–376.

Pinsky, L., Mendelson, J., & Lajoie, R. Can language disorder not due to peripheral deafness be an isolated expression of prenatal rubella? *Pediatrics*, 1973, *52*, 296–298.

Prechtl, H. F. R., & Dijkstra, J. Neurological diagnosis of cerebral injury in the newborn. *In* B. S. ten Berge (Ed.), *Prenatal care.* Groningen, The Netherlands: P. Noorhoff, 1960.

Prechtl, H. F. R., & Stemmer, C. J. The choreiform syndrome in children. *Developmental Medicine and Child Neurology*, 1962, *4*, 119–127.

Quinn, P. D., & Rapoport, J. L. Minor physical anomalies and neurologic status in hyperactive boys. *Pediatrics*, 1974, *53*, 742–747.

Richardson, J. A. Physical factors in reading failure. *Australian Journal of Education*, 1958, *2*, 1–10.

Roberts, J., & Baird, J. T. *Behavior patterns of children in school: United States.* Rockville, Md.: Vital and Health Statistics, Series 11, HEW, Division of Health Examination Statistics, February 1972.

Robinson, N. M., & Robinson, H. B. A follow-up study of children of low birth weight and control children at school age. *Pediatrics*, 1965, *35*, 425–433.

Rogers, M. E., Lilienfeld, A. M., & Pasamanick, B. Prenatal and paranatal factors in the development of childhood behavior disorders. *Acta Psychiatrica et Neurologica Scandanavica*, 1955, Suppl. 102.

Rosenberg, J. B., & Weller, G. M. Minor physical anomalies and academic performance in young school children. *Developmental Medicine and Child Neurology*, 1973, *15*, 131–135.

Rubin, R. A. Sex differences in effects of kindergarten attendance on development of school readiness and language skills. *Elementary School Journal*, 1972, *72*, 265–274.

Rubin, R. A. Preschool application of the Metropolitan Readiness Tests: Validity, reliability and preschool norms. *Educational and Psychological Measurement*, 1974, *34*(2), 417–422.

Rubin, R. A., & Balow, B. Learning and behavior disorders: A longitudinal study. *Exceptional Children*, 1971, *38*, 293–299.

Rubin, R. A., & Balow, B. *Perinatal and early childhood conditions related to academic achievement in the elementary school years.* Paper presented at the annual meeting of the Council for Exceptional Children, Los Angeles, April 1975a.

Rubin, R. A., & Balow, B. *Relationships between Bayley infant scales and measures of cognitive development and school achievement.* Minneapolis: NIE, Project No. 6-1176, Interim Report No. 21, Department of Psychoeducational Studies, University of Minnesota, December 1975b.

Rubin, R., & Balow, B. *A longitudinal survey of school behavior problems.* (USOE, NIE, Project No. 6-1176 Interim Report No. 25) Department of Psychoeducational Studies, University of Minnesota, February 1977.

Rubin, R. A., Balow, B., & Dorle, J. *The relationship of maternal and infant variables to school readiness.* Paper presented at the annual meeting of the American Psychological Association, Chicago, August 1975.

Rubin, R. A., Balow, B., & Hara, C. *Relationship of bilirubin levels in infancy to later intellectual development.* Minneapolis: NIE, Project No. 6-1176, Interim Report No. 20) Department of Psychoeducational Studies, University of Minnesota, April 1975.

Rubin, R. A., Krus, P., & Balow, B. Factors in special class placement. *Exceptional Children,* 1973, *39,* 525–532.

Rubin, R. A., Rosenblatt, C., & Balow, B. Psychological and educational sequelae of prematurity. *Pediatrics,* 1973, *52,* 352–363.

Rutt C. N., & Offord, D. R. Prenatal and perinatal complications in childhood schizophrenics and their siblings. *Journal of Nervous and Mental Disease,* 1971, *152,* 324–331.

Rutter, M., Graham, P., & Yule, W. A neuropsychiatric study in childhood. *Clinics in Developmental Medicine,* 1970, 35–36.

Safer, D. J. A familial factor in minimal brain dysfunction. *Behavior Genetics,* 1973, *3,* 175–186.

Sameroff, A. J., & Chandler, M. J. Perinatal risk and the continuum of caretaking casualty. *In* F. Horowitz, M. Hetherington, S. Scarr-Salapatek, & G. Siegel (Eds.), *Review of child development research,* Vol. 4. Chicago: Society for Research in Child Development, 1975.

Schacter, F. F., & Apgar, V. Perinatal anoxia and psychologic signs of brain damage in childhood. *Pediatrics,* 1959, *24,* 1016–1025.

Shipe, D., Vandenberg, S., & Williams, R. D. B. Neonatal Apgar ratings as related to intelligence and behavior in preschool children. *Child Development,* 1968, *39,* 861–866.

Smith, A. C., Flick, G. L., Ferriss, G. S., & Sellmann, A. H. Prediction of developmental outcome at seven years from prenatal, perinatal and postnatal events. *Child Development,* 1972, *43,* 495–507.

Stewart, M. A., Pitts, F. N., Jr., Craig, A. G., & Dieruf, W. The hyperactive child syndrome. *American Journal of Orthopsychiatry,* 1966, *36,* 861–867.

Taft, L. T., & Goldfarb, W. Prenatal and perinatal factors in childhood schizophrenia. *Developmental Medicine and Childhood Neurology,* 1964, *6,* 32–43.

Tapia, F. Girls with conditions more commonly seen in boys: A pilot study. *Diseases of the Nervous System,* 1968, *29,* 323–326.

Terris, M., Lapouse, R., & Monk, M. A. The relation of prematurity and previous fetal loss to childhood schizophrenia. *American Journal of Psychiatry,* 1964, *121,* 476–481.

Uddenberg, G. Diagnostic studies in prematures. *Acta Psychiatrica et Neurologica Scandanavica,* 1955, Suppl. 104.

Versacci, C. J. An epidemiological study of the relation between children's birth record information and reading achievement. Unpublished doctoral dissertation, Temple University, 1966.

Vorster, D. An investigation into the part played by organic factors in childhood schizophrenia. *Journal of Mental Science* (British Journal of Psychiatry), 1960, *106*, 494–522.

Waldrop, M. F., & Halverson, C. F., Jr. Minor physical anomalies and hyperactive behavior in young children. *In* J. Hellmuth (Ed.), *The exceptional infant:* Vol. 2. *Studies in abnormalities.* New York: Brunner/Mazel, 1971.

Wenar, C. The reliability of developmental histories: Summary and evaluation of evidence. *Psychosomatic Medicine,* 1963, *25,* 505–509.

Wenar, C., & Coulter, J. B. A reliable study of developmental histories. *Child Development,* 1962, *33,* 453.

Wender, P. H. Some speculations concerning a possible biochemical basis of minimal brain dysfunction. *Annals of the New York Academy of Science,* 1973, *205,* 18–28.

Werner, E. E., Bierman, J. M., & French, F. E. *The children of Kauai: A longitudinal study from the prenatal period to age ten.* Honolulu: University of Hawaii Press, 1971.

Werry, J. S., & Quay, H. C. The prevalence of behavior symptoms in younger elementary school children. *American Journal of Orthopsychiatry,* 1971, *41,* 136–143.

Werry, J. S., Weiss, G., & Douglas, V. Studies on the hyperactive child: I. Some preliminary findings. *Canadian Psychiatric Association Journal,* 1964, *9,* 120–130.

Whittam, H., Simon, G. B., & Mittler, P. J. The early development of psychotic children and their sibs. *Developmental Medicine and Child Neurology,* 1966, *8,* 552–560.

Wiener, G. Scholastic achievement at age 12–13 of prematurely born infants. *Journal of Special Education,* 1968, *2,* 237–250.

Wiener, G., Rider, R. V., Oppel, W. C., & Harper, P. A. Correlates of low birthweight: Psychological status at eight to ten years of age. *Pediatric Research,* 1968, *2,* 110–118.

Winer, B. *Statistical principles in experimental design.* New York: McGraw-Hill, 1962.

Wortis, H., Braine, M., Cutler, R., & Freedman, A. Deviant behavior in 2½-year-old premature children. *Child Development,* 1964, *35,* 871–879.

Zitrin, A., Ferber, P., & Cohen, D. Pre- and paranatal factors in mental disorders of children. *Journal of Nervous and Mental Diseases,* 1964, *139,* 357–361.

5 Social-Skills Training with Children

Melinda L. Combs and
Diana Arezzo Slaby

1. Introduction

The complex social skills necessary for confident, responsive, and mutually beneficial interaction with other people are certainly among the most important skills a child must learn. A person's social facility has profound implications for nearly every facet of life—both in childhood and in adulthood. A lack of social skills may lead directly to problems in interpersonal relationships or may interfere indirectly with optimal functioning in school, occupational, and recreational activities. Yet, as frequently noted, the training of even the most basic social skills has been almost completely neglected in American schools (e.g., Winnett & Winkler, 1972; Lazarus, 1973). Researchers and clinicians have only recently begun to investigate methods of fostering specific social skills in children.

1.1. Definition

The term *social skill* has not been precisely defined for either theoretical or practical purposes. It is apparently assumed that everyone knows what is meant. In formulating a definition, we should consider such issues as how the value of a given skill is assessed, by whom, and for whose benefit. The value of a particular social skill in a child may be assessed from a number of different perspectives: (1) the effect on overall group functioning from the point of view of an adult group-leader (e.g., a teacher's assessment of appropriate social skills in a

Melinda L. Combs • Children's Orthopedic Hospital and Medical Center and University of Washington, Seattle, Washington. Present address: Children's Behavioral Services, 6171 W. Charleston Blvd., Las Vegas, Nevada. Diana Arezzo Slaby • Children's Orthopedic Hospital and Medical Center and University of Washington, Seattle, Washington. The authors jointly consider their individual contributions to the chapter of equal importance.

classroom); (2) the effect on the child's popularity from the point of view of peers; or (3) the effect on the child's own feelings of social competence. These different sources of assessment may lead to discrepant or even contradictory definitions of what constitutes a valuable social skill. For example, a child's resistance to peer pressure may be negatively valued by the group leader because of its disruptive potential, and may have a detrimental effect on peer popularity. This "skill" may nevertheless be very important from the point of view of the child's own social and moral development. Researchers of social skills have not attempted to directly assess the value to the child of particular social skills. Rather, they have depended largely on either peer-popularity measures or on adult presumptions of what would be a valuable social skill. A definition of *social skills* should reflect these different perspectives.

Social skills, as conceptualized in this chapter, refers to positive skills that are at least minimally acceptable according to societal norms and that are not harmful to others. This excludes exploitive, deceitful, or aggressive "skills," which may be of individual benefit. Skills that are of mutual benefit to the user and others, such as cooperative skills, are clearly valuable social skills. Also included are skills that are of primary immediate benefit to others, such as altruistic behaviors (Bryan & London, 1970). Finally, the word *skill* is taken to imply a relatively specific behavior pattern—rather than a global attribute—and competence (i.e., the knowledge and ability to perform in a certain way) rather than performance alone.

Thus, we come to our definition of a *social skill* as the ability to interact with others in a given social context in specific ways that are societally acceptable or valued and at the same time personally beneficial, mutually beneficial, or beneficial primarily to others.

1.2. The Need for Social-Skills Training

Social skills are learned and used by children in interaction with a variety of people, including parents and teachers. However, this chapter focuses on peer interaction as perhaps the most important forum for the development of social skills. Many children go through school with few friends or with no friends at all (Gronlund, 1959). Children who interact very little with peers (i.e., "social isolates") and children who show other signs of poor peer relations are considerably more likely than others to have additional adjustment problems. They exhibit a greater incidence of:

1. School maladjustment (Gronlund & Anderson, 1963).
2. Dropping out of school (Ullmann, 1957).

3. "Delinquency" (Roff, Sells & Golden, 1972).
4. Bad-conduct discharges from military service (Roff, 1961).
5. Adult mental-health problems (Cowen, Pederson, Babigan, Izzo, & Trost, 1973; Kohn & Clausen, 1955; Roff, 1970).

Kohn and Clausen (1955) reported that the proportion of adults diagnosed as manic-depressive and schizophrenic who had been social isolates as children was approximately one-third, compared to proportions near zero in normal control groups.

It has often been noted that an adequate opportunity for peer interaction may be necessary to provide a child with the practice and feedback required to develop social skills (e.g., Hartup, 1976). It is conversely true that an initial deficit in social skills may seriously limit the extent or the quality of a child's peer-interaction experience and thereby further impede the development of appropriate positive social skills. Children normally show a marked increase during the preschool years in their use of "social reinforcers," such as showing positive attention, approval, and affection to each other (Charlesworth & Hartup, 1967). It may be that if young children are initially deficient in the use of social reinforcers, they will be handicapped in their later development of the more complex behavioral repertoires needed for effective social functioning.

Several studies have indicated that unpopular children are in fact deficient in a variety of social skills, such as initiating play, cooperating, communicating needs and emotions accurately, and responding to peers with appropriate affection, approval, or help (e.g., Gottman, Gonso, & Rasmussen, 1975; Hartup, Glazer, & Charlesworth, 1967). Ineffective social contacts resulting from a child's lack of social skills may cause the child to be ignored or actively rejected by peers. Such negative social experience could be expected to encourage further maladaptive responses, such as withdrawal from social interaction, hostile or annoying verbalizations toward peers, or retaliatory physical aggression. These negative behaviors are likely to make children even less popular with their peers (Hartup *et al.*, 1967), thus setting up a vicious circle. To make matters worse, disruptive social behaviors are often maintained and increased unwittingly by adults who reinforce them with abundant attention (Bandura, 1973) or by peers who submit or react strongly (Patterson, Littman, & Bricker, 1967). For example, Patterson and his colleagues (1967) found that 80% of the aggressive incidents observed in a preschool class were directly rewarded by such victim reactions as giving up objects, crying, or running away. Children who are initially ineffective in gaining peer reinforcement through prosocial behaviors can readily fall into a cycle that leads to the increasing use of seriously negative social behaviors to gain control, recognition, and attention. Thus, while social deficits almost certainly play a role in the development of isolation, they may also be a factor in the etiology of aggression. These possibilities, together with the evidence that poor peer relationships in childhood are related to serious later adjustment problems, point to the need for early identification of specific social-skills deficits and for early social-skills training for those children who are seriously deficient.

Some of the research discussed in this chapter deals with social-skills training for a population of children who might be considered "deviant" or "abnormal," many of whom are labeled *social isolates*. However, the authors feel that there are factors within our particular society that pose a much broader problem than the training of a relatively small number of "deviant" children. For example, a heavy emphasis is placed on competition between individuals or groups rather than on cooperative accomplishment for its own sake. Many sanctioned competitive activities, such as boxing or football, include components of physical aggression. There is some evidence that a competitive environment tends to foster belligerent, noncooperative peer interaction (e.g., Davitz, 1952; Sherif & Sherif, 1953, 1964). In contrast to child-rearing practices in other cultures, such as modern Israel and the USSR, children in the United States are generally provided with no systematic training in cooperation or in prosocial methods of solving interpersonal problems (Bronfrenbrenner, 1970). At the same time, our children are exposed to frequent and salient models of both gratuitous aggression and aggressive solutions to problems. Aggressive modeling situations that have been shown to influence children's social behavior adversely include the widespread parental use of hostile verbal discipline and physical punishment (Bandura, 1973; Becker, 1964), physical abuse between parents and against children (Parke, 1975), and rampant media violence (Liebert, Neale, & Davidson, 1973).

The authors believe that social skills cannot be trained, practiced, or researched effectively in isolation from the total "normal" peer-group setting. For example, social skills acquired in a clinical setting would not be likely to be maintained by a child who returned to either a classroom or a city street where opportunities for cooperation were limited, where peers were unresponsive to her (his) newly acquired skills, and where negative behaviors were modeled and rewarded. For this reason, much of the research discussed here deals with factors that foster the development of prosocial peer-interaction skills in normal children and in everyday settings. Routine efforts by parents and teachers are clearly needed to help all children develop valuable prosocial skills and to help prevent the development of serious social-interaction problems. In addition, work with normal children is necessary to provide a basis for the development of specialized techniques for deficient children.

Some may object to adult intervention in children's activities with peers. However, in the absence of effective adult guidance, many normal children develop serious problems in social interaction because of either an initial lack of social skills or the direct learning of negative behaviors from peers. Children learn social behaviors through peer interaction, whether or not adults intervene. For example, Patterson and his colleagues (1967) described an unfortunate chain of events that resulted in dramatic increases in aggression in a number of preschool children over the course of a year of extensive observation. Initially nonaggressive children observed the aggression of peers, frequently became victims themselves, and subsequently began to adopt defensive aggressive strategies. If defensive aggression was effective, they began to initiate aggressive attacks. When these attacks were typically rewarded by peer submission or reaction, aggression increased sharply. These observations suggest that with regard to aggressors and victims, "Let them handle it themselves" does not always represent the best strategy for adult supervisors.

This type of negative pattern can be altered through deliberate adult intervention designed to foster cooperation, control aggression, and teach children assertive skills for dealing effectively with peer aggression in ways that are neither aggressive nor submissive (D. Slaby, 1976). It has been pointed out that intervention that helps children develop such positive social skills does not limit their choices but rather allows them more freedom of choice in their peer interactions (Roedell, R. Slaby & Robinson, 1977). A child who has assertive skills can choose to use them instead of necessarily relying on defensive aggression. A child who has the skills to initiate play and communicate with peers may still choose to spend a good deal of time alone. But that child will be able to interact effectively when she (he) wants to or when the situation requires it. On the other hand, a socially unskilled child may be alone or "isolated" out of necessity rather than by choice.

Furthermore, there appears to be an interaction between different social behaviors, so that negative behaviors may be more likely to develop in the absence of adequate positive skills. The child who is belligerent or physically aggressive or who is a "tattletale" or a "cry baby" may demonstrate these behaviors not out of choice or preference but rather because she (he) lacks the skills for more appropriate social interaction. There is some evidence, for example, that aggressive and cooperative behaviors in children may be incompatible in the sense that training that strengthens behavior of either type simultaneously weakens behavior of the other type. In one study, a group of children whose cooperative behaviors were increased through contingent teacher attention to verbal cooperation showed simultaneously less verbal and physical aggression (Slaby & Crowley, 1977). When the children's aggressive behaviors were similarly increased through attention to verbal aggression, they simultaneously showed less peer cooperation. Other training procedures designed to increase aspects of positive interaction alone have led to a decrease in negative or inappropriate behaviors (e.g., Allen, Hart, Buell, Harris, & Wolf, 1964; Brown & Elliot, 1965; Strain, Shores, & Kerr, 1976).

These findings indicate the importance of training in positive social skills, not only to increase desirable behaviors *per se* but also to provide children with viable alternatives to negative behaviors. Although more subtle and specific ethical questions require continued consideration, the authors feel that there is clear ethical justification and need for the active fostering of prosocial skills in children—both on a routine basis and in training programs for children with specific deficits.

1.3. Research Approaches and Trends

Social behaviors toward peers, including both prosocial skills and negative behaviors, are learned by children in three major ways: (1) adult guidance, instruction, and reinforcement; (2) observation of social behaviors (and their consequences) displayed by adults, peers, and media models; and (3) direct experience in interacting with peers and working out social problems (Roedell *et al.*, 1977). The research reviewed in this chapter is organized into three major procedural approaches to effecting changes in social skills, roughly corresponding to these three types of learning: (1) shaping procedures using contingent adult reinforcement alone; (2) modeling or combined modeling and reinforcement procedures; and (3) direct training procedures that make more explicit use of the child's cognitive and verbal facilities. This third category has become increasingly important; it includes coaching, role playing, rehearsal, and teaching children to use behavior-management techniques themselves.

Concomitant with trends in training procedures, there have also been changes in the goals of training. A large number of studies, using both reinforcement and modeling techniques, have had as their goal a simple increase in the amount of social interaction between children. This broad approach has limited usefulness when one is dealing with the complex problems of children's social interaction. Other studies have focused on the effecting of changes in general categories of behavior, such as cooperation, helping behavior, and aggression. A third category of goals, which tend to be the goals set by the proponents of the more recent verbal–cognitive approaches, involves training more *specific* social skills and problem-solving techniques. These may include such skills as asking a peer for help or responding to a peer's misbehavior in particular situations.

2. Identifying Valuable Social Skills

An initial step in the development of successful intervention techniques should be the identification of those peer-interaction behaviors and attributes that are correlates of social effectiveness. Social-status measures have been the most commonly used indicators of social effectiveness.

2.1. Correlates of Social Status

Peer acceptance (or "popularity") basically refers to the degree to which a child's peers evaluate her (him) highly or wish to have some form of associative contact with her (him). *Peer rejection* refers to the extent to which a child is negatively evaluated or actively avoided by peers. Research indicates that low peer acceptance is by no means equivalent to peer rejection; rather, it may reflect only indifference (Hartup, 1970). *Social status* and *sociometric status* are more general, inclusive terms used to refer to peer acceptance, peer rejection, or measures that combine both. Originally the term *sociometric rating* was used to refer only to mutual social-status ratings by peers within a group. More recently, all techniques designed to measure social status have come to be referred to as *sociometric instruments* (Hartup, 1970). Measured sociometric status may be based on paper-and-pencil ratings (or choices) made by the children themselves about their peers or made by teachers or group leaders. Occasionally, sociometric evaluations have been derived either from naturalistic behavioral observations or from structured-response measures, such as the pattern of actual sharing behavior among peers in a forced-choice situation.

Peer acceptance, for children from preschool age through adolescence, has been consistently found to be directly associated with such characteristics as friendliness (e.g., Marshall & McCandless, 1957; Moore, 1967); social visibility (e.g., Clifford, 1963); and outgoingness or social participation (e.g., Baron, 1951; Bonney & Powell, 1953). In addition to these rather global attributes, high peer acceptance has been associated with the following measures of sensitivity, responsiveness, and generosity in peer interaction:

1. The extent to which nurturance is given to peers (Moore & Updegraff, 1964).
2. The frequency with which the child dispenses positive social reinforcers to peers (Gottman, Gonso, & Rasmussen, 1975; Hartup *et al.*, 1967).
3. The frequency with which "kindness" is expressed to peers (Smith, 1950).
4. Willingness both to give and to receive friendly overtures and to respond positively to dependent behaviors of peers (Campbell & Yarrow, 1961).
5. Sensitivity to the social overtures of other children (Klaus, 1959).

Consistent with these correlational findings, it has been demonstrated experimentally that increased sharing of reinforcement by children raises the sociometric evaluation they receive (Karen, 1965). Surprisingly, of all these studies in which peer acceptance was found to be related to positive behaviors, only one included peer rejection as a second measure of social status (Hartup *et al.*, 1967). In this study, peer rejection was found to be *unrelated* to friendly or "socially reinforcing" behaviors.

In reference to negative behaviors, peer rejection has consistently been found to be related to measures of aggression (e.g., Dunnington, 1957; Hartup *et al.*, 1967; Moore, 1967). However, findings on the relationship between peer *acceptance* and aggression have been inconsistent or have indicated no significant correlation for preschool and school-aged children (Hartup, 1970). The verbal and physical aggression displayed by nonpopular or rejected children tends to be immature, indirect, unprovoked, or disruptive compared to the more socially acceptable forms of aggression displayed by popular children (Campbell & Yarrow, 1961; Dunnington, 1957; Lesser, 1959; Winder & Rau, 1962). In one dramatic example, a strong negative correlation (-0.69) was found between popularity and indirect aggressiveness in grade-school boys, whereas a positive correlation (0.31) was found between popularity and provoked physical aggression (Lesser, 1959). This finding illustrates the importance of contextual factors in the determination of both the appropriateness and the social consequences of a given behavior, such as an aggressive or a submissive act. These contextual factors have been too little considered in the correlational research on social behaviors and in much of the training research to be discussed.

It should be noted that sociometric ratings often provide measures of a comparative nature within a fixed group. Peer acceptance is typically gauged by such questions as "Which three of your classmates do you like best?" Regardless of whether most of the children in the class are socially skilled or socially unskilled, approximately the same small number will be rated high on such a measure of peer acceptance. Individual social-training procedures have led to improvements in the social functioning not only of the target children but also of others in the class (e.g., Cooke & Apolloni, 1976; Strain, Shores, & Kerr, 1976). In such cases of overall changes within a group, comparative measures of individual social status might not be expected to reflect the full extent of improvements made by individual children. Measures are needed to evaluate the *absolute* quality of peer interaction for individual children or for the group as a whole.

Peer popularity has been overemphasized at the expense of other potential measures of social effectiveness. Two examples of very different areas of social functioning that might profitably be studied in this regard are "instrumental competence" (socially responsible, independent, nonsubmissive, and purposive behaviors) and "expressive competence" (behaviors related to the expression of feelings, spontaneity, and social intimacy) (Baumrind, 1972). Value judgments with regard to goals will have to be made by professionals, children, and parents. However, as a prerequisite, research is clearly needed to assess the potential effects of social-skills training or other measures of social functioning in addition to peer popularity.

In the vast majority of the studies cited above, only peer acceptance was measured. Peer rejection has received far less attention, both empirically and theoretically. Yet, active rejection by peers would seem to constitute a serious problem for the child, whereas being very popular (highly accepted) is certainly not a prerequisite for social adjustment in every child. Peer rejection is presumably more closely related to the peer-interaction difficulties found to be predictive of later adjustment problems. Thus, knowing the correlates of peer rejection may be more important than knowing the correlates of peer acceptance—both for developing strategies to help prevent peer rejection and for developing training programs to help individual children who are rejected by peers. Peer acceptance and rejection are not simple opposites on a bipolar dimension. When both measures are taken, the negative correlation between them is only moderate, and in some cases, no significant correlation is found (Hartup, 1970). Also, each of these measures has a different set of correlates. For example, if Hartup and his colleagues (1967) had used only peer acceptance as a measure of social status, their conclusion would have been that a child's rate of aversive behaviors toward peers is unrelated to social status. By taking the unusual step of including a peer-rejection measure of social status, they found that aversive behaviors are indeed related to peer rejection. There is need for increased use of peer-rejection measures.

Causal inferences about the relationships between social behaviors and social status must be limited, since the available research is almost exclusively correlational. As Moore (1967) has stated, "It is just as reasonable to hypothesize that being well-liked inspires a child to perform friendly behaviors as it is to hypothesize that performing these behaviors causes the child to be well-liked" (p. 236). Hartup (1970) has pointed out that the direction of causality is probably reciprocal. However, the application of more efficient research techniques, including experimental manipulation of social skills, is needed to clarify the causal nature of the relationship between various skills and peer acceptance. Furthermore, all of the studies cited were based on children of essentially normal social adjustment. Comparable studies of correlates of social status based on children referred to clinical settings or on other children with serious behavior problems are lacking.

2.2. Peer Reinforcement and Reciprocity

The study by Hartup et al. (1967) may help to provide an explanation for the findings on correlates of social status. These invesitgators conceptualized preschool-aged children as direct agents of both positive and negative reinforcement for peers. Observed peer behaviors that were categorized as "generalized positive reinforcers" included approving or positively attending; giving affection, help, or tangible objects; and submitting or acquiescing. "Generalized negative reinforcers" included noncompliance with peers; uncooperative or disruptive behaviors; verbal insults or attacks; and physical aggression. It was found that peer acceptance (the number of positive sociometric choices received from peers) was postively correlated with the frequency of giving positive reinforcement to peers, a finding that partially replicated an earlier study (Marshall and McCandless, 1957). In addition, in two of the three replications, peer rejection (number of negative choices received) was significantly correlated with the frequency of giving negative reinforcement. These findings indicate that reinforcement principles operating within the peer group, independent of adult intervention, may go a long way in explaining the findings on behavioral correlates of social status. Interaction that is reinforcing to peers may play an important role in the emergence of interpersonal attraction in children.

Findings on *reciprocity* in peer interactions further support this learning-theory interpretation. Preschool and grade-school children who give high levels of positive reinforcement to peers not only are more highly accepted but also receive higher levels of reinforcement from peers (Charlesworth & Hartup, 1967; Fagot & Patterson, 1969; Gottman et al., 1975). As would also be expected from learning theory, children are more likely to continue in a given activity when peer reinforcement is received (Charlesworth & Hartup, 1967). Kohn (1966) found that the rate of positive social initiations by kindergarten children was positively correlated with positive initiations received.

The studies taken together suggest a potential positive cycle of increased prosocial peer interaction, development of social skills, and increased peer acceptance. Since many of the findings involve preschool-aged children, the importance of the early development of positive social behaviors with peers becomes obvious. Evidence as to whether reciprocity is involved in the use of *negative* social reinforcement between peers would provide valuable information about a potential negative cycle of increased aversive peer interaction, development of negative behaviors, and peer rejection. Such evidence has not yet been reported.

2.3. Specific Social Skills and Discriminant Validity

In order to provide information of greater value for planning training strategies, researchers need to focus on specific trainable skills. The finding that a popular child tends to engage in a high frequency of positively reinforcing social interactions provides little information regarding the specific skills that facilitate these positive interactions.

In an important recent study, Gottman, Gonso, and Rasmussen (1975) have advanced the previous research on peer reciprocity. In addition to using social-status and peer-reinforcement measures, they independently assessed a variety of specific social skills displayed by grade-school children in performing six selected tasks. The skills for each task were assessed in terms of specific behavioral categories. For example, assessed skills in the "making friends" task included greeting, asking for information, extending inclusion, and giving information. Using behavioral measures derived from naturalistic classroom observations, Gottman and his colleagues replicated the finding that popular children dispense and receive more positive reinforcement than unpopular children. In addition, they found that the popular children demonstrated higher levels of specific social skills on two of the six selected tasks: the "making-friends" task and the "referential-communication" task, involving communicating meaning to a listener by giving clues in a word game. Popularity had previously been found to be related to other communication skills (Rubin, 1972; Rubin, 1973, as statistically reanalyzed by Gottman *et al.*, 1975).

Gottman and his colleagues (1975) found that other "social-skills" tasks chosen *a priori* as potential correlates of social status were not necessarily so related, even when performance differences across age were as predicted. They concluded that it is improper to label performance on a task as a "social skill" simply because it seems logical or because older children do better than younger children on that task. They wrote, "It may be necessary to validate the task by showing that performance on the task has discriminant validity with reference to a criterion [of successful social interaction] such as sociometric status." (p. 717). Gottman and his colleagues have suggested that failure to seek empirical support in choosing the skills to be trained may be partially responsible for the ineffectiveness of interventions that have used sociometric status as the dependent measure. Reviews indicate that such interventions with isolate children have generally resulted in small gains and a return-to-baseline effect (Asher, Oden, & Gottman, 1977; Bonney, 1971).

Research has so far been limited primarily to global correlates of social status. What is needed is empirical validation of *specific* social skills as correlates not only of social status but also of other qualitative and diversified measures of social effectiveness. In addition, the causal relationships between social skills and criterion measures, which are suggested by correlational findings, need to be clarified through the wider use of manipulative experimental designs. Only with such experimental validation can practitioners design specific social-skills training programs that are based on more than clinical intuitions.

In summary, peer acceptance is related to a variety of measures of friendliness, outgoingness, social responsiveness, generosity, and social participation. Highly accepted children give and receive more positive social reinforcement in peer interaction than less accepted children and may have greater command of certain specific social skills. Peer rejection (studied to a far lesser extent than peer acceptance) is related to the giving and receiving of negative social reinforcement in terms of peer interaction, aversive behavior, and verbal and physical aggression. Reciprocity has been experimentally demonstrated in children's positive social interactions but has not yet been assessed for negative social interactions.

3. Training Through Contingent Reinforcement

Research on the application of operant-conditioning principles to the shaping children's social behaviors has tended to focus on the young child. In the early research, contingent attention from adults was used as the primary source of reinforcement, but recently peer influences have become evident in operant-training procedures. Many studies have set as their goal an increase in the amount of social interaction engaged in by children who are considered social isolates.

One of the first applications of the shaping and reversal procedures generally used in these studies resulted in the rapid elimination of excessive crawling behavior in a 3-year-old (Harris, Johnston, Kelley, & Wolf, 1964). The procedure involved contingent teacher attention to the child for successive approximations of on-feet behavior and nonattention for crawling. The child's social interaction was found to increase sharply and to become more diversified as she spent more time on her feet. This study provides dramatic evidence of the close relationship between contingent teacher attention and both appropriate and inappropriate behavior. Prior to training, the girl was observed to receive more attention when crawling than when on her feet. Thus, the training procedure involved not simply adding attentional contingencies to the crawling behavior but rather *switching* the adult attention from inappropriate to appropriate behaviors.

The necessity of switching previously misapplied contingencies is frequently overlooked in programs designed to shape social behaviors. Adults typically show an unfortunate tendency to attend to children's inappropriate or disruptive social behaviors by scolding, reasoning, or simply reacting. On the other hand, adults typically pay little attention to appropriate social behaviors since these behaviors do not seem to require a reaction. Experts giving advice often completely disregard the enormous reinforcing potential of adult attention in almost any form, and they may inadvertently encourage parents, teachers, and therapists to give attention to inappropriate social behavior. Such advice includes:

1. Repeat or "reflect" a child's aggressive phrases (Axline, 1969).
2. Use "active listening" with the child at crisis times (e.g., "parent effectiveness training," Gordon, 1970).
3. Encourage an isolate child to play with peers.
4. "Distract" or "redirect" a child engaged in socially disruptive behavior.
5. Provide a physically aggressive child with "an alternative target" for her (his) aggression.
6. Reason with a misbehaving child about the social consequences of misbehavior.

Potential benefits of some of these practices have been empirically demonstrated, as in the case of the use of reasoning in discipline (Hoffman, 1970). On the other hand, providing alternative targets for aggression or "reflecting" aggressive phrases are examples of common practices clearly *contraindicated* by research evidence (Berkowitz, 1973; R. Slaby & Crowley, 1977). The timing of adult intervention—that is, whether it is contingent on appropriate or on *inappropriate* behaviors—is a critical and often overlooked determinant of the behavioral consequences of any intervention. For example, Hoffman (1970) has drawn together convincing evidence that the use of reasoning in discipline is beneficial in fostering mature moral development, yet he failed to note that reasoning consistently following social *misbehavior* is more likely to reinforce than to discourage it. The importance of the research discussed in this section is highlighted by the frequent misuse of adult attention to inadvertently reinforce the inappropriate social behavior of children.

3.1. Adult Contingencies

In two early operant-training studies of social interaction, it was found that two preschool children who spent little time in interaction with peers attracted or maintained adult attention when engaged in isolate play (Allen, Hart, Buell, Harris, & Wolf, 1964; Johnston, Kelley, Harris, Wolf, & Baer, 1964). Teachers initially shaped approximations to peer contact by attending when the children merely approached and watched peers play and later attended only to actual peer interaction. This contingent-reinforcement procedure resulted in a marked decline in isolate play, and a two- to threefold increase in social play. During the reversal phase, teacher attention to solitary play resulted in a rapid return to baseline levels of isolate play. Reinstatement of the experimental treatment again resulted in increased peer interaction. As peer interaction was experimentally increased, one target child stopped directing inappropriate vocalizations and complaints to adults (Allen *et al.*, 1964), illustrating the point that increasing positive social behaviors may indirectly reduce negative behaviors. Follow-up observation at the same facility, made 26 days after the completion of one study (Allen *et al.*, 1964) and during the following school year for the other study (Johnston *et al.*, 1964), indicated that the target children's social play continued in roughly the same high proportions achieved during treatment. However, the almost immediate return to baseline levels of social interaction during the reversal phases in both studies would seem to indicate that the behaviors shaped in treatment were dependent to a great extent on the continuation of the adult-controlled contingencies. Studies in this area have generally been characterized by a lack of adequate follow-up evaluation or by poor follow-up results. For example, in a study comparing the effects of modeling and reinforcement procedures, O'Connor (1972) substantially increased social interaction in isolate children through reinforcement procedures alone but found that the social behaviors returned to baseline levels in follow-up observations just three weeks after treatment (O'Connor, 1972).

Rather than shaping overall amounts of peer interaction, Hart, Reynolds, Baer, Brawley, and Harris (1968) shaped cooperative peer interaction in a 5-year-old girl initially low in cooperative behaviors. In addition, they compared the effects of contingent and noncontingent social reinforcement from adults. Cooperative play was defined as an activity engaged in with another child, such as pulling or being pulled in a wagon, working on a joint project, or sharing. Teachers prompted other children to initiate cooperative interaction with the target child. The girl herself was reinforced initially for verbalizations when in the proximity of peers, then for participation in potentially cooperative situations, and finally only for actual cooperative play. Contingent reinforcement resulted in reliable increases in cooperative play. On the other hand, randomly delivered noncontingent reinforcement failed to have an effect, whether presented intermittently or continuously. Thus, a smaller amount of contingent reinforcement was more effective than an abundant (continuous) amount of noncontingent reinforcement. The investigators noted that this finding is in contradiction to the popular assumption that children display inappropriate social behaviors as a result of too little overall positive attention from adults. Again, the shaped behaviors remained highly dependent on the immediate adult contingencies, changing rapidly as periods of contingent and noncontingent reinforcement were experimentally alternated.

Pinkston, Reese, LeBlanc, and Baer (1973) reduced the amount of physical aggression displayed by a highly aggressive preschool boy by instructing teachers to ignore his aggressive behavior while attending instead to the victim of his aggression. Teachers focused exclusively on reducing aggression at first and only subsequently used contingent attention to increase his nonaggressive social interaction. Although these investigators chose to accomplish the two training goals in sequence, others have found it effective to apply contingencies simultaneously to alternative behaviors. For example, instructions have been given both to ignore aggression and to reinforce nonaggressive interaction (e.g., Brown & Elliot, 1965). "Time-out" (i.e., brief isolation) procedures have also been used successfully to control aggressive behaviors while cooperative behaviors were simultaneously shaped (e.g., Allen, Benning, & Drummond, 1972). Applying behavioral intervention strategies simultaneously for aggressive and cooperative behaviors may well provide added efficiency, to the extent that these two types of behavior are incompatible. It would be of interest to compare empirically either simultaneous or sequential intervention for aggression and cooperation—or for other pairs of related social behaviors.

3.2. Peer Influences

Early operant-training studies, such as those described above, used contingent social reinforcement directly from adults to shape behavior for individual target children. However, research has clearly demonstrated the important role of social reinforcement between peers themselves (e.g., Hartup et al., 1967; Charlesworth & Hartup, 1967). Peer reinforcement influences almost certainly operate, to some extent, both in the presence and in the absence of additional adult influences. Adults are frequently completely absent from child activities, such as free play or games, which would appear to be particularly important for the development of independent peer-interaction skills. If behaviors shaped by adults are not supported by peer reinforcement in the natural setting, there is reason to believe that they will not be maintained. More recent operant-training research on social skills involves peers in intervention strategies and examines the effects of intervention on nontarget children as well as on target children (e.g., Kirby & Toler, 1970; Strain, Shores, & Kerr, 1976; Strain & Timm, 1974).

Kirby and Toler (1970) increased the rate of peer interaction of a socially isolated 5-year-old boy by inducing the child to give material positive reinforcement to his peers. The target child asked classmates individually for their candy choice (thus interacting verbally) and then gave them the candy of their choice (thus interacting physically). After giving out all the candy, he himself was reinforced with teacher praise, five cents, and candy. Observations during a 60-minute free-play period immediately following the distribution of the candy indicated that the child was spending well over 50% of the time with other children, compared to 13% during baseline observations prior to treatment. Both the child's cooperative play and his proximity to peers increased, and the amount of time spent with adults decreased in each successive treatment period. In the reversal period, there was a drop in time spent with peers to 31%, but this is not as sharp a drop as has generally been found in studies that utilize adult contingencies alone. Unfortunately, follow-up results were not reported.

Kirby and Toler's interpretation is that treatment effects may be due to either instructions to pass out the candy, teacher reinforcement for doing so, or the target child's acquisition of reinforcing properties "by virtue of being paired with primary reinforcement" (p. 309). Surprisingly, they failed to note the possibility of reciprocal positive peer influences. Peers may well have acted differently toward the target child (in ways that encouraged social interaction) because of the positive *social* reinforcement involved in being asked for their candy preferences, receiving something from the target child, and interacting at least briefly with him. To answer these important questions, investigators might monitor changes in the social behavior not only of the child who dispenses reinforcement but also of the peers who receive it. Within this context, sequential analysis of mutual social behaviors between peers may be particularly useful. As is discussed later, several investigators have expanded this general line of research to include teaching children to give peers social reinforcers, such as smiles or compliments, and teaching children to give reinforcement to peers contingent on particular behaviors displayed by those peers (e.g., Crowder, 1975; Wahler, 1967).

A disturbing finding of the Kirby and Toler study is that the overall increase in social interaction in the target child was accompanied by a major increase in the amount of aggression he displayed, to a level that "might have been considered a problem by many people" (p. 313). The authors speculated that "hopefully, less aggressive modes of interaction would develop as a result of continued social experience" (p. 313). This comment reflects a common belief in the beneficial effects of increased social interaction or experience *per se*—a belief that is not empirically supported in the area of aggression. As described in the introduction of this chapter, the findings of Patterson and his colleagues (1967) dramatically demonstrated that once aggression occurs in the young child, the most likely result of "social experience" is increased aggression due to peer reinforcement of aggression. It is not sufficient to depend on qualitative changes in behavior to develop as by-products of quantitative increases in peer interaction.

Strain and Timm (1974) investigated the effects of contingent adult social reinforcement on social interaction between a preschool girl, described as both isolate and "hyperactive," and her peers. Both initiated and respondent positive behaviors were reinforced with adult praise and physical contact. The two experimental conditions, used in a reversal design, were (1) reinforcement given to the target child alone for appropriate interaction with peers; and (2) reinforcement given to the peers alone for appropriate interaction with the target child. Both conditions resulted in increased positive social behaviors by *both* the target child and her peers. The unusual procedure of assessing continuous sequences of initiator–responder units of behavior between children enabled the investigators to conclude that changes in the behavior emitted by the recipient of adult reinforcement were accompanied by concomitant changes in the behavior of other children not directly reinforced. Strain and Timm attempted to explain these results by suggesting a "spillover effect" of adult social reinforcement to those children not directly targeted. In their words, "Adult proximity as well as non-verbal events such as smiles may have inadvertently affected the [nonreinforced] partner's response rate" (p. 589).

This narrow operant-learning interpretation disregards other theoretically important explanations for this key finding. For example, *changes in direct peer behaviors* could explain the increased positive social interaction in the non-adult-reinforced partners. Since the adult-reinforced children initiated significantly more positive interactions during treatment than previously, this changed peer behavior itself would be expected to produce more positive respondent behavior from partners (Charlesworth & Hartup, 1967; Gottman *et al.*, 1975). Furthermore, simply observing increased positive social behaviors in peers might be expected to affect the observer's behavior through *observational learning* (Bandura, 1968). A related interpretation is that the adult's praise and attention for positive social behaviors increased the likelihood of occurrence of those behaviors by providing *informational cues* to the other children indicating which behaviors were valued and likely to be reinforced. The information-cue value of reinforcement deserves broader consideration in the area of social development (e.g., Bandura, 1973).

In a more recent attempt to investigate what they had called "spillover" effects, Strain, Shores, and Kerr (1976) examined the effects on social interaction of teacher prompts in conjunction with contingent social reinforcement. Three preschool boys who gave low rates of social reinforcement to peers were selected to serve as target children. Either one or two boys at a time received verbal and physical "prompts" by teachers to approach or interact with peers, as well as adult social reinforcement contingent on appropriate social behaviors. Reliable increases in the positive social behaviors of the target children, as well as decreases in negative social behaviors, were obtained during intervention periods. The target child who displayed the most isolate play prior to treatment showed the least increase in positive social behavior, perhaps because of this child's greater susceptibility to a factor apparently overlooked by the investigators: the teacher prompts, which were administered when a child was *not* interacting with peers, may have partially counteracted the treatment effect by serving to reinforce isolate play. The positive spillover effect of intervention on nontargeted peers was replicated from the earlier study. This effect was found to be greater during periods when intervention was simultaneously directed at two, rather than at one, of the target children. Again the relative instability of the treatment effect was suggested by the fact that behaviors changed rapidly with changed adult contingencies. The investigators suggested that individual differences in behavior repertoires or histories may help to identify those children who require direct intervention and those who can benefit most from the indirect (spillover) effects of intervention aimed primarily at others.

3.3. Individual versus Group Application of Contingencies

Applying reinforcement contingencies to either one or several target children, while deliberately avoiding direct intervention with others, is a valuable strategy for the investigation of certain research issues, such as spillover effects. However, the findings of Strain and his associates raise the question of whether exclusive targeting within a group setting is the most valuable clinical or education practice. Both the finding that spillover effects were greater when two children, rather than one, were targeted (Strain et al., 1976) and the finding that a problem child benefited from contingencies applied to her peers (Strain & Timm, 1974) would seem to indicate the benefits of a broader application of social contingencies.

In the introduction to this chapter, we emphasized the importance of fostering prosocial skills in all children for their own sake and to ensure naturalistic peer support for "deficient" children. There may be specifiable advantages to the application of positive behavioral methods to an entire group, especially in light of the lack of demonstrated stability of the effects of contingencies applied solely to individual children. These possible advantages include (1) greater consistency in the application of reinforcement across children and across situations and (2) increased opportunities for positive peer influences, modeling, and cueing effects. In addition, situations might be designed to take advantage of the fact that children behave more cooperatively after operating within a group orientation and after working together toward a superordinate goal (e.g., Bryan, 1975; Kagan & Madsen, 1971; Sherif & Sherif, 1964; Stendler, Damrin, & Haines, 1951). Children also tend to like each other better after working together to achieve a common goal (Heber & Heber, 1957). The resulting increase in cooperation or friendliness could be further enhanced by the use of group-reinforcement contingencies. Children rewarded for achieving group goals, in both laboratory and naturalistic settings, have consistently been observed to be friendlier, more cooperative, and less antagonistic toward each other, whereas children who compete for individual rewards may become less generous and less cooperative (Bryan, 1975; Nelson & Madsen, 1969).

The authors of this chapter have found it to be clinically effective to treat preschool children with diverse behavior problems by applying reinforcement contingencies with consistency to the entire day treatment group (D. Slaby, 1976). Several investigators have achieved impressive training effects by applying behavioral contingencies to an entire group. Brown and Elliot (1965) effected a highly significant decrease in the aggressive behavior of preschool boys by instructing teachers to ignore aggression and simultaneously to praise or attend to any cooperative behaviors in all 27 boys in the class. Teachers were asked to let the most aggressive boys see that others received attention for cooperation. Interestingly, the authors noted that the initially skeptical teachers were very impressed with "the effect upon two very aggressive boys, both of whom became friendly and cooperative to a degree not thought possible" (p. 107). R. Slaby and Crowley (1977) effectively shaped overall classroom levels of both verbal and physical cooperative behaviors by instructing teachers to attend to as many instances of verbal cooperation as possible as they occurred in a normal preschool class. Treatment was effective despite the fact that the teachers were able to attend to an average of only 14% of the total instances of verbal cooperation that occurred in the busy classroom. This result indicates that broadly applied reinforcement on a partial schedule can be sufficient for effective training.

Important research questions for the future involve the relative effectiveness of operant intervention strategies that are either directed exclusively at target children or applied to an entire group. Of interest would be the specific effects of each of these approaches on particular problem children, on other children, and on the functioning of the group as a whole.

3.4. Concluding Comments on Contingent Reinforcement

This area of training research has certainly demonstrated the influence of contingent adult reinforcement—at least, while it is being administered—on children's social interaction. Unfortunately, the stability of behavior changes obtained through these means alone has not been demonstrated. Perhaps treatment lasting longer than the usual very brief intervention period would be more likely to produce stable effects. It has been reported on the basis of case studies that the gradual fading of reinforcement may result in longer-lasting effects (Baer & Wolf, 1972), but this widely held view needs to be tested more rigorously in the area of peer interaction.

The direct effects of adult-administered contingencies have been heavily stressed, perhaps as a carry-over from early operant-training studies of children's less complex behaviors. One result of this emphasis on adult reinforcement is that the social reinforcement effect of peers has often been overlooked—even when the experimental results themselves seem conducive to such an explanation (e.g., Kirby & Toler, 1970; Strain & Timm, 1974). Researchers would do well to give greater consideration to the influence of peers, both as a possible additional factor in adult contingency studies and as a potential primary source of planned behavior change. O'Connor (1972) has suggested that as an alternative to adult social reinforcement, future research might focus on a means of reinforcement delivery that would occur more naturally from within the context of the performance of the behavior. Peer delivery of social reinforcement would appear to be a logical choice.

Reliance on adult contingencies has disadvantages. The adult who inadvertently increases a child's dependence on adults by providing too much attention in peer-group settings may do a disservice to the child. Children who spend a great deal of time interacting with adults tend to be less popular with peers, and, in addition, emotional dependence on adults may interfere with the normal age-developmental shift to more peer interaction and less adult interaction (e.g., Maccoby & Masters, 1970; Moore & Updegraff, 1964). Isolate children may be particularly susceptible to this danger of excessive dependency on adults. O'Connor (1972) has suggested that in attempting to reinforce peer interaction, an adult may actually interfere with and disrupt that interaction. Supporting this contention, in one study, the amount of peer interaction unexpectedly increased in the postexperimental period after adult praise for social interaction had been withdrawn (Evers & Schwarz, 1973). Roedell and her associates (1977) have pointed out that it requires some finesse for adults to provide positive reinforcement without turning children's interactions into several separate child–adult interactions. They suggest that a teacher might smile or make a brief comment directed at an entire cooperative group and then move on, avoiding prolonged interaction. Alternatively, the teacher might bring additional materials to the group, thus encouraging group cooperation and potentially prolonging the play by adding new resources.

Operant methods rely on the occurrence of the desired behavior, or approximations to it, which can then be reinforced and gradually shaped. This approach, if relied on exclusively, may be excessively time-consuming or even completely unfeasible with certain children who show extremes of isolated, aggressive, or disruptive behaviors. In general, the exclusive use of operant techniques is most successful in shaping simple behaviors, such as "on-feet" behavior (Harris et al., 1964), or broadly defined classes of existing behavior, such as amount of general cooperative interaction (e.g., Allen et al., 1964; Hart et al., 1968). Operant shaping used alone is not well suited to the teaching of specific, complex, or completely new social skills, such as particular verbal means of initiating interaction or solving social conflicts. Bandura (1965) has facetiously illustrated the inadequacy of operant shaping for teaching someone to drive a car. Similarly, teaching complex new social skills would also seem to require the inclusion of modeling, cueing, direct guided practice, or other methods that rely on cognitive mediation. The demonstrated influence of operant principles in the social area can be used potentially in conjunction with these other approaches to increase the power and efficiency of the training methods. This area of research should also make all those who work with children aware of the reinforcing potential of adult attention and the possible inadvertent misapplication of this powerful source of reinforcement.

4. Training through Observational Learning

It has been amply demonstrated that children can acquire new behaviors by observation alone and that modeling procedures can be effectively used to eliminate various patterns of avoidance behavior (Bandura, 1969; Bandura & Menlove, 1968; Poulos & Davidson, 1971). O'Connor (1969) hypothesized that modeling procedures could be used to teach new social behaviors and to extinguish social fears in children.

4.1. Modeling Films

O'Connor (1969) selected a group of preschool children who had exhibited long-standing social withdrawal according to the teacher's report and who also displayed isolate behaviors in the classroom as assessed by behavioral observations. Half of these isolate children were shown a 23-minute film in which an initially withdrawn child engaged in increasingly complex social interaction in a preschool setting. Participation in peer activities was followed by reinforcing consequences for the child model in the film. The other half of the group of isolate children were shown a neutral control film unrelated to peer interaction. Behavioral observations in the classroom immediately following the film viewing indicated that those children who had viewed the experimental modeling film showed a dramatic increase in the frequency and quality of their social interactions. Only one of the six children in this group continued to be rated as socially withdrawn by the teachers. On the other hand, the children who had viewed the control film remained withdrawn and isolated from their peers.

In a more recent study, O'Connor (1972) examined the contribution of shaping procedures used in conjunction with the symbolic modeling procedure of the earlier study. The isolate preschool children viewed either the modeling or the control film. Subsequently, half of the children in each film condition also received social reinforcement in the classroom contingent on social orienting and social interaction with peers. Thus, the four conditons consisted of: modeling only; shaping only; both modeling and shaping; and neither type of intervention (control). O'Connor replicated his earlier finding of increased social interaction for the modeling-only group. He also demonstrated a treatment effect of approximately equal magnitude for the shaping-only intervention. The combined procedures were no more effective at increasing social interaction than either alone. This same result was also obtained by Evers and Schwarz (1973) in a similarly designed study using the same modeling film. Unlike O'Connor, these investigators used a reinforcing agent who was familiar to the children and consequently might have been expected to be more effective.

An important finding of O'Connor's (1972) study was that the high levels of peer interaction achieved in both of the conditions that involved modeling were maintained in follow-up assessments at approximately three and six weeks after treatment. In contrast, the effects of shaping alone were not evident in follow-up assessments, indicating that the symbolic modeling procedure produced more stable changes than did the shaping procedure. By way of explanation, O'Connor suggested that those isolated children who viewed the modeling film may have been exposed to *new* social behaviors that increased their social repertoires. In addition, since the modeled interactions depicted graduated levels of potential threat, a facilitating gradual reduction in anxiety may have occurred in the viewers. The positive consequences that followed appropriate social behavior in the modeling film may also have facilitated performance of the modeled behavior. In contrast, the shaping procedure used in O'Connor's study did not include the presentation of novel responses or possibilities for desensitization to social fears.

Keller and Carlson (1974) assessed the training effects of videotapes depicting selected behavioral components of social interaction. Isolate children were selected on the basis of low frequencies of (1) overall peer interaction; (2) giving positive reinforcement to peers; and

(3) receiving positive reinforcement from peers. Children in the modeling condition viewed a different video-taped sequence on each of four consecutive days. Each tape depicted children engaged in preschool activities and emphasized one of the following socially reinforcing behaviors: imitating; smiling and laughing; token giving; or affectionately touching other children. Children in the modeling condition, in contrast to those in the control group (who viewed nature films), showed a significant increase in all three criterion measures of social behavior in the classroom immediately following intervention and also three weeks later in follow-up observation. Only those specific behaviors that had been highest in the children's pretreatment hierarchy of social skills increased in frequency. There were no increases in those behaviors that initially had occurred only very infrequently. Keller and Carlson concluded that in this case, the symbolic modeling procedure raised the probability of occurrence of previously learned social responses—perhaps by orienting the children's attention to possible sources of reinforcement in the natural enviroment—but did not result in the transmission of novel social behaviors. This conclusion suggests that although there are indications that modeling may be more effective than shaping alone in transmitting lasting new social behaviors (e.g., O'Connor, 1972), still more explicit or directive methods may be required to teach certain kinds of new social skills or to teach skills to children with serious deficiencies.

The demonstrated beneficial influence of even a single exposure to selected modeling films has far-reaching implications. Here is a form of "training" that might be applied effectively and at minimal cost for selected behavior problems, such as social withdrawal. The fact that Evers and Schwarz (1973) were able to replicate O'Connor's findings when they used the same modeling film suggests the possibility of developing effective materials for use on a large scale. Direct professional involvement is apparently not required. Modeling films might also be used more widely as an adjunct to other forms of intervention. Finally, these findings suggest that regular network or public television may have great potential influence as a means of fostering prosocial behaviors in millions of children. In contrast to this promising potential, the primary modeling influence of much of current television programming is to foster aggression in children (Liebert *et al.*, 1973).

4.2. Live Models

Cooke and Apolloni (1976) used other training techniques in combination with live modeling to teach social–emotional behaviors to a group of four grade-school children who had been diagnosed as "learning-disabled." Using a multiple-baseline design, they attempted to increase initially low levels of (1) smiling; (2) sharing; (3) positive physical contacting; and (4) verbal complimenting. One skill was trained in each session in a room outside of the classroom. After distributing an identical set of toys to each of the target children, the trainer talked briefly about the skill being trained at that session, modeled it for the children, prompted each child to try the behavior, and used contingent intermittent praise for prompted or spontaneous occurrences of the behavior. Behavioral observations were made during the training sessions and also during a "generalization" session immediately following training. During the generalization session, three untrained classmates were brought into the room, given the same set of toys, and left alone to play with the target children.

Procedures were effective in increasing each trained behavior, within the respective training sessions, for all target children. During the initial training session, when only smiling was being specifically trained, there was nevertheless an increase in sharing and positive physical contacting in two of the target children. The training in smiling alone also increased both the smiling and the positive physical contacting displayed by all target children during the following generalization session when the adult was absent. Training of the other three social behaviors was not as effective in that only one of the target children maintained increases during the generalization session. A particularly interesting result was that all of the *untrained* children increased their rates of smiling and sharing during the generalization sessions that followed the respective training sessions for those behaviors in the target children. Increases in positive physical contacting for the untrained children followed a pattern similar to the increases in this behavior in the target children. The achieved increases in social skills were maintained in a follow-up assessment four weeks later.

Thus, Cooke and Apolloni demonstrated that directly teaching particular social skills can have two kinds of desirable indirect effects: (1) increases in other positive social behaviors in the trained children; and (2) increases in positive social behaviors in other (untrained) children merely by virtue of contact with the trained children. The design of this study rules out Strain and Timm's (1974) explanation of spillover effects in terms of the proximity of nontarget children to the adult reinforcer. The increased positive social behaviors of the untrained children in this study appear to have occurred in direct response to the experimentally increased positive social behaviors of the trained children. This finding provides experimental support for the correlational findings on peer reciprocity. It is also interesting to note that training in smiling clearly had the most dramatic response-generalization effects, although comparisons are not completely valid since smiling was trained first. It may be that smiling was the skill most effectively trained through the use of this short-term training procedure because it is the simplest of the trained skills. Future research may focus on the long-range effectiveness of training in more complex social skills.

By providing live examples of prosocial behavior as part of the everyday classroom routine, Yarrow, Scott, and Waxler (1973) demonstrated the powerful modeling effect an adult can have in a natural setting. Adults demonstrated such behaviors as helping a kitten find its hidden food and showing concern about another's injury. The models described their own actions and used the word *help*. They also used pictures and props during the intervention period to portray situations in which individuals needed help. Adult models who had previously built a nurturant relationship with the children were more effective in producing an increase in helping behavior than those who had not. Follow-up treatment effects were evident several weeks after the experiment.

Thus, modeling has been demonstrated to be an effective technique for training social behaviors. In sharp contrast to the operant studies reported earlier, nearly all of the modeling studies we have reported have included follow-up evaluations. All of these follow-up evaluations have indicated stability of the treatment effects, at least for the relatively short follow-up intervals. This finding suggests that procedures that include modeling may be more effective in producing lasting training effects than operant procedures alone, a conclusion that is supported by studies that have made this direct comparison (O'Connor, 1972; Evers & Schwarz, 1973).

In both operant and modeling studies, there has been a heavy emphasis on increasing the frequency of peer interaction in social isolates or in other children who show low levels of social participation. This training goal can be empirically justified, to some extent, by research indicating that social isolates may have considerable adjustment problems and that social participation is correlated with peer acceptance. However, exclusive emphasis on the quantity of peer interaction has serious limitations. For example, if peer interaction alone is increased in a previously isolated child, without any attempt at the teaching of specific social skills, a conceivable peer reaction might be, "What a kid; he used to play by himself all the time and now he's always hanging around" (Oden & Asher, 1975, p. 2.). Much of the previous research has disregarded questions of which qualitative deficits may indicate a need for intervention and which specific qualitative social skills may be most beneficially trained. Those operant and modeling studies that have used measures other than total frequency of peer interaction have still tended to use globally defined categories of behavior, such as cooperative or socially reinforcing behaviors. In this chapter, we began with a definition of *social skill* that included specificity of behavior as well as a demonstrated benefit of a personal, mutual, or altruistic nature. By these criteria, such globally defined social behaviors would not strictly be considered "social skills."

5. Cognitive Mediation in Social-Skills Training

The operant and modeling studies reviewed have given very little systematic attention to the role of the verbal and cognitive system in children's responses to training. Nevertheless, several training programs have added some degree of verbal prompts, instructions, or descriptions to the basic shaping or modeling strategies (e.g., Cooke & Apolloni, 1976; Strain *et al.*, 1976; Yarrow *et al.*, 1973). In addition, the shaping methods themselves have provided verbal cues in addition to reinforcement, and the modeling films have provided narrative sound tracks describing the filmed action. However, as Oden, Asher, and Hymel pointed out, "The contributions of such verbal components . . . have not been systematically assessed in terms of children's social learning" (1976, p. 2).

In the remainder of this chapter, the discussion turns to training methods that rely more explicitly on verbal and cognitive processes and that involve the child more directly and actively in training. These methods include coaching, role playing, rehearsal, guided practice, information exchange and feedback, and teaching children to use behavior-management techniques themselves. These methods are sometimes used in combination with shaping and modeling procedures, and they are especially well suited to the training of novel, complex, and situation-specific skills. Essentially verbal social skills, such as assertiveness, are emphasized here.

5.1. Coaching

Oden and her associates (1976) described *coaching* as a training method that "relies heavily on the verbal transmission of cues, concepts, and rules" (p. 2). They have successfully coached third- and fourth-grade isolate children to become more popular. Isolate children were selected on the basis of a peer sociometric measure rather than on the more commonly used frequency-of-interaction measure. They were assigned to one of three conditions: coaching, peer pairing, or control. The *coaching* procedure consisted of six sessions in which the isolate children were first individually instructed in concepts of how to play with other children; then given an opportunity to practice, actually playing specially selected social games with a peer partner; and finally provided with feedback on their play behavior. Four concepts were selected for coaching because they correspond to behaviors that correlate with peer acceptance: (1) participating in play activities; (2) cooperating with peers by taking turns and sharing; (3) communicating with peers by talking; and (4) supporting peers by giving attention and help. The *peer-pairing* procedure involved playing the same social games with a peer partner but without the coaching and feedback periods. The *control* procedure involved playing solitary games without interacting with the peer partner. Only children in the coaching condition achieved a significant pre- to posttreatment increase (both from their "peer partners" and from nonpartners) in sociometric ratings that specifically assessed how much peers liked playing with them. However, differential treatment effects were not evident either in sociometric ratings concerning *working* with peers or in observational assessments of play behavior during the experimental sessions. Interestingly, follow-up sociometric ratings concerning play, made by a different group of peers approximately one year later, indicated that the coached children had made still further gains.

The work of Oden and her associates is of particular interest from a methodological point of view. Skills were selected for training based on their demonstrated correlation with the criterion measure of social status, and a long-term follow-up assessment was included one year after treatment. Specific *verbal* forms of interaction were coached, including asking questions, praising the partner, listening to the partner, and offering an alternative in case of disagreement. When prompts have been used in other research, they have typically been designed to encourage physical rather than specifically verbal forms of interaction (e.g., Strain *et al.*, 1976). The coaching procedure involved a combination of training procedures specifically designed to help children learn to evaluate the social consequences of their behavior. The specific components of the coaching procedure—didactic discussion, independent practice, and feedback—are found in other research to be discussed in this section.

5.2. Role-Playing and Active Problem-Solving

Coaching procedures that attempt to induce children by verbal means alone to perform prosocial behaviors of little immediate personal benefit may not be successful. Staub (1971) hypothesized that willingness to help others requires not only empathy with the needy other but also knowledge of the skills to help effectively. He designed a study to compare the effectiveness of "induction" and role playing in increasing young children's willingness to help others and to share. In the induction procedure, an adult described situations in which someone required help, asked children how help might be provided, and suggested further helpful acts. In the role-playing condition, pairs of children acted out situations in which one person needed help and another provided help, and they subsequently exchanged roles. An adult suggested further helping acts for children to perform after each child had run out of ideas. A control group of children enacted scenes unrelated to helping. Staub found that children who had role-played helping situations demonstrated significantly more helping and sharing behaviors both immediately after treatment and five to seven days later. Neither the control procedure *nor* induction had a significant effect on prosocial peer behaviors. An important component of the effective role-playing treatment was that children were actively involved both in deciding on particular ways to provide help and in acting out the solutions.

In a classic study (Chittenden, 1942), preschool children were encouraged to participate actively in discussions of alternative solutions to a variety of social-conflict situations. Although the children did not role-play the solutions themselves, an adult graphically demonstrated various aggressive and cooperative solutions and the respective consequences using a set of dolls. For example, one of the conflict situations involved two children who both wanted to play with the same wagon. In the aggressive solution, the two dolls fought, the wagon broke, and both were unhappy. The alternative cooperative solution involved demonstrating how both dolls could be satisfied by taking turns with the wagon. The children who observed such dramas and had a chance to discuss them became less aggressive and more cooperative in their preschool play. Follow-up treatment effects were evident as long as one month after training.

Representative of recent trends, a game format has been devised to teach children and preadolescents verbal and nonverbal components of basic social skills (Rathjen, Hiniker, & Rathjen, 1976). Goals of the game include demonstration of available behavioral alternatives and their social consequences, so as to allow evaluation by the children. Modeling, practice, and feedback are provided. Innovative features of the procedure include built-in peer feedback regarding the appropriateness of the skills for a particular social context (i.e., ethnic group, age level); and a hierarchy of social skills that range up to complex and primarily verbal skills such as expressing opinions, disclosing feelings, and handling criticism. Preliminary evaluation of the effectiveness of this procedure in improving observable social skills appears very promising.

Spivack and Shure (1974) have devised a 10-week program designed to help preschool children learn to generate and evaluate their own alternative solutions to interpersonal conflicts and to identify and interpret emotional cues from others. Social conflicts and emotional changes in characters are portrayed by means of scripts, stories, and role-played situations with puppets. Children are given the opportunity to practice problem solving by trying out their own solutions and receiving feedback. Children are also encouraged to label and discuss their own feelings and to identify emotions in others by using behaviors as a guide. Thus, skills related to social problem-solving and emotional responsiveness are fostered. Problem-solving skills have been found to be correlated with social adjustment (Spivack & Shure, 1974), and emotional responsiveness has been found to be correlated with peer acceptance (as discussed above).

Perhaps more than any other training program for young children, the program of Spivack and Shure (1974) encourages the child to generate independent, creative, and flexible problem-solving approaches and to evaluate them on the basis of the "potential consequences rather than the absolute merits of a particular solution to a problem" (p. 29). This approach is highly unusual in that it gives the child a great deal of credit and responsibility and it takes the child's own point of view as the main perspective from which to judge the value of a social skill. Spivack and Shure have reported that the longer children participated in the program, the fewer aggressive solutions they offered in the dramatized situations. They also reported that the children's behavioral adjustment, as rated by the teachers, improved as a result of their increasing ability to think through the consequences of their own actions. Although further empirical support is needed to evaluate the treatment effects, this program represents an important innovation in the area of social-skills training.

We have seen that role playing and fostering active involvement in solving interpersonal problems are effective techniques for training social skills in normal children. These methods also have special applications for children with particular behavior problems. For example, Ross, Ross, and Evans (1971) designed an elaborate procedure to treat a 6-year-old boy for extreme phobiclike avoidance of peer interaction. One purpose of the procedure was to build social skills, since the child's extreme social withdrawal was presumed to derive largely from a marked deficit in social functioning. The target child was initially reinforced for interaction with an adult male "model." He subsequently watched the model participate in a graduated series of social interactions with other children and with another adult. Finally, the model gradually involved the child in a variety of social situations through discussion, role playing, guided practice, and specific training. Pictures, stories, and movies were also used to provide symbolic modeling.

The treatment was found to be effective in increasing the child's social interactions and in reducing his specific avoidance behaviors in the classroom to levels approximately equal to those observed in socially competent control children. In generalization tests administered two months later, the child successfully initiated and effectively maintained social interactions with unfamiliar children whom he encountered in novel settings. An important component of the procedure used in this study was the child's gradual introduction into direct involvement. Initially, the model deliberately exhibited the fear and hesitancy characteristic of the child's problems. During early exchanges between the model and another adult, little attention was given to the target child; however, the child soon began to offer reassuring information to the model, similar to what he had heard the other adult suggest. This gradual, nondemanding approach apparently functioned as a desensitization procedure for social fear.

5.3. Teaching Children Assertiveness and Behavior-Management Skills

Increased interest in the value of assertiveness skills for adults (e.g., Goldsmith & McFall, 1975; Hersen & Eisler, 1976; Twentyman & McFall, 1975) has just begun to be reflected in the child research (Bornstein, Bellack, & Hersen, 1977; Maccoby & Jacklin, 1976). Assertiveness has not been generally recognized as a valuable social skill for children. In fact, in two notable studies (Charlesworth & Hartup, 1967; Hartup et al., 1967), "submission" has been categorized as one type of positive reinforcement between peers—a category that was found to have beneficial correlates for the child. This categorization ignores the fact that an important positive social skill is knowing when and how to say "no" and when to refuse to submit to the frequent inappropriate demands received from peers. In fact, it has been shown that submission to a peer's aggressive demands reinforces the aggressor and leads to increased aggressive attacks on the submissive child (Patterson et al., 1967). The social consequences of aggression have been shown to vary dramatically with the forms of aggression used and with such contextual factors as provocation. Similarly, submission or assertive nonsubmission might be expected to have different social consequences, depending on the form of the behaviors and the contextual factors. This is an important research question.

Children are faced daily with situations that call for assertive behavior, yet they typically receive very little guidance in learning appropriate responses. For example, few children know how to respond with verbal assertiveness when another child attacks, intrudes, or takes objects. Most react instead in ways that often have negative consequences for both themselves and for the aggressor—by fussing, running away, submitting, retaliating physically or verbally, or seeking an adult's assistance. Similarly, many children do not know how to ask peers appropriately for objects, for help, or for a chance to participate in activities. A lack of these skills in initiating peer interaction may lead the child to grab toys, barge in on peers, or withdraw. Assertiveness skills would serve the important function of aiding children in finding their *own* solutions to potentially difficult social problems. Yet, the very specific verbal skills of assertiveness, which even many adults lack, are unlikely to be acquired by children through everyday observation or through operant shaping procedures.

The use of behavioral rehearsal, coaching, modeling and feedback have been effective in teaching assertive behavior to college students (e.g., Twentyman & McFall, 1975). These same methods have been used successfully by Bornstein and his associates (1977) in the only reported study of explicit assertiveness training in children. The training occurred in the context of rehearsing—with two adult role-models—interpersonal encounters that required assertive responses. Target behaviors were sequentially trained in unassertive gradeschool children initially showing the following deficits: (1) poor eye-contact, (2) short speech duration, (3) inaudible responses; and (4) inability to make requests for new behaviors from others. Improvements occurred both on the target behaviors of eye contact, speech duration, voice level, and ability to make requests; and also on independent overall assertiveness ratings. The improvements were maintained in two- and four-week follow-up sessions. However, all assessments were made in role-playing situations with adults, and there was no test of generalization to peer interaction in the natural environment.

The authors have used a combination of methods to train specific verbal assertive skills in preschool children with behavior problems. Unlike most other training programs, *in vivo* practice is stressed. Teachers provide direct guidance by telling children exactly what they can say in a given situation as it actually occurs in the classroom. The teacher might intervene in a potentially explosive situation *before* aggression occurs and firmly offer suggestions of verbal alternatives such as, "You can ask for that." Peers are far more likely to cooperate, even with a previously rough or bossy child who approaches them in a friendly way and asks appropriately. Teachers can then praise the use of verbal statements, the peer cooperation that may follow, or the acceptance of a peer's "no" for an answer. Children are taught in the same way that it is all right to say "no" and how to do so, sometimes adding phrases such as, "You can have it when I'm done."

The teaching of these social skills is assisted by the use of active role-playing with a doll both in the target situations themselves and in structured practice sessions. The child and the teacher alternately use the doll to play the role of the child protagonist, the reacting peer, or the teacher, while the other responds directly to the doll in a reciprocal role. The consequences of typical inappropriate social behaviors and alternative appropriate behaviors are role-played and discussed. Examples of specific trained reactions to peer behaviors include: (1) saying, "No hitting" instead of hitting back; (2) holding onto a toy and saying, "I'm playing with this now," instead of letting a peer grab it away; (3) saying, "Please don't lean on me—I don't like that," instead of shoving; (4) telling a bossy peer, "No, I want to do it my way," instead of submitting; and (5) ignoring a peer's insults instead of reacting. Trained responses that involve the child's taking initiative include: (1) trading or asking peers for objects instead of grabbing; (2) asking peers for permission to interact instead of barging in on them; (3) asking for help in a "regular voice" instead of whining; and (4) making friendly suggestions instead of bossy demands. Children as young as three years of age have shown facility and enthusiasm in role-playing these situations, have verbally demonstrated an understanding of the depicted consequences, and have subsequently been observed to use the new skills with their peers (D. Slaby, 1976).

In responding to peers with effective assertiveness, children are likely to foster appropriate behaviors in peers. There has been a growing interest in explicitly training children to shape appropriate behaviors in their peers by teaching them the basic principles of behavior management. Children have been used as agents of behavior change in academic and social settings (Graubard, Rosenburg, & Miller, 1971; Johnson & Bailey, 1974). Wahler (1967), for example, found that preschool children could be taught, through direct instruction and role playing, to use contingent attention to decrease aggression in one boy and to increase cooperation in another. Similarly, Solomon and Wahler (1973) found that a sixth-grade child's disruptive behaviors decreased when classmates were trained to stop attending to these behaviors. Children who themselves exhibited behavior problems have been trained to act effectively as contingency managers for peers with equally severe behavior problems (Nelson, Worell, & Polsgrove, 1973).

The use of children as therapeutic agents for peers could increase the effectiveness of intervention strategies by extending treatment to settings that are out of the range of adult control. Similarly, children could be used as peer contingency-managers in areas where the strength of adult reinforcement is low. In addition to being used as agents of adult-initiated behavior change in peers, children have been taught the effective application of behavior-management procedures to problem behaviors of their own choosing. Crowder (1975) successfully taught elementary-school children to define and record behaviors and to apply behavior-management techniques to themselves, siblings, parents, and friends.

Children's demonstrated ability to understand and use behavioral methods suggests the potential benefits of further involving children in setting and implementing specific goals for change in their own social behavior. Children can provide a direct source of information for designing training programs maximally beneficial to themselves. They can gain a sense of accomplishment in this way, and the probability of success in training may be increased because children have a high stake in achieving the goals they have helped to set. Children may also be able to generalize their successful behaviors more readily if the methods and goals of the training program are made explicit to them. The authors have personally observed striking clinical benefits of such direct involvement of even very young children.

6. Summary and Concluding Comments

Little attention has been given in this country to deliberately fostering prosocial peer-interaction skills in children. Factors presented in this chapter that indicate the need for routine as well as specialized social skills training include:

1. Evidence that poor peer relationships are related to serious adjustment problems in later life.
2. Evidence suggesting that an initial deficit in social skills can lead to a cyclical pattern of increased levels of both peer rejection and inappropriate social behavior.
3. Societal factors that may currently be operating to foster a high degree of antisocial behavior.
4. The need for appropriate peer support for skills that may be trained individually in "deficient" children.

Our definition of *social skills* represented an attempt to take into account several different possible perspectives for assessing the value of a given skill. We have seen in the research reviewed that the personal perspective of the child herself (himself) has received little attention, compared with adult or peer-popularity sources of assessment. Recent work that has considered the child's perspective includes the cognitive social-skills training program of Spivack and Shure (1974), the teaching of assertiveness skills to children (D. Slaby, 1976), and the teaching of behavior-management skills to children (e.g., Crowder, 1975).

The definition delineated a social skill as a *specific* behavior, but most of the reviewed studies have involved quantitative measures of either peer interaction or some other relatively global category of behavior. We have noted, in particular, a need for research on highly specific verbal skills. The definition also included a demonstrated benefit to be derived from the use of social skills, and again the research has been weak in providing such empirical demonstration. Sociometric status has been used recently as a criterion measure for social-skills training. We have discussed the need to develop other diversified and individualized measures of social effectiveness for use as criterion measures. This review clearly indicates that such criterion measures should be used more widely for two important purposes: (1) selecting children to be trained; and (2) carrying out "discriminant-validity" research to determine which trainable social skills are *in fact* valuable with regard to the criterion.

Research has indicated the effectiveness of contingent adult attention in shaping general aspects of peer interaction, but the stability of these effects has not been demonstrated. The limitations of the exclusive use of operant techniques have been discussed, both in regard to teaching complex skills and in regard to the potential for adult interference in peer interaction. Film-modeling techniques have been shown to have dramatic effects on children's isolate behavior, and these effects appear to be more stable than effects produced by the exclusive use of operant techniques. In both operant-learning and modeling studies, investigators have shown that the training of particular children may have indirect beneficial influences on other children who may have observed the training process (e.g., Strain *et al.*, 1976) or who did *not* observe the training process but merely interacted with the trained children (Cooke & Apolloni, 1976). We have interpreted these findings as contributing to other evidence that children exert a substantial influence over each other's behavior in specific and often reciprocal ways.

The more cognitive or verbal approaches to social-skills training are new, but initial research indicates that they have promise for the effective and efficient training of specific skills. In addition to verbal "coaching" alone, actual practice (in the form of role playing or re-hearsal) and feedback appear to be important. Compared to operant or modeling techniques, these methods serve to involve the child more actively in thinking about, talking about, practicing, and examining the consequences of given social skills. This active and explicit in-volvement might be predicted to lead to greater understanding, in-ternalization, and generalization of learning effects. The practice situa-tions in which adults have provided direct training or guidance have all involved hypothetical or dramatized social interactions. A proce-dure that has not yet been experimentally tested, but that appears to have potential clinical value, consists of teaching specific skills within a group setting in the *actual* social situations in which they are required (D. Slaby, 1976). Cuing, practice, and the "natural" reinforce-ment of successful interaction would seem to be especially potent at times when something is actually at stake for the child. The use of cog-nitive training approaches does not rule out the concomitant use of contingent reinforcement or modeling influences. Some of the most impressive studies we have reviewed have combined all of these methods to achieve effective results.

A few brief methodological points may be noted. There is a clear need for follow-up evaluations, and at longer intervals than have gen-erally been reported. The interventions reported have all been rela-tively short-term, generally ranging from one session to several weeks of treatment. It may be that long-range stability in treatment effects will not be reliably demonstrated unless longer-lasting and perhaps more comprehensive interventions are designed and assessed. Some type of social validation of the importance and usefulness of trained skills should be included as part of the pre- and postassessment of in-tervention techniques (for example, Minkin, Braukmann, Minkin, Timbers, Timbers, Fixsen, Phillips, & Wolf, 1976). Sequential analysis of behavior may be particularly useful in the analyzing of reciprocal peer influences as they occur both with and without training interven-tion. A developmental approach has been lacking in the training re-search. The age-developmental level of the child would certainly be expected to be important in determining the appropriateness ess of particular social skills, as well as the relative effectiveness of various training approaches. Finally, training studies have focused almost ex-clusively on children who show low levels of social participation or high levels of aggression. Child clinicians and teachers are aware of a large number of children who do not fall into these two categories but who are nevertheless in special need of social-skills training—for ex-ample, children who are boistrous, immature, passive, or otherwise socially inept.

We need to define more accurately the social needs of individual children and to design programs to assist children with a wider variety of needs. Hopefully, in the future we will attempt not simply to increase interaction or popularity but also to help children learn particular skills involved in effective, rewarding interaction. We will not simply attempt to decrease aggressive acts, but also to teach children prosocial and assertive behaviors designed specifically to replace aggression as a means of meeting particular needs. Social-skills training, as viewed in this chapter, is not only a way to correct inappropriate behavior in problem children but also a potentially important way to improve the lives of all children.

Acknowledgment

The authors wish to thank Dr. Ronald G. Slaby for his valuable suggestions and editorial assistance in the preparation of this chapter.

References

Allen, K. E., Benning, P. M., & Drummond, T. Integration of normal and handicapped children in a behavior modification preschool: A case study. Paper presented at the Third Annual Conference on Behavior Analysis in Education, Lawrence, Kansas, May 1972.

Allen, K. E., Hart, B., Buell, J. S., Harris, F. R., & Wolf, M. M. Effects of social reinforcement on isolate behavior of a nursery school child. *Child Development,* 1964, *35,* 511–518.

Asher, S. R., Oden, S. L., & Gottman, J. M. Children's friendships in school settings. *In* L. G. Katz (Ed.), *Current topics in early childhood education,* Vol. 1. Norwood, N.J.: Ablex, 1977.

Axline, V. *Play therapy.* New York: Ballantine, 1969.

Baer, D. M., & Wolf, M. M. Recent examples of behavior modification in preschool settings. *In* C. Neuringer & J. L. Michael (Eds.), *Behavior modification in clinical psychology.* New York: Appleton-Century-Crofts, 1972.

Bandura, A. Vicarious processes: A case of no-trial learning. *In* L. Berkowitz (Ed.), *Advances in experimental social psychology,* Vol. 2. New York: Academic Press, 1965.

Bandura, A. Social learning theory of identificatory processes. *In* D. Goslin (Ed.), *Handbook of socialization theory and research.* New York: Rand McNally, 1969.

Bandura, A. *Aggression: A social learning analysis.* Englewood Cliffs, N.J.: Prentice-Hall, 1973.

Bandura, A., & Menlove, F. L. Factors determining vicarious extinction of avoidance behavior through symbolic modeling. *Journal of Personality and Social Psychology,* 1968, *8,* 99–108.

Baron, D. Personal–social characteristics and classroom social status: A sociometric study of 5th and 6th grade girls. *Sociometry,* 1951, *14,* 32–41.

Baumrind, D. Socialization and instrumental competence in young children. *In* W. W. Hartup (Ed.), *The young child: Reviews of research,* Vol. 2. Washington, D.C.: National Association for the Education of Young Children, 1972.

Becker, W. C. Consequences of different kinds of parental discipline. *In* L. W. Hoffmann & M. L. Hoffman (Eds.), *Review of child development research,* Vol. 1. New York: Russell Sage, 1964.

Berkowitz, L. Control of aggression. *In* B. M. Caldwell & H. N. Ricciuti (Eds.), *Review of child development research* Vol. 3. Chicago: The University of Chicago Press, 1973.

Bonney, M. E. Assessment of efforts to aid socially isolated elementary school pupils. *Journal of Educational Research,* 1971, *64,* 359–364.

Bonney, M. E., & Powell, J. Differences in social behavior between sociometrically high and sociometrically low children. *Journal of Educational Research,* 1953, *46,* 481–495.

Bornstein, M. R., Bellack, A. S., & Hersen, M. Social skills training for unassertive children: A multiple baseline analysis. *Journal of Applied Behavior Analysis,* 1977, in press.

Bronfrenbrenner, U. *Two worlds of childhood: U.S. and U.S.S.R.* New York: Russell Sage Foundation, 1970.

Brown, P., & Elliot, R. Control of aggression in a nursery school class. *Journal of Experimental Child Psychology,* 1965, *2,* 103–107.

Bryan, J. H. Children's cooperation and helping behavior. *In* M. Hetherington (Ed.), *Review of child development research,* Vol. 5. Chicago: University of Chicago Press, 1975.

Bryan, J. H., & London, P. Altruistic behavior by children. *Psychological Bulletin,* 1970, *73,* 200–211.

Campbell, J. D., & Yarrow, M. R. Perceptual and behavioral correlates of social effectiveness. *Sociometry,* 1961, *24,* 1–20.

Charlesworth, R., & Hartup, W. Positive social reinforcement in the nursery school peer group. *Child Development,* 1967, *38,* 993–1002.

Chittenden, G. E. An experimental study in measuring and modifying assertive behavior in young children. *Monographs of the Society for Research in Child Development,* 1942, *7.*

Clifford, E. Social visibility. *Child Development,* 1963, *34,* 799–808.

Cooke, T., & Apolloni, T. Developing positive social-emotional behaviors: A study of training and generalization effects. *Journal of Applied Behavior Analysis,* 1976, *9,* 65–78.

Cowen, E. L., Pederson, A., Babigan, H., Izzo, L. D., & Trost, M. A. Long-term follow-up of early detected vulnerable children. *Journal of Consulting and Clinical Psychology,* 1973, *41,* 438–446.

Crowder, J. Teaching elementary school children the application of principles and techniques of applied behavior analysis. Paper presented at the Ninth Annual Convention of Association for Advancement of Behavior Therapy, San Francisco, Calif., December 1975.

Davitz, J. R. The effects of previous training on postfrustration behavior. *Journal of Abnormal and Social Psychology,* 1952, *47,* 309–315.

Dunnington, M. J. Behavioral differences of sociometric status groups in a nursery school. *Child Development,* 1957, *28,* 103–111.

Evers, W., & Schwarz, J. Modifying social withdrawal in preschoolers: the effects of filmed modeling and teacher praise. *Journal of Abnormal Child Psychology,* 1973, *1,* 248–256.

Fagot, B., & Patterson, G. R. An *in vivo* analysis of reinforcing contingencies for sex-role behavior in the preschool child. *Developmental Psychology,* 1969, *1,* 593–567.

Goldsmith, J. G., & McFall, R. M. Development and evaluation of an interpersonal skill-training program for psychiatric inpatients. *Journal of Abnormal Psychology,* 1975, *84,* 51–58.

Gordon, T. *Parent effectiveness training.* New York: Peter H. Wyden, 1970.

Gottman, J., Gonso, J., & Rasmussen, B. Social interaction, social competence and friendship in children. *Child Development*, 1975, *46*, 709–718.

Graubard, P., Rosenberg, H., & Miller, M. B. Student applications of behavior modification to teachers and environments or ecological approaches to social deviancy. In E. Ramp & B. Hopkins (Eds.), *A new direction for education: Behavior analysis*, 1971. Lawrence: University of Kansas, 1971.

Gronlund, H., & Anderson, L. Personality characteristics of socially accepted, socially neglected and socially rejected junior high school pupils. *In* J. Seidman (Ed.), *Educating for mental health*. New York: Crowell, 1963.

Gronlund, N. E. *Sociometry in the classroom*. New York: Harper & Brothers, 1959.

Harris, F. R., Johnston, M. K., Kelley, C. S., & Wolf, M. M. Effects of positive social reinforcement on regressed crawling of a nursery school child. *Journal of Educational Psychology*, 1964, *55*, 35–41.

Hart, B. M., Reynolds, N. J., Baer, D., Brawley, E. R., & Harris, F. R. Effects of contingent and noncontingent social reinforcement on the cooperative play of a preschool child. *Journal of Applied Behavior Analysis*, 1968, *1*, 73–78.

Hartup, W. Peer interaction and social organization. *In* P. H. Mussen (Ed.), *Carmichael's manual of child psychology*, Vol. 2. New York: Wiley, 1970.

Hartup, W. Peer interaction and the behavioral development of the individual child. *In* E. Schopler & R. J. Reichler (Eds.), *Child development, deviations and treatment*. New York: Plenum, 1976.

Hartup, W., Glazer, J., & Charlesworth, R. Peer reinforcement and sociometric status. *Child Development*, 1967, *38*, 1017–1024.

Heber, R. F., & Heber, M. E. The effects of group failure and success on social status. *Journal of Educational Psychology*, 1957, *48*, 129–134.

Hersen, M., & Eisler, R. M. Social skills training. *In* W. E. Craighead, A. Kazdin, & M. J. Mahoney (Eds.), *Behavior Modification: Principles, issues and applications*. Boston: Houghton Mifflin, 1976.

Hoffman, M. L. Moral development. *In* P. H. Mussen (Ed.), *Carmichael's manual of child psychology*, Vol. 2. New York: Wiley, 1970.

Johnson, M., & Bailey, J. Cross age tutoring: Fifth graders as arithmetic tutors for kindergarten children. *Journal of Applied Behavior Analysis*, 1974, *7*, 223–232.

Johnston, M. K., Kelley, C. S., Harris, F. R., Wolf, M. M., & Baer, D. M. Effects of positive social reinforcement on isolate behavior of a nursery school child. Unpublished manuscript, University of Washington, 1964.

Kagan, J., & Madsen, M. C. Cooperation and competition of Mexican, Mexican-American, and Angloamerican children of two ages under four instructional sets. *Developmental Psychology*, 1971, *5*, 32–38.

Karen, R. L. Operant conditioning of social preferences. Unpublished doctoral dissertation, Arizona State University, 1965.

Keller, M., & Carlson, P. The use of symbolic modeling to promote social skills in preschool children with low levels of social responsiveness. *Child Development*, 1974, *45*, 912–919.

Kirby, F. D., & Toler, H. C. Modification of preschool isolate behavior: A case study *Journal of Applied Behavior Analysis*, 1970, *3*, 309–314.

Klaus, R. A. Interrelationships of attributes that accepted and rejected children ascribe to their peers. Unpublished doctoral dissertation, George Peabody College for Teachers, 1959.

Kohn, M. The child as a determinant of his peers' approach to him. *Journal of Genetic Psychology*, 1966, *109*, 91–100.

Kohn, M., & Clausen, J. Social isolation and schizophrenia. *American Sociological Review*, 1955, *20*, 265–273.

Lazarus, A. A. On assertive behavior: A brief note. *Behavior Therapy*, 1973, *4*, 697–699.

Lesser, G. S. The relationship between various forms of aggression and popularity among lower-class children. *Journal of Educational Psychology*, 1959, *50*, 20–25.

Liebert, R. M., Neale, J. M., & Davidson, E. S. *The early window: Effects of television on children and youth.* New York: Pergamon Press, 1973.

Maccoby, E., & Jacklin, C. Assertion and how it grows: early sex differences & similarities. Paper presented at the first Society for Research in Child Development Western Regional Conference, Emeryville, Calif., 1976.

Maccoby, E. E., & Masters, J. Attachment and dependency. In P. H. Mussen (Ed.), *Carmichael's manual of child psychology*, Vol. 2. New York: Wiley, 1970.

Marshall, R. J., & McCandless, B. R. A study in prediction of social behavior of preschool children. *Child Development*, 1957, *28*, 149–159.

Minkin, N., Braukmann, C. J., Minkin, B. L., Timbers, G. D., Timbers, B. J., Fixsen, D. L., Phillips, E. L., & Wolf, M. M. The social validation and training of conversational skills. *Journal of Applied Behavior Analysis*, 1976, *9*, 127–139.

Moore, S. G. Correlates of peer acceptance in nursery school children. In W. Hartup & N. Smothergill (Eds.), *The young child: Reviews of research*, Vol. 1. Washington, D.C.: National Association for the Education of Young Children, 1967.

Moore, S. G., & Updegraff, R. Sociometric status of preschool children as related to age, sex, nurturance-giving, and dependence. *Child Development*, 1964, *35*, 519–524.

Nelson, C., Worell, J., & Polsgrove, L. Behaviorally disordered peers as contingency managers. *Behavior Therapy*, 1973, *4*, 270–276.

Nelson, L., & Madsen, M. C. Cooperation and competition in four-year-olds as a function of reward contingency and subculture. *Developmental Psychology*, 1969, *1*, 340–344.

O'Connor, R. D. Modification of social withdrawal through symbolic modeling. *Journal of Applied Behavior Analysis*, 1969, *2*, 15–22.

O'Connor, R. D. Relative efficacy of modeling, shaping, and the combined procedures for modification of social withdrawal. *Journal of Abnormal Psychology*, 1972, *79*, 327–334.

Oden, S., & Asher, S. Coaching children in social skills for friendship making. Paper presented at the biennial meeting of the Society for Research in Child Development, Denver, Colo., April 1975.

Oden, S., Asher, S., & Hymel, S. Coaching third and fourth grade isolated children in social skills. Paper presented at the meeting of American Educational Research Association, San Francisco, Calif., April 1976.

Parke, R. D. Child abuse: an interdisciplinary approach. In M. Hetherington (Ed.), *Review of child development research*, Vol. 5. Chicago: University of Chicago Press, 1975.

Patterson, G. R., Littman, R. A., & Bricker, W. Assertive behavior in children: A step toward a theory of aggression. *Monographs of the Society for Research in Child Development*, 1967, *32*, 1–43.

Pinkston, E., Reese, N., LeBlanc, J., & Baer, D. Independent control of a preschool child's aggression and peer interaction by contingent teacher attention. *Journal of Applied Behavior Analysis*, 1973, *6*, 115–124.

Poulos, R. W., & Davidson, E. S. Effects of a short modeling film on fearful children's attitudes toward the dental situation. Unpublished manuscript. State University of New York at Stony Brook, 1971.

Rathjen, D., Hiniker, A., & Rathjen, E. Incorporation of behavioral techniques in a game format to teach children social skills. Paper presented at the Tenth Annual Convention of the Association for Advancement of Behavior Therapy, New York City, December 1976.

Roedell, W. C., Slaby, R. G., & Robinson, H. B. *Social development in young children.* Monterey, Calif.: Brooks/Cole, 1977.

Roff, M. Childhood social interactions and young adult bad conduct. *Journal of Abnormal Social Psychology,* 1961, *63,* 333–337.

Roff, M. Some life history factors in relation to various types of adult maladjustment. In M. Roff & D. Ricks (Eds.), *Life history research in psychopathology.* Minneapolis: University of Minnesota Press, 1970.

Roff, M., Sells, B., & Golden, M. Social adjustment and personality development in children. Minneapolis: University of Minnesota Press, 1972.

Ross, D., Ross, S., & Evans, T. A. The modification of extreme social withdrawal by modification with guided practice. *Journal of Behavior Therapy and Experimental Psychiatry,* 1971, *2,* 273–279.

Rubin, K. H. Relationship between egocentric communication and popularity among peers. *Developmental Psychology,* 1972, *7,* 364.

Rubin, K. H. Egocentrism in childhood: A unitary construct? *Child Development,* 1973, *44,* 102–110.

Sherif, M., & Sherif, C. W. *Groups in harmony and tension.* New York: Harper, 1953.

Sherif, M., & Sherif, C. W. *Reference groups.* New York: Harper & Row, 1964.

Slaby, D. A. Day treatment and parent training programs. Unpublished manuscript. Children's Orthopedic Hospital and Medical Center, Seattle, Wash., 1976.

Slaby, R. G., & Crowley, C. G. Modification of cooperation and aggression through teacher attention to children's speech. *Journal of Experimental Child Psychology,* 1977, *23,* 442–458.

Smith, G. H. Sociometric study of best-liked and least-liked children. *Elementary School Journal,* 1950, *51,* 77–85.

Solomon, R. W., & Wahler, R. G. Peer reinforcement of classroom problem behavior. *Journal of Applied Behavior Analysis,* 1973, *6,* 49–56.

Spivack, G., & Shure, M. *Social adjustment of young children.* San Francisco: Jossey-Bass, 1974.

Staub, E. The use of role playing and induction in children's learning of helping and sharing behavior. *Child Development,* 1971, *42,* 805–816.

Stendler, C. B., Damrin, D., & Haines, A. C. Studies in cooperation and competition: I. The effects of working for group and individual rewards on the social climate of children's groups. *Journal of Genetic Psychology,* 1951, *79,* 173–198.

Strain, P., Shores, R., & Kerr, M. An experimental analysis of "spillover" effects on the social interaction of behaviorally handicapped preschool children. *Journal of Applied Behavior Analysis,* 1976, *9,* 31–40.

Strain, P., & Timm, M. An experimental analysis of social interaction between a behaviorally disordered preschool child and her classroom peers. *Journal of Applied Behavior Analysis,* 1974, *7,* 583–590.

Twentyman, C., & McFall, R. Behavioral training of social skills in shy males. *Journal of Consulting and Clinical Psychology,* 1975, *43,* 384–395.

Ullmann, C. A. Teachers, peers, and tests as predictors of adjustment. *Journal of Educational Psychology,* 1957, *48,* 257–267.

Wahler, R. Child-child interactions in free field settings: Some experimental analyses. *Journal of Experimental Child Psychology,* 1967, *5,* 278–293.

Winder, C. L., & Rau, L. Parental attitudes associated with social deviance in preadolescent boys. *Journal of Abnormal Social Psychology,* 1962, *64,* 418–424.

Winnett, R. A., & Winkler, R. C. Current behavior modification in the classroom: Be still, be quiet, be docile. *Journal of Applied Behavior Analysis,* 1972, *5,* 499–504.

Yarrow, M. R., Scott, P. M., & Waxler, C. Z. Learning consideration for others. *Developmental Psychology,* 1973, *8,* 240–260.

6   Use of Biofeedback in the Treatment of Seizure Disorders and Hyperactivity

Joel F. Lubar
and Margaret N. Shouse

During the past 15 years, considerable basic research and applied effort has been directed toward developing methods for controlling internal physiological processes. These processes include autonomic functions, both unit and gross (summated) neuromuscular activity, and central neural electrophysiological responses, all of which may be modifiable through the application of behavioral methods. Psychophysiology is the discipline most concerned with this type of research. A relatively new applied branch of psychophysiology, now known as *biofeedback*, is undergoing rapid development to fulfill basic research and clinical needs related to the control of physiological processes.

In this chapter, we examine two new areas of considerable potential that have employed biofeedback methods. These are the control of epileptic seizures and management of the behavior of hyperkinetic children. Currently, there is widespread interest in these two potential applications of biofeedback, perhaps because of promising initial successes. The following discussion focuses on a description of the use of biofeedback methodology, a general consideration of epilepsy, and the use of biofeedback in treating severe or refractory epilepsy. We then

Joel F. Lubar • Department of Psychology, University of Tennessee, Knoxville, Tennessee. Margaret N. Shouse • School of Medicine, University of California at Los Angeles, Los Angeles, California. The research reported here was supported by grants from the Physicians' Medical Education and Research Foundation, the Knox Children Foundation, and the Tom's International Foundation.

discuss the hyperkinetic syndrome and the preliminary research that
has now been completed in our laboratory directed toward the management of this behavior problem.

1. Biofeedback

1.1. Definitions of Biofeedback and Brief Historical Overview

Biofeedback is a methodology for acquiring learned control over
internal processes. Essentially, biofeedback is operant conditioning of
autonomic, electrophysiological, and neuromuscular responses. The
procedure usually involves making an extroceptive stimulus contingent upon some clearly delineated change of an internal response,
resulting in control of the targeted response. This process may take
place with or without awareness on the part of the organism as to exactly what manipulations must be performed to bring about such control. Feedback-mediated control of physiological activity has been
demonstrated in a variety of species, including rats, cats, monkeys,
and humans. The target responses are usually of the following types:
(1) electromyographic activity (EMG) representing activity of specific
muscles; (2) autonomic activity that can be detected in a variety of
organ systems; or (3) electrophysiological activity, that is, brain
waves, evoked potentials, and possibly even slow potential shifts
within the nervous system. The extroceptive stimulus is usually a light
or a tone that provides the subject with information about the internal
response. It tells the subject that the internal response has taken place
and may even provide information dealing with the magnitude of the
response, that is, its amplitude or frequency or some other parameter.
The extroceptive stimulus can also act as a primary or secondary reinforcer in that its contingent presentation can change the probability
that the internal response will occur.

Whereas psychophysiology is primarily concerned with the problem of how autonomic, electrophysiological, or neuromuscular responses are learned, clinical biofeedback is directed at taking advantage of mediating responses in order to increase the rate of learning.
Hence, the client might be trained to think "relaxed thoughts" and to
try to remain as rested as possible in order to lower his EMG activity
and blood pressure, to decrease his heart rate, to increase his gastrointestinal motility, or to bring about a variety of other autonomic responses that are part of the general parasympathetic profile.

A major concern in current biofeedback research is eliminating or
accounting for the possibility of placebo effects that may explain the

desired results. In the studies presented here dealing with epilepsy and hyperkinesis, control procedures are discussed in detail. One of the most potent control procedures is the use of the ABA design, a variety of which is illustrated in our hyperkinesis work. In this type of design, data are collected systematically across several conditions. First, there is a baseline or pretreatment condition, then treatment intervention, and finally a return to the baseline condition. As Blanchard and Young (1974) have pointed out, "if changes in the target symptom occur in going from A to B and then revert when going from B to A . . . this constitutes a very strong evidence that B is the casual variable for changes in that symptom." (p. 575).

Other control procedures involve the introduction of *noncontingent* reinforcement either before treatment is undertaken or at some time during the treatment regimen. It is essential that the patient or subject not be aware that any change in contingencies has occurred. Other procedures involve the use of yoked controls or no-feedback controls, who are observed throughout the period of treatment along with the experimental group and compared on their target responses. This procedure is also exemplified in the hyperkinesis research to be discussed later.

1.2. Areas of Biofeedback Application

There are currently a number of areas in which clinical applications of biofeedback are being explored. These include the management of systolic and diastolic blood pressures (Schwartz & Shapiro, 1973; Elder, Ruiz, Deabler, & Dillenkoffer, 1973), cardiac arrhythmias (Bleecker & Engel, 1973), and the control of stress-related conditions, including tension and migraine headache, anxiety, and lower-back pain. Also, initial controlled studies of tension headache have been carried out by Budzynski, Stoyva, Adler, and Mullaney (1973), as have studies of both migraine and tension headaches by Sargent, Green, and Walters (1973).

Biofeedback has been applied to the rehabilitation of patients who have suffered from neuromuscular disease, stroke, or spinal-cord injury. Considerable effort here has been exemplified in the work of Basmajian (1972) and Brudny, Korein, Levidow, Brynbaum, Liberman, and Friedmann (1974). The interest in this area is currently expanding, so that many physical therapists have learned to integrate electromyographic-feedback techniques as part of their methodology for the rehabilitation of patients with neuromuscular dysfunction.

A recent area of feedback research and application involves the control of the gastrointestinal tract. Engel, Nikoomanesh, and Schuster

206 JOEL F. LUBAR AND MARGARET N. SHOUSE

(1974) have shown that it is possible to operant-condition the rectosphincteric response for the control of fecal incontinence. A more widespread application is the use of biofeedback for the management of ulcerative conditions in various portions of the intestinal tract (Welgan, 1974).

Many systems can also be monitored for the control of brain-wave (EEG) activity. For example, there has been a great deal of interest in the behavioral control of alpha rhythms. Kamiya (1969), Lynch and Paskewitz (1971), and Beatty (1973) have shown that alpha rhythms (8–13 Hz recorded from the occipital regions of the human scalp) can be manipulated when feedback or reward is provided for changes in the density of this activity. Although the evidence is far from clear, alpha-feedback training has been linked with states of relaxation that may also be associated with low levels of arousal. Other types of electroencephalographic control seem to be much more specific. In the ensuing discussion, emphasis is placed on the behavioral control of a rhythm (sensorimotor rhythm) that is recorded over the sensorimotor cortical regions of the human or mammalian brain. This activity of 12–15 Hz is associated with the inhibition of motor responses and perhaps the generation of spindles during sleep. Current applications of sensorimotor-rhythm (SMR) conditioning include epilepsy (Sterman & Friar, 1972; Sterman, MacDonald, & Stone, 1974; Finley, 1975, 1977; Seifert & Lubar, 1975; Lubar, 1975, 1977; Lubar & Bahler, 1976) and specific types of insomnia in which cerebral mechanisms involved in the generation of Stage 2 sleep spindles might be deficient (Hauri, 1976). The newest application of SMR conditioning, which is described here in detail for the first time, is the management of the hyperkinetic syndrome in children.

It is important to leave the impression that there is *not* a specific biofeedback treatment for every type of functional, psychomatic, or medical disorder for which biofeedback has been tried. Perhaps the most powerful effects can be obtained when several modalities of feedback are combined within a treatment program that may also include psychotherapy. Schwartz (1975) has effectively argued that many autonomic and electrophysiological responses that are highly correlated are also involved in a particular altered state. For example, the state of deep relaxation appears to be correlated with theta brain-wave activity (4–7 Hz) or the alpha rhythm (8–13 Hz) and also decreased levels of frontalis muscle EMG and EMG recorded from limb flexors. Also, increased peripheral skin temperature, slow and even respiration, and perhaps lowered heart rate and blood pressure occur in deep relaxation. This is what Gellhorn (1968) has called the "state of parasympathetic dominance." In those psychogenic or physiological conditions for which stress levels are high, it appears to be desirable to shift the balance toward the parasympathetic to a considerable extent. In order for a patient to accomplish this and maintain such control in stressful life situations, the combination of multiple feedback for several modalities plus desensitization techniques appears to offer the most potent approach.

2. Epilepsy: General Considerations

2.1. Definition and Incidence of Seizure Disorders and Epilepsy

Epilepsy is a complex entity. The definition of the term is complicated because of its many forms and etiology. The epilepsy branch of the National Institutes of Health has provided the following definition (Cereghino, 1976): "Epilepsy is defined as a chronic brain disorder of various etiologies characterized by *recurrent* seizures due to excessive discharge of cerebral neurons." Therefore, a single epileptic seizure or occasional epileptic seizures—such as febrile convulsions or those that occur during childbirth—and isolated seizures occurring from severe illness, drug intoxication, or alcoholism are not a part of true epilepsy. Also, an epileptic seizure is associated with a variety of clinical and laboratory manifestations.

A seizure is defined as an "attack of cerebral origin affecting a person in an apparent good health or causing a sudden aggravation of a chronic pathologic state" (Cereghino, 1976). There are at least seven types of seizures: those of epileptic origin, of anoxic origin due to toxicity, of metabolic origin, of psychic origin, associated with sleep, and of undetermined origin and not related to the above features.

Taking into account the varied nature of epilepsy and seizure disorders, we can consider the incidence of this disease entity. There are two relevant measures here. One is the *incidence per se* of epilepsy, which refers to the number of new cases per year. The best estimate at the present time according to the Epilepsy Foundation of America is approximately 50 cases per 100,000 new cases per year. *Prevalence* refers to the number of cases in a defined population at any given time. For all forms of epilepsy taken together, the best current estimate of its prevalence is about 1 case in 250 individuals, or approximately 4 out of every 1,000. Based on these two statistics, it is clear that epilepsy is an extremely widespread disease. It is definitely not a condition that is only genetically or congenitally based. A severe head injury as a result of an automobile accident, a cerebrovascular accident (i.e., a stroke or an embolism), and many degenerative neurological diseases of central origin can also lead to the formation of single or multiple epileptic foci. Therefore, any individual can become an epileptic at any time during his life.

The prevalence and incidence figures stated above are for "epilepsy." If we also include seizure disorders that can come about as a result of tumors, drug intoxication, and a variety of other causes, the total number of individuals suffering from seizure disorders and epilepsy is far higher than the cited figures. Another important statistic is that for all types of epilepsy and many types of seizure disorders, only about 75% of existing cases have achived adequate control of their seizures through the use of a variety of anticonvulsant medications, many of which can have serious and even debilitating side effects. It is for this relatively large group of individuals with poorly managed seizures that an alternative treatment is needed; the biofeedback approach also holds potential for those people who have achieved seizure control with chemotherapy but who would like an alternative to their medications. Finally, the incidence and prevalence of epilepsy is not evenly distributed across all age levels (Masland, 1976). Epilepsy and seizure disorders are much more prevalent in children, particularly since a proportion of these disorders arise from febrile convulsions occurring in infancy- and birth-related trauma. Again, it is particularly important that a supplementive or alternative means of seizure management be developed for the child instead of a reliance on the use of anticonvulsants for this epileptic population.

2.2. Types of Epilepsy

Epilepsy, as we have seen, is not a single disease entity. The definition and classification of different types of seizures has been an area of considerable confusion. The International League against Epilepsy has, on the basis of both clinical and EEG features of epileptic seizures, developed an International Classification of Epileptic Seizures (Gastaut, 1970). The classification is presented in Table 1. This classification attempts to eliminate some of the old and imprecise terminology. Hence, both petit mal and grand mal seizures are classified as generalized seizures, whereas psychomotor and sensory seizures are classified as partial. An important point is that any seizure that is initially partial—including Jacksonian, autonomic, psychomotor, psychosensory, etc., from the older classifications—may over time become *secondarily generalized*. That is, after a period of time these partial

TABLE 1
International Classification of Epileptic Seizures

Partial Seizures (seizures beginning locally)
1. Partial seizures with elementary symptomatology (generally without impairment of consciousness)
   a. With motor symptoms (includes Jacksonian seizures)
   b. With special sensory or somatosensory symptoms
   c. With autonomic symptoms
   d. Compound forms
2. Partial seizures with complex symptomatology (generally with impairment of consciousness)
   (temporal lobe or psychomotor seizures)
   a. With impairment of consciousness only
   b. With cognitive symptomatology
   c. With affective symptomatology
   d. With "psychosensory" symptomatology
   e. With "psychomotor" symptomatology (automatisms)
   f. Compound forms
3. Partial seizures secondarily generalized
Generalized Seizures (bilaterally symmetrical and without local onset)
   a. Absences (petit mal)
   b. Bilateral massive epileptic myoclonus
   c. Infantile spasms
   d. Clonic seizures
   e. Tonic seizures
   f. Tonic-clonic seizures (grand mal)
   g. Atonic seizures
   h. Akinetic seizures
Unilateral Seizures (or predominantly unilateral)
Unclassified Epileptic Seizures (due to incomplete data)

seizures may develop into a generalized seizure of the tonic-clonic or "grand mal" type. Part of the rationale behind the various therapeutic approaches, whether they be chemotherapy, surgical, or otherwise, is to prevent this secondary generalization from taking place.

Current research using biofeedback as a means of controlling epileptic seizures has been the most successful for seizures that have motor manifestations. These include partial seizures with motor symptoms (Jacksonian) and partial seizures with complex symptomatology (psychomotor). This category also includes generalized seizures of the tonic-clonic (grand mal), atonic, and akinetic types. Relatively little work has been done with purely sensory seizures and with individuals who have generalized absences (petit mal) because individual seizure events are very difficult to demarcate in the latter for the purposes of keeping seizure logs. The cases presented here represent a variety of seizure types treated in adolescents and young adults.

3. The Use of Biofeedback in the Treatment of Epilepsy

3.1. Initial Studies in Animals

In 1963, Brazier described a 13–14 Hz EEG rhythm recorded from the sensorimotor cortex in cats. A related "somatomotor rhythm" (rhythm *en arceau* or mu rhythm) of 9 Hz was described earlier by Gastaut (1952). He suggested that this EEG activity represented "inhibition of sensory and motor representation at the level of the rolandic cortex" (Gastaut, Naquet, & Gastaut, 1965). Both the sensorimotor rhythm, as the faster activity has become designated, and mu rhythm are examples of a larger group of synchronous cortical rhythms that can be recorded from the brains of many species. Andersen and Andersson (1968) have developed an elegant model to deal with the neurophysiology of synchronous EEG activity. Such activity represents a type of "cortical idling" that is associated mentally or physically with decreased activity in certain cerebral systems. This is why the alpha rhythm (occipital 8–13 Hz), which is dominant in the human, is often correlated with relaxed mental states; theta rhythm (4–7 Hz) is associated with deeper states of relaxation and the transitional state between sleep and wakefulness. In all mammals, in contrast, desynchronized cortical high-frequency and low-amplitude EEG is usually associated with increased levels of arousal, problem solving, or other complex mental activities, and is most often characterized by beta activity (greater than 14 Hz).

Physiologically, the sensorimotor rhythm (SMR), which ranges from 12 Hz to 16 Hz in cats and 12 Hz to 15 Hz in humans and perhaps other primates, is associated with the cortical inhibition of ongoing motor activity (Roth, Sterman & Clemente, 1967). Sterman, Lopresti, and Fairchild (1969) and Sterman (1976) have demonstrated that the operant conditioning of the SMR is possible in cats and that its acquisition is correlated with behavioral immobility and increased resistance to epileptic seizures induced by the potent convulsant chemical monomethylhydrazine.

A brief description of what is known of the cerebral pathways that may mediate the sensorimotor rhythm is necessary to an understanding of how this change in seizure thresholds might come about. SMR can be recorded from specific subcortical structures of the somatosensory system and in nuclei and pathways of the motor system. These include the thalamic nuclei ventralis posterolateralis (VPL) and ventralis lateralis (VL). During the acquisition of SMR through operant conditioning, there is a suppression of unit discharge in cats from large neuronal elements in the red nucleus (Harper & Sterman, 1972), as well as a change in the firing pattern and inhibition of units in VPL. Furthermore, the outflow of the cerebellum, which is inhibitory according to Eccles, Ito, & Szentagothai (1967), projects to the red nucleus and to the VL nucleus of the thalamus, whose projections in turn modulate outflow of the motor cortex.

One link between these neurophysiological and anatomical findings and epilepsy comes from the work of Dr. Irving S. Cooper. Cooper has been able to control intractable seizures in some epileptics through the implantation of stimulating electrodes in the cerebellar cortex. Electrical impulses are delivered continuously over several months by a portable implanted stimulator. Perhaps the mechanism for this seizure control is via the establishment of SMR or related inhibitory activity in the efferent pathways from the cerebellum to the thalamus, which in turn act upon the motor cortex.

The precise mechanisms by which SMR might change seizure thresholds is not yet known. Perhaps it is through the activation of inhibitory transmitters such as gamma amino butyric acid (GABA), which may produce enough thalamic inhibitory postsynaptic potentials (IPSPs) to develop sufficient inhibition to increase seizure thresholds. Eccles *et al.* (1967) has shown that efferent cerebellar inhibition may operate upon the red nucleus, the VL thalamus, and perhaps the sensorimotor cortex through the release of GABA. The resultant effect in epilepsy may be to increase the threshold for paroxysmal discharge (Jovanovic, 1974). Jovanovic's model of epilepsy further supposes that there are different central-nervous-system (CNS) levels where natural barriers to uncontrolled or paroxysmal discharges exist. He proposed that there are cortical, thalamic, brain-stem, and spinal-cord barriers. In the case of partial seizures, the temporal lobe or the hippocampal formation may also be the site of such barriers. If all these barriers are inoperative, the patient experiences *status epilepticus* (a continual state of seizure). If a few of these barriers are disrupted, the patient experiences seizure activity in the form of slow waves and spikes but is not aware of anything unusual. If additional barriers are disrupted, the patient might experience both EEG and some clinical changes, including confusion, dizziness, disorientation, and affective changes. If more, but not all, barriers have broken down, overt seizures may occur in conjunction with the abnormal EEG activity. Although a complete model cannot be proposed at the present time, current electro-physiological and behavioral studies employing SMR conditioning tend to indicate that the conditioning procedure might reestablish barriers that have become ineffective by increasing inhibitory activity in ascending pathways that modulate the efferent flow of signals via the motor system.

3.2. SMR Conditioning in Human Epileptics

Based on the preliminary animal studies indicating that Rolandic rhythms between 12 Hz and 16 Hz might be involved in neural inhibition and the modulation of seizure thresholds, Sterman & Friar (1972) showed that behavioral control of this EEG activity appeared to be associated with decreased seizures in a human epileptic. Behavioral control of seizures has been attempted previously. Efron (1957) paired an olfactory stimulus with a visual stimulus, a silver bracelet for an epileptic experiencing olfactory seizures. The patient learned that staring at the bracelet became effective in blocking the development of these seizures. This patient remained free of clinical seizures for more than one year. Other experimenters, including Stevens, Milstein, & Dodds (1967), have used paroxysmal activity as a conditioned stimulus for epileptics, paired with a noxious unconditioned stimulus, for example an electric shock. The use of aversive conditioning has not been particularly successful in the control of seizures. Forster (1966) has worked with patients whose seizures were triggered by specific sensory stimuli. Through the use of desensitization techniques, he has trained patients to become aware of stimuli that are associated with impending seizures. These approaches do not act to change seizure thresholds, but they help patients to become aware of seizure events and to develop strategies for overcoming them.

Following the initial success of Sterman's laboratory in training a human epileptic to suppress her seizures through SMR conditioning, our laboratory, Finley's, and several others have also successfully trained epileptics using this methodology. Although results with humans over the past five years have been very encouraging, Kaplan (1975) reported that biofeedback training of 12–15 Hz activity in two epileptics did not alter their clinical EEGs, seizures, or EEG spectral power in the range of frequencies that were trained. She did find, however, the 6–12 Hz activity resulted in some degree of seizure reduction in other patients. Kaplan's methodology differed significantly, however, from that used by other laboratories that have been successful in dealing with epilepsy. One of the basic differences in her procedure was that she did not inhibit SMR feedback when slow waves were present. As a result, her patients were given partial reinforcement for slow-wave activity, which may have actually increased this paroxysmal activity and counteracted any positive effects of the SMR conditioning procedure. She also used different electrode placements than did the investigators who have been successful; her placements were not located directly over the sensorimotor cortex. In addition to the SMR, both Sterman's and Wyler's laboratories (Wyler, Lockhard, Ward, & Finch, 1976) are demonstrating that operant conditioning of higher frequencies (18 Hz to 23 Hz) is also effective in decreasing seizures, especially when the conditioning electrodes are applied directly over sites of cortical epileptic foci. Our work indicates that while 18–23 Hz activity is being conditioned, there is also an increase in 12–15 Hz activity and that both SMR and higher-frequency activity might be enhanced by these procedures. The combined effect would tend to decrease the spectral power of EEG activity in the lower-frequency ranges (less than 10 Hz) as well as to decrease EEG amplitude, which in turn would act to produce a "mirror image" of the cortical epileptogenic EEG pattern (i.e., low voltage, high frequency).

3.3. Research Employing Epileptics in Our Laboratory

3.3.1. Subjects

Although our laboratory during the past three years has worked with 12 epileptics, this discussion concentrates primarily on those subjects who represent the youngest group. These include 4 males and 2 females. The ages of 5 of the subjects range between 15 and 19. A 6th subject to be discussed (G.C.) is a 30-year-old male. Table 2 presents detailed data regarding types of seizures, duration of the seizure condition, and daily medications. These patients have been in treatment for a minimum of one year and some for more than two years. Currently, all of these patients are being weaned from the treatment program, which initially consists of three sessions per week.

During an initial interview, the requirements of the study were described in detail to each of their patients and their parents and/or family. It was explained that all treatments were provided without cost and that the patient would agree to attend three weekly training sessions and maintain his seizure records with compulsive accuracy. The seizure records would contain information on the duration, the severity, and the type of each seizure that occurred during waking hours, as well as documenting as many nocturnal seizures as it was possible to record.

Each patient was told that there would be no guarantee concerning the effectiveness of the treatment and that if for any reason the

TABLE
Seizure, EEG, and

	K.S.	G.M.[a]	S.R.
Age, sex	15, female	17, male	19, female
Duration of disorder	13 years	12 years	13 years
Diagnosis and EEG	Generalized myo-clonic seizures: 8–9 Hz background alpha with multiple high-voltage spikes	Partial seizures: with complex symptomatology (psychomotor) and secondarily general-ized clonic seizures: 7–8 Hz background alpha, mild retarda-tion	Atonic seizures: 8–10 Hz background alpha, polyspike, and slow waves; brain damage, severe retardation
Daily medication regimen at start of training	Phenobarbitol: 100 mg	Dilantin: 400 mg Mysoline: 100 mg	Meberal: 350 mg Dilantin: 200 mg Tegretol: 600 mg Ritalin: 50 mg
Most recent medications	Phenobarbitol: 100 mg	Dilantin: 400 mg Mysoline: 750 mg	Same as above

[a] In October 1975, G.M.'s medication was changed to: Dilantin, 400 mg; Mysoline, 250 mg; Tegretol, 600 mg. This medication change occurred after the seizure graph shown in Figure 3 was completed.

treatment were to be terminated, a long-term follow-up ranging from months to perhaps years would be undertaken. This follow-up would include a continual monitoring of blood levels of anticonvulsant medi-cation and a maintenance of seizure records. All patients in our re-search program have been referred to us by neurologists, with whom we have been in close contact during all phases of the treatment pro-gram.

3.3.2. Methodology

Bilateral electrode placements and bipolar recordings were used in this work. Grass (E5SH) cup electrodes were placed over skull loca-tions C3 and T3 for the left hemisphere and C4–T4 for the right hemi-sphere according to the international 10–20 system of electrode place-ment. An ear-clip electrode was used as a ground. Electrode sites were cleansed with alcohol followed by acetone, and electrodes were held in place by electrode paste, cotton, and overlying gauze, which was wrapped several times around the head. Interelectrode impedances of less than 10 kΩ were considered acceptable.

2
Medications for Epileptics

M.T.	C.D.	G.C.
19, male	17, male	30, male
15 years	11 years	25 years
Partial right-temporal-lobe seizures: with complex symptoms (psychomotor): 9–10 Hz background alpha	Mixed seizure disorder: generalized tonic-clonic (grand mal), absences and partial with complex symptoms: bilateral paroxysms left frontal 8–9 Hz background alpha	Partial seizures: with elementary motor symptoms (Jacksonian) and with complex symptoms; evidence of left temporal calcification
Dilantin: 400 mg Mysoline: 750 mg Tegretol: 200 mg	Dilantin: 360 mg Zorontin: 1000 mg	Phenurone: 1500 mg Tegretol: 1200 mg
Dilantin: 200 mg Mysoline: 750 mg	Dilantin: 200 mg Zorontin: 800 mg	Phenurone: 500 mg Tegretol: 1200 mg

Our previous publications (Seifert & Lubar, 1975; Lubar & Bahler, 1976) provide a detailed description and a block diagram of the basic system used in this research. The electronics were designed to very precisely detect 12–15 Hz activity. Briefly, the electronics worked in the following way. Scalp EEG signals were amplified by Grass P511-E preamplifiers and then were passed through a clipping circuit, which partially attenuated signals greater than 40 μV and full clipped signals greater than 60 μV microvolts back to 40 μV. This procedure is essential when one is using active band-pass filters to minimize filter ringing, which could produce artifacts and false feedback. SMR activity between 12 Hz and 15 Hz was detected by a precisely tuned and stable 14-pole active band-pass filter of elliptical design (Frequency Devices Incorporated). This filter has a roll-off of 80 db within the first octave, with side lobes at harmonic frequencies of greater than 40-db attenuation as compared with the center frequency of 13.5 Hz. The elliptic filter, unlike filters of the Butterworth and Chebyshev designs that have been used in previous studies of SMR conditioning, is less subject to ringing artifact and more precise in its ability to detect the frequency band of interest because its response is flat between 12 Hz and 15 Hz.

Next, the output of the SMR filter was subjected to a zero-crossing digital analysis. Feedback criteria for amplitude based on the output of the SMR filter could be varied from session to session in order for the learning process to be maximized. A fixed duration of 6 cycles of filter output exceeding a preset microvolt criterion for 0.5 sec was used for all training sessions.

In addition to this main SMR analysis, the EEG recorded from active electrode sites was split and sent to two additional circuits. One circuit inhibited SMR feedback whenever slow-wave epileptiform activity, spikes, or gross movement occurred. The latter were detected by a 4–8 Hz active band-pass filter of the Butterworth design with 24-db-per-octave roll-off (White Instrument Company, Austin, Texas). A third circuit was provided to detect EMG activity from active EEG scalp electrodes. Whenever this EMG activity exceeded a preset microvolt level, SMR circuits were again inhibited. The use of an EMG inhibitory circuit has not been reported previously and was added to our system after our earlier reports (Seifert & Lubar, 1975; Lubar & Bahler, 1976). The purpose of this EMG inhibit circuit was to aid the patient in achieving a relaxed state and to further exclude artifacts that might result in false feedback from the main processing circuitry.

All three circuits keyed feedback for the patient. Figure 1 shows an oscillographic recording that displays the functions of each of the discriminator circuits used in data processing as well as the contingent and noncontingent EEG and feedback.

3.3.3. Data Analysis

During the training session, an on-line analysis was carried out in which the data were processed and analyzed continuously. At the end of each minute, a teletype automatically printed out: (1) the minute number; (2) the number of wave forms processed by the 12–15 Hz filter that exceeded a fixed amplitude setting and was *independent* of inhibit-circuit activity; (3) the number of wave forms (12–15 Hz) that exceeded the amplitude for that particular session and was contingent upon the absence of artifacts detected by inhibitory circuits; and (4) the number of times all criteria were met and feedback was presented to the patient. From this information, additional analyses could be carried out off-line. One type of off-line analysis involved EEG recording on FM tape. This EEG was subjected later to power spectral analysis performed by a PDP-11 computer using the Fast Fourier transform routine and plotted with compressed isometric routines to be illustrated later (Bickford and Fleming, 1970).

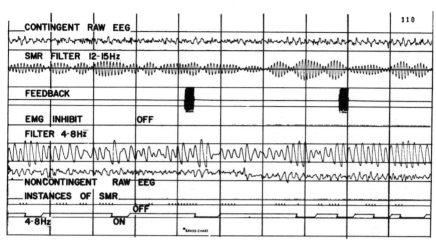

a

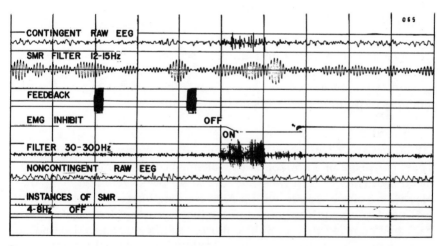

b

FIGURE 1. Paper channels for EEG printout. Note in particular the operation of inhibit circuits for EMG activity and for epileptiform slow-waves linked to their filter outputs. Paper channel 5 shows the operation of the 4–8 Hz filter in panel (a) and the raw EMG signal from the active electrodes in panel (b).

Clinical EEGs taken before training began were compared with clinical EEGs taken at the beginning of weaning or after a long period of training had been completed. EEG recordings made during the early training sessions were compared with those of later sessions. The most important dependent variable was the seizure records, which would show whether the biofeedback training was effective clinically.

3.3.4. Daily Training Routine

Training sessions were 40 min long and were held three times a week for each patient. During each session, both right and left hemispheres independently received contingent feedback training; the first and last 5 min of that session served as a habituation period for the purpose of establishing a baseline. These baseline measurements were taken from the same hemisphere on a given day; however, the order of training of the hemispheres alternated with each succeeding session. Following the 5 min of baseline recording without feedback, 15 min of feedback were presented for the hemisphere for which the initial baseline was obtained. Next, 15 min of feedback were provided for the contralateral hemisphere, followed by a final 5-min baseline obtained from the same hemisphere from which the initial baseline had been taken. Hence, on a given day, the training sequence might be baseline–left side, feedback–left side, feedback–right side, baseline–left side, followed in the next training session by a similar sequence starting with the right hemisphere. Since a large number of training sessions were employed for each patient, the patients received equal amounts of training for each side of the brain.

3.3.5. Feedback

A variety of different modalities of feedback were employed. These consisted of a horizontal row of small colored lamps that illuminated sequentially each time the criteria for SMR were met. This display was typically paired with a 2000-Hz tone beep. A digital display was used as an optional mode of feedback. To supplement the feedback that signaled that an SMR criterion had been achieved based on both amplitude and duration, an additional tone of 400 Hz was provided for each wave form of the SMR filter that met the only amplitude criterion. This additional signal provided patients with information concerning how close they had come to achieving the criterion for SMR duration as well as providing a more continuous feedback mode.

Feedback keyed by the 4–8 Hz filter was presented to the patient in the form of two large (28.5 × 8.0 cm) green panels that indicated the presence of slow-wave activity, spikes, or gross body movement when they were not illuminated. This also inhibited the feedback for 12–15 Hz. Patients were told to "keep the green lights on." The inhibit circuit for EMG blocked feedback for SMR but not for 4–8 Hz activity. So patients could infer that when the green panels were illuminated but there was no SMR feedback, they might be producing excessive EMG activity. During the last year we have installed a large (61.0 × 8.0 cm) red prismatic plastic panel that when illuminated indicates a condition of excessive EMG activity.

The training room was carpeted and moderately illuminated. External sounds were eliminated or greatly attenuated by soundproofing and the use of a low-level white-noise generator. The patients were seated in a large overstuffed recliner, and the experimenter could observe them through a one-way glass and communicate when necessary by means of an intercom.

3.3.6. Results

The results of our studies involve an analysis of the effect of training on seizure activity. We also examined changes in the EEG that might reflect the normalization of the seizure process and directed analyses toward determining whether patients did in fact show an increase in the amount of 12–15 Hz activity (SMR) during acquisition of the task. A further approach designed to elucidate the degree to which the EEG had been modified by training was by means of spectral analyses sampled periodically throughout the training period. Other spectral analyses were done by use of the clinical EEG, which took into account other electrode placements besides those actively trained. These were obtained before training and after training was completed. The cases described here are illustrative of the results that we have obtained. The primary results are described for the cases that are illustrated in Figure 2, but occasionally data are drawn from other patients in our total population of 12 cases.

Seizure data is shown in Figure 2. It is very important to emphasize that each case has to be considered separately. It is completely unacceptable to combine data from different patients into single graphs because each patient represents a different typology of epilepsy with different environmental and medical factors that affect each patient's seizures. As shown in Figure 2, all of the patients showed changes in seizure level correlated with training. These were most marked in cases K.S., G.M., M.T., and C.D., and less so in cases S.R. and G.C. Each of the cases illustrates some important points. For example, in case K.S. the decline in seizures over a period of nearly two years is very marked. The correlation between seizure activity and training days was −0.59. This correlation was significant ($t = 2.93$, $df = 16$,

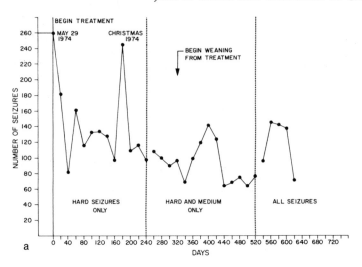

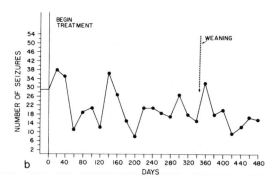

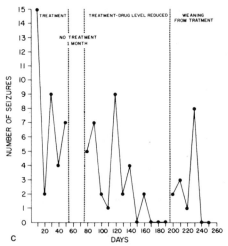

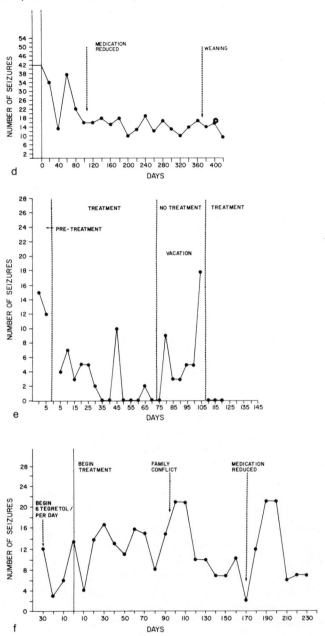

Figure 2. Seizure frequencies as a function of training condition for patients. (a) K.S., female, (b) S.R., female, (c) C.D., male, (d) G.M., male, (e) M.T., male, and (f) G.C., male.

$p < 0.02$). Note that during the course of training, the quality of the seizures changed. During the first portion of training, the "hard seizures" were severe myoclonic jerks of the head in which the head was maximally turned to one side. Later, these seizures differentiated into a second type called medium seizures, which consisted of deviation of the eyes and turning of the head, but head jerks were absent. Finally, in the third portion of her graph (all seizures), the severe seizures virtually disappeared and were replaced by mild head-turning and in some cases only seizure discharges in the EEG without overt clinical seizure. This graph also illustrates an important point mentioned before—that is, that excitement can cause a change in seizures as evidenced by the peak on Christmas Day of 1974. Overall, this patient had shown a significant decrease in seizure activity of greater than 60% as well as a decrease in the intensity and the duration of her seizures. K.S. is now being treated approximately once per month, with her seizures under much better control than initially.

Case G.M. also illustrates a long-term decrease in seizure activity. This patient did so well that his Mysoline medication was reduced after 110 days of treatment. When it appeared that it was not possible to reduce seizures further, weaning was instituted approximately 340 days after training had started. This patient is no longer in training and is experiencing very mild seizures.

S.R. represents a different problem. Her record is highly variable. This patient experienced akinetic seizures and has experienced progressive brain damage as a result of falling to a cement pavement many times per month without the help of protective reflexes. The patient is severely retarded with an IQ of less than 40. As a result of the severe retardation and associated brain damage, her record is more variable but still illustrates an approximate 40% decrease in seizure activity. Weaning was instituted and her seizure level remained decreased. At the present time, a medication reduction is being considered for S.R. The correlation of seizures over time was -0.36 for S.R. and -0.28 for G.M., neither of which is statistically significant. G.M.'s seizure reduction was clinically significant, however. The lack of a significant correlation is due to a long period in which the seizures remained at a reduced level. Despite the lack of a strong negative correlation, it is clear from an examination of Figure 2 that G.M.'s seizures remained at a consistently lower level than initially for a period of more than one year.

Two of the patients achieved the ideal—that is, seizure-free periods. M.T.'s seizures correlated -0.58 over training ($t = 2.47$, $df = 12$, $p < 0.05$). This patient, a psychomotor epileptic, illustrates the potential effectiveness of SMR training for this type of partial epilepsy.

The graph also illustrates another important point. M.T. elected to go on vacation between Day 75 and Day 105. From our work, and that of Finley's laboratory, we have learned that abrupt withdrawal from treatment leads to a rapid increase in seizure activity, particularly if withdrawal is early in the treatment program. However, M.T. quickly reacquired the SMR task and his seizures again returned to zero. This patient has now been out of treatment for nearly 18 months and has continued to do very well.

C.D., who also attained a zero level of seizures for periods of up to two weeks at a time, was withdrawn from treatment abruptly after approximately 55 days so that his medication could be adjusted. This patient was severely overmedicated at the beginning of the treatment program, but following a rapid reduction of seizures by 50%, his medication was adjusted. Note that after medication reduction, C.D. was able to reduce his seizures to the zero point. Weaning for this patient was rather abrupt at first but was made more gradual later on. This patient is no longer in training and is experiencing a small fraction of the tonic-clonic seizures that he did originally. The correlation of C.D.'s seizures over time was $-.069$, which was significant ($t = 3.71$, $df = 15$, $p < 0.01$).

Another partially successful case is illustrated in patient G.C. This patient is much older than the others (25 years), has a difficult family situation, and has partial seizures with complex symptoms (psychomotor). We have found that psychomotor seizures are somewhat more difficult to control than generalized tonic-clonic seizures and other seizures of a motor type. To make matters more difficult, before G.C. was taken into treatment he was placed on a new (Tegretol) medication, and showed an immediate reduction in seizures followed by an increase above the initial reading. It was at this point that training was instituted. A difficult home situation lead to a sustained increase in seizures during the middle of the training period. However, after 170 days of training, this patient was finally able to achieve a lower seizure level than during the best period for which the Tegretol was administered before SMR training. At this point, in consultation with the referring neurologist, Phenurone medication was reduced. This resulted in a transient increase in seizures followed by a reduction. G.C. has now been in training for more than one year. Phenurone medication has been further reduced and his seizure level is finally reduced markedly compared to initial levels (by more than 70%).

This case illustrates another important point, that the effects of SMR training do not always occur early in the treatment sequence. In the cases of M.T. and C.D., rapid early reductions were obtained. G.C. required more than one year of intensive training in order to

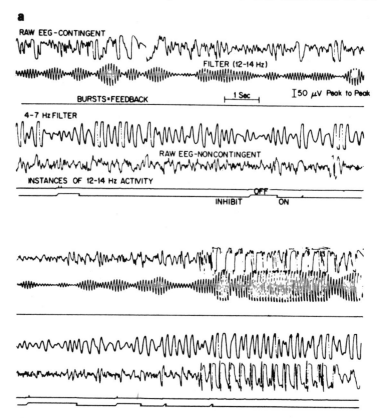

FIGURE 3a and b. Records from the clinical EEG sampled three months apart during training for patient K. S. Normalization is apparent in the set of Tracing B as compared with Tracing a. This normalization is demonstrated by a decrease in slow-wave epileptiform activity and an overall increase in the amount of SMR reinforcement. Furthermore,

bring seizures under better control. In all of these cases, as well as others from our population, there has been a reduction not only in the number of seizures but also in their intensity and duration, that is, the overall severity of the seizure condition. Changes in the EEG are illustrated in Figures 3 and 4 for three patients. These records are typical and were not specifically selected to show the effects. Such normalization has also been seen in patients trained in Finley's and Sterman's laboratories. Such positive EEG changes have been varified by spectral analyses. They consist primarily of three elements: (1) the reduction in epileptogenic slow-wave spike, polyspike, and other abnormal discharge patterns; (2) an overall reduction in the amplitude of the EEG;

b

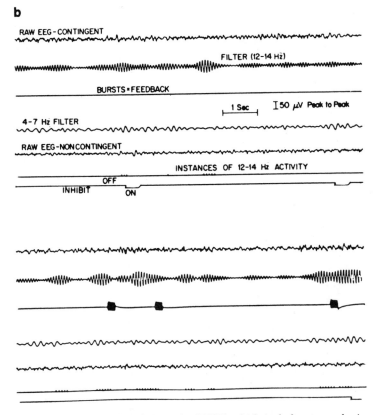

Record a shows a highly disorganized EEG, which includes a myoclonic seizure. Both records were obtained with identical calibrations and are representative samples of the types of positive changes that occur in many patients who have successfully decreased their seizures through biofeedback training.

and (3) an increase in the amount of higher-frequency activity above 12 Hz. All three processes tend to transform the abnormal EEG into a more normal appearing pattern. In all cases the normalization was accompanied by increased instances of reinforcement and decreased activity of the inhibitory channels.

Figure 5 illustrates the acquisition of SMR activity over sessions. Note that in the early sessions (18–46), with the exception of Sessions 44–46, there is a clear increase in the percentage of SMR over sessions. There is also a slight increase in the amount of SMR activity during baseline as well as when feedback was provided. However, in the later

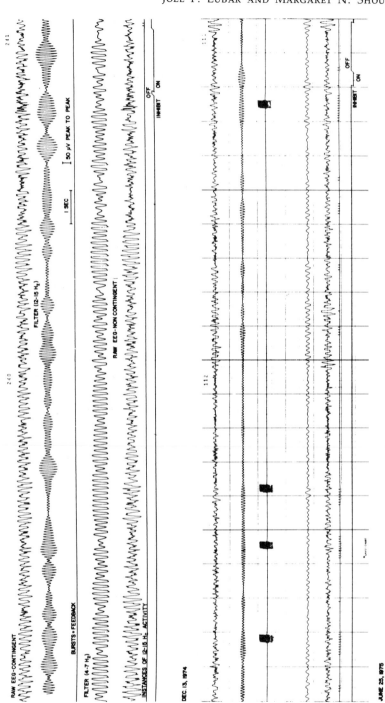

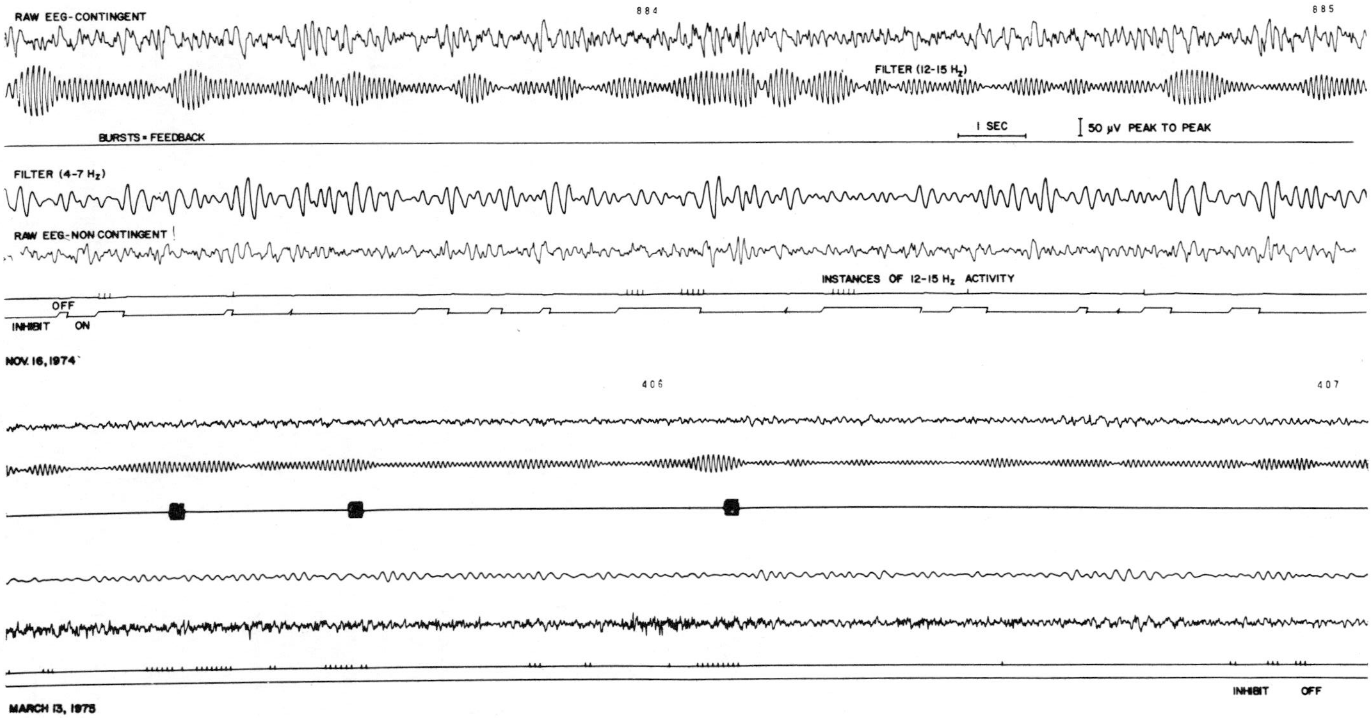

Figure 4a and b. EEG changes for patients G.B. and G.M. Patient G.B., a 29-year-old female, is from our larger population of epileptics. This patient suffered partial complex seizures. In both cases, there is considerable normalization of epileptogenic EEGs as recorded from electrode sites C3–T3 and C4–T4. This normalization is characterized by decreased high-amplitude slow-wave activity, decreased overall EEG amplitude and, increased activity in the SMR feedback circuits. Identical calibrations were used.

block of sessions, there is a further increase in the SMR, both with and without feedback. The latter illustrates the operation of a carry-over effect. It appears to be essential that such carry-over occur; otherwise the training would have very little meaning. The philosophy behind biofeedback training for seizure control is not just for the patient to be able to control EEG activity while connected to the equipment but, perhaps as envisioned by Sterman, to facilitate a "reorganization" of the nervous system so that seizure thresholds are altered both during and between training sessions.

Figure 6 is an example of changes that can be seen from Fast Fourier spectral analyses. Note that in the early sessions (Sessions 1, 15, and 30), there is considerable activity between 0 and 10 Hz, with the majority of peaks around 5–7 Hz. This represents the slow-wave paroxysmal activity. In the later sessions (Sessions 45 and 54), there is a decrease in the slow-wave epileptogenic activity and a strong peak has developed at 13 Hz, representing SMR that has been trained. E1, whose data are not illustrated in Figure 2, is from our larger population of 12 patients. This patient (19-year-old female) also showed a marked reduction of seizures and is now virtually seizure-free. She has been out of training for nearly two years, and her seizure data were discussed in previous publications (Seifert & Lubar, 1975; Lubar & Bahler, 1976).

In spectral analyses of the clinical EEG of E1 taken before training, there was considerable slow-wave activity in central and occipital leads. There was also a peak at approximately 9–10 Hz in the occipital and temporal leads. The latter was due to this patient's alpha rhythm. After training, there was a slight reduction in the slower frequencies and the appearance of a 13-Hz peak in the central, temporal, and occipital placements. There was also a disappearance of alpha activity in the latter two electrode sites. This finding tends to indicate that alpha rhythm and SMR are not only distinct entities but perhaps negatively correlated. One other point concerning alpha rhythm is that in most epileptics, alpha is slowed between 7 Hz and 10 Hz, whereas in non-epileptics it occurs between 8 Hz and 13 Hz. Because sensorimotor rhythm is between 12 and 15 Hz it is unlikely that the SMR training has been confounded by alpha conditioning.

3.4. Control Procedures: Evaluation of Overall Results of SMR Training

In various laboratories that are applying SMR methodology for epilepsy, several control procedures have been used. These are necessary because the frequency of epileptic seizures varies considerably over long periods of time. In some patients, the seizure frequencies are

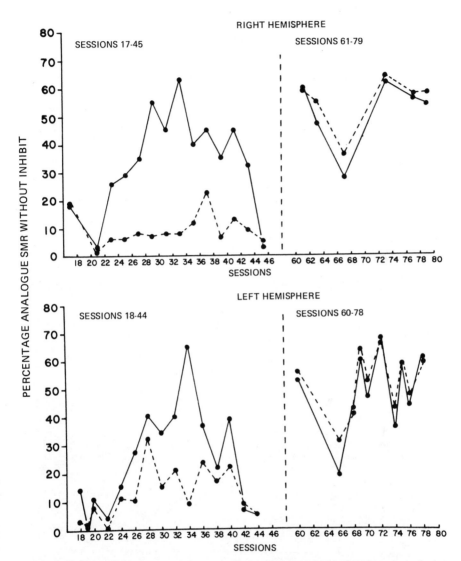

FIGURE 5. Percentage SMR for left and right hemispheres over blocks of sessions during baseline and feedback for patient G.C. There is a significant difference between the amount of SMR activity during baseline and feedback for the early block of sessions as shown in the left portion of the diagram. Feedback generally resulted in higher levels of SMR. During later blocks of sessions, both feedback and baseline levels of SMR increased. As described in the text, this increase indicates a carry-over effect of the training from feedback to baseline sessions. The amplitude criterion level for SMR reinforcement was 6 μV. For this particular measure, SMR is processed by a separate circuit from that used in feedback. This circuit was not inhibited by a 4–8 Hz slow waves or excessive EMG activity. Baseline - - -, feedback ——.

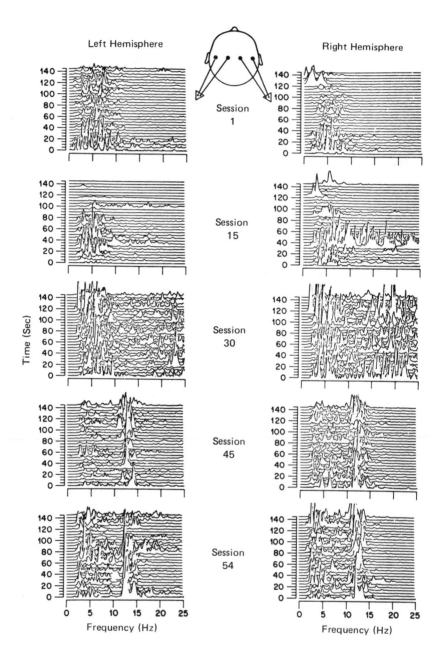

FIGURE 6. Spectral displays with compressed isometric routines for 19-year-old grand mal epileptic. As described in the text, there is an increase in 13-Hz activity in later sessions associated with a decrease in slow-wave epileptogenic activity.

cyclical over a period of years. In others, changes in medication cause immediate alterations in seizure frequency, as do other environmental and medical factors discussed previously. In addition, when patients are first brought into an SMR training program, they may have expectancies that lead to placebo effects, and some patients begin to comply with their medication requirements more stringently. To control for these and other problems that might confuse the preliminary positive results that have been obtained so far, several control procedures have been used by various researchers. One is the employment of noncontingent reinforcement, as reported by Finley (1975), in which a severe epileptic was given noncontingent reinforcement without his knowledge for a seven-week period. During this time, the percentage of SMR decreased associated with an increase in seizure events and the deterioration of the EEG. Following this period, contingent reinforcement was reinstituted and the patient showed improvement.

Kuhlman (1977) has employed a different procedure. He preceded feedback training with a prolonged period of noncontingent reinforcement specifically to introduce a control procedure during that period at the beginning of a training program when placebo effects might be strongest. During this time, Kuhlman's patients did not show positive changes in either seizure frequency or EEG but did following the initiation of contingent training.

Another approach is to use the ABA design described earlier. Sterman's laboratory is currently employing such techniques. In these studies, some patients are initially trained to produce 12–15 Hz activity (A condition) followed by a B period, when 6–9 Hz is reinforced and 12–15 Hz is inhibited. The B period is finally followed again by an A period, when 12–15 Hz is reinforced and 6–9 Hz is inhibited. Patients undergoing this training procedure have evidenced seizure reductions during the SMR portion of the program but have experienced a decrease in their seizure reductions and, in some cases, an increase in seizures in the B portion, followed by an improvement in the last A portion of the program.

Other patients are currently being trained first to produce slow-wave activity with inhibition of SMR, which does not lead to improvement, followed by SMR conditioning, which leads to an improvement. This is followed by a second 6–9 Hz training period with 12–15 Hz inhibited. Interestingly, once patients have been given SMR training, further training on 6–9 Hz does not lead to more seizures. Finally, these patients are given an opportunity to end their training program with more SMR training and again experience an improvement in seizure control.

Sterman and Lubar (research in progress) are trying to determine if other frequencies might be helpful in the training of epileptics. Currently, it appears that feedback-trained inhibition of slow-wave epileptogenic activity (2–8 Hz) by itself is not sufficient for obtaining seizure reductions. Another alternative is to reinforce fast activity (12-Hz to 18-Hz activity) representing the mirror image of the epileptic EEG without inhibition for the slow activity. This procedure produces a mixed result, with one of two patients showing an improvement and the other not responding.

Wyler (1977) has trained 19–25 Hz activity and has obtained improvements in several epileptic patients. Sterman is currently training some patients on 18–23 Hz and obtaining improvements as well. It therefore appears that learning to increase EEG activity between 12 Hz and 25 Hz is beneficial, with perhaps 12–15 Hz being the most beneficial and the higher frequencies being of secondary importance in the normalization of the epileptic EEG.

Summarizing the results from all of the laboratories that have published their results, a total of 30 epileptics have now been trained on either 12–15 Hz or higher frequencies for seizure reductions. Of these, 25% or 83% have shown significant seizure reductions. This is an encouraging beginning for the development of a new modality of treatment. Currently, all laboratories cited in this chapter are continuing actively to engage more patients in EEG biofeedback training. It is clear that studies of a much larger scope are needed before this training can become a meaningful clinical modality.

4. Future Directions

Almost all of the research dealing with the biofeedback control of seizures has been carried out on a restricted population of patients, primarily adolescents and young adults. Clearly, there is a need to work with older and younger populations. It is essential to determine the youngest group for whom this type of training might be meaningful and also to determine the effectiveness of biofeedback for children who have various degrees of brain damage. To this end, our laboratory is embarking on a field test of SMR training at the Chileda Institute for Educational Development at Stevens Point, Wisconsin. The Chileda Institute is a nonprofit organization providing a controlled environment for severely brain damaged, epileptic, and hyperkinetic children. The pilot study started in the fall of 1976 with children ages 6–13 who have severe uncontrolled seizures, which are in some cases compounded by brain damage and hyperkinesis. The same methodology and instrumentation used in our laboratory have been installed at

Chileda Institute. This instrumentation was developed by our laboratory for this field study. Preliminary results are already encouraging.

Research in other directions is needed to varify the effectiveness of SMR or other forms of EEG feedback training in seizure control. Currently, Lubar and Sterman (research in progress) are studying the effect of EEG biofeedback training on a large number of selected EEG frequency bands between 0 Hz and 27 Hz. The purpose is to determine how the various frequencies change as the EEG is modified by feedback training. Preliminary off-line analyses from tape-recorded training sessions indicate that as patients acquire either 12–15 Hz or 18–23 Hz activity, there is a normalization of the abnormal EEG. This normalization is reflected in an increase in the percentage of spectral power representing activity between 16 Hz and 27 Hz and a decrease in the relative (percentage of) spectral power for activity between 0 Hz and 11 Hz. In contrast, training 6–9 Hz activity is contraindicated for epileptics, as it increases the amount of slow-wave activity and decreases the amount of fast activity. If a more accurate picture of what is happening to the entire EEG spectrum as a function of training is to be provided, on-line spectral analyses are essential. Currently, none of the laboratories engaged in epilepsy feedback research have done on-line spectral analyses; however, our laboratory will move in this direction this year. With the use of an on-line spectral analysis, it would be possible, for example, to show a patient his progress, and to indicate where plateaus have occurred, and perhaps to give him better feedback information to speed up the normalizing process.

Another area in which progress is needed is in the development of an objective electronic method of seizure detection. Currently, there is no way of making a reliable 24-hour record of seizure events that is free of artifacts as a result of movement and other types of electronic interference. Another future development will involve the use of portable equipment. Currently, Sterman's laboratory has provided some patients with portable EEG equipment that can be taken home. Other laboratories involved in this research area are also in the process of developing portable equipment that can be used in either the home or the clinic.

It is clear from the findings presented that EEG biofeedback presents an interesting new modality that has shown considerable promise for dealing with the very difficult problem of epilepsy. This problem is a multidisciplinary one, and the psychologist alone cannot be responsible for the treatment of this complexity. Clearly, biofeedback should be used only in a clinical setting after a thorough medical diagnosis has been made. There should be interaction between the biofeedback trainer—whether a psychologist, a neurophysiologist, or a member of a related discipline—and the neurologist who has referred the patient. Such a dialogue is essential for a continual evaluation of results. Medical participation in a biofeedback application of this type is both the ethical and the legal responsibility of the biofeedback practitioner.

Finally, there is the question of the practicality of a biofeedback approach. The management of epilepsy is a very difficult task. The results reported here show that biofeedback training is also a tedious procedure that requires months and perhaps years for a satisfactory result. Clearly, this approach is not suited to the patient who has relatively few seizures or whose seizures can be controlled by moderate doses of medications that have relatively few unpleasant side effects. The use of biofeedback for the clinical or hospital outpatient treatment of epilepsy is going to be costly. It is important that charitable organizations, public agencies, and insurance companies help to defray some of these costs.

Many epileptics have very poor self-images. Biofeedback provides a method whereby the patient can gain varying degrees of control over what appears to be an overwhelmingly devastating disorder. For patients who opt to employ biofeedback to control their seizures, there is a promise of less psychological dependency. There is also a feeling of accomplishment in controlling one's own destiny, in as much as it is possible in the case of epilepsy.

It is also hoped that better anticonvulsant medications will appear that will be less debilitating and more potent. Certainly neither the pharmacological or the biofeedback approach should be considered to be in competition with each other. We have shown that when they are combined, a more satisfactory result is obtained, as the patient gains control over his own electrophysiological processes.

5. Hyperkinesis: General Considerations

5.1. Definition of the Disorder

The lack of agreement on the identifying features of hyperkinesis is reflected in estimates of its prevalence, which currently range from 5% to 22% of all elementary-school children (e.g., Minskoff, 1973). Nevertheless, a uniform set of research criteria may be derived from those characteristics most frequently agreed on by researchers. These include:

   1. Consensus of parents, teachers, and pediatricians on the coincidence of the two fundamental symptoms: undirected, cease-

less motor activity and abbreviated attention span (American Psychiatric Association, 1968).

2. The gender of the hyperkinetic population, which is predominately male.

3. The course of the syndrome, which typically spans the 6-year to 12-year age range (Menkes, Rowe, & Menkes, 1967).

4. The absence of specific sensorimotor deficients and other functional or physical handicaps (e.g., mental retardation), through which the syndrome's manifestations may be simulated.

Adopting such criteria not only appears justified on the basis of the available normative data (Wender, 1971) but should also yield incidence estimates of hyperkinesis in a more conservative and manageable range. Nevertheless, even these prerequisites are infrequently employed in a systematic fashion, and the resulting confusion has especially applied to organic interpretations of the hyperkinetic syndrome (Werry & Sprague, 1970; Omenn, 1973).

5.2. Hyperkinesis as a Brain-Damage Syndrome

Despite the diversity of opinion on the disorder's etiology, an organic substrate has been customarily assumed for hyperkinesis, and chemotherapy has been the preferred treatment. Historically, attention to hyperkinesis as a brain-damage syndrome emanated from the frequency with which overactivity characterized early postencephalitic cases (Hohman, 1922). The disorder's traditional association with brain damage is exemplified by frequent allusions in the medical literature to minimal brain dysfunction (MBD) and hyperkinesis as interchangeable labels for the syndrome. This practice may be attributed to the following findings relating hyperkinetic subjects to the normal population:

1. A 50% coincidence of a history of the disorder between hyperkinetic children raised by biological parents and full sibs raised in foster settings in contrast to a 14% coincidence of the disorder in half-sibs raised in foster settings (Wender, 1971).

2. A higher coincidence between hyperkinetic behavioral manifestations and a specific history of generalized brain damage, particularly encephalitis (Hohman, 1922).

3. A higher probability for hyperkinesis to be diagnosed in males (Wender, 1971), suggesting sex-linked holandric transmission.

4. A higher coincidence between a history of pre- and perinatal birth complications and subsequent diagnosis of hyperkinesis (Stewart, Pitts, Craig, & Dierak, 1966).

5. Reliable differential MBD diagnoses on the Reitan battery rela-

tive to normal children and children with severe cases of brain damage (Reitan & Boll, 1973).

Nevertheless, a number of factors militate against a brain-damage theory of origin. For example, even though a significantly higher percentage of hyperkinetic subjects display specific neurological diseases and "soft neurological signs" than do nonhyperkinetics (Satterfield, 1973), the coincidence of hyperkinesis and other disorders such as encephalitis (Bond & Smith, 1935) and epilepsy, or pre- and perinatal incidents such as accidental poisoning during early childhood (Stewart, et al., 1966), has rarely accounted for a very large proportion of the children diagnosed as hyperkinetic. In addition, the empirical basis on which hereditary estimates are based is extremely meager. No studies, for example, have been reported on the frequency of the disorder in first-degree relatives; also, only 14 sets of siblings participated in the adoption study cited above (Omenn, 1973; Wender, 1971), and the single twin-study available (Lopez, 1965) is inconclusive because a disproportionate number of the fraternal twins were of unlike sex. Finally, although Reitan and Boll (1973) have successfully identified hyperkinetic symptoms with moderate but significant deficits on Reitan's battery, they failed to include a control group of children displaying a history of disruptive behavior problems that are not typically associated with neurological origins. Knights and Tymchuk (1969) were unable to differentiate two such groups on the Halstead categories test, which is a highly reliable diagnostic sub-test of the Reitan examination. Until some clarification of these data is provided, only an insubstantial case can be made for brain damage as a necessary or even likely concomitant of hyperkinesis.

5.3. Treatment of Hyperkinetic Children

The equivocal basis for brain damage as a causal factor in hyperkinesis further obscures the puzzling outcomes reported with chemotherapy. The fact that sedatives exacerbate symptoms in hyperkinetic subjects apparently contradicts the somnolent effects otherwise obtained with these drugs. In contrast, the unprecedented therapeutic success of stimulant drugs, such as methylphenidate and the amphetamines, is contrary to the presumed excitatory nature of the disorder (e.g., Millichap, 1968). On the other hand, the paradoxical stimulant-drug effect does not appear to be a completely generalized phenomenon in the disorder, since moderate therapeutic benefits with tranquilizing agents have been reported in hyperkinetic children to whom stimulant drugs were either not administered or were unsuccessfully applied (e.g., Millichap, 1973).

Such evidence on the disorder's nature, symptoms, and treatment hardly yields a uniform profile of the syndrome. Although few would speculate that all diagnosed cases of hyperkinesis are properly admissible under the same rubric, one recently identified moderator variabler, CNS arousal level, may clarify many of the controversies.

5.4. CNS Arousal as an Integrative Mechanism in the Hyperkinetic Disorder

In the past decade, evidence has accumulated to suggest two meaningful subgroups of hyperkinetic subjects, one having reduced CNS arousal and the other displaying heightened CNS arousal (Satterfield, Cantwell, Lesser, & Rodesin, 1972). Excessive overactivity in low-arousal subjects is presumed to reflect the overcompensatory behavior of an otherwise sluggish organism. The selective effectiveness of stimulant medication in reducing these subjects' overactivity may therefore be explained by drugs' enhancing their physiological arousal level. In contrast, high-arousal subjects, whose excessive motor activity is presumably commensurate with the excitable state of the nervous system, should respond most favorably to CNS depressants. Establishing CNS arousal level as a moderating influence in the disorder may therefore account for the paradoxical calming effects associated with stimulant-drug administration in some hyperkinetic children and may permit more reliable predictions about the successful clinical application of both stimulants and depressants.

Low- and high-arousal children have been separated on the basis of three CNS-arousal indices taken individually (Satterfield, 1973; Satterfield, Lesser, Saul, & Cantwell, 1973; Satterfield & Dawson, 1971; Stevens, Sachdeo & Milstein, 1968) or in concert (Satterfield et al., 1972). Generally speaking, low-arousal subjects are characterized by excessive synchronized slow-wave activity in the waking EEG (e.g., Stevens et al., 1968), which suggests low arousal because alertness is typified by a faster, low-amplitude EEG (e.g., Penfield & Jasper, 1954); reduced GSR conductance (e.g., Satterfield et al., 1972), which indicates reduced sympathetic and reticular arousal (Duffy, 1962); and enhanced auditory evoked-response amplitudes (Satterfield et al., 1972), which indicate relaxation, reduced alertness (Guerrero-Figuera & Heath, 1964), and possibly abbreviated attention span (Satterfield, 1965). Subjects differing from controls in the low-arousal direction also displayed more severe disruptive-behavior symptoms (Stevens et al., 1968; Satterfield et al., 1972) and benefited most from stimulant-drug therapy (Satterfield & Dawson, 1971; Satterfield et al., 1972). Finally, medication produced moderate changes toward increased arousal in conjunction with substantial decreases in behavior problems.

High-arousal subjects, on the other hand, displayed less slow-wave activity, higher GSR conductance, and lower-amplitude evoked cortical responses. They also showed the least behavioral disturbance, and although there is no direct evidence that they selectively benefit from CNS depressants, these subjects responded less well, if not unfavorably, to stimulant-drug therapy. Posttreatment data indicated either unchanged or exacerbated behavioral disturbance combined with exceedingly reduced CNS arousal (Satterfield *et al.*, 1972).

These data are consistent with the rate-dependency findings in human and animal subjects in demonstrating that stimulant-drug treatment may affect motor activity either by increasing relatively low base-rates or by decreasing relatively high base-rates (e.g., Millichap, 1973; Stretch & Dalrymple, 1968). Furthermore, analogous drug effects on GSR and EEG base-rates in human subjects indicate levels of CNS arousal as a physiological mediator for the differing drug effects on hyperkinetic behavior.

6. SMR Biofeedback as an Independent Test of the Arousal Hypothesis and a Potential Treatment Modality

Even if stimulant drugs were demonstrably more effective for hyperkinetic children with reduced arousal, the role of arousal would remain uncertain since these drugs are known to affect both arousal (reticular) and motor systems concurrently (e.g., Millichap, 1968). A more conclusive assessment of CNS arousal functions in hyperkinesis has been investigated in our laboratory by the conditioning of increases in SMR, which, as shown in epileptics, is an EEG activity associated first with enhanced peripheral motor inhibition and second with changes in CNS arousal measures.

Because of its association with these two characteristics of hyperkinetic children, SMR biofeedback training should provide a convenient test of the arousal hypothesis. Contingent increases in SMR should result in reduced motor activity in all hyperkinetic subjects, increased physiological arousal in low-arousal subjects, and decreased physiological arousal in high-arousal children. This outcome would strengthen the arousal hypothesis. On the other hand, the exclusive display of training effects in either arousal level or motor activity would contraindicate the relevance of arousal as a primary factor in the disorder. In either case, a favorable outcome would provide a set of therapeutic procedures independent of the drug issue and perhaps of independent value when the use of drugs is contraindicated.

6.1. Project Description

6.1.1. Goals

The goals of our project were:

1. To subdivide hyperkinetic subjects on the basis of CNS arousal level.
2. To demonstrate more severe pretreatment overactivity and better treatment effects with stimulant drug (Ritalin) medication in subjects with *reduced* CNS arousal level than in subjects with *elevated* CNS arousal level.
3. To show greater treatment effects in low-arousal hyperkinetic subjects with drugs and SMR training than can be obtained with medication alone.
4. To demonstrate that positive treatment effects can be maintained with SMR training after medication is withdrawn.

6.1.2. Subjects

6.1.2.1. Hyperkinetic Subjects. In order to participate in all phases of the research (see Table 3), hyperkinetic subjects (total sample $n = 12$) had to meet a dual set of criteria. First, a uniform set of diagnostic criteria were required for admission to the initial baseline study. A child was considered an acceptable representative of the hyperkinetic population if he was:

1. Male.
2. Within the age range of 6–12 years.
3. Diagnosed as hyperkinetic by a pediatrician who considered the case severe enough to warrant medication.
4. Regularly taking methylphenidate (Ritalin).
5. Diagnosed as hyperkinetic according to the Stewart teacher questionnaire, requiring definite indication of at least six symptoms, including overactivity and short attention span (Stewart *et al.*, 1966).
6. Without specific sensory deficits or any other functional or physical illness (e.g., mental retardation or epilepsy) that might contribute to or otherwise be confounded with the target syndrome.

Second, participation in the SMR training sequence (training $n = 4$) was dependent upon pretraining arousal and behavioral profiles to be described later. The remaining eight subjects who did not participate in the SMR training sequence served as hyperkinetic control subjects.

TABLE 3

Number of Laboratory and Classroom Observation Sessions Conducted during Six Experimental Phases

		Baseline Sequence			Biofeedback Sequence		
	Experimental subjects	I No drug	II Drug only	III Drug & 12–14+ 4–7 Hz– feedback	IV Drug & 12–14 Hz– 4–7 Hz+ feedback	V Drug & 12–14+ 4–7 Hz– feedback	VI No drugs & 12–14 Hz+ 4–7 Hz– feedback
Behavioral sessions	1	6	6	78	38	30	24
	2	6	6	60	30	24	24
	3[a]	6	6	74	—	—	6
	4	6	6	68	26	24	26
Laboratory sessions	1	15	15	45	15	15	15
	2	15	15	30	15	15	15
	3[a]	15	15	30	—	—	15
	4	15	15	30	15	15	15
Laboratory sessions	Hyperkinetic (5–12) & normal	6	6	—	—	—	6
Behavioral sessions	(1–12) control subjects	15	15	—	—	—	15

[a]Training was discontinued in this subject following Phase III; nevertheless, at the end of the training period for the other subjects (Phase VI), additional baseline sessions were obtained for this subject.

6.1.2.2. *Normal Control Subjects.* Twelve normal (nonhyperkinetic) control subjects were also selected from a group of children nominated by the teachers of each hyperkinetic subject. At least two children from each class were nominated, and the final selection was based on the relevant matching characteristics (age, sex, IQ). In addition, the absence of criteria 3, 4, and 5 above for hyperkinetic subjects was required for each normal control.

6.1.3. Experimental Design

Initial baseline sessions (hyperkinetic $n = 12$) under no-drug (I) and drug-only (II) conditions were conducted in the absence of EEG biofeedback. Reference to these pretraining data permit assessments of the training procedure's therapeutic effects whether the drug regimen was sustained or withdrawn. The same dosage levels were maintained during all phases (II–V) employing chemotherapy.

The feedback contingency implemented in Phase III (training $n = 4$) required the production of 12–14 Hz EEG activity and the inhibition of 4-Hz to 4–7 Hz activity. A contingent increase in SMR production (12–14 Hz +; 4–7 Hz −) was followed by a contingency reversal (12–14 Hz −; 4–7 Hz +) in Phase IV. If pretraining performance levels under the drug-only condition (II) were resumed, the feedback manipulation used in training was assumed to produce whatever changes were evidenced during that time. The original contingency (12–14 Hz +; 4–7 Hz −) was reinstated during Phase V. In the final training phase (VI), the same EEG contingency was maintained after medication was withdrawn.

At the end of the training sequence, baseline measures under the no-drug condition (VI) were reassessed in all hyperkinetic subjects ($n = 12$). Baseline measures were also obtained from all 12 normal children before and at the end of the training period as indicated in Table 3.

6.1.4. Classroom and Laboratory Procedures

Classroom and laboratory apparatus and procedures have been described in detail elsewhere (Shouse, 1976; Lubar & Shouse, 1976). In addition to the 6 stimulus categories, 13 behavior categories selected as indices of overactivity and short attention span have been adapted, largely intact from a larger sample described in detail by Wahler, House, and Stanbaugh (1975).

The following physiological responses were monitored in the laboratory:

1. 4–7 Hz events: each 4–7 Hz signal above 12.5 μV:
2. SMR events: each 12–14 Hz signal above 5 μV in the absence of 12–14 Hz events:

3. SMR bursts: 6 cycles of SMR within 0.5 sec:
4. Background EEG:
5. Auditory evoked cortical responses:
6. EMG criterions: each set of 50 integrated EMG signals of predetermined amplitude between Hz 30 and 300 Hz.
7. GSR: basal skin resistance in response to 18 μA constant current read at 30-sec intervals and converted to conductance units (μmhos).

7. Results—Hyperkinesis Study

7.1. Pretraining Data

7.1.1. No-Drug Comparisons of Hyperkinetic and Normal Subjects

Overall differences between hyperkinetic and normal children on questionnaire, behavioral, and physiological measures during the no-drug condition are provided in Table 4. Hyperkinetic subjects differed significantly from normal ones in producing a higher frequency of parent- and teacher-reported developmental problems and symptoms of overactivity and distractibility. They also exhibited fewer desirable behaviors and more frequent undesirable and social behaviors in the classroom setting. In contrast to the questionnaire and behavioral findings, differences between the two groups in laboratory performance were confined to the relative dearth of SMR anticipated in hyperkinetic subjects. This statistically significant result was consistent with the EEG rhythm's noted correlation with behavioral immobility (Shouse, 1976).

7.1.2. Arousal Differences during the No-Drug Condition

A rank ordering of hyperkinetic and normal subjects as a function of physiological arousal level is presented in Figure 7. The distribution of these data demarcates the four hyperkinetic subjects who consistently showed reduced-arousal characteristics relative to normal control subjects and to the remainder of the hyperkinetic population. In the absence of high-arousal characteristics, the latter were labeled *hyperkinetic control subjects* to reflect extensive overlap with normal children on physiological measures.

Table 4 summarizes the performance of the three groups on all questionnaire, behavioral, and physiological measures during the no-drug condition. The statistical analyses presented confirmed advance predictions that the low-arousal subjects would display more severe

TABLE 4

Phase I (No-Drug) Differences in Laboratory Questionnaire and Behavioral Indices as a Function of Subjects' Arousal Level

	Low-arousal[b] hyperkinetics (n = 4)	Hyperkinetic controls (n = 8)	Normal controls (n = 12)
Laboratory data[a]			
Mean amplitude evoked cortical response (P2 μV)	19.8	15.2	14.5
Mean GSR conductance (μmhos)	4.7	17.5	19.5
Mean number of SMR bursts per minute	5.9	9.1	11.23
Mean number of EMG criterions per minute	70.12	113.1	118.2
Stewart questionnaire data			
Mean number of parent-reported symptoms (n = 47)	24.25	14.125	4.17
Mean number of parent-reported developmental anomalies (n = 30)	9.75	11.0	2.25
Mean number of teacher-reported symptoms (n = 37)	19.0	10.05	2.05
Behavioral data			
Mean number of undesirable behaviors (n = 6)	31.35	21.28	14.41
Mean number of desirable behaviors (n = 3)	12.39	27.28	50.83
Mean number of social behaviors (n = 4)	28.75	14.25	15.3

[a]Laboratory and behavioral data were assessed over days; consequently, the degrees of freedom were 5 and 14, respectively, for dependent t tests.

[b]Low-arousal versus hyperkinetic controls: *Evoked response amplitudes:* $t = 3.53$, $df = 5$, $p < 0.05$. *GSR conductance:* $t = -3.53$, $p < 0.05$. *EMG:* $t = 3.25$, $df = 5$, $p < 0.05$. *SMR:* $t = 3.72$, $df = 5$, $p < 0.05$. *Undesirable behaviors:* $t = 3.38$, $df = 14$, $p < 0.05$. *Desirable behaviors:* $t = 1.86$, $df = 14$, $p < 0.05$. *Social behaviors:* $t = 2.62$, $df = 14$, $p < 0.05$. *Parent-reported developmental problem:* $t = -6.7$, $df = 10$, $p < 0.05$. *Parent-reported symptoms:* $t = 2.95$, $df = 10$, $p < 0.05$. *Teacher-reported symptoms:* $t = 4.4$, $df = 10$, $p < 0.05$.

symptom profiles than hyperkinetic control subjects. According to qualitative assessments of questionnaire items, low-arousal subjects were more likely to be characterized as overactive, extraverted, and oppositional but were less likely than hyperkinetic control subjects to show severe attentional deficits. Also, although low-arousal subjects exhibited fewer parent-reported developmental problems than hyperkinetic control subjects, they were more likely to display problems in sensorimotor development (e.g., deficient large-muscle coordination, speech and hearing impediments) and to have experienced more medical problems at an early age (poor health in the first year, accidental injuries requiring emergency-room visits).

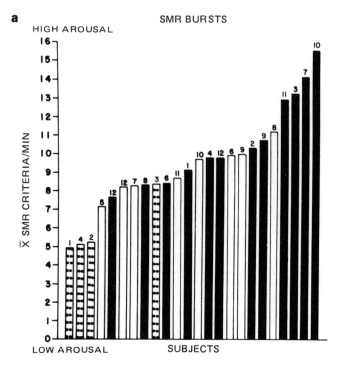

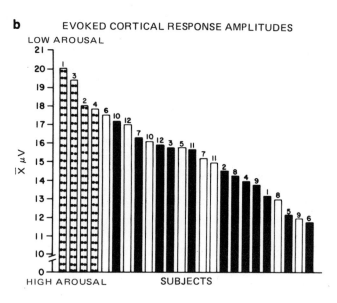

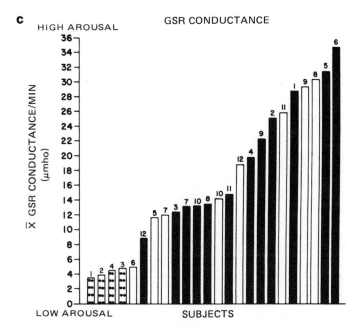

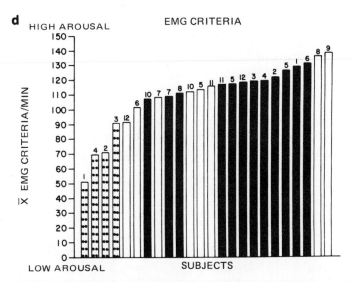

FIGURE 7a-d. Phase I (no-drug) laboratory results: hyperkinetic versus normal children as a function of arousal level. ⊞ Low arousal hyperkinetic subjects, □ hyperkinetic control subjects, ■ normal control subjects.

Table 5

*Phase I (No-Drug) versus Phase II (Drug-Only) Changes on Laboratory,
Questionnaire, and Behavioral Indices as a Function of Subjects' Arousal Level*

	Low-arousal[a] hyperkinetic	Hyperkinetic control	Normal control
Laboratory data			
Mean amplitude evoked cortical			
responses	Subjects	Subjects	Subjects
(P2 μV)	−3.0	+.9	+.35
Mean GSR conductance (μmhos)	+2.9	+.9	+1.25
Mean number of SMR bursts per minute	+4.42	+1.52	−1.6
Questionnaire data			
Mean number of teacher-reported symptoms	−5.75	−1.97	+2.25
Behavioral data			
Mean number of undesirable behaviors ($n = 6$)	−7.36	−2.24	+.51
Mean number of desirable behaviors ($n = 3$)	4.68	1.69	−.94
Mean number of social behaviors ($n = 4$)	−14.0	−.25	+.75

[a]*Low-arousal versus hyperkinetic controls: evoked responses:* $t = -2.12$, $df = 5$, $p < 0.05$. *GSR conductance:*
$t = 0.99$, $df = 5$, $p > 0.1$. *EMG:* $t = 2.5$, $df = 5$, $p < 0.05$. *SMR:* $t = 5.9$, $df = 5$, $p < 0.05$. *Undesirable
behaviors:* $t = -4.15$, $df = 14$, $p < 0.05$. *Desirable behaviors:* $t = 1.98$, $df = 14$, $p < 0.05$. *Social behaviors:*
$t = 5.8$, $df = 14$, $p < 0.05$. *Teacher-reported symptoms:* $t = 3.28$, $df = 19$, $p < 0.05$.

7.1.3. No-Drug and Drug-Only Comparisions

An analysis of change scores (no drug versus drug only) following
the administration of Ritalin is presented in Table 5. As expected, low-
arousal subjects benefited more by stimultant-drug medication than
did control hyperkinetics, whose performance did not significantly
differ from that in unmedicated normal subjects. Finally, although
low-arousal subjects exhibited significant change toward increased
physiological arousal level and improved classroom conduct, they still
displayed fewer desirable and more undesirable behaviors than did
either control group.

7.2. Training Data

7.2.1. Laboratory Findings

Figure 8 presents evidence supporting the notions that contingent
EEG feedback can produce orderly changes in SMR production relative
to daily and pretraining baselines and that corresponding changes in
EMG occur in the opposite direction as training progresses. SMR and
EMG values during the training sequence represent the following
ratio:

$$\frac{\overline{X} \text{ criterions per minute during initial 15-min feedback period}}{\overline{X} \text{ criterions per minute during initial 5-min feedback period}}$$

Comparable values are provided for pretraining baseline sessions when no feedback was presented.

Acquisition of the SMR task was demonstrated in three of four subjects. After six months of unsuccessful training, Subject 3's training was terminated. In Subjects 1, 2, and 4, negligible training effects occurring during early SMR training sessions were successively replaced by substantial increases in SMR ratios. Pretraining performance levels were temporarily resumed following a three-week lapse in SMR training for Subject 1 and the contingency-reversal phase in all three subjects. Original training effects were recovered when the SMR contingency was reinstated and were sustained following some variability in Phase VI, when medication was gradually withdrawn (5 mg/week). Finally, the inverse relationship between SMR and EMG is supported by moderate but statistically insignificant outcomes in the brief pretraining phases and by statistically significant ones during the three SMR training phases.

Power spectral analyses similar to those reported earlier for our epileptic patients were conducted during initial 5-min baseline periods for the four low-arousal hyperkinetics. The results of these analyses showed the following trends. Relative to the no-drug condition, there was a decline in slow-wave activity between 4 Hz and 7 Hz during the drug-only phase for all subjects. This change was not accompanied by a noticeable increase in the 12–14 Hz activity range, although slight to moderate increases in the 12–18 Hz activity subsequently appeared in the three subjects who responded to the feedback procedure. A temporary reversal in the latter trend during SMR counterconditioning (Phase IV) confirmed that the observed redistribution of power reflects treatment influences above and beyond those expected to accompany maturation alone. Finally, these changes were sustained during SMR conditioning in the absence of medication (Phase VI), thus supporting the effectiveness of the training procedures. As in the case of our epileptics, a baseline shift in the EEG appears to be reasonable if valid extrapolations from the laboratory to general experience are to be made.

Although the changes observed in the feedback-to-baseline ratios and in the spectral analyses were in the predicted direction, the disparity in the magnitude of effects shown in the two types of data is significant. One reason for this difference is that all three of the successfully trained children gritted their teeth during the initial 5-min baseline period. This action resulted in the spurious reduction of initial SMR base-rates. In addition, since EMG electrodes were attached to the chin, artifically high levels of baseline EMG also occurred. Since monetary rewards were based on SMR production during feedback relative to the initial baseline only, this practice tended to assure not only training success but also a highly negative correlation between

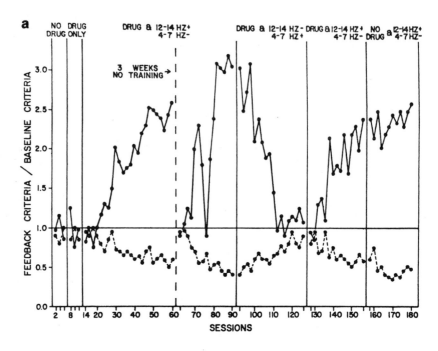

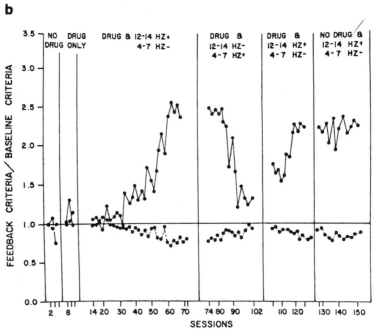

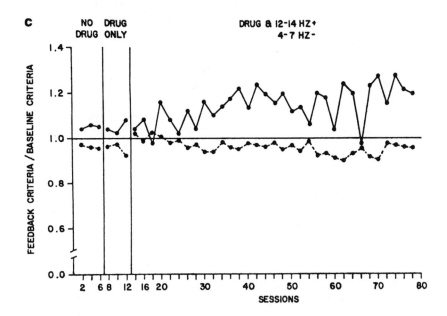

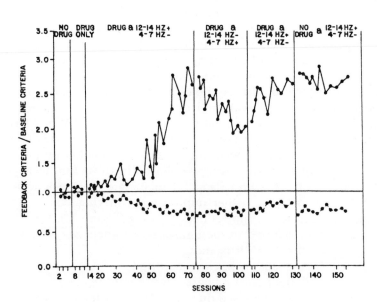

FIGURE 8a–d. SMR and EMG ratios over time for the four training subjects. ●——● 12–14 Hz, ● -- ● EMG.

SMR and EMG on a daily basis. Although monetary rewards were suspended following ostensible signs of the artifact in the EEG, verbal reports at the end of the training indicated that subjects continued to supplement their performance in a similar, if more subtle, fashion. The persistence of the artifact no doubt accounts for the remarkable appearance of the learning curves as well as for the modest changes found in the EEG spectra. Nevertheless, the fact that some evidence of a baseline shift in the EEG occurred in spite of teeth gritting strengthens our basis for postulating a carry-over effect from the laboratory setting.

7.2.2. Classroom Observations

Figures 9 through 12 present the average number of daily events scored per week for eight categories under six conditions in Subjects 1, 2, 3, and 4, respectively. Reliabilities were computed for two independent observers in half the sessions of each condition. Using the formula:

$$\frac{\text{Number of categories of agreement}}{\text{Number of categories of agreement and disagreement}}$$

the average reliabilities per session for Subjects 1, 2, 3, and 4 were greater than 80%.

Combining medication and SMR training was intended to enhance the level of improvement already achieved with drugs alone. The eight behaviors included in Figures 9 through 12 exhibit the predicted changes during SMR training. Relative to the no-drug phase, improvement in at least six of those categories was displayed during the drug-only phase in all four subjects. Generally, decreases in undirected activities, out-of-seat, and oppositional behaviors were accompanied by increased cooperation and schoolwork. When drugs and effective SMR training were combined (Subjects 1, 2, and 4), even further improvement occurred in the behaviors benefited by medication, and substantial changes were evidenced in those that were not. As expected, Subject 3, who failed to demonstrate SMR task acquisition, also failed to show further improvement in classroom conduct following the inception of biofeedback training (Figure 11).

Five behaviors omitted in the figures failed to change in the predicted direction during SMR training. One undirected activity (self-talk) and all four social behaviors occurred at moderate or high frequencies during the no-drug phase. Uniform decreases in them following drug-only were reversed during SMR conditioning in Subjects 1, 2, and 4, although the pretraining levels under no-drug were not resumed.

Changes in stimulus categories are also omitted. Positive and neg-

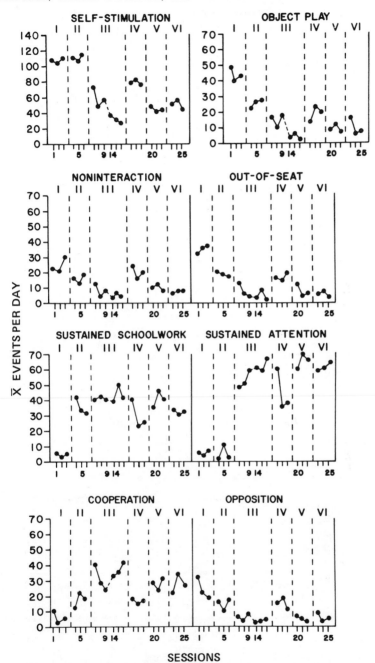

FIGURE 9. Changes in eight behaviors during SMR training: Subject 1. I No drug, II drug only, III drug and 12–14 Hz$^+$ 4–7 Hz$^-$, IV drug and 12–14 Hz$^-$ 4–7 Hz$^+$, V drug and 12–14 Hz$^+$ 4–7 Hz$^-$, VI no drug and 12–14 Hz$^+$ 4–7 Hz$^-$.

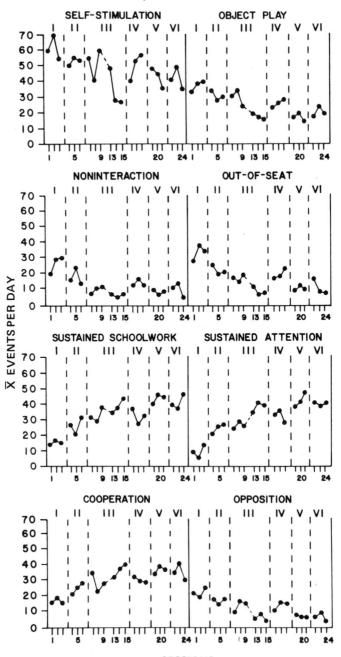

FIGURE 10. Changes in eight behaviors during SMR training: Subject 2. I No drug, II drug only, III drug and 12–14 Hz$^+$ 4–7 Hz$^-$, IV drug and 12–14 Hz$^-$ 4–7 Hz$^+$, V drug and 12–14 Hz$^+$ 4–7 Hz$^-$, VI no drug and 12–14 Hz$^+$ 4–7 Hz$^-$.

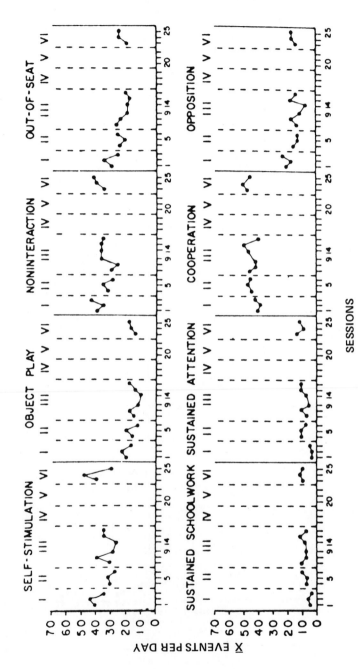

FIGURE 11. Absence of change in eight behaviors during ineffective SMR training: Subject 3. I No drug, II drug only, III drug and 12–14 Hz$^+$ 4–7 Hz$^-$, IV drug and 12–14 Hz$^-$ 4–7 Hz$^+$, V drug and 12–14 Hz$^+$ 4–7 Hz$^+$, VI no drug and 12–14 Hz$^+$ 4–7 Hz$^-$.

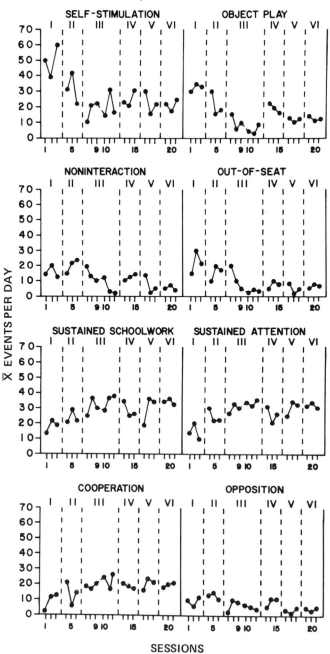

Figure 12. Changes in eight behaviors during SMR training: Subject 4. I No drug, II drug only, III drug and 12–14 Hz$^+$ 4–7 Hz$^-$, IV drug and 12–14 Hz$^-$ 4–7 Hz$^+$, V drug and 12–14 Hz$^+$, 4–7 Hz$^-$, VI no drug and 12–14 Hz$^+$ 4–7 Hz$^-$.

ative instructions as well as negative social attention from both teachers and peers occurred infrequently during the study regardless of the experimental condition. However, relative to the no-drug phase, positive social attention from peers decreased in the drug-only condition in all subjects and during both treatment conditions in Subjects 1, 2, and 4. Although this reduction varied inversely with improvement in the child's hyperkinetic behaviors in general, it varied most often as a direct function of reductions in self-initiated social approaches to peers. The correlation between the two events was fairly consistent in each subject across conditions, despite overall reductions in their frequency following the no-drug phase. It would be difficult, then, to conclude that changes in peer reinforcement contributed directly, or even positively, to the observed changes in the target indices of hyperactivity. Rather, it would appear that treatment-related reductions in subject-initiated social approaches stimulated the decline in this reinforcement category.

7.2.3. Pretraining versus Posttraining Analyses

An analysis of the training data suggested not only that combining medication and SMR conditioning leads to more desirable changes in hyperkinetic behaviors than the changes resulting from the use of drugs alone but also that these benefits are sustained following the withdrawal of medication. These contentions are supported and extended by the data presented in Figures 13 and 14, which show physiological and behavioral changes during the no-drug (I), drug-only (II), and no-drug-and-SMR training (VI) phases in all subjects and in Table 9-6, which presents the mean change in all dependent measures between the drug-only (II) and the no-drug-and-SMR training (VI) phases. Physiological and behavioral benefits associated with SMR training are indicated by the following findings:

1. A greater degree of improvement shown by low-arousal subjects during SMR training alone (Phase VI) than during medication alone (Phase II).
2. A better treatment outcome by the end of training (Phase VI versus Phase II) in low-arousal subjects than in hyperkinetic control subjects who did not participate in training and whose physiological and behavioral profile remained relatively stable regardless of the administration or withdrawal of medication.
3. The increasing resemblance between the posttraining profiles of SMR-trained and normal control subjects for many of the measures.

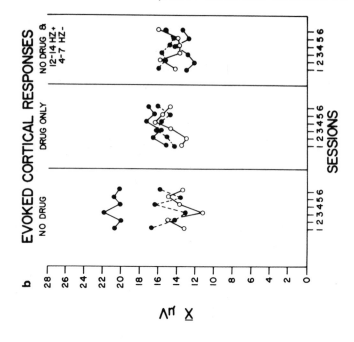

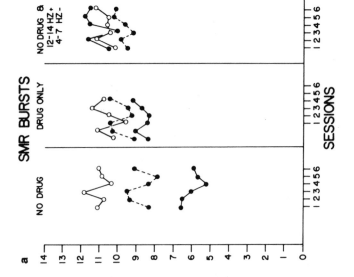

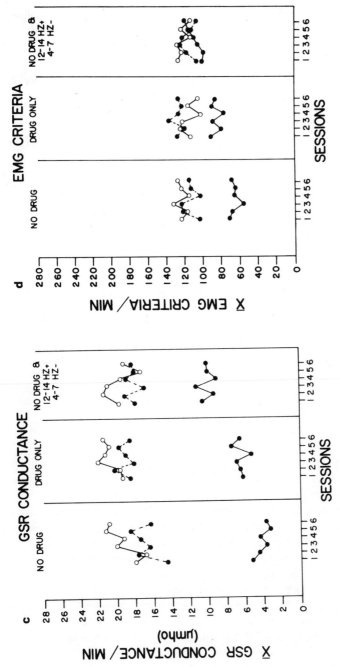

Figure 13a–d. Daily changes in four laboratory measures during Phase I (no drug, left panel), Phase II (drug only, center panel), and Phase VI (no drug and SMR training, right panel) in low-arousal and control hyperkinetic subjects and normal control children. Low-arousal hyperkinetic versus normal control during Phase VI: EMG: $t = 0.11$, $df = 0.5$, $p > 0.1$: Evoked response amplitude: $t = 1.11$, $df = 5$, $p > 0.1$: SMR bursts: $t = 1.57$, $df = 5$, $p = 0.1$: GSR: $t = 6.8$, $df = 5$, $p > 0.05$. ●——● Low arousal, hyperkinetic subjects, ●--● hyperkinetic control subjects, ○——○ normal control subjects.

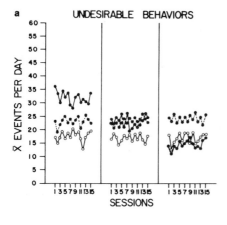

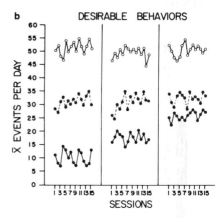

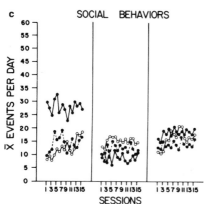

FIGURE 14a-c. Daily changes in (a) desirable, (b) undesirable, and (c) social behaviors during Phase I (no drug, left panel), Phase II (drug only, center panel), Phase VI (no drug and SMR training, right panel) in low-arousal and control hyperkinetic subjects and normal control children. Low-arousal hyperkinetic versus normal control children during Phase VI: *Undesirable behaviors:* $t = 0.93$, $df = 14$, $p > 0.1$: *Desirable behaviors:* $t = 2.72$, $df = 14$, $p < 0.05$: *Social behaviors:* $t = 0.16$, $df = 14, p > 0.1$. ●——● Low arousal, hyperkinetic subjects, ●--● hyperkinetic control subjects, ○——○ normal control subjects.

All training-related changes in low-arousal subjects were in the predicted direction and were statistically significant relative to their own drug-only performance and to the performance of hyperkinetic controls during Phases II and VI, shown in Table 6. Additionally, relative to normal controls, the absolute posttraining values in low-arousal subjects showed incomplete normalization only in GSR conductance and desirable behaviors (Figures 13 and 14). Otherwise, SMR-trained subjects could not be differentiated physiologically or behaviorally from normal subjects by the end of the study.

The greatest improvement appears to have occurred in undesirable behaviors, which primarily reflected motor disturbance. This finding is supported both by the selective normalization of undesirable behaviors in the classroom and by the tendency for teachers to continue complaining only of attentional deficits in Phase VI, even

TABLE 6

Phase II (Drug Only) versus Phase VI (No Drug and SMR Training) Changes on Laboratory, Questionnaire, and Behavioral Indices as a Function of Subjects' Arousal Level

	Low-arousal hyperkinetics $(n = 3)$[a]	Hyperkinetic controls $(n = 8)$	Normal controls $(n = 12)$
Laboratory data			
Mean-amplitude-evoked cortical response (P2 μV)	−3.9[b]	+4.5[c]	+.27[d]
Mean GSR conductance (μmhos)	+3.6	−.15	−.10
Mean number of SMR bursts per minute	+2.97	−0.3	−.24
Mean number of EMG criterions per minute	+14.07	−2.25	+1.8
Questionnaire data			
Mean number of teacher-reported symptoms	−6.25	+2.0	−.16
Behavioral data			
Mean number of undesirable behaviors	−8.3	+1.3	−.22
Mean number of desirable behaviors	+9.58	+.52	+1.58
Mean number of social behaviors	+4.25	+2.0	+.75

[a]The low-arousal subject (3) who failed to acquire the SMR task is not included in the statistical analyses.
[b]DRUG alone versus SMR alone in low-arousal subjects: Evoked-response amplitudes: $t = 2.8$, $df = 5$, $p < 0.05$. GSR: $t = 2.27$, $df = 0.05$, $p < 0.05$. SMR bursts: $t = -2.96$, $df = 5$, $p < 0.55$. EMG: $t = 2.8$, $df = 5$, $p < 0.05$.
[c]Low-arousal versus hyperkinetic controls: Evoked-response amplitude: $t = 2.0$, $df = 5$, $p < 0.05$. GSR: $t = 2.27$, $df = 5$, $p < 0.05$. SMR bursts: $t = 2.96$, $df = 5$, $p < 0.05$. Teacher-reported symptoms: $t = 3.0$, $df = 2$, $p < 0.05$. Undesirable behaviors: $t = 4.5$, $df = 14$, $p < 0.05$. Desirable behaviors: $t = 3.48$, $df = 14$, $p < 0.05$. Social behaviors: $t = 2.37$, $df = 14$, $p < 0.05$.
[d]Low-arousal versus normal controls: Evoked response: $t = 0.87$, $df = 6$, $p > 0.1$. GSR: $t = 0.96$, $df = 6$, $p > 0.1$. SMR bursts: $t = 0.86$, $df = 6$, $p > 0.1$. EMG: $t = 0.77$, $df = 6$, $p > 0.1$. Teacher-reported symptoms: $t = 1.99$, $df = 6$, $p < 0.05$. Undesirable behaviors: $t = 1.10$, $df = 14$, $p > 0.1$. Desirable behaviors: $t = 1.6$, $df = 14$, $p > 0.1$. Social behaviors: $t = 1.41$, $df = 14$, $p > 0.1$.

though improvement in both overactivity and distractibility were reported. In contrast, desirable behaviors, which primarily reflected attention span, showed incomplete remission by the end of training. These findings suggest a greater relative role for motor functions in a successful training outcome.

8. Conclusions

The effectiveness of the biofeedback technique in dealing with hyperkinesis is supported by the fact that the combined effects of drug administration and SMR training resulted in substantial improvement above and beyond the effects of drugs alone. Further support derives from the maintenance of positive treatment effects with SMR training after medication was withdrawn. The loss of improvement following SMR counterconditioning tends to minimize the role of extraneous influences (e.g., maturation) on treatment outcomes. Finally, the fact that the subject who failed to acquire the SMR task also failed to develop associated physiological and beahvioral changes lends additional credence to these assertions.

These findings clearly implicate both CNS arousal level and central motor-system functions in the development of the hyperkinetic syndrome and its treatment. However, since SMR acquisition, normalization of CNS arousal indices, and behavioral improvement appear to have emerged concurrently, it is difficult to determine whether the observed behavioral outcomes reflect primary changes in CNS arousal or whether the arousal changes represent a secondary effect from enhanced motor control.

An analysis of individual differences in laboratory and classroom performance suggests a greater relative role for enhanced motor control than for arousal level in training success. Two interrelated factors in the no-drug condition may have influenced susceptibility to treatment in the four training subjects. First, pretreatment laboratory data indicated a greater relative dearth of SMR in the subjects who responded most favorably both to medication and to SMR training (Subjects 1, 4, 2, and 3, respectively). Although SMR has also been considered here as a CNS arousal index, the other, more traditional physiological measures of arousal were consistently less effective in predicting treatment outcomes. Second, the interview and behavioral assessments designate excessive overactivity as the dominant problem area in children with reduced SMR production. In contrast, the subject who failed to demonstrate acquisition of the SMR task not only produced the highest pretreatment level of SMR but also displayed abbreviated attention span rather than overactivity as his principal behavioral deficit.

Pretreatment levels of SMR, then, most conveniently and reliably indexed both the severity of the original motor deficits and the subsequent success of both treatments in mitigating those symptoms. These findings not only reconfirm the relationship between SMR and behavioral immobility but also suggest the EEG rhythm's potential value as a diagnostic and prognostic tool in the disorder, especially when overactivity is a central feature. These findings are also consistent with recent research linking reduced production of the Rolandic rhythm in epileptics who have a primary motor symptomatology to a higher probability of successful treatment outcomes during SMR biofeedback training (Sterman, 1976).

Despite these promising findings, a cautious interpretation is particularly warranted in view of the heterogeneous symptom profiles typically included in MBD diagnoses, the specificity of the physiological- and behavioral-symptom profiles considered here, and the inability to produce feedback-related changes in one of the four subjects. The possibility exists that short attention span, although partially controlled by medication, may have interfered with successful training in the one negative case. This outcome could restrict the procedure's therapeutic utility on a larger scale since some degree of reduced attention span is symptomatic of the disorder. A considerable increase in the subject population is necessary before adequate evaluation is possible either of the procedure's general application to hyperkinesis or of its basis in CNS mechanisms of arousal or motor control.

ACKNOWLEDGMENTS

The authors would like to acknowledge Ms. Renee Culver and Mr. Tom Curlee of Biotechniques Incorporated and the ORTEC Corporation, for the development of the instrumentation used in this research, and Ms. Charlotte Gasker for the preparation and typing of this manuscript. We gratefully acknowledge Dr. Ted Mott, Department of Nuclear Engineering of the University of Tennessee, for the use of their facilities in carrying out the spectral analyses presented here and for their kind technical assistance. We would like to acknowledge Dr. Hammond Pride, Dr. Robert Crawford, Dr. William Paulsen, and Dr. Stephen Natelson, for referring the hyperkinetic and epileptic subjects, and the teachers of the hyperkinetic subjects for nominating the normal control children and for cooperating with the classroom observation team. We also acknowledge John Maltry and Bret Boring for technical assistance in the laboratory; Mr. William Bahler, who has worked diligently with the epileptic patients; and Jack Dryden, Steven Soaf, and other undergraduate assistants, who helped in the behavioral observations required for the hyperkinesis research. The research reported here on hyperkinesis is based on a doctoral dissertation by M. E. Shouse, University of Tennessee, 1976.

References

American Psychiatric Association. *Diagnostic and statistical manual of mental disorders,* No. D-SM-11, 1968.

Andersen, P., & Andersson, S. A. Physiological basis of the alpha rhythm. New York: Appleton-Century-Crofts, 1968.

Basmajian, J. V. Electromyography comes of age. *Science,* 1972, *176,* 603–609.

Battini, C., Moruzzi, G., Palestini, M., Rossi, G. F., & Zanchetti, A. Persistent patterns of wakefulness in the pre-trigiminal midpointine preparation. *Science,* 1958, *128,* 30–32.

Beatty, J. Similar effects of feedback signals and instructional information on EEG activity. *Physiology and Behavior*, 1973, *9*, 151–154.

Bickford, R. G., & Fleming, N. *EDAS-1 data analysis system*. San Diego: School of Medicine, University of California, 1970.

Blanchard, E. B., and Young, L. D. Clinical applications of biofeedback training. *Archives of General Psychiatry*, 1974, *30*, 573–589.

Bleecker, E. R., & Engel, B. T. Learned control of ventricular rate in patients with atrial fibrillation. *Psychomatic Medicine*, 1973, *35*, 161–170.

Bond, E. D., & Smith, L. H. Postencephalitic behavior disorders. *American Journal of Psychiatry*, 1935, *92*, 17.

Brazier, M. A. B. The problem of periodicity in the electroencephalogram: Studies in the cat. *Electroencephalography and Clinical Neurophysiology*, 1963, *15*, 287–29.

Brudny, J., Korein, J., Levidow, L., Brynbaum, B. B., Liberman, A., & Friedmann, L. W. Sensory feedback therapy as a modality of treatment in central nervous system disorders of voluntary movement. *Neurology*, 1974, *24*, 925–932.

Budznyski, T. H., Stoyva, J. M., Adler, C. S., & Mullaney, D. J. EMG biofeedback and tension headache: A controlled outcome study. *Psychosomatic Medicine*, 1973, *35*, 484–496.

Cereghino, J. J. Epidemiology and basic statistics on the epilepsies: Where are we. Paper presented at the Fifth National Conference on the Epilepsies, Washington, D.C., 1976.

Denhoff, E. The natural life history of children with minimal brain dysfunction. *Annals of the New York Academy of Sciences*, 1973, *205*, 188–205.

Duffy, E. *Activation and behavior*. New York: Wiley, 1962.

Eccles, J. C., Ito, M., & Szentagothai, J. *The cerebellum as a neuronal machine*. New York: Springer, 1967.

Efron, R. The conditional inhibition of uncinate fits. *Brain*, 1957, *80*, 251–262.

Elder, S. T., Ruiz, Z. R., Deabler, H. L., & Dillenkoffer, R. L. Instrumental conditioning of diastolic blood pressure in hypertensive patients. *Journal of Applied Behavior Analysis*, 1973, *6*, 377–382.

Engel, B. T., Nikoomanesh, P., & Schuster, M. M. Operant conditioning of rectosphincteric responses in the treatment of fecal incontinence. *New England Journal of Medicine*, 1974, *290*, 646–649.

Feldman, S. M., & Waller, H. K. Dissociation of electrocortical activation and behavioral arousal. *Nature*, 1960, *196*, 1320–1322.

Finley, W. W. Seven weeks noncontingent feedback after one year of SMR biofeedback treatment in a severe epileptic: Follow-up study. *Proceedings of the Biofeedback Research Society Meeting*, Monterey, Calif., 1975.

Finley, W. W. Operant conditioning of the EEG in two patients with epilepsy: Methodologic and clinical considerations. *Pavlovian Journal of Biological Science*, 1977, I *In press*.

Finley, W. W., Smith, H. A., & Etherton, M. D. Reduction of seizures and normalization of the EEG in a severe epileptic following sensorimotor biofeedback training: Preliminary study. *Biological Psychology*, 1975, *2*, 189–203.

Fischer, K. C., & Wilson, W. P. Methylphenidate and the hyperkinetic state. *Diseases of the Nervous System*, 1971, *32*, 695–698.

Forster, F. M. Conditioning in sensory evoked seizures. *Conditional Reflex*, 1966, *1*, 224–234.

Gastaut, H. Étude electrocorticographique de la réactivite des rythmes rolandiques. *Review of Neurology*, 1952, *87*, 176.

Gastaut, H. Clinical and electroencephalographical classification of epileptic seizures. *Epilepsia*, 1970, *11*, 102–113.

Gastaut, H., Naquet, R., & Gastaut, Y. A study of the mu rhythm in subjects lacking one or more limbs. *Electroencephalography and Clinical Neurophysiology*, 1965, *18*, 720–721.

Gazzaniga, M. S. Brain theory and minimal brain dysfunction. *Annals of the New York Academy of Sciences*, 1973, *205*, 89–92.

Gelhorn, E. Central nervous system tuning and its implications for neuropsychiatry. *Journal of Nervous and Mental Disease*, 1968, *147*, 148–162.

Greenfield, N. S., & Sternbach, R. A. (Eds.). *Handbook of psychophysiology*. New York: Holt, Rinehart, and Winston, 1972.

Guerrero-Figueroa, R., & Heath, R. G. Evoked responses and changes during attentive factors in man. *Archives of Neurology*, 1964, *10*, 74–84.

Hallgreen, B. Specific dyslexia. *Acta Psychiatry Scandanavica Supplement*, 1950, *65*, 83.

Harper, R. M., & Sterman, M. B. Subcortical unit activity during a conditioned 12–14 Hz sensorimotor EEG rhythm in the cat. *Federation Proceedings*, 1972, *31*, 404.

Hauri, P. Biofeedback as a treatment for insomnia. *Proceedings of the Biofeedback Research Society*, seventh annual meeting, Colorado Springs, 1976, p. 34.

Hohman, L. B. Post-encephalitic behavior disorders in children. *Johns Hopkins Hospital Bulletin*, 1922, *380*, 372.

Jovanovic, U. J. *Psychomotor epilepsy: a polydimensional study*. Springfield, Ill.: Charles C Thomas, 1974.

Kamiya, J. Operant control of the EEG alpha rhythm and some of its reported effects on consciousness. *In* C. T. Tart (Ed.), *Altered states of consciousness*. New York: Wiley, 1969, pp. 507–517.

Kaplan, B. J. Biofeedback in epileptics: Equivocal relationship of reinforced EEG frequency to seizure reduction. *Epilepsia*, 1975, *16*, 477–485.

Knights, R. M., & Tymchuk, A. J. An evaluation of the Halstead-Reiton category tests for children. *Cortex*, 1969, *4*, 403–414.

Kuhlman, W. N., & Allison, T. EEG feedback training in the treatment of epilepsy: Some questions and some answers. *Pavlovian Journal of Biological Science*, 1977, *In press*.

Lopez, R. E. Hyperactivity in twins. *Canadian Psychiatric Association Journal*, 1965, *10*, 421.

Lubar, J. F. Behavioral management of epilepsy through sensorimotor rhythm EEG biofeedback conditioning. *National Spokesman*, 1975, *8*, 6–7.

Lubar, J. F. Electroencephalographic biofeedback methodology and the management of epilepsy. *Pavlovian Journal of Biological Science*, 1977, *In press*.

Lubar, J. F., & Bahler, W. W. Behavioral management of epileptic seizures following EEG biofeedback training of the sensorimotor rhythm. *Biofeedback and Self-Regulation*, 1976, *1*, 77–104.

Lubar, J. F., & Shouse, M. N. EEG and behavioral changes in a hyperkinetic child concurrent with training of the sensorimotor rhythm (SMR): A preliminary report. *Biofeedback and Self-Regulation*, 1976, *1*, 293–301.

Lynch, J. J., & Paskewitz, D. A. On the mechanisms of the feedback control of human brain wave activity. *Journal of Nervous and Mental Disease*, 1971, *153*, 205–217.

Masland, R. L. Epidemidogy and basic statistics on the epilepsies: Where are we? Paper presented at the Fifth National Conference on the Epilepsies, Washington, D.C., 1976.

Menkes, M. M., Rowe, J. S., & Menkes, J. H. A 25 year follow-up study on the hyperkinetic child with minimal brain dysfunction. *Pediatrics*, 1967, *39*, 393.

Millichap, J. G. Drugs in the management of hyperkinetic and perceptually handicapped children: Council on drugs. *Journal of the American Medical Association*, 1968, *206*, 1527–1530.

Millichap, J. G. Drugs in the management of minimal brain dysfunction. *Annals of the New York Academy of Sciences*, 1973, 205, 321–334.

Minskoff, J. G. Differential approaches to prevalence estimates of learning disabilities. *Annals of the New York Academy of Sciences*, 1973, 205, 139–145.

Omenn, G. S. Genetic approaches to the syndrome of minimal brain dysfunction. *Annals of the New York Academy of Sciences*, 1973, 205, 212–311.

Penfield, W., & Jasper, H. H. *Epilepsy and the functional anatomy of the human brain*. Boston: Little, Brown, 1954.

Reitan, R. M., & Boll., T. J. Neuropsychological correlates of minimal brain dysfunction. *Annals of the New York Academy of Sciences*, 1973, 205, 65–88.

Roth, S. R., Sterman, M. B., & Clemente, C. D. Comparison of EEG correlates of reinforcement, internal inhibition, and sleep. *Electroencephalography and Clinical Neurophysiology*, 1967, 23, 509–520.

Sargent, J. D., Green, E. E., & Walters, D. Preliminary report on the use of autogenic feedback training in the treatment of migraine and tension headaches. *Psychosomatic Medicine*, 1973, 35, 129–135.

Satterfield, J. H. Evoked cortical response enhancement and attention in man: A study of responses to auditory and shock stimuli. *Electroencephalography and Clinical Neurophysiology*, 1965, 19, 470–475.

Satterfield, J. H. EEG issues in children with minimal brain dysfunction. *Seminars in Psychiatry*, 1973, 5, 35–46.

Satterfield, J. H., Cantwell, D. P., Lesser, L. I., & Rodesin, R. L. Physiological studies of the hyperkinetic child: I. *American Journal of Psychiatry*, 1972, 128, 1418–14 Satterfield, J. H., & Dawson, M. E. Electrodermal correlates of hyperactivity in children. *Psychophysiology*, 1971, 80, 191–197.

Satterfield, J. H., & Dawson, M. E. Electrodermal correlates of hyperactivity in children. *Psychophysiology*, 1971, 80, 191–197.

Satterfield, J. H., Lesser, R. I., Saul, R. E., & Cantwell, D. P. EEG aspects in the diagnosis and treatment of minimal brain dysfunction. *Annals of the New York Academy of Science*, 1973, 205, 274–282.

Schwartz, G. E. Biofeedback self regulations and patterning of physiological processes. *American Scientist*, 1975, 63, 314–324.

Schwartz, G. E., & Shapiro, D. Biofeedback and essential hypertension: Current findings and theoretical concerns. *Seminars in Psychiatry*, 1973, 5, 493–503.

Seifert, A. R., & Lubar, J. F. Reduction of epileptic seizures through EEG biofeedback training. *Biological Psychology*, 1975, 3, 81–109.

Sharpless, S., & Jasper, H. H. Habituation of the arousal reaction. *Brain*, 1956, 79, 555–680.

Shouse, M. N. The role of CNS arousal levels in the management of hyperkinesis: Methylphenidate and EEG biofeedback training. Doctoral dissertation, University of Tennessee, 1976.

Sterman, M. B. Effects of brain surgery and EEG operant conditioning on seizure latency following monomethylhydrazine intoxication in the cat. *Experimental Neurology*, 1976, 50, 757–765.

Sterman, M. B. Sensorimotor EEG operant conditioning and experimental and clinical effects. *Pavlovian Journal of Biological Science* 1977, *In press*.

Sterman, M. B. & Friar, L. Suppression of seizures in an epileptic following sensorimotor EEG feedback training. *Electroencephalography and Clinical Neurophysiology*, 1972, 33, 89–95.

Sterman, M. B., LoPresti, R. W., & Fairchild, M. D. *Electroencephalographic and behavioral studies of monomethylhydrazine toxicity in the cat*. Technical Report AMRL-TR-69-3, Air Systems Command, Wright-Patterson Air Force Base, Ohio, 1969.

Sterman, M. B., MacDonald, L. R., & Stone, R. K. Biofeedback training of the sensorimotor electroencephalographic rhythm in man: Effects on epilepsy. *Epilepsia,* 1974, *15,* 395–416.

Sterman, M. B. & Wywricka, W. A. EEG correlates of sleep evidence for separate forebrain substrates. *Brain Research,* 1967, *6,* 143–163.

Stevens, J. R., Milstein, V. M., & Dodds, S. A. Endogenous spike discharges as conditioned stimuli in man. *Electroencephalography and Clinical Neurophysiology,* 1967, *23,* 57–66.

Stevens, J. R., Sachdeo, K., & Milstein, V. Behavior disorders of childhood and the electroencephalogram. *Archives Neurology,* 1968, *18,* 160.

Stewart, M. A. Hyperactive children. *Scientific American,* 1970, *222,* 94–98.

Stewart, M. A., Pitts, F. N., Craig, A. G., & Dierak, W. The hyperactive child syndrome. *American Journal of Orthopsychiatry,* 1966, *36,* 861–867.

Stewart, M. A., Thack, B. T., & Freidin, M. *Diseases of the Nervous System,* 1970, *31,* 403–407.

Stretch, R., & Dalrymple, D. *Psychopharmacologia,* 1968, *13,* 49–64.

Vanderberg, S. G. Contributions of twin research to psychology. *Psychological Bulletin,* 1966, *66,* 327.

Vanderberg, S. G. Possible hereditary factors in minimal brain dysfunction. *Annals of the New York Academy of Sciences,* 1973, *205,* 223–230.

Wahler, R. G., House, A. E., & Stanbaugh, E. E. *Ecological Assessment of Child Problem Behavior.* New York: Pergamon Press, 1975.

Welgan, P. R. Learned control of gastric acid secretions in ulcer patients. *Psychosomatic Medicine,* 1974, *36,* 411–419.

Wender, P. H. *Minimal brain dysfunction in children.* New York: Wiley-Interscience, 1971.

Werry, J. S., & Sprague, R. L. Hyperactivity. *In* C. G. Costello (Ed.), *Symptoms of psychopathology.* New York: Wiley, 1970, pp. 397–417.

Wyler, A. R. Operant conditioning of single epileptic neurons and its application to human epilepsy. *Pavlovian Journal of Biological Science,* 1977, *In press.*

Wyler, A. R., Lockard, J. S., Ward, A. A., & Finch, C. A., Conditioned EEG desynchronization and seizure occurrence in patients. *Experimental Neurology,* 1977, in press.

Wywricka, W., & Sterman, M. B. Instrumental conditioning of sensorimotor cortex EEG spindles in the walking cat. *Physiology and Behavior,* 1968, *31,* 703–707.

7 Assessment and Treatment of Childhood Gender Problems

George A. Rekers

Sex-role development and the normal processes of gender identification have been investigated by child psychologists for several decades (Maccoby, 1966; Maccoby & Jacklin, 1974; Mischel, 1970; Mussen, 1969). Normal boys occasionally display behaviors that are socially assigned to girls and women, such as using cosmetics or wanting to nurse and bear children. Similarly, but with considerably less risk of social disapproval in our American society, girls sometimes behave as boys and will be referred to as tomboys. This exploration and flexibility of sex-typed behavior, typical of many boys and girls, is a part of the normal socialization process. On rare occasions, however, behavior that may have begun as a curiosity-induced exploration of sex-role stereotypes becomes a compulsive, excessive, and persistent pattern. One such example is the pathological hypermasculinity of boys who are destructive, independent, belligerent, uncontrolled, or aggressive to the point of interpersonal violence and lack gentleness or sensitivity to others (Harrington, 1970). These exaggeratedly "masculine" boys may come to the attention of the child clinical psychologist and require psychological intervention. Another extreme is the cross-gender identified boy who insists that he is a girl or wants to become a girl and rejects his male role and status. It has only been in the last decade that such gender-disturbed children have been systematically investigated. Although child *developmental* psychologists have amassed a substantial body of research on the normal sex-typing process during the past 40 years, child *clinical* psychologists have only

GEORGE A. REKERS • Fuller Theological Seminary, Graduate School of Psychology, Pasadena, California, and University of California at Los Angeles, Los Angeles, California. Present address: Department of Psychiatry, University of Florida, Gainesville, Florida.
 This chapter is based on research supported by USPHS grants MH21803 and MH28240.

recently focused attention on the assessment and treatment of atypical sex-role development.

1. The Childhood Gender Disturbances

Four general types of childhood gender disturbance may be distinguished: (1) excessive femininity in boys; (2) excessive masculinity in boys; (3) excessive femininity in girls; and (4) excessive masculinity in girls. Of these four potential types of gender disturbance in children, the systematic research deals almost exclusively with the case of the extremely feminine boy. This state of the literature is, in part, a function of the finding that problems of gender dysphoria and sexual deviations occur more frequently in males than in females (Green & Money, 1969; Kinsey, Pomeroy, & Martin, 1948; Money & Ehrhardt, 1972; Stoller, 1968b) and of the relatively greater concern by American parents over feminine sex-role behavior in their sons. Therefore, this review is confined to the early identification and treatment of cross-gender disturbance in male children.

Rosen, Rekers, and Friar (1977) have differentiated two basic syndromes: "Gender behavior disturbance" and "cross-gender identification" in physically normal boys who display feminine sex-typed behavior. The boy with gender-behavior disturbance has adopted cross-gender clothing preferences, the actual or imagined use of cosmetic articles, feminine gestures and behavior mannerisms, feminine vocal inflection and predominantly feminine speech content, an aversion to masculine sex-typed activities coupled with a preference for girl playmates, feminine activities, and female roles in play. On the other hand, the boy with cross-gender identification not only behaves in a feminine way but truly wishes to be or fantasizes or believes that he is a girl (Greenson, 1966; Stoller, 1964, 1965, 1968a), evidenced by his stated desire or preference to be a girl or a mother and to bear children and breast-feed infants and/or to have his penis removed (Rekers, 1972, 1977b; Rekers & Lovaas, 1974).

Clinically speaking, it is probable that the prognosis and treatment of gender behavior disturbance and gender identity disturbance are not the same, but research on this question has not yet been conducted. The developmental histories of both of these types of gender-disturbed boys parallel the retrospective reports of adult male transsexuals, transvestites, and some effeminate homosexuals. The feminine behaviors used as the initial screening criteria may exist in several contexts; that is, some children who exhibit these behaviors may develop adult gender and sexual problems, while others may develop a normal adult adjustment. It is unfortunate that there are no published studies that report the base rate for gender disturbances in the general population of boys. Adequate longitudinal data do not exist to indicate what percentage of feminine boys spontaneously outgrow gender disturbance, what percentage grow up to become adult transsexuals, what percentage develop to be heterosexual transvesites, or what percentage become adult male homosexuals, for example.

2. The Diagnostic Assessment of Gender-Disturbed Boys

The diagnosis of gender disturbances must be based on the clinical data that have been obtained retrospectively from adult cases (e.g., Benjamin, 1966; Green & Money, 1969), from the prospective data available (Green, 1974; Lebovitz, 1972; Zuger, 1966), and on developmental theories (e.g., Bentler, 1976). Having investigated approximately 100 young boys referred for gender disturbances, the research team of Drs. Rekers, Bentler, Lovaas, & Rosen at UCLA has identified a number of factors that are relevant to the diagnostic process and has formulated some specific diagnostic procedures based on the research to date (see Bates & Bentler, 1973; Bates, Bentler, & Thompson, 1973; Bates, Skilbeck, Smith, & Bentler, 1974; Rekers, 1975; Rekers, Amaro-Plotkin, & Low, 1977a; Rekers, Lovaas, & Low, 1974; Rekers, Willis, Yates, Rosen, & Low, 1977c; Rekers & Yates, 1976; Rosen, et al., 1977; Rosen & Teague, 1974; Skilbeck, Bates, & Bentler, 1975).

Rekers (1976) proposed that the degree of gender behavior disturbance be conceptualized as a continuum, and he developed a five-point clinical rating scale ranging from (1) profound cross-gender behavior through (2) severe, (3) moderate, and (4) mild cross-gender behavior, to (5) no cross-gender behavior of clinical significance. Similarly, a clinical judgment can be made regarding the gender identity of the child by the use of a five-point continuum from (1) profound cross-gender identity through (2) moderate cross-gender identity, (3) gender identity confusion, (4) mild gender identity confusion, to (5) normal gender identity.

An accurate assessment of gender disturbance in boys necessitates the acquisition of data from numerous sources, such as parental report, clinic playroom observations, field observations, psychological testing, and parent and child interviews. In addition, an adequate pediatric evaluation consists of a medical history; a physical examination, including examination of the external genitals; chromosome analysis, including 2 cells karyotyped and 15 counted; and sex chromatin studies (Rekers et al., 1977c; Rekers, Yates, Willis, Rosen, & Taubman,

1976). In standard medical practice, baseline endocrinological studies are considered unnecessary unless abnormalities are detected in the physical exam (B. F. Crandall, personal communication, 1973).

2.1. Clinic Assessment of Sex-Typed Play Behavior

Many methods devised by developmental psychologists for measuring sex-typed play in children have imposed some critical limitations on the kind of conclusions to be drawn from the data, for example, by involving only the child's initial choice of a toy (Brown, 1956; Sutton-Smith, Rosenberg, & Morgan, 1963) or by requiring that an adult be present for the test administration (Rabban, 1950). Rekers (1972) therefore developed a method that (1) employed stimuli related to significant differences in the sex-typed play behavior of normal boys and girls; (2) provided meaningful data through the use of repeated dependent measures over time; (3) did not require the presence of a male or female experimenter to eliminate a potential source of variance; and (4) could be administered to a range of children from ages 3 years to 8 years. The specific procedure consisted of unobtrusive recording of the individual child's continuous play with sex-typed toys from behind a one-way mirror.

In a normative validation study using this procedure, Rekers and Yates (1976) recorded children's continuous play in four sessions totaling 20 minutes rather than measuring only the initial choice of a sex-typed toy. One toy table had both masculine and feminine clothing and grooming toys on it; the other table had toys associated with maternal nurturance (such as baby dolls) and toys associated with masculine assertive play (cowboys and Indians and dart guns). The play behavior of 60 normal boys, 60 normal girls, and 15 gender-disturbed boys was recorded from behind a one-way mirror by two independent observers. An analysis of variance found a significant sex effect, indicating that the measures discriminated between the sex-typed play preferences of normal males and females. No significant age effects or age–sex interactions were obtained. Figure 1 presents the mean percentage of feminine play for both normal groups and for the group of gender-disturbed (feminoid) boys. A large-sample approximation of the Mann–Whitney U test found that the feminine play of the gender-disturbed boys was significantly higher than that of the normal boys and there were no significant differences in the occurrence of feminine play between the normal girls and the gender-disturbed boys.

These results provide the base rate data necessary to formulate an assessment-decision rule for the diagnosis of "gender disturbance" in boys. Specifically, the clinical child psychologist could administer this

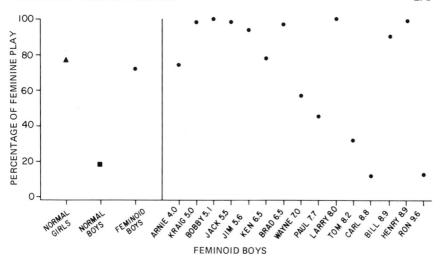

FIGURE 1. Group means for feminine play by normal girls, normal boys, and feminoid boys; and feminine play by individual feminoid boys in order of age in years and months. (From Rekers & Yates, 1976. Copyright © 1976 by the American Psychological Association. Reprinted by permission.)

simple play task and require that a boy obtain a score that exceeded the mean of the gender-disturbed group (72%) before making the diagnosis of gender disturbance. Since 56% feminine play was the highest score obtained in the group of normal boys, "false positives" using this decision rule should be extremely rare. With this same decision rule, however, these data indicate that the proportion of false negatives would approximate 33%. This would not constitute a serious clinical diagnostic problem, so long as the clinical child psychologist used more than one data source before finalizing the diagnosis.

The results of the intrasubject replication study of cross-gender identified boys reported by Rekers (1975) underscore the necessity of assessing the child during solitary play, in contrast with play in the presence of various observers. This investigation explored various potential discriminative stimuli for feminine and masculine sex-typed play with the sex-typed toys described above. With an ABA reversal design, certain stimulus conditions (such as the presence of father or mother or a male or female stranger) were found to be discriminative for reliable intrasubject changes in sex-typed play. Sex-typed play was found to vary as a function of the social situation and the type of play response required. All the boys played predominantly feminine while alone in the playroom. While no single environmental stimulus was consistently discriminative for masculine play across children, at least one stimulus condition was found for each subject under which he played predominantly masculine. Figure 2 illustrates this finding for one of the subjects in this study. This figure indicates that during the baseline sessions in which this gender-disturbed boy was alone, he played predominantly feminine with the dress-up toys (sessions 1–7) and exclusively feminine with the affect toys (sessions 1–6). This gender-disturbed boy played exclusively feminine at both tables in his mother's presence. But his sex-typed play reversed with his father's presence (see sessions 11 and 13 on the top portion of the figure and

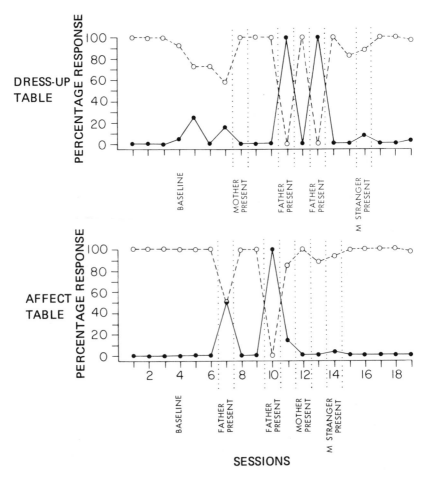

Figure 2. Percentage of occurrence of feminine mannerisms in the clinic as a function of baseline stimulus conditions. ●—● Masculine, ○---○ feminine.

sessions 7 and 10 on the lower portion of the figure). Interestingly, the father's stimulus control was not generalized to another male adult (see session 16 at the dress-up table and session 14 at the affect table).

The data indicated that childhood gender disturbance is character- ized by stimulus-specificity and response-specificity of sex-typed mas- culine and feminine play behaviors. These findings complicate the diagnostic procedure for identifying cross-gender problems in chil- dren. The boy's sex-typed behavior differs potentially in the presence of his mother, his father, a male clinical psychologist, or a female clinical psychologist. The data indicate that only sex-typed play in an "alone" condition is reliably correlated with the clinical diagnosis of "childhood cross-gender identification."

2.2. Clinic Assessment of Sex-Typed Mannerisms

Rekers and his colleagues have similarly developed reliable obser- vational measures of several "feminine" behavior mannerisms ob- served in gender-disturbed boys. Rekers et al. (1977a) obtained base rate data in normal children on the occurrence of eight of these expres- sive gestures that had been previously observed in gender-disturbed boys: (1) hand clasp—operationally defined as touching the hands together in front of the body; (2) hyperextension—moving the hands in the direction of the posterior surface of the forearm while the elbow is either flexed or extended; (3) limp wrist—flexing the wrist toward the palmar surface of the forearm and/or the upper arm while the elbow is either flexed or extended; (4) flutters—a rapid succession of up and down movements of the forearm and/or upper arm while the wrist remains relaxed; (5) palming—touching the palm(s) to the back, front, or sides of the head above ear level; (6) hands on hips—resting the palm(s) or back of the hand(s) on the waist or the hip; (7) flexed elbow—walking or standing with the arm(s) held so that the angle be- tween the forearm and the upper arm is between 0° and 135° (approxi- mately); and (8) arm fold—placing hands on opposite arms on the area above the elbow. Although these kinds of behavioral mannerisms in boys have been labeled effeminate by clinicians and the general public, no data previously existed on the occurrence of such gestures in the normal population of children. After having developed these opera- tional definitions of "effeminate gestures" and after extensive pilot in- vestigation, Rekers et al. (1977a) recorded these gestures in 48 Cauca- sian boys and girls of two age groups—4–5 years and 11–12 years—while the children performed a standardized play task requir- ing gross motor movements.

Analysis of variance showed a significant overall difference between the gestures in normal boys and normal girls. Three of the gestures were found to discriminate significantly between the sexes: limp wrist, flutters, and flexed elbow. Differences between the age groups were not significant, nor was there a significant interaction between age and sex, suggesting that sex-related gestures are already well established by age 5 years. The base rate for performance of all eight gestures is generally low, ranging from 0% to about 12%. Three of the gestures were not observed at all among the older boys. It would appear, then, that even a moderate frequency rate for these behaviors would mark a girl or especially a boy as being different and would possibly provoke the peer ridicule that is suffered by gender-disturbed boys. Some behavioral mannerisms may differentiate the gender-disturbed boy from both normal boys and normal girls, suggesting that the gender-disturbed boy is not simply "feminine." In any case, an unusually high frequency rate of any of these gestures would be one diagnostic sign for a serious problem of social adjustment, if not gender disturbance (Bates, Bentler, & Thompson, 1973; Rekers et al., 1974; Stoller, 1970). Rekers et al. (1977c) did not find the kind of discriminative stimulus control over sex-typed mannerisms in gender-disturbed boys that was found previously in the sex-typed play behavior of those boys. The occurrence of these sex-typed mannerisms could therefore be recorded during a play session as one useful diagnostic tool for discriminating the gender-disturbed boy from the normal boy.

2.3. Assessment of Sex-Typed Behavior in the Natural Environment

Rekers and his colleagues have recorded the gender-disturbed boy's masculine and feminine behaviors in the home and school environments by teaching the parents a time-sampling procedure using daily behavior checklists and by using trained behavioral observers in the child's natural environments (Rekers, 1972; Rekers & Lovaas, 1974; Rekers et al., 1974; Rekers et al., 1977c; Rekers, Yates, Willis, Rosen, & Taubman, 1976; Rekers & Varni, 1977). The parents also provided a behavioral history of the child's gender development on the Rekers Behavior Checklist of Childhood Gender Problems (Rekers, 1972). Data are also obtained from school psychologists, pediatricians, teachers, and others who are significant adults in the child's daily life, when such data collection does not pose a risk of labeling the child adversely in some setting. Professor P. M. Bentler and his colleagues at UCLA have developed and validated two instruments that are helpful in the diagnosis of the degree of gender behavior disturbance: the

Child Behavior and Attitude Questionnaire and the Child Game Participation Questionnaire (based on the research on normal and gender-disturbed boys reported in Bates & Bentler, 1973; Bates, Bentler, & Thompson, 1973). The scores from these inventories provide a quantitative measure of the degree of effeminate behavior as contrasted to the standardization grouping of normal boys and girls, aged 4–10 years.

2.4. Conventional Psychological Testing

In addition to the referral information, parent reports, developmental history data, and *in vivo* behavioral observations in the clinic and natural environments, certain tests have been found to be helpful in the diagnostic process:

1. The Wechsler Intelligence Scale for Children could be administered to screen the child for deficits in intellectual functioning that might interfere with normal identification and sex-role learning processes.
2. Human figure drawings provide one type of data that, in combination with other supporting evidence, can be an indicator of cross-gender identification problems (Green, 1974; Green, Fuller, & Rutley, 1972a; Rosen *et al.*, 1977; Skilbeck, Bates, & Bentler, 1975). For some gender-disturbed children this Draw-a-Person Test can be unenlightening, but in other cases it can be very revealing.
3. Rosen *et al.* (1977) recommend the standard administration of the Schneidman Make-a-Picture Story test, in which identification can be measured by the ratio of total number of male to female figures in the stories generated by the child and by the sex of the main characters.
4. Similarly recommended is a standard administration of the Bene–Anthony Family Relations Test (Bene & Anthony, 1957) to obtain a quantitative measure of how the child feels toward each member of his family, focusing on the correlation between the gender of each family member and the child's incoming and outgoing feelings for them. These test results can also be analyzed for defenses and overall degree of disturbance. Low involvement with the father and a high degree of involvement with the mother corroborates the diagnosis of a gender identity problem as distinguished from a gender behavior disturbance (Rosen & Teague, 1974).

5. The Brown "IT" Scale for Children has not been of diagnostic utility except for children under age 6 years (Rosen *et al.*, 1977).

2.5. Parent and Child Clinical Interviews

The clinician should interview each parent and the child, separately and together, in order to explore individual attitudes, the mother–son relationship, and the father–son relationship. The clinician should interpret the interview data together with the other assessment-data sources to derive the differential diagnosis. Rosen *et al.* (1977) have discussed this diagnostic process in detail. The evaluation of the severity of the gender disturbance relies on a weighing of the qualitative and quantitative aspects of the sex-typed behaviors recorded. The age of onset is another important variable, since gender identification appears to develop at the age of 1½–2 years and is typically established by age 5 or 6 years. In other cases, in which atypical sex-typed behavior has not occurred at any significant frequency until age 8 or later, it is less likely that a true cross-gender identity is present, and the more appropriate diagnosis would be some level of gender behavior disturbance. In some cases, some data sources may strongly suggest a cross-gender identity problem, while other classic indicators are missing or perhaps ambiguous. In such cases, a diagnosis of "gender identity confusion" or "moderate cross-gender identification" may be more appropriate than "profound cross-gender identification." In cases in which there is only a single indicator of a gender identity problem in the absence of other corroborative data, the diagnosis of "mild gender identity confusion" is recommended along with a diagnosis on the continuum of gender behavior disturbance (i.e., mild, moderate, marked, or extreme).

3. The Rationale for Treatment Intervention

There are numerous interrelated reasons for intervening in the life of a boy diagnosed with a gender disturbance. The clinical rationale for intervention has been discussed at length by a number of investigators (Bates, Skilbeck, Smith, & Bentler, 1975; Green, 1974; Rekers, 1977a; Rekers & Lovaas, 1974; Rekers, Bentler, Rosen, & Lovaas, 1977b; Stoller, 1968a, 1970–1971; Rosen, Rekers, & Bentler, 1978). Therefore, the rationale will be only briefly summarized here.

3.1. The Psychological Maladjustment of Gender-Disturbed Children

Gender-disturbed boys manifest psychological maladjustment requiring intervention. At the emotional level, the boy suffers unhappiness and is rigid and obsessive-compulsive with feminine sex-typed behavior. At the cognitive level, there is conflict and confusion in identity and self-concept. There is the dissonance between rigidly held self-labels and the reality demands of society. At the social level, the child faces serious peer rejection, ridicule, and isolation as a function of his deviance. A gender-disturbed boy is typically scapegoated in cruel ways and must tolerate the indignitites of insulting labels such as "sissy," "fag," "queer," and "girly" (Green, 1974; Green, Newman, & Stoller, 1972b; Rekers & Lovaas, 1974; Rekers et al., 1974; Rekers et al., 1977c; Stoller, 1970–1971). While society could afford to become more tolerant with individuals with sex-role deviations, the facts remain that it is not tolerant, and realistically speaking, it is potentially more difficult (if not impossible) to modify society's behaviors than to modify the boy's behaviors in order to relieve an individual's suffering.

But the psychological maladjustment of the gender-disturbed child goes beyond mere social rejection from the peer group, because it involves the elements of unhappiness, obsessive-compulsive trends, isolation and withdrawal, negativistic behavior, detachment, inability to form close interpersonal peer relationships, and low self-esteem (Rekers et al., 1977b). The gender disturbance therefore constitutes a psychological distortion in itself and generates the secondary maladjustment problems. Treatment of the gender disturbance, then, would seek first to ameliorate the psychological disorder and secondarily the associated social maladjustment. This latter goal in itself provides a sufficient rationale to intervene in the child's life, but there are additional implications of his maladjustment that strengthen the intervention rationale.

3.2. Prevention of Adult Sexual Perversions

Intervention in atypical sex-role development in childhood may be the only effective manner of preventing the severe sexual perversions that are highly resistant to psychological treatment in adulthood. Although it is not yet possible to formulate a differential prognosis for the pretranssexual, the pretransvestite, and the prehomosexual child, gender-disturbed boys have been demonstrated to be at high risk for any one of those three conditions in adulthood. Although questions remain regarding the etiological variables in deviant sex-role development (Bentler, 1976; Money, 1970a,b; Rosen, 1969; Zuger, 1970a,b), the available longitudinal data indicate that boyhood effeminate behavior is fairly predictive of male homosexuality (Bakwin, 1968; Green, 1974; Lebovitz, 1972; Zuger, 1966, 1970a; Zuger & Taylor, 1969) and is retrospectively reported by adult male homosexuals (Bieber *et al.*, 1962; Evans, 1969; Holemon & Winokur, 1965), adult male transvestites (Prince & Bentler, 1972), and adult male transsexuals (Benjamin, 1966; Bentler, 1976; Green & Money, 1969). The majority of adult transsexuals and transvestites do retrospectively report that their cross-gender behavior began in early childhood (Green, 1974; Money & Primrose, 1968; Prince & Bentler, 1972; Walinder, 1967; Zuger, 1966), and therefore all available evidence indicates that childhood gender identity and childhood gender behavior disturbances are strongly predictive of homosexual-orientation disturbance, transsexualism, or transvestism in adulthood (Green, 1974; Green & Money, 1961, 1969; Stoller, 1968b, 1970–1971; Pauly, 1969). In the case of males with gender identity problems in adulthood, the majority have experienced substantial deviation from appropriate sex-role behavior and identity by age 5 years. Our best prediction—based on all the literature—is that a gender-disturbed boy will be at high risk for transsexualism, transvestism, or homosexuality.

There is only one published report of the successful psychological treatment of an adult transsexual, aged 17 years (Barlow, Reynolds, & Agras, 1973). Because adult transsexuals are extremely discontented and because efforts to change their gender identity to match their anatomy have generally failed (Baker, 1969; Benjamin, 1969; Pauly, 1969), many clinicians have concluded that surgical and hormonal sex-reassignment is the only ameliorative treatment available (e.g., Green & Money, 1969; Randell, 1970). With the numerous legal, ethical, psychological, and surgical problems raised with attempted sex reassignment procedures (see articles in Green & Money, 1969), attempts to change the individual's behavior during the formative childhood years may be preferable to changing the adult's body (Greenson, 1966; Stoller, 1970–1971).

Transvestic behavior is a highly probable prognostic outcome if the gender-disturbed child does not become a transsexual. In adulthood, the results of compulsive cross-dressing behavior range from a disruption of normal heterosexual relationships to a disabling sense of guilt and fear of disclosure. There are legal and informal sanctions against cross-dressing in public places, violations of which lead to social ostracism, personal isolation, and the threat of arrest, fines, or imprisonment (see Money, 1968). With rare exception, adults with compulsive transvestic behavior recognize it as at least awkward and, in many cases, as severely distressing, and consequently they seek out therapeutic assistance for the condition. The Statement of Ethical Standards of the American Psychological Association (1972) requires that the psychologist be sensitive to the social codes and the moral expectations of the community in which the client resides. In this ethical context, responsible clinical child psychologists cooperate with parents' requests to decrease the frequency of cross-dressing behavior in their child.

If the gender-disturbed child does not develop to be transsexual or transvestic in adulthood, the evidence indicates that he will probably develop as an effeminate male homosexual. Even though differential prognoses cannot be made of the "prehomosexual" boy, it is ethically and legally appropriate for the psychologist to cooperate with the parent's therapeutic objective of preventing homosexual adjustment for clinical reasons (Hatterer, 1970; Socarides, 1970), for professional ethical reasons (acting in consonance with the social codes of the community), or for moral reasons (see Evans, 1975; Rekers, 1977a).

3.3. Prevention of Problems Secondary to Adult Gender Problems

The gender-disturbed boy is a high risk for adult gender disturbance, and intervention in childhood is appropriate since adult gender disturbance is highly correlated with other serious emotional, social, and economic maladjustments. The psychopathology most frequently accompanying transsexualism is depression (Pauly, 1969), which is present in 67% of male transsexuals, with suicidal ideation in 60% and actual suicide attempts reported in 17–20% of the cases cited in various studies (Pauly, 1965; Walinder, 1967). Self-mutilation in the form of autocastration or autopenectomy was attempted in 18% and accomplished in 9% of one series of cases (Dewhurst & Gordon, 1969; Pauly, 1969). Investigations of the social and economic aspects of transsexualism (Hoenig, Kenna, & Youd, 1970) indicate that such individuals show a high proportion of educational and work maladjustments and criminal and other antisocial behavior. In addition to the problems with hormonal and sex reassignment, the cost of such medical intervention ranges from $6,000 to $10,000, and even after sex-reassignment therapy, many of these individuals do not attain normal psychological adjustment; many become sexually promiscuous in an attempt to validate their sexual identity, and many turn to prostitution. Kando (1973) reported research that shows that gender-disturbed adults have extremely rigid sex-role conceptions; that is, they are not androgynous. This rigidity indicates potential maladaptation in the context of recent psychological research emphasizing the positive adaptive value of androgyny (Bem, 1974; Ellis & Bentler, 1973). The third basic reason for treating gender-disturbed boys, then, would be to prevent the emotional, social, economic, and legal problems associated with gender disturbance in adulthood.

3.4. Cooperation with Appropriate Parental Concern over Gender Deviance

The parents of many gender-disturbed children request professional intervention when the cross-gender behaviors persist and become a compulsive pattern. When the parents seek to prevent sexual deviance in their child and to improve the child's social and psychological adjustment, it is consistent with professional ethics to provide treatment (see Rekers, 1977a; Rosen et al., 1978).

An appropriate ethical goal for treatment intervention is to increase the life options of the individual (Gray, 1971). "By increasing the number of responses available to an individual, he is 'freed' from previous limitations imposed by such things as learning deficits and fears and anxieties that have led to avoidance responses" (Thoresen & Mahoney, 1974, p. 5). Although many sex-role stereotypes are very arbitrarily defined by our culture, there are a few gender role expectations that are realistic rather than arbitrary. For example, girls but not boys may realistically develop fantasies and the behavioral skills associated with the maternal role of pregnancy, childbirth, and breast-feeding infants. Even some of the arbitrary distinctions (for example, only women are expected to wear skirts and dresses in daily life in the American culture) do not necessarily hinder the freedom of individuals to develop to their potential; when this is the case, it seems more appropriate for the compulsive cross-dresser to change, rather than to require that the benign proscription of the entire society change. But sex-role stereotypes that hinder individuals' freedom of development (as in the case of stereotyping "doctor" as masculine and "nurse" as feminine) should be abolished.

The therapeutic goal is to reduce the inappropriate sex-role rigidity in the gender-disturbed child. For example, promoting nurturance toward infants in both boys and girls is desirable, but intervention is necessary for the boy who desires to bear and breast-feed babies himself. Adjustment to biological limitations is a necessary socialization lesson for the boy. Reasonable sex-role flexibility and satisfaction with one's physical sex status are the therapeutic goals.

4. The Research on Intervention Techniques

The intervention strategy for an individual gender-disturbed boy must be based upon the findings of the medical, behavioral, and other psychological assessment data obtained with the procedures summarized above. Of course, problems of hermaphroditism, detected in the medical evaluation, would require specialized pediatric consultation. But it is extremely rare to detect an abnormality in any of the five physical variables of sex in gender-disturbed children who are evaluated with current methods of biomedical testing. Social learning variables have been considered to be the main source of sex-role deviance (Litin, Giffin, & Johnson, 1956; Lukianowicz, 1959; Money, Hampson, & Hampson, 1955; Pauly, 1969; and Stoller, 1969), although biological abnormalities may be a potential contributing factor (e.g., Evans, 1972; Money & Ehrhardt, 1972; Zuger, 1970a). Although there have been several recent case histories reporting environmentally induced changes in childhood gender-role behavior (Bates *et al.*, 1975; Bentler, 1968; Dupont, 1968; Green, 1974; Green *et al.*, 1972b; Myrick, 1970; Stoller, 1970–1971), this review focuses on the studies in which replication procedures have reliably identified the treatment variables.

If the pretreatment assessment procedures have established that an individual boy has a cross-gender *identity* disturbance, the therapist would select any of the following techniques that may be applicable to that individual case in order to increase appropriate masculine behaviors and to decrease the compulsive feminine behaviors. On the other hand, if the individual boy has gender *behavior* disturbance, many of the techniques designed to decrease feminine behaviors would be of limited use, since the primary therapeutic emphasis would be on the acquisition of masculine behaviors to increase sex-role flexibility, in conjunction with the decrease of one or two discrete feminine behaviors such as compulsive cross-dressing.

4.1. Treatment Techniques in the Clinic Setting

To increase the potential generalization and maintenance of the treatment effects, particular focus in the clinic setting has been placed upon training the child's parents to be the therapeutic agents. But some of the more detailed techniques of discrimination training and behavior shaping for more complex gender behaviors require the skills of professional therapists.

4.1.1. Clinic Treatment of Sex-Typed Play

If the gender-disturbed child is found to play predominantly feminine during the pretreatment baseline sessions in the presence of one or both of the parents, it is appropriate to train the parents in social reinforcement techniques designed to increase appropriate sex-typed behavior. It is desirable to conduct this training in the clinic setting, where the therapist can closely supervise the parents' acquisition of behavior-shaping skills.

Using an intrasubject replication design, Rekers and his colleagues have developed a set of therapeutic procedures whereby a parent, a guardian, or another adult is trained to apply social reinforcement procedures in clinic play sessions. With the sex-typed toys described by Rabban (1950) on a small table, Rekers and his colleagues seated the mother and the boy in a playroom. The mother wore a "bug-in-the-ear" device to allow the therapist to communicate directly with her without the boy's overhearing the conversation. The mother sat with a large book or a magazine in her lap. She was given specific instructions to attend to the boy's masculine verbal and play behavior by smiling and complimenting his play and to ignore feminine behavior by picking up a book to "read." In several 10-minute play sessions spaced over one hour, the child played in the mother's presence while the experimenter prompted the parent to extinguish feminine behavior and socially reinforce masculine behavior. The therapist verbally reinforced the parent for correct responses and gradually faded out the prompting instruction. In the research studies, the experimental procedure followed the ABABABA reversal, intrasubject replication design, in which A represented a baseline and reversal condition in which no differential reinforcement was given and B represented the treatment sessions. In several studies, Rekers and his colleagues demonstrated these procedures to be successful in decreasing compulsive feminine play and verbal behavior (Rekers, 1972, 1976; Rekers & Varni, 1977; Varni & Rekers, 1975).

If gender-disturbed boys had genuine *behavioral deficits* in the area of gender-appropriate play and verbal responses, a social learning theorist might expect that these kinds of therapeutic reinforcement contingencies would result in an acquisition learning curve for masculine behavior and an extinction curve for feminine behavior. Because these gender-disturbed boys have had long clinical histories of predominant cross-gender behavior, one might expect that the acquisition of masculine behaviors and the extinction of feminine behaviors would be a very gradual process, requiring complex behavior-shaping features to establish masculine patterns of play behavior and a verbal repertoire of predominantly masculine or neutral themes. In contrast, however, appropriate masculine play and verbal behaviors do exist in the gender-disturbed boys' behavioral repertoires prior to treatment. Immediate change to masculine behavior is typically found with the institution of the therapeutic contingency. This change represents the boy's discrimination of the reinforcement contingency rather than a more complex process of response acquisition.

The treatment effects of these clinic procedures have tended to be narrowly specific to the particular stimulus environment in which they were introduced. When generalization has occurred, however, it has been where it would be most expected: in stimulus environments that are the most similar to the treatment environment. The amount of treatment generalization obtained may be a function of which particular response is treated and the stimulus parameters of the treatment setting. For this reason, Rekers *et al.* (1976) programmed a series of similar treatment procedures in different environments (i.e., play alone, mother present, father present, and the use of different therapy rooms). This revision in the treatment procedures substantially eliminated the stimulus-specificity of the behavioral treatment effects. In this subsequent study, as in the previous intrasubject studies, both generalization test sessions and reversal sessions were conducted in alone and adult-attending conditions. As in the previous studies, the child's mother was prompted through the "bug-in-the-ear" device to reinforce masculine behavior and to extinguish feminine behavior. Then, in addition to the preceding contingencies, another procedure was added in which the mother verbally prompted her son not to play with the feminine toys. The child's father was alternated as the therapeutic agent in this treatment condition, in an effort to maximize the generalization of the treatment effects. Next, the child played alone with the therapy toys while his mother waited just outside the playroom wearing the "bug-in-the-ear." The investigators observed the child's play from behind a one-way mirror, and when the child initiated feminine play, his mother was immediately instructed to enter the playroom and to repeat the verbal prompt asking her son not to play with the feminine toys. Finally, the investigators conducted this procedure similarly in a different clinic room to increase the probability of generalization of the treatment effects to the child's play alone.

4.1.2. Clinic Treatment of "Feminine" Speech

For some of the gender-disturbed boys, a high "feminine" vocal inflection coupled with predominantly "feminine" speech content constitutes one of the most socially salient aspects of their cross-gender behavior. Rekers *et al.* (1974) reported a behavioral observation procedure in which audio tapes can be reliably scored by independent observers for feminine vocal inflection and sex-typed speech content. For behavior coding, *feminine vocal inflection* was defined as a boy's verbal pronunciation of any word with a vocal pitch markedly higher than his normal range of vocal inflection. *Feminine speech content* was defined as words denoting feminine sex-typed objects (e.g., lipstick), feminine persons (e.g., sister), and feminine sex-typed activities (e.g., putting on a dress). *Masculine speech content* consisted of words denoting masculine sex-typed objects (e.g., man's suit), masculine persons (e.g., fireman), and masculine sex-typed activities (e.g., camping with the Boy Scouts). In addition, the *neutral speech* category consisted of any speech considered ambiguous as to sex-typed content and references to non-sex-typed objects (e.g., the telephone), to persons whose gender is left unspecified (e.g., a swimmer), and to non-sex-typed activities (e.g., watching television). Each verbal phrase can be assigned to one of these mutually exclusive content categories. The information of clinical significance is the percentage of feminine speech and masculine speech, calculated with reference to the total number of seconds of verbal behavior (total = feminine + masculine + neutral).

Rekers *et al.* (1974) reported the treatment of a gender-disturbed boy who told elaborate fantasized stories with extensive feminine content while drawing pictures on a chalkboard in the clinic setting. With the use of an ABA reversal design, differential social reinforcement was delivered contingent upon appropriate sex-typed speech. An assistant reinforced the boy's questions regarding masculine or neutral topics by giving short, nonleading direct answers that expressed positive interest. Feminine speech was extinguished by the withdrawal of social attention and by statements expressing disinterest: "I'm not interested in that." Control was thus obtained over the feminine speech content, and the data suggested a generalized suppression effect from speech content to speech inflection. Masculine speech content was found to be an inverse function of the rate of feminine content under the differential reinforcement conditions.

4.1.3. Clinic Treatment of Cross-Gender Mannerisms

Rekers *et al.* (1976) designed a response-cost and verbal-prompt procedure to modify a gender-disturbed boy's cross-gender mannerisms. While the child participated in a game of throwing a tennis ball at a target, two independent observers recorded the occurrence of his two predominant types of cross-gender mannerisms: (1) "flexed elbow," operationally defined as standing with arms raised with a limp wrist, and (2) "feminine running," defined as running with elbows flexed but arms turned away from body with hands raised approximately to shoulder level. During baseline sessions, the child earned tokens for playing the throwing game. Then the target mannerisms were explained to the boy, and he was given additional "free" tokens prior to each treatment session. The response-cost contingency involved a loss of one token for each instance of flexed elbow or feminine running. Simultaneously, a verbal prompt was administered contingent upon the occurrence of each target behavior; for example, on each occurrence of flexed elbow, the assistant said, "No, Bobby, keep your arms down." Between the game-playing sessions, the assistant trained the child in appropriate running movements by modeling the behavior and then asking the child to imitate, using manual guidance where necessary.

The boy's parents were trained to identify the target behaviors on videotape and to administer the same contingencies in both the clinic and the home setting. In order to prevent the kind of setting discrimination characteristic of earlier treatments and methods, the treatment contingencies were instituted in the home on the same day that they were introduced in the clinic. Intervention then continued for nine months. All running essentially ceased during the treatment sessions, rendering the data inconclusive regarding a potential therapeutic change in feminine running. The occurrence of flexed elbow decreased sufficiently so that the boy ceased to appear effeminate. Recordings made by observers in the school setting confirmed that the flexed-elbow mannerisms had decreased to the normal frequency among the boy's peers, thereby removing a potential source of future labeling and ostracism by the peer group.

Although the response-cost contingencies have successfully decreased cross-gender mannerisms, the children appeared to have had initial difficulties in discriminating the target behaviors. Consequently, another study was designed to provide discrimination training with a videotape feedback procedure (Rekers et al., 1977c). In this study, reliable observational measures were obtained for the subtypes of mannerisms that had been investigated in normal boys and girls by Rekers et al. (1977a). This procedure was suggested by a gender-disturbed boy's own expressed concern that he was unaware of the things he did that resulted in peer ostracism.

Like all the other gender-disturbed boys that have been studied, this particular boy's feminine play occurred under specifiable conditions—in this case, with dress-up toys but not with the affect toys. When his foster mother spontaneously cautioned him against "playing like a girl" in the clinic, his feminine play with the dress-up toys was suppressed. These observations are typical of those we have recorded for all the gender-disturbed boys that we have studied. In the case of this particular boy, the mannerisms occurred under a variety of stimulus conditions—with two different sets of toys and in the alone condition as well as in various people-present conditions. This boy's mannerisms appeared to be suppressed in the presence of male strangers as compared with other stimulus conditions. The finding of clinical significance, however, was that his mannerisms (unlike his feminine play behavior) were *not* suppressed by the foster mother's verbal instructions to "stop playing like a girl" in the clinic. In the absence of conclusive evidence of discriminative stimulus control over mannerisms, we questioned whether this boy could, indeed, discriminate his own mannerisms as "feminine" or "masculine." The boy himself told us that he did not know what he did that people referred to as "girlish movements." In this context, therefore, we developed (1) procedures to assess his discrimination of his own cross-gender mannerisms; (2) procedures to train him to discriminate those mannerisms; and (3) procedures to suppress the mannerisms.

The therapist explained the target mannerisms of finger extension, hand clasp, hyperextension, limp wrist and flutters to the boy and demonstrated them by manually guiding the boy through the movements that constituted each target behavior. The therapist then explained to the boy that he would watch a 5-minute segment of a videotape of himself and that he would earn one penny for each mannerism he correctly identified. During a baseline pretest condition, the boy was asked to identify the target mannerism. The therapist stopped the tape to reinforce him with a penny for each correct attempt. Then, in the self-observation training sessions for each 5-minute taped segment, the boy was again given one penny for each correctly identified mannerism. Unlike the pretest session, however, when he failed to identify a target mannerism, the therapist stopped the tape to explain that a mannerism had been missed and immediately replayed the tape to point out the missed mannerism. After a criterion of the total target mannerisms had been reached on three separate trials, a new segment of the tape was introduced. Again, the first presentation of the new tape segment was a pretest used to assess generalization of the self-observation training effect.

The data indicated that this boy could not identify the target cross-gender mannerisms before the discrimination training. But with training feedback, his acquisition was rapid. He became progressively better in discriminating his mannerisms from one test session to another, and he was clearly pleased with this acquired ability. After this boy had been trained to identify his target mannerisms from the videotape, there was no evidence that this learning transferred to *in vivo* recognition of these mannerisms. It was clinically necessary to treat his mannerisms with explicit reinforcement contingencies in both the clinic and the home setting. In the clinic setting, therefore, a response-cost and verbal-prompt procedure was introduced contingent upon the occurrence of one of the mannerisms—limping the wrist. The data indicated that limping the wrist decreased, with concurrent decreases in hyperextensions and the residual class of mannerisms (containing feminine gait, flexing the elbow, finger extension, flutters, hand clasp, hands-on-hips, and palming).

Compared with previous cases (Rekers, 1972; Rekers & Lovaas, 1974; Rekers *et al.*, 1974; Rekers *et al.*, 1976), this boy's cross-gender mannerisms decreased more quickly with the application of extrinsic contingencies. It is possible that the self-observation pretraining was the critical factor. But on the other hand, the relatively more efficient treatment result may have been a joint function of (1) the prior self-observation training; (2) the relatively more easily discriminable contingency for a single subclass of mannerisms; and (3) the addition of the verbal cuing, which provided a clear connection between response and consequence. More research is needed to determine the relative advantage of teaching a child to discriminate particular complex behaviors prior to the introduction of contingencies for their occurrence. The obtained response generalization that occurred across subtypes of mannerisms seems to suggest that the individually defined cross-gender mannerisms may together form a single *response class*.

4.2. Treatment Techniques in the Home Setting

In the context of previous findings that have shown the effects of child behavior therapy to be setting-specific (e.g., Wahler, 1969), Rekers and his colleagues have designed treatment procedures to be applied in the major living environments of the gender-disturbed child. The intervention procedures introduced in the clinic setting have sought (1) to demonstrate that environmental variables control sex-typed behavior in gender-disturbed boys; (2) to train the child's parents in behavior-shaping procedures so that they may become the major therapeutic agents for their own child in the home environment; and (3) to supply more specialized behavioral intervention for difficult cross-gender behavior, such as mannerisms, that require more complicated training procedures than can be carried out by parents or teachers in the natural environment (for example, discrimination training with videotape feedback).

The gender-disturbed boys' sex-typed behaviors have therefore been systematically observed and recorded in the home setting before and during treatment intervention in the clinic. Parents have been trained to record child behavior on a daily behavior checklist form that consists of descriptions of frequently occurring feminine behaviors and infrequently occurring masculine behaviors. The behavior checklists are individually designed for each child, based upon referral information, interviews with the parents, and observations of the child's behavior by the investigators in the clinic and home settings. These behavior checklists would include any of the following behaviors that are relevant to an individual child:

1. Play with girls.
2. Play with female dolls.
3. Feminine gesture mannerisms, including any of the gestures that have been operationally defined in the study by Rekers *et al.* (1977a).
4. Play acting of a feminine role, which consists of imitative behaviors modeled after the child's mother, a female schoolteacher, television actresses, and similar female figures (also Flip Wilson, a male comedian who cross-dresses and assumes a female role—and has been a favorite TV personality among gender-disturbed boys).
5. Feminine speech inflection.
6. Masculine play, including any play activity with a male peer if the sex-typed behavior is masculine (e.g., playing cowboys) or neutral (e.g., playing checkers).
7. Play acting of a masculine role, consisting of imitative behaviors modeled after a child's father, a male schoolteacher, or other male figures.

The child's parent is instructed to observe and record his/her son's behavior for 10 minutes at several specific times daily, according to schedules mutually arranged with the investigators. The parent records the behavior by placing a check after the description of each behavior observed during that time period. Observer reliability for this time-sampling procedure is checked periodically throughout the investigation by home visits made by assistants.

By and large, the data from these home observations have indicated that the clinic-treatment effects have not generalized to the home setting, even in the cases in which a parent was trained to be a therapeutic agent in the clinic. For this reason, it has been necessary to introduce treatment procedures in the home setting itself. Even in cases in which the child's mother has been instructed to carry out the same kind of social reinforcement contingencies in the home that have been mastered in the clinic procedure, the sex-typed behavior of the gender-disturbed boy has not significantly changed.

Rekers and colleagues have therefore introduced more explicit reinforcement-control procedures in the home setting by training the mothers to mediate a token reinforcement system (Rekers, 1972; Rekers & Lovaas, 1974; Rekers *et al.*, 1974; Rekers *et al.*, 1977c). The parents are asked to read a programmed booklet for laymen explaining the application of reinforcement principles to child behavior problems (either Patterson & Gullion, 1968, or Patterson, 1971). The investigators then provide the parents with more detailed instruction on the administration of a token system as it would be specifically applied to the child's gender problems. To assure that the instructions are accurately carried out by the parents, an assistant is sent to the home on a number of occasions to observe the parent–child interaction and to answer questions regarding the practical day-to-day operation of the token system. This instruction in the home supplements the regular clinic visits made by the parent for ongoing supervision and formulation of the treatment procedures.

The parents select, with our consultation, a set of back-up reinforcers (see Sherman & Baer, 1969) according to the boy's unique preferences for certain candies and rewarding activities (e.g., TV time). Red and blue standard poker chips have been used as the tokens. The blue tokens, which serve as secondary positive reinforcers (S^{r+}), are directly exchanged by the child for the back-up reinforcers according to a "price list" set by the parents (e.g., five blue tokens required for a candy bar). The red tokens (S^{r-}) are typically discriminative for a response-cost condition in which the red tokens are subtracted from accumulated blue tokens on a one-for-one basis.

In some cases, it is desirable not to use the token-economy system for gender-related behaviors until it has been successfully applied to nongender behaviors in the home. Rekers and Lovaas (1974) have suggested three reasons for this procedure: (1) to test the parents' ability to manage the contingencies consistently; (2) to establish a clear discrimination between S^{r+} and S^{r-} contingencies for the child; and (3) to determine the strength of the S^{r-} contingency necessary to suppress an undesired behavior in the individual child. During this initial period, the parent practices the token-economy system and records the tokens given and the behaviors treated on individualized mimeographed forms. To further guard against the possibility of inappropriate application of a token-reinforcement system to gender behaviors, Rekers and his colleagues have required a written contract, which is cosigned by the parents and the investigators and which specifies that continued intervention in the home setting is contingent upon the parent's success in taking reliable observational data in the home and in gaining control over a nongender behavior.

After the token-reinforcement system has been successfully applied to the boy's nongender behaviors in the home, it is extended to one gender-related behavior at a time. To avoid the possibility of overwhelming the boy with too many contingencies all at once, we have chosen to apply the positive and negative token contingencies to one behavior at a time. Generally speaking, it is preferable to start with the giving of blue tokens for masculine play behavior with other boys. Where this is not possible, masculine play behavior could be reinforced for the child as he plays alone in the home setting. In subsequent stages, one feminine sex-typed behavior is selected and the parent verbalizes the new contingency and then incorporates it in a continuous schedule by giving a red token for each observed incident of that feminine behavior. After the first feminine behavior has been suppressed for several weeks, this contingency is then introduced for a second feminine behavior in addition to the first. Similarly, the S^{r-} contingency is extended to third, fourth, and fifth feminine behaviors successively after each of the preceding feminine behaviors have been successfully suppressed. In the intrasubject research studies presented by Rekers and his colleagues, these successive interventions permit a replication of the S^{r-} contingency across behaviors in a multiple-baseline design.

The results of these parent-mediated token-reinforcement procedures can be illustrated with the data obtained for a 5-year-old gender-disturbed boy and an 8½-year-old boy.

Figure 3 indicates the baseline rate of four separate feminine behaviors that were recorded for the 5-year-old boy in his home for four weeks prior to treatment. During this baseline period, play with girls and feminine gestures occurred at the relatively high frequency of 18–70%, while play with dolls and taking the female role in play occurred at a more moderate rate of 0–12%. These were the four most pronounced feminine behaviors displayed by this boy in the home setting. The figure indicates that in Week 5, the token-reinforcement system was begun for nongender behaviors. Beginning with Week 7, the mother was trained to use special reinforcement procedures to decrease feminine behaviors in the clinic setting. These two initial interventions continued through Week 11. Inspection of the data on Figure 3 indicates that no systematic change in feminine behavior at home can be attributed to either one of these interventions.

The token system at home was extended to play with dolls at the beginning of Week 12. Figure 3 indicates that playing with dolls decreased completely and remained at zero every week after this contingency was in effect. At Week 21, the red tokens were introduced for feminine gestures, which had varied between 0% and 50% during the baseline period. When the red tokens were applied by the mother for feminine gestures, they dropped to zero and (with the exception of Week 22) stayed at zero in subsequent observations. Since playing with girls was not affected by the contingencies for doll play and femi-

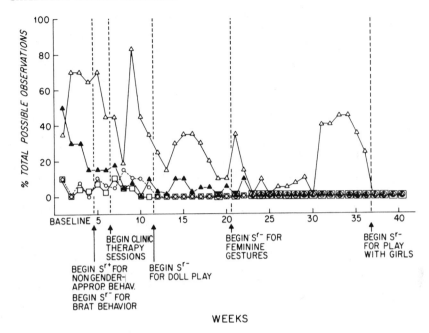

FIGURE 3. Percentage of feminine behavior per week as a function of token reinforcement intervention in the home. Δ Plays with girls, ○ plays with dolls, ▲ feminine gestures, □ female role play.

nine gestures, the final intervention began at Week 37 with the introduction of red tokens for the boy's compulsive play with girls.

In each case, the application of the token-reinforcement contingency was successful in suppressing the undesirable feminine behaviors.

A similar therapeutic effect was obtained by use of the response-cost contingency applied to the gender behaviors of an 8½-year-old boy (Rekers *et al.*, 1974). The first treatment step in the home was the positive reinforcement of masculine play with brother during a daily half-hour play period. From the first reinforced play period, the boy's masculine play with his brother rose to 100% during that play period and remained between 94% and 100% for each play period thereafter. However, there was no immediate stimulus generalization from the reinforced play period to a nonreinforced observation period until the S^{r+} contingency had been in effect for 12 weeks.

The second home intervention involved the introduction of a response-cost contingency for feminine gestures that resulted in an immediate and enduring decrease in the frequency of those gestures. The third intervention was the introduction of the red tokens for feminine speech, which was broadly defined to include both feminine speech content and feminine vocal inflection. This intervention led to a shift in speech content from a ratio of predominantly feminine to a ratio of predominantly masculine and to a decrease of feminine vocal inflection.

This boy's play with his sister consisted almost exclusively of feminine sex-typed activities. In this context, the clinical decision was made that the possible therapeutic benefits of discouraging feminine play with the sister would outweigh the possible negative side effects of discouraging the boy from playing with his sister altogether. When the response-cost contingency was applied, the boy's feminine play with his sister ceased. Finally, the play acting of feminine roles did not require specific treatment, since it ceased during the course of treatment for the other feminine behaviors.

Rekers *et al.* (1977c) reported similar procedures in the home setting in which an explicit "verbal prompt" was superimposed upon the token-mediated response contingency. The data suggested that an explicit verbal labeling by the parent may assist the child to discriminate feminine speech and feminine mannerisms as they occur. The parent was trained in this relatively more complicated method of verbal cuing, in conjunction with the token-mediation contingency, in a behavioral-rehearsal procedure in which an assistant played the role of the child and demonstrated a target behavior while the parent practiced the application of the verbal-prompt and response-cost procedure in the clinic setting. In addition, once the parent had mastered the combined response-cost and verbal-prompt intervention, it was introduced for the target behavior simultaneously in the clinic by the therapist and in the home by the parent.

Bates *et al.* (1975) reported a related clinical study of a group of gender-disturbed boys in which parents were involved in administering behavioral treatment procedures. In contrast with the treatment strategy employed by Rekers and his colleagues, these other investigators did not include procedures specifically to decrease the boys' effeminate mannerisms and feminine play interests but instead focused on the acquisition of masculine behaviors and social skills. The parents were taught to apply social and material reinforcers and token systems in the home setting concurrent with individual social reinforcement contingent upon athletic and masculine behaviors performed in the clinic setting.

The findings of Bates *et al.* (1975) and Rekers and his colleagues demonstrated the importance of obtaining (1) reliable observational data on the boy's sex-typed behavior during treatment to monitor the

child's progress under treatment mediated by his parents and (2) reliability checks on the parents' observational data. These points were underscored by Green's (1974) report of his attempt to replicate Rekers's
(1972) parent-mediated therapy procedures for three gender-disturbed
boys. Green provided parents with verbal instructions to administer
the same type of point-economy reinforcement procedures, including
response-cost contingencies. He did not pretrain the parents with
clinic shaping procedures and he did not obtain reliable observational
data on the child's behavior, which might have served to evaluate the
intervention outcome. Green briefly discussed the difficulties he encountered in attempting to train the parents to discriminate specific
feminine behaviors and to carry out the planned reinforcement procedures. Green's partial replication omitted the two components of (1)
specifically training the parent to observe sex-typed behavior reliably
in the clinic and the home and (2) pretraining the parent carefully in
the clinic setting prior to introducing instructions for similar intervention in the home. In reporting his three treatment failures, Green concluded that in the absence of any experimental control procedures, he
was unable to evaluate whether sex-typed behavior is amenable to
change by reinforcement. He also drew attention to the issue of parental cooperation in mediating contingencies in the home. Actually, "cooperation" may not be possible when adequate training has not been
provided in behavioral observation and behavior-shaping procedures.
The independent investigations by Bates and his colleagues and
Rekers and his colleagues do demonstrate that treatment success is
possible when appropriate training and supervision are provided to
the parents in their role of mediating treatment contingencies for their
own child in the home environment.

5. Other Treatment Strategies

A number of other treatment strategies appear to have clinical
usefulness for the comprehensive treatment of gender-disturbed boys.

5.1. Management in the School Setting

Myrick (1970) presented a case study of a 9-year-old effeminate
boy attending elementary school. Rather than treating the boy directly, the therapist developed strategies to be carried out by the
child's teachers. The boy's classroom teacher and physical education
teacher carried out behavior modification procedures, and the
physical education teacher "tutored" the boy in fundamental athletic

skills, basic game concepts, and successive approximations of the skills required in regular class activities. Significant changes were recorded in pre- and postexperimental measures of playground behavior, lunch room behavior, physical education activities, a class sociogram, and a thematic differential.

The treatment effects of neither the clinic nor home settings can be expected to generalize to the school setting (Rekers et al., 1974). Consequently, Rekers and his colleagues have extended treatment to the school environment in the form of a point-economy system. Following the same model as the intervention in the home setting, a response-cost contingency was applied to non-gender-related problem behaviors before it was applied to gender-relevant behaviors. Rekers and colleagues (1974) reported an intrasubject study involving contingencies mediated by classroom teachers. The dependent measure was obtained by a time-sampling technique using the behavior checklist completed both by the teachers and by independent observers. For an 8½-year-old boy, the checklist items were (1) feminine-gesture mannerisms; (2) feminine speech, either content or inflection; and (3) items grouped as "brat behaviors" (the teacher's term): (a) creating a class disturbance, (b) bossing another child, (c) behaving rudely to the teacher, and (d) teasing another child. The teacher recorded the boy's behavior for 30 minutes at three predetermined times daily. The recording consisted of placing a check after the description of each behavior that was observed one or more times during that time period. An observer, posing as a student teacher, conducted observer-reliability checks.

After a baseline of 18 schooldays, a response-cost contingency was applied to the boy's four brat behaviors. In the presence of the teacher, Dr. Rekers explained to the boy that he would automatically receive 10 points at the beginning of each schoolday. He would lose 1 point each time he created a class disturbance, bossed another child, behaved rudely to the teacher, or teased another child. During the day, the teacher would say to the boy, "One point," to indicate (without his classmates' knowing) that he had lost 1 point for the behavior in which he was currently engaging. Toward the end of the schoolday, the teacher subtracted the points he had lost and he received two minutes of free time for each point remaining.

When the response-cost contingency was introduced for the "brat behaviors," they were entirely suppressed. When the response-cost contingency was extended to feminine-gesture mannerisms, these behaviors decreased slowly. While the response-cost contingency had not been extended to include feminine speech, that behavior ceased entirely. Apparently, the effect of the response-cost contingency on feminine mannerisms generalized to feminine speech.

When this boy was transferred for summer school to a new classrooom with a new teacher, his feminine mannerisms and feminine speech both returned to the baseline levels, and his brat behaviors substantially increased. This circumstance replicated the initial baseline condition, in which no contingency was in effect, providing an ABA reversal replication. Then, when the boy was transferred to yet another room for the beginning of the fall semester, his undesirable behaviors continued, but at a lower frequency. When the teacher in that classroom introduced the response-cost procedure for both feminine mannerisms and brat behaviors, these behaviors ceased immediately. This final condition also replicated the generalization effect from mannerisms to speech that was earlier observed in the first classroom. In summary, the contingency management procedures did lead to a decrease of the feminine behavior; however, the treatment effect in the school was stimulus-specific to the classroom setting; that is, it did not generalize across classrooms.

5.2. Athletic-Behavior Shaping

A specific set of training procedures has been developed to shape athletic behaviors in gender-disturbed boys (Rekers et al., 1974; Rekers et al., 1977c). To enable these boys to gain social reinforcement from their peer group, and to provide competing responses to the cross-gender behavior, training is provided in various athletic skills such as throwing a football, socking a playground ball, kicking a kickball, and shooting baskets. Training is provided in one skill at a time. Once substantial improvement is demonstrated according to a preestablished criterion, training is provided for a second skill. With the use of a multiple-baseline design, a number of children have been trained in several skills each. A male college student models the target behavior and reinforces successive approximations of the desired responses with verbal praise and candy. Test sessions are interspersed at regular intervals so that progress can be measured. The percentage of successful throws (for example) is recorded, and a measure of motivation is calculated as the percentage of time in which the boy attempts the behavior. The acquisition of such athletic skills has been achieved. In many cases, it appears to be even more clinically significant that the boy changes in his approach to playing ball. In the context of individualized training from the college student, some of the boy's fears appear to be desensitized and he learns that playing ball can be intrinsically enjoyable. One boy became involved in neighborhood athletic play and began to derive pleasure from imagining himself as a professional football player. Another boy attained a level of competence that allowed him to compete with his peers without feelings of failure and accompanying anxiety. This boy succeeded to the extent of being elected captain of the kickball team at school (Rekers, 1977b).

5.3. Individual Verbal Therapy

At present, there is no systematic research available on environmentally induced changes in childhood sex-role behavior as a function of individual psychotherapeutic techniques, although a few case histories of such changes have been published. Greenson (1966, 1968) has summarized the clinical notes of his psychoanalytically oriented psychotherapy of a "transvestite boy" aged 5 years at the beginning of treatment. Dupont (1968) described the treatment of mild transvestic behavior in an 8-year-old boy. Rather than treating the boy or his mother, the therapist met for only one session with the father, who agreed to terminate verbal and physical punishment for the deviant behavior and to give the boy his attention and affection contingent upon normal gender behavior. Although Dupont obtained no systematic data in this uncontrolled case study, he reported that after one week, the parents observed no further transvestite behavior for the next 12 years.

Bentler (1968) reported the successful treatment of three adolescent boys aged 11, 13, and 16 years. In individual therapy sessions conducted once weekly, Bentler systematically expressed disapproval for effeminate behavior, encouraged conversation about heterosexual dating, play-acted rehearsals of heterosexual social interaction, encouraged heterosexual encounters, and encouraged frequent masturbation with heterosexual fantasy rather than transvestic fantasy. After 4–12 months of weekly therapy sessions, cross-dressing ceased, masturbation with heterosexual fantasy increased, masculine interests increased, and social dating behavior increased. No follow-up evaluations are available on these children.

In commenting on the psychotherapy for "extremely feminine boys," Stoller (1970–1971) saw the treatment as "reeducation" rather than emphasizing insight. He described the clinical necessity of involving the mothers and the fathers in treatment. An "interim report" by Green et al. (1972b) provides more case material on the boys described by Stoller. In clinical case summaries, these therapists described a psychotherapy procedure consisting of (1) developing a close relationship between a male therapist and the boy; (2) intervening in parental encouragement of feminine behavior; (3) altering the abnormally close relationship between mother and son; (4) enhancing the father–son relationship; and (5) altering the father's role within the family. The five cases, aged 5–12 years, resulted in treatment success ranging from "only modest" change to "considerable shift in . . . gender-role orientation."

Although a number of individual verbal therapy techniques have been used with gender-disturbed boys, none of the treatment variables have been subjected to experimental investigation, and only clinical case reports are available for the generation of hypotheses in this frontier research area.

5.4. Group Therapy

Green and Fuller (1973) and Green (1974) have provided a clinical summary of the treatment of several "very feminine young boys" aged 4–9 years. The boys were treated in a group on a weekly basis for one year, and the available mothers and fathers were treated in separate groups with the goal of enhancing masculine identification in the boys. Since no reliability data were obtained on the behavior ratings made by parents before and after treatment, an evaluation of the results of this treatment is not possible. The authors have discussed the problems in evaluating their anecdotal report, in the absence of systematic objective data.

Bates et al. (1975) developed groups of gender-disturbed boys in which masculine and prosocial behaviors were systematically reinforced with structured point-economy systems and individual behavioral charting. At the clinic, these boys' groups were conducted concurrently with parents' groups that attempted to increase the parents' cooperative behavior as well as to reinforce their successful use of behavioral intervention strategies in the home. Unfortunately, the treatment outcomes were not subjected to controlled comparisons with any systematic or objective outcome measures, since the major focus of this research program was to develop and validate the kinds of new assessment techniques for boys with gender disturbance that were nonexistent at the time of their preintervention evaluation of the subjects (Bates & Bentler, 1973; Bates, Bentler, & Thompson, 1973; Bates, et al., 1974). The pioneering research by these investigators in the area of the measurement of gender disturbance has provided the necessary assessment techniques for future treatment research with gender-disturbed boys.

5.5 Companionship Therapy

Some of the boys lack a stable relationship with a father figure. To partially compensate for this, Rekers and colleagues assigned male college students to build "buddy" relationships with gender-disturbed boys. Interactions between the boy and the college student included informal athletic sessions, tumbling lessons, trips to the park, regular treats such as ice cream, and occasional trips to the beach. The goals were to model appropriate masculine behavior, to provide the boy with a stable male figure with whom he could make positive associations, and to provide a companionship relationship in which the boy could receive gratification from empathetic understanding (Rekers et al., 1974).

5.6. Self-Regulation of Sex-Role Behavior

With the use of extrinsic reinforcement contingencies, childhood gender disturbance has been successfully treated by intervention for multiple sex-role behaviors in multiple environments. The traditional office-visit model of mental health service delivery has been supplemented by staff visits to the home, play, and school environments of the child. These visits were necessary in view of the finding of stimulus-specificity of the extrinsic reinforcement effects. Although parents and teachers have been effectively trained to take on therapeutic roles for the gender-disturbed child, the treatment successes of Rekers and his colleagues as contrasted with the treatment failures of Green (1974) have underlined the importance of extensive supervision of these paraprofessionals. To minimize the potential stimulus-specificity and response-specificity of the treatment effects and to increase the cost efficiency of intervention procedures for childhood gender disturbance, self-control strategies have been successfully introduced to alter patterns of sex-typed behavior in gender-disturbed boys (Rekers & Varni, 1977; Varni & Rekers, 1975).

In the first study conducted (Rekers & Varni, 1977), a 6-year-old gender-disturbed boy was successfully treated with a parent-mediated extrinsic social reinforcement procedure, but an ABA reversal design demonstrated the effects to be stimulus-specific. Since this initial part of the study replicated previous findings, the boy was then successfully trained to use a wrist counter to self-monitor his masculine play. The boy was told that he could play with any toy while alone in a playroom but that he could press the counter only when playing with "boys' toys." A "bug-in-the-ear" device was used for training the self-monitoring response in a behavioral-cuing procedure that was gradually faded out over time. For example, the investigator prompted from the observation room, "Okay, if you played only with the boys' toys for the last two minutes, you can press the wrist counter." An ABA reversal replication demonstrated the reactive effect of this self-monitoring procedure, but the effect extinguished over time. To maximize the probable therapeutic outcome, a self-reinforcement contingency was introduced. The boy was taught to give himself a small piece of candy for each point recorded on his wrist counter. This self-reinforcement procedure, in combination with the self-monitoring instruction, produced exclusive masculine play that was replicated in a BAB reversal design. An independent clinical psychological evaluation, conducted 12 months after the termination of treatment, found no evidence of feminine behaviors or any other emotional disturbance. A 24-month follow-up found occasional cross-gender behaviors recurring in this boy.

Similar results were obtained in a subsequent study in which a 4-year-old gender-disturbed boy was taught to self-monitor and self-reinforce his sex-typed play after an external reinforcement intervention had not produced the desired generalization effects (Varni & Rekers, 1975). In the clinic setting, self-monitoring with the wrist counter produced (1) high and stable rates of masculine sex-typed play and (2) a treatment generalization effect to another set of sex-typed toys. In the preschool setting, moderately high base rate frequencies of cross-dress-up play, feminine role play, and play with girls were recorded. Self-monitoring for cross-dress-up play resulted in an initial reactive effect that extinguished over four sessions. Then a self-reinforcement procedure was superimposed upon the self-monitoring of cross-dress-up play, resulting in a substantial decrease in cross-dressing and response generalization to feminine-role play but not to play with girls. Response maintenance of these therapeutic gains was demonstrated by a one-year follow-up evaluation.

These self-monitoring and self-reinforcement procedures, therefore, hold potential for greater efficiency than external social-reinforcement techniques for the treatment of childhood gender disturbance. These self-regulation strategies have resulted in greater treatment generalization with relatively less investment of professional time. Additional research is required, however, to investigate the possibility of enhanced response maintenance and generalization of the treatment effects with self-regulation approaches to the treatment of sex-role deviance in children.

6. Longitudinal Follow-up Assessment

Behavioral treatment techniques have resulted in adaptive changes in sex-role behaviors in the gender-disturbed boys reported by Dr. Rekers and his colleagues and Dr. Bates and his colleagues. A

total of more than 40 children have been treated by these two independent treatment teams with similar positive outcomes. We may conclude with some confidence that these behavioral treatment effects
would be obtained in other boys, particularly in younger children.
Upon completion of 8–15 months of the behavioral treatment program,
each child that Rekers and his colleagues have treated obtains an independent clinical psychological evaluation. In progress is a study that
will follow these children longitudinally to determine their later adolescent and adulthood adjustment. Only such follow-up data will allow
us to claim a preventive treatment for the adult sexual deviations of
transsexualism, transvestism, and some forms of homosexuality. Sci-
entifically speaking, such follow-up data would need to be compared
to outcome data on gender-disturbed individuals who have been
identified in young childhood and followed through adolescence and
early adulthood, such as the untreated cases that are currently being
followed longitudinally by Green (1974; Green & Money, 1961). For
ethical reasons, Rekers and his colleagues have specifically chosen not
to conduct a group-designed study in which some children are offered
treatment and treatment is withheld from a "control" group of gender-
disturbed boys (Rekers, 1977a; Rosen et al., 1978).

The Although one can currently entertain optimism about the behavioral treatment of childhood gender disturbances, until follow-up data
are available it remains wise to hold several reservations. First, we do
not know the extent to which we may have produced changes in future preference of sex mates. It is possible that adulthood preference of
sex mate is a response that is independent of the ones we have treated
in childhood. Second, a reversal in gender identification from a feminine identification to a masculine one in these boys may or may not
result in a normal gender identity in adulthood. Third, it is possible
that gender behavior changes achieved in childhood may not be predictive of normal gender behavior in adulthood if the treatment has
resulted in a shift in cross-gender behavior from the overt modes to
the covert level of fantasy. For this reason, follow-up assessment must
involve a measure of the intrapsychic concerns, wishes, and fantasies
of the children as they grow up, in addition to measures of overt behavior and stated sexual preferences.

The follow-up data that have been obtained thus far, however, indicate that the changes accompanying treatment have been very comprehensive. The longitudinal follow-up evaluation conducted by
Rekers consisted of the same assessment battery and interviews that
were conducted in the preintervention assessment. An independent
clinical psychologist conducted evaluations and submitted written reports. Let us summarize the follow-up evaluations conducted on 7

children who are representative of approximately 22 children on whom we have obtained follow-up data. Rekers (1977b) reported on the three-year follow-up of a black, gender-disturbed 7-year-old boy, Wayne, whose treatment had been described by Rekers (1972). The independent follow-up of this boy at age 10 found predominantly masculine play behavior and no evidence of a gender disturbance. Rekers (1977b) also reported on two follow-up evaluations of a 4-year, 11-month-old boy whose treatment had been reported by Rekers and Lovaas (1974). A follow-up evaluation 26 months after termination of treatment revealed durability of the treatment effects with no resumption of cross-gender identification. The boy was found to be relatively less skilled at some desired masculine play behaviors, however. For this reason, a male college student made weekly visits to the home for several months to conduct athletic training in conjunction with the boy's father. An additional follow-up evaluation was conducted three and a half years after the treatment by an independent clinical psychologist who again interviewed the boy and the family members and administered the complete battery of psychological tests. The boy was found to have normal gender identity and emotional, social, and academic adjustment.

Similarly, a one-year and two-year evaluation after the completion of treatment of an 8½-year-old boy, reported by Rekers et al. (1974), revealed stable therapeutic gains in a boy who previously had evidenced a profound cross-gender identification. An evaluation of another gender-behavior-disturbed boy, aged 8 years at the time of referral for treatment, revealed that by age 12 years, no gender behavior problems persisted. However, this boy (whose treatment is reported in Rekers et al., 1977c) was later referred for treatment for some family conflicts and for one incident of homosexual play with the foster brother.

Another boy, who was 5 years old at time of initial evaluation and was then found to have a gender identity problem, was followed up 25 months after the completion of treatment. The independent psychologist formulated a posttreatment diagnosis of "mildly effeminate and no cross-gender identification." No evidence of any other mental disorder was found (see Rekers et al., 1976). Similarly, the follow-up evaluations of the children treated with self-regulation procedures have revealed normalization of gender identity and gender behavior one and two years after treatment (Rekers & Varni, 1977; Varni & Rekers, 1975).

In each case, we have found a cognitive change in terms of gender identity as a function of overt, nonverbal gender behavior changes. This has been our finding to the extent that we can measure gender identity by the child's own spontaneous statements and by means of the projective testing and other personality testing that we have described above in our discussion of the diagnostic assessment procedures we have employed. But pending follow-up on these and similarly treated children whose data can be compared to those of the untreated children followed by Green, we can only entertain tentative hope that an effective preventive treatment has been isolated for the adult conditions of transvestism, transsexualism, and effeminate male homosexuality.

References

American Psychological Association. *Ethical standards of psychologists.* As amended, 1972.

Baker, H. J. Transsexualism: Problems in treatment. *American Journal of Psychiatry*, 1969, *125*, 1412–1418.

Bakwin, H. Deviant gender-role behavior in children: Relation to homosexuality. *Pediatrics*, 1968, *41*, 620–629.

Barlow, D. H., Reynolds, E. J., & Agras, W. S. Gender identity change in a transsexual. *Archives of General Psychiatry*, 1973, *28*, 569–576.

Bates, J. E., & Bentler, P. M. Play activities of normal and effeminate boys. *Developmental Psychology*, 1973, *9*, 20–27.

Bates, J. E., Bentler, P. M., & Thompson, S. Measurement of deviant gender development in boys. *Child Development*, 1973, *44*, 591–598.

Bates, J. E., Skilbeck, W. M., Smith, K. V. R., & Bentler, P. M. Gender role abnormalities in boys: An analysis of clinical ratings. *Journal of Abnormal Child Psychology*, 1974, *2*, 1–16.

Bates, J. E., Skilbeck, W. M., Smith, K. V. R., & Bentler, P. M. Intervention with families of gender-disturbed boys. *American Journal of Orthopsychiatry*, 1975, *45*, 150–157.

Bem, S. L. The measurement of psychological androgyny. *Journal of Consulting and Clinical Psychology*, 1974, *42*, 155–162.

Bene, E., & Anthony, J. *Manual for the family relations test.* London: National Foundation for Educational Research, 1957.

Benjamin, H. *The transsexual phenomenon.* New York: Julian Press, 1966.

Benjamin, H. Newer aspects of the transsexual phenomenon. *Journal of Sex Research*, 1969, *5*, 135–144.

Bentler, P. M. A note on the treatment of adolescent sex problems. *Journal of Child Psychology and Psychiatry*, 1968, *9*, 125–129.

Bentler, P. M. A typology of transsexualism: Gender identity theory and data. *Archives of Sexual Behavior*, 1976, *5*, 567–584.

Bieber, I., Dain, H. J., Dince, P. R., Drellich, M. G., Grand, H. G., Gundlach, R. H., Kremer, M. W., Rifkin, A. H., Wilber, C. B., & Bieber, T. B. *Homosexuality: A psychoanalytic study.* New York: Basic Books, 1962.

Brown, D. G. Sex-role preference in young children. *Psychological Monographs: General and Applied*, 1956, *70* (14, Whole No. 421), 1–19.

Dewhurst, C. J., & Gordon, R. R. *The intersexual disorders.* London: Failli Tindall & Cassell, 1969.

Dupont, H. Social learning theory and the treatment of transvestite behavior in an eight-year-old boy. *Psychotherapy: Theory, Research, and Practice,* 1968, 5, 44–45.

Ellis, L. J., & Bentler, P. M. Traditional sex-determined role standards and sex-stereotypes. *Journal of Personality and Social Psychology,* 1973, 25, 28–34.

Evans, R. B. Childhood parental relationships of homosexual men. *Journal of Consulting and Clinical Psychology,* 1969, 33, 129–135.

Evans, R. B. Physical and biochemical characteristics of homosexual men. *Journal of Consulting and Clinical Psychology,* 1972, 39, 140–147.

Evans, T. D. Homosexuality: Christian ethics and psychological research. *Journal of Psychology and Theology,* 1975, 3, 94–98.

Gray, S. W. Ethical issues in research in early childhood education. *Children,* 1971, 18, 83–89.

Green, R. *Sexual identity conflict in children and adults.* New York: Basic Books, 1974.

Green, R., & Fuller, M. Group therapy with feminine boys and their parents. *International Journal of Group Psychotherapy,* 1973, 23, 54–68.

Green, R., Fuller, M., & Rutley, B. IT-scale for children and Draw-a-Person Test: 30 feminine vs. 25 masculine boys. *Journal of Personality Assessment,* 1972a, 36, 349–352.

Green, R., & Money, J. Effeminacy in prepubertal boys: Summary of eleven cases and recommendations for case management. *Pediatrics,* 1961, 27, 286–291.

Green, R., & Money, J. *Transsexualism and sex reassignment.* Baltimore: Johns Hopkins, 1969.

Green, R., Newman, L. E., & Stoller, R. J. Treatment of boyhood "transsexualism"—An interim report of four years' experience. *Archives of General Psychiatry,* 1972b, 26, 213–217.

Greenson, R. R. A transvestite boy and a hypothesis. *International Journal of Psychoanalysis,* 1966, 47, 396–403.

Greenson, R. R. Dis-identifying from mother: Its special importance for the boy. *International Journal of Psycho-Analysis,* 1968, 49, 370–374.

Harrington, C. C. *Errors in sex-role behavior in teenage boys.* New York: Teachers College Press, 1970.

Hatterer, L. J. *Changing homosexuality in the male: Treatment for men troubled by homosexuality.* New York: McGraw-Hill, 1970.

Hoenig, J., Kenna, J., & Youd, A. Social and economic aspects of transsexualism. *British Journal of Psychiatry,* 1970, 117, 163–172.

Holemon, E. R., & Winokur, G. Effeminate homosexuality: A disease of childhood. *American Journal of Orthopsychiatry,* 1965, 35, 48–56.

Kando, T. M. *Sex change: The achievement of gender identity by feminized transsexuals.* Springfield, Ill.: Charles C Thomas, 1973.

Kinsey, A. C., Pomeroy, W. B., & Martin, C. E. *Sexual behavior in the human male.* Philadelphia: W. B. Saunders, 1948.

Lebovitz, P. S. Feminine behavior in boys: Aspects of its outcome. *American Journal of Psychiatry,* 1972, 128, 1283–1289.

Litin, E. M., Giffin, M. E., & Johnson, A. M. Parental influence in unusual sexual behavior in children. *Psychoanalytic Quarterly,* 1956, 25, 37–55.

Lukianowicz, N. Survey of various aspects of transvestism in the light of our present knowledge. *Journal of Nervous and Mental Disease,* 1959, 128, 36–64.

Maccoby, E. E. (Ed.). *The development of sex differences.* Stanford, Calif.: Stanford University Press, 1966.

Maccoby, E. E., & Jacklin, C. N. *The psychology of sex differences.* Stanford, Calif.: Stanford University Press, 1974.

Mischel, W. Sex-typing and socialization. *In* P. H. Mussen (Ed.), *Carmichael's manual of child psychology,* 3rd ed., Vol. II. New York: Wiley, 1970.

Money, J. *Sex-errors of the body: Dilemmas, education, counseling.* Baltimore: Johns Hopkins, 1968.

Money, J. Critique of Dr. Zuger's manuscript. *Psychosomatic Medicine*, 1970a, *32*, 463–465.

Money, J. Sexual dimorphism and homosexual gender identity. *Psychological Bulletin*, 1970b, *74*, 425–440.

Money, J., & Ehrhardt, A. A. *Man and woman, boy and girl: The differentiation and dimorphism of gender identity from conception to maturity.* Baltimore: Johns Hopkins University Press, 1972.

Money, J., Hampson, J., & Hampson, J. L. An examination of some basic concepts: Evidence of human hermaphroditism. *Bulletin of the Johns Hopkins Hospital*, 1955, *97*, 301–319.

Money, J., & Primrose, C. Sexual dimorphism and dissociation in the psychology of male transsexuals. *Journal of Nervous and Mental Disease*, 1968, *147*, 472–486.

Mussen, P. H. Early sex-role development. *In* D. A. Goslin (Ed.), *Handbook of socialization theory and research.* Chicago: Rand McNally, 1969.

Myrick, R. D. The counselor–consultant and the effeminate boy. *Personnel and Guidance Journal*, 1970, *48*, 355–361.

Patterson, G. R. *Families: Applications of social learning to family life.* Champaign, Ill.: Research Press, 1971.

Patterson, G. R., & Gullion, M. E. *Living with children: New methods for parents and teachers.* Champaign, Ill.: Research Press, 1968.

Pauly, I. Male psychosexual inversion: Transsexualism: A review of 100 cases. *Archives of General Psychiatry*, 1965, *13*, 172–181.

Pauly, I. Adult manifestations of male transsexualism. *In* R. Green & J. Money (Eds.), *Transsexualism and sex reassignment.* Baltimore: Johns Hopkins, 1969.

Prince, C. V., & Bentler, P. M. A survey of 504 cases of transvestism. *Psychological Reports*, 1972, *31*, 903–917.

Rabban, M. Sex-role identification in young children in two diverse social groups. *Genetic Psychology Monographs*, 1950, *42*, 81–158.

Randell, J. An emerging entity. *International Journal of Psychiatry*, 1970, *9*, 275–277.

Rekers, G. A. Pathological sex-role development in boys: Behavioral treatment and assessment. *Dissertation Abstracts International*, 1972, *33*, 3321B. (University Microfilms No. 72-33, 978).

Rekers, G. A. Stimulus control over sex-typed play in cross-gender identified boys. *Journal of Experimental Child Psychology*, 1975, *20*, 136–148.

Rekers, G. A. *Atypical sex-role development: Assessment, intervention, and ethics.* Invited paper presented at the Western Regional Conference, Society for Research in Child Development, Emeryville, Calif., April 1976.

Rekers, G. A. Atypical gender development and psychosocial adjustment. *Journal of Applied Behavior Analysis*, 1977a, *10*, in press.

Rekers, G. A. Sexual problems: Behavior modification. *In* B. B. Wolman (Ed.), *Handbook of treatment of mental disorders in childhood and adolescence.* Englewood Cliffs, N.J.: Prentice-Hall, 1977b.

Rekers, G. A., Amaro-Plotkin, H., & Low, B. P. Sex-typed mannerisms in normal boys and girls as a function of sex and age. *Child Development*, 1977a, *48*, 275–278.

Rekers, G. A., Bentler, P. M., Rosen, A. C., & Lovaas, O. I. Child gender disturbances: A clinical rationale for intervention. *Psychotherapy: Theory, Research, and Practice*, 1977b, *14*, 1–8.

Rekers, G. A., & Lovaas, O. I. Experimental analysis of cross-sex behavior in male children. *Research Relating to Children*, 1971, *28*, 68. (Abstract)

Rekers, G. A., & Lovaas, O. I. Behavioral treatment of deviant sex-role behaviors in a male child. *Journal of Applied Behavior Analysis*, 1974, *7*, 173–190.

Rekers, G. A., Lovaas, O. I., & Low, B. P. The behavioral treatment of a "transsexual" preadolescent boy. *Journal of Abnormal Child Psychology*, 1974, *2*, 99–116.

Rekers, G. A., & Varni, J. W. Self-monitoring and self-reinforcement processes in a pre-transsexual boy. *Behaviour Research and Therapy*, 1977, *15*, 177–180.

Rekers, G. A., Willis, T. J., Yates, C. E., Rosen, A. C., & Low, B. P. Assessment of childhood gender behavior change. *Journal of Child Psychology and Psychiatry*, 1977c, *18*, 53–65.

Rekers, G. A., & Yates, C. E. Sex-typed play in feminoid boys vs. normal boys and girls. *Journal of Abnormal Child Psychology*, 1976, *4*, 1–8.

Rekers, G. A., Yates, C. E., Willis, T. J., Rosen, A. C., & Taubman, M. Childhood gender identity change: Operant control over sex-typed play and mannerisms. *Journal of Behavior Therapy and Experimental Psychiatry*, 1976, *7*, 51–57.

Rosen, A. C. The intersex: Gender identity, genetics, and mental health. In S. Plog & R. Edgerton (Eds.), *Changing perspectives in mental illness*. New York: Holt, 1969.

Rosen, A. C., Rekers, G. A., & Bentler, P. M. Ethical issues in the treatment of children. *Journal of Social Issues*, 1978, *34*, in press.

Rosen, A. C., Rekers, G. A., & Friar, L. R. Theoretical and diagnostic issues in child gender disturbances. *Journal of Sex Research*, 1977, *13*, in press.

Rosen, A. C., & Teague, J. Case studies in development of masculinity and femininity in male children. *Psychological Reports*, 1974, *34*, 971–983.

Sherman, J. A., & Baer, D. M. Appraisal of operant therapy techniques with children and adults. In C. M. Franks (Ed.), *Behavior therapy: Appraisal and status*. New York: McGraw-Hill, 1969.

Skilbeck, W. M., Bates, J. E., & Bentler, P. M. Human figure drawings of gender-problem and school-problem boys. *Journal of Abnormal Child Psychology*, 1975, *3*, 191–199.

Socarides, C. W. Homosexuality and medicine. *Journal of the American Medical Association*, 1970, *212*, 1199–1202.

Stoller, R. J. A contribution to the study of gender identity. *International Journal of Psychoanalysis*, 1964, *45*, 220–226.

Stoller, R. J. Passing in the continuum of gender identity. In J. Marmer (Ed.), *Sexual inversion: The multiple roots of homosexuality*. New York: Basic Books, 1965.

Stoller, R. J. Male childhood transsexualism. *Journal of the American Academy of Child Psychiatry*, 1968a, *7*, 193–209.

Stoller, R. J. *Sex and gender: The development of masculinity and femininity*. New York: Science House, 1968b.

Stoller, R. J. Parental influences in male transsexualism. In R. Green & J. Money (Eds.), *Transsexualism and sex reassignment*. Baltimore, Md., Johns Hopkins University Press, 1969.

Stoller, R. J. Psychotherapy of extremely feminine boys. *International Journal of Psychiatry*, 1970–1971, *9*, 278–280.

Sutton-Smith, B., Rosenberg, B. G., & Morgan, E. R. Development of sex differences in play choices during preadolescence. *Child Development*, 1963, *34*, 119–126.

Thoresen, C. E., & Mahoney, M. J. *Behavioral self-control*. New York: Holt, 1974.

Varni, J. W., & Rekers, G. A., *Behavioral self-control treatment of "cross-gender identity" behaviors*. Paper presented at the meeting of the Association for the Advancement of Behavior Therapy. San Francisco, California, December, 1975.

Wahler, R. G. Setting generality: Some specific and general effects of child behavior therapy. *Journal of Applied Behavior Analysis*, 1969, *2*, 239–246.

Walinder, J. *Transsexualism: A study of forty-three cases.* Göteborg, Sweden: Scandinavian University Books, 1967.

Zuger, B. Effeminate behavior present in boys from early childhood: 1. The clinical syndrome and follow-up studies. *Journal of Pediatrics,* 1966, *69,* 1098–1107.

Zuger, B. Gender role determination: A critical review of the evidence from hermaphroditism. *Psychosomatic Medicine,* 1970a, *32,* 449–467.

Zuger, B. The role of familial factors in persistent effeminate behavior in boys. *American Journal of Psychiatry,* 1970b, *126,* 1167–1170.

Zuger, B., & Taylor, P. Effeminate behavior present in boys from early childhood: II. Comparison with similar symptoms in non-effeminate boys. *Pediatrics,* 1969, *44,* 375–380.

8   *Uses of Modeling in Child Treatment*

KAREN D. KIRKLAND
AND MARK H. THELEN

1. Overview

Learning by observation and imitation of other people's behavior is an everyday affair for most children and a central process in the acquisition of a wide variety of new behaviors. Extensive research has shown that modeling is an effective way for children to acquire, strengthen, and weaken behaviors. Given frequent naturalistic observation of imitation among children and the voluminous experimental literature on the topic, it is not surprising that *modeling* is a common term in developmental psychology. The next step that occurred in the evolution of the field was the application of modeling techniques to the treatment of clinical problems with children. A number of practitioners and researchers have begun to bridge the gap between the experimental and the applied realms by demonstrating that modeling is an effective strategy for the treatment of a variety of childhood disorders.

This review is intended to provide the reader with concrete descriptions of modeling procedures and guidelines regarding ways to design clinical treatment programs. Also, the reader will be informed of methods for quick and effective treatment of various childhood disorders and will be guided in making significant contributions to our present understanding of modeling in therapy.

In support of these goals, we describe experimental, analogue, applied, and anecdotal research on modeling treatment with children. Since the scope of this paper includes adolescents, the term *children* is intended to include adolescents unless otherwise indicated. Experimental studies on the use of modeling to extinguish fears of people,

KAREN D. KIRKLAND AND MARK H. THELEN • Department of Psychology, University of Missouri at Columbia, Columbia, Missouri.

animals, visits to the physician, and inanimate stimuli are reviewed here. Special considerations and the application of modeling to the treatment of autistic, mentally retarded, and distractible children are described, in addition to the treatment of interpersonal problems, such as social aggression and delinquency. Specific situational and organismic variables that may enhance the effects of modeling treatment are reviewed to assist in the development of treatment strategies tailored to meet the individual needs of each client. In concluding the review, we provide a variety of speculative notions regarding relevant yet neglected areas of research and a discussion of general issues related to modeling treatment.

2. Modeling with Fearful Children

Many childhood disorders involve learned patterns of fearfulness. These problems are often difficult to treat because of the reward that results from avoidance of the feared stimulus. In addition, positive reinforcing consequences may serve to maintain childhood fears (e.g., playing at home because of a school phobia). Phobias and avoidance patterns often develop as a result of emotional or physical discomfort that occurs in a particular situation, then becomes associated with a variety of additional settings or objects. Such fears may be learned by direct experience and/or by observation of other people.

Research has shown promising treatment effects using modeling to reduce fears, phobias, and avoidance behaviors. Treatment programs usually consist of exposing the fearful child to a model who calmly encounters the feared situation. Observation of a calm model who behaves appropriately without receiving negative consequences is likely to reduce the threatening stimulus value of the feared situation and thereby to strengthen the child's willingness to approach the feared situation.

2.1. Animal Fears

Most of the early experimental research on modeling dealt with the reduction of children's fear of animals. This section is intended to provide descriptions of modeling procedures and evidence that modeling is a highly effective method of eliminating specific animal fears. Macfarlane, Allen, and Honzik (1954) reported that fear of dogs was the most frequent fear among 3-year-olds but that over time such fears usually subsided without treatment. Since animal fears are quite common among children, they merit treatment commensurate with age-appropriateness, the severity level, and the degree of interference with daily activities. For example, if a child's avoidance of dogs continues long after peers have naturally "outgrown" such fears, and if the child avoids settings where a dog might appear (e.g., the school playground), then treatment is clearly appropriate. However, in less severe cases, practitioners must decide on a case-by-case basis whether treatment is indicated.

Long before modeling became a popular topic and procedure, Mary Cover Jones (1924a,b) eliminated a young child's fear of animals by a treatment procedure that included exposing the child to peer models who played with a rabbit and showed no fear. Albert Bandura and his colleagues have conducted a variety of experiments using modeling to reduce children's fear of animals. For example, Bandura, Grusec, and Menlove (1967) assessed the effects of peer modeling and the affective quality of the modeling context by assigning dog-phobic preschool children to one of four treatment conditions. One group of youngsters watched a live child model fearlessly engage in gradually more threatening interactions with a dog in the context of an ongoing party complete with colored hats and prizes. A second group observed the identical modeling sequence in a neutral context. Children in a third treatment group observed the dog within a positive context but with the model absent. The final group of children attended the party but observed neither the dog nor the model. Behavioral posttests administered immediately and at a one-month follow-up revealed that regardless of context, the children who had observed a model improved significantly in their ability to approach two dogs over the children who had not observed a model.

Bandura and Menlove (1968) found that children who watched single or multiple models were more willing to approach live dogs than children who did not observe models. Children who observed multiple models performed better than those who observed only one model on a posttest of remaining confined in a playpen with a dog.

A variety of experimental studies using modeling to reduce children's fear of snakes have documented positive effects similar to those obtained in studies using dog-phobic children (Bandura, Blanchard, & Ritter, 1969; Ritter, 1968; Weissbrod & Bryan, 1973). In summary, exposure to fearless models is a consistently effective method for the reduction of specific animal fears in children, particularly when multiple models and live guided participation are used. Since modeling treatment for children's animal phobias is effective, is inexpensive to administer, and requires minimal professional time, it appears to be an excellent treatment for focal fears and phobias.

2.2. Inanimate Fears

Modeling has also been used to reduce a variety of inanimate fears. Although research is somewhat sparse, it generally suggests that any specific fear is amenable to treatment with modeling if the client observes a model encountering the feared situation, then practices the modeled behavior in graduated steps.

Several experiments have demonstrated that modeling reduces fears of inanimate stimuli. For example, Ritter's (1969) study showed that modeling reduced fear of heights in adolescents and adults and that guided practice produced better results than verbal instructions or passive observation of models.

Lewis (1974) used modeling films to reduce children's fear of swimming by exposing one group of children to a film of three initially fearful (coping) models who eventually played in a swimming pool. After seeing the film, the children were physically guided by the experimenter through a series of water activities. The second experimental group received only the modeling portion of the treatment, and a third group received only the participation phase. Although the modeling-plus-participation treatment was the most effective in the reduction of water fears, both modeling alone and participation alone were more effective than a no-treatment control condition. While a mild fear of water would probably not interfere with children's normal development, a severe fear of water could be debilitating. Therefore, it might be desirable for camp counselors and swimming teachers to use models and gradual exposure to water to accommodate extremely fearful children. In the future, researchers might devise modeling programs to treat children who are severely afraid of athletic activities (e.g., horseback riding, skiing, gymnastics), of transportation vehicles (e.g., cars, buses, airplanes), or of natural phenomena (e.g., lightning, thunder, darkness). In addition to reducing these fears, it is important to teach children appropriate precautions to ensure that their experience will be safe and enjoyable.

2.3. Dental and Medical Fears

Avoidance of dental and medical treatment is a common yet potentially life-threatening reaction that is often learned in childhood and may extend into adulthood. The routine and preventive use of modeling films to prepare patients for medical and dental treatment could spare thousands of people the misery and dread associated with office visits and hospitalization. Such preventive preparation would probably make medical staff's work easier, contribute to superior health care, and encourage individuals to seek treatment when appropriate.

Melamed, Weinstein, Hawes, and Katin-Borland (1975) demonstrated a successful reduction of disruptive dental-treatment behavior as a result of exposure to a film that depicted a 4-year-old child who successfully coped with his anxieties during dental treatment and received verbal praise and a toy for his cooperative behavior. Other researchers (Johnson & Machen, 1973; Machen & Johnson, 1974; Melamed, Hawes, Heiby & Glick, 1975; White & Davis, 1974) have also demonstrated an effective reduction of dental fears via modeling.

In a study with important implications for the prevention of negative reactions, Melamed and Siegel (1975) assessed the effect of preparing young children for surgery with modeling. The treatment group was shown a film depicting a 7-year-old boy who encountered various events associated with hospitalization (e.g., separation from parents, medical procedures, and recovery). Narration by the child model described initial fears and successful efforts to cope with them. The control group was shown a film unrelated to hospitalization. On behavioral, self-report, and physiological measures of state anxiety, the treatment group consistently evidenced less anxiety than the control group.

Two studies (Vernon, 1973; Vernon & Bailey, 1974) showed that children who observed film models receiving general anesthesia were rated by observers as less upset than controls prior to (but not during) anesthesia induction. Vernon (1974) found that observation of film models who received injections and demonstrated moderate yet realistic pain reactions reduced children's rated levels of pain and upset.

In summary, physicians and dentists might use modeling to reduce children's fear and disruptive behavior during examination and treatment. Routine use of modeling films in a preventive way would probably contribute to better health care and decrease the frequency of severe medical phobias. Future research might explore whether repeated exposure to modeling films at each visit is needed to maintain fear reduction and whether young children might respond better to modeling since they have had fewer opportunities to develop severe fears.

Based on our review, it appears that modeling is an efficient and effective treatment that can be used to reduce any fear that is relatively situation- or object-specific. Although fear reduction can be expected after short-term treatment, the clinician should check with the client several times following formal treatment to guarantee that generalization to the naturalistic environment occurs and that appropriate responses are maintained over time.

3. Modeling with Socially Maladjusted Children

Many childhood problems involve the lack of adequate social skills and the presence of antisocial behavior or both. These problems often impair learning and the enjoyment of social rewards. Modeling treatment for interpersonal problems usually consists of the elimination of disturbing behaviors and social avoidance patterns, as well as training in new skills.

3.1. Social Withdrawal

Research has demonstrated successful reduction of social isolation through the use of modeling therapy with nursery-school children. For example, O'Connor (1969) showed preselected social isolates 11 film scenes depicting a child who initially observed social interactions, then joined in the activities with positive consequences. Behavioral measures revealed that social withdrawal was sharply reduced as a result of film treatment compared with no change for control-group children.

Evers and Schwarz (1973) treated 13 socially withdrawn nursery-school children with either exposure to a modeling tape or exposure to the modeling tape plus teacher reward for classroom interaction. Results showed that compared to base rate, exposure to a film of appropriate social behavior reduced social isolation with or without praise and that improvement was maintained at a four-week follow-up.

Ross, Ross, and Evans (1971) treated a severely withdrawn 6-year-old boy over a seven-week period. During the first phase of the program, imitation of the model was established with rewards for imitation. The adult model interacted with other children to demonstrate appropriate behavior, then the child participated in a graduated series of pleasant activities with other children. Descriptive results indicated that modeling with guided participation increased the child's adaptive social skills.

Keller and Carlson (1974) treated a group of socially isolated preschool children with exposure to videotapes depicting children engaged in socially rewarding behaviors. Untreated control children viewed a nature film. Results showed that children in the modeling group increased the amount of social reward that they gave to and received from peers. Also, their social interaction increased more than that of the control children.

In summary, the short-term effects of modeling in the treatment of severe childhood social withdrawal generally have been successful, but follow-up data are somewhat weak. Treatment effects may be difficult to maintain because social withdrawal represents a generalized rather than a focal fear or because treatment involves a combination of new-skills training and fear reduction. Future research is needed to clarify the conditions under which modeling is effective in the reduction of social withdrawal on a long-term basis.

3.2. Social Aggression

Social aggression is a particularly disturbing interpersonal behavior that merits treatment because of its antisocial and destructive consequences. Aggressive behavior can interfere with the acquisition and use of new skills and knowledge, and impair the development of satisfying social relationships. Limited research shows short-term reduction in aggression as a result of modeling. However, it appears that positive consequences in the natural environment are necessary to maintain nonaggressive behavior.

Chittenden (1942) conducted a study designed to teach children nonaggressive reactions to frustration. She exposed children to a series of plays depicting aggressive and then cooperative solutions to interpersonal problem situations and facilitated discussion of the advantages of cooperation. The results indicated that the children who observed the modeling plays showed a decrease in domination and aggression in response to frustration at nursery school. In a similar program, Gittelman (1965) modified the rated aggressive behavior of a group of children by having them watch each other role-play solutions to frustrating situations.

Sarason and Ganzer (1973) used modeling to reduce antisocial behavior and teach new, adaptive ways of dealing with common problem situations. A group of male juvenile delinquents observed social models who demonstrated such skills as how to apply for a job, how to resist peer pressure, and how to delay gratification. The boys practiced imitation of the modeled behavior and received feedback regarding their performance. A second group of delinquents attended group meetings in which the same topics were discussed but no modeling or imitation occurred. Boys in the control group received no special treatment. Both the modeling and the discussion treatment-groups showed positive changes in attitudes and behavior, as well as less recidivism than the control group.

Thelen, Fry, Dollinger, and Paul (1976) applied modeling strategies to the treatment of juvenile delinquents living in a group home. Boys in the modeling condition observed a series of 14 videotapes in which a model portrayed initial difficulty but gradual ability to cope with a variety of day-to-day interpersonal situations. After individually viewing each modeling tape, the delinquent and the experimenter role-played the filmed interactions. Control subjects observed lecture tapes that emphasized similar social skills. Staff behavior-ratings indicated that the boys in the modeling condition had better home adjustment during the five-week treatment period, but this improvement was not maintained during the four-week follow-up. Control subjects showed no changes in behavior. The authors suggested that the naturalistic social reinforcement of the critical behaviors after treatment was not sufficiently positive to maintain the behavior changes that resulted from modeling treatment. Additional research is needed to establish strategies for enhancing transfer of training and maintenance effects in the natural environment.

4. Modeling with Distractible Children

Several researchers have attempted to decrease distractibility and impulsivity in children. For example, Nixon (1969) provided an anecdotal description of modeling therapy to increase task-related behavior among hyperactive elementary-school children. The author used a modeling film that demonstrated the difference between distractible behavior and on-task behavior, then showed contingent model reinforcement for desirable behavior. Next, the children received a direct contingent reward from their teachers for appropriate behavior. The school staff noted marked changes in the behavior of some, but not all, of the children and no deterioration of any child's behavior. Additional research is needed to assess the singular effect of modeling and reward as well as the degree of change that results from such combined treatments.

Thomas (1974) attempted to alter the attending-to-task behavior of first-grade public-school children with attention-span difficulties. Although not a clinical population, these children were identified by school staff as being highly distractible. Two treatment groups were exposed to a series of video tapes depicting positive attending behavior by a variety of models. One treatment group was told that their teacher would like them to act the way the child in the films did, and the other group was shown the films with no instructions. Classroom ratings indicated that both treatment groups increased their attending behavior more than no-treatment control children and that neither treatment group was superior to the other. In summary, although these two anecdotal reports suggest that modeling is effective in reducing distractible behavior, more rigorous research evidence is necessary.

5. Modeling with Severely Deficient Children

Some childhood problems involve extreme deficiencies in the behavioral skills that are appropriate, or even critical, for a given age. Although wide variability exists in children's developmental rates, parents often become appropriately alarmed and seek help when their children exhibit deficits in basic areas of functioning, especially when bizarre and undesirable responses accompany the deficit condition.

Modeling treatment is quite difficult and time-consuming in cases in which children are labeled mentally retarded or autistic. With these populations, remedial and preparatory training programs that include a variety of strategies must often precede modeling treatment (e.g., Lovaas, Freitag, & Whalen, 1967). For example, autistic children are often preoccupied with self-stimulatory and repetitive behaviors that must be eliminated with punishment before new skills can be learned. Some children are almost completely unresponsive to people, including the model, and therefore must be taught to pay attention to as well as to imitate the model. After learning these prerequisite behaviors, children with behavioral deficits are usually responsive to modeling programs (e.g., Baer, Peterson, & Sherman, 1967; Metz, 1965).

5.1. Autism

Most research with autistic children does not use modeling as it is strictly defined but rather uses a combination of treatments that includes modeling as an adjunctive technique. For example, Lovaas *et al.* (1967) demonstrated improvements in the behavior of autistic and schizophrenic children using rewards, shaping, prompts, and modeling to establish speaking skills. Punishment was used to extinguish bizarre, self-stimulatory, and social-withdrawal behaviors. The children's behavior was gradually shaped, so that modeling and adjunctive techniques could be used to train the children in a variety of social and intellectual skills, such as personal hygiene, sex-role behaviors, playing games, and nonverbal expression.

Using a similar combination of techniques, Lovaas, Berberich, Perloff, and Schaeffer (1966) taught language skills to two previously mute schizophrenic children. Their treatment program consisted of giving food rewards for sounds that resembled words spoken by the adult trainer and giving physical and verbal punishment for off-task behavior. The children learned to respond verbally to physical prompts, which were gradually faded out, and to imitate a variety of words.

Other researchers have described language-training programs

with autistic children (Coleman & Stedman, 1974; Koegel & Rincover, 1974; Schell, Stark, & Giddan, 1967; Stark, Giddan, & Meisel, 1968) and with mentally retarded children (Butz & Hasazi, 1973; Marshall & Hegrenes, 1970). These intensive programs typically involve a broad combination of operant and modeling techniques (e.g., training in looking behavior, imitation, and vocal responding).

5.2. Mental Retardation

A number of researchers have demonstrated the efficacy of modeling and adjunctive techniques to teach new self-care skills to mentally retarded children. Modeling tends to be an excellent teaching method, particularly with children who have difficulty learning via more traditional techniques (e.g., lectures). For example, Butterfield and Parson (1973) taught a retarded mongoloid boy to chew solid food with a program of modeling, shaping, and differential reward. Eaton and Brown (1974) used modeling and reward to train 13 mentally retarded youths in appropriate mealtime behavior. Using verbal instruction, modeling, and manual guidance, O'Brien and Azrin (1972) trained 12 institutionalized retardates in the use of proper table manners.

Horner and Keilitz (1975) used verbal instructions, modeling, and prompts with social reward to teach eight mentally retarded adolescents to brush their teeth. Using both live and videotaped models, Stephan, Stephano, and Talkington (1973) trained mental retardates to identify parts of the telephone, to call the police, and to take messages for other people.

The effect of goal-setting and imitation strategies on the work-performance skills of retarded male adolescents was investigated by Kleibhan (1967). Feedback about daily work level was given to each boy in the goal-setting group, and each was asked to state his expected work rate for the following day. Boys in the imitation group worked with a productive male model and were asked to notice what a fine job the model did. Control subjects received no special treatment. Both goal-setting and imitation treatments increased work production to more than that of the control group, and no difference was found between the two treatments.

Marburg, Houston, and Holmes (1976) conducted a study in which mentally retarded children received rewards for imitation from either one or three models. Results showed that all the children learned to imitate both previously rewarded and nonrewarded behaviors. Generalized imitation was eight times greater for the children trained with multiple models than for those trained with single models.

In summary, remedial training programs are often necessary to prepare autistic and mentally retarded children for modeling treatment. Such remedial programs often include a combination of operant shaping, reward, punishment, and modeling techniques. When unwanted behaviors are reduced and the ability to imitate has been established, these children are capable of acquiring a variey of simple social, motor, and intellectual skills. Research evidence suggests that reward for imitation increases attention to models and accurate imitation. In addition, variable schedules of reward may be used to maintain a high level of imitation and transfer of training. Limited research suggests that multiple models strengthen response generalization.

6. Modeling-Program Development

We have reviewed a number of different kinds of behavioral problems in which modeling has been used. However, the practical application of modeling therapy to behavioral problems necessarily involves many other considerations. This section is designed to assist the practitioner or applied-research scientist in the process of systematically devising a modeling program for a specific child or population. Program considerations might involve pretraining, client and model characteristics, and treatment procedures.

A major thrust of this section is toward the optimal refinement of the modeling treatment for a given type of client. In support of this purpose, experimental-research findings that relate to program-development decisions are described. The reader should keep in mind, however, that most of the research cited in this section was conducted with nonclinical populations. Thus, the techniques should be adopted cautiously, pending verification and replication in more clinical settings.

6.1. Client Characteristics

When researchers and practitioners develop a modeling-therapy program, they might be aware that some children may be more suitable for and responsive to modeling treatment than other children. Research is available that can help us to identify some "client characteristics" that, when present in a given child or population, tend to support the use of a modeling treatment.

For example, Thelen, Paul, Dollinger, and Roberts (1975) found that in unstructured situations, younger children imitate more than their older counterparts. Other research has indicated that children with a cognitive set to cooperate are more likely to imitate than children with a competitive, resistant set (Mausner & Block, 1957). In addition, highly dependent children imitate more than children with low dependence (Ross, 1966). Hence, limited research supports the use of modeling with dependent, cooperative, or young children.

Theorists have suggested that people are more likely to imitate when they are uncertain about how to respond (Thelen, Dollinger & Kirkland, 1976; Walters & Amoroso, 1967; Walters, Bowen, & Parke, 1964). Research support for this notion is provided by Gelfand (1962) and Kanareff and Lanzetta (1960), who found that children who have failure experiences prior to modeling treatment imitate more than children with prior success experiences. This might suggest that modeling scenes be introduced immediately after a child experiences a failure in the natural environment, since the child may be more likely to imitate at that time.

According to Bandura (1969), attention to modeling scenes and cognitive retention of that information are necessary for imitative learning to occur. Therefore, children with attentional or cognitive deficiencies may be unsuitable candidates for treatment with modeling unless special pretraining efforts are successful (e.g., Lovaas et al., 1967). In summary, practitioners might profitably attend to certain population characteristics when they devise individualized modeling programs.

6.2. Model Characteristics

In addition to guidelines on client characteristics, information about facilitative model characteristics is available and highlights the importance of selecting models carefully. However, since most of the relevant research was not conducted with child clinical populations, the reader should extrapolate cautiously from the following research until additional clinical research is available.

Several guidelines are available to assist practitioners in deciding whether to select a model of the same sex as the client or the opposite sex. Fryrear and Thelen (1969) have suggested that females imitate females and males imitate males only when the child observer perceives the modeled behavior as sex-appropriate. However, since most clinical behavior is not "sex-linked," the model's sex may not be an important variable. When multiple models are used, it might be advisable to use both female and male models.

At present, few clear guidelines are available to indicate whether child or adult models are more effective with child clinical populations. Positive treatment effects have been obtained in separate studies using adult models (e.g., Horner & Keilitz, 1975; Lovaas *et al.*, 1966, 1967; Marburg *et al.*, 1976) and child models (e.g., Bandura, Grusec, & Menlove, 1967; Lewis, 1974; Melamed & Siegel, 1975; Weissbrod & Bryan, 1973). Therefore, research is needed to assess the effect of model age and to clarify whether adult or peer models might be differentially effective with given target behaviors.

Program planners may wish to increase the salience of modeling cues by incorporating one or several model attributes that have been shown to facilitate modeling-treatment effects. For example, Roberts, Santogrossi, and Thelen (1976) found that positive emotional expression by the model increased imitation. Mischel and Grusec (1966) found that a rewarding female model elicited more imitation than a nonrewarding female model. Other research has demonstrated that models who control resources of value to the child elicit a high rate of imitation (Bandura *et al.*, 1963; Grusec & Mischel, 1966; Hetherington & Frankie, 1967). Since research suggests that model affect, nurturance, and power tend to facilitate imitation, program planners might use models who possess these characteristics (e.g., parents, teachers, and staff members).

6.3. Model Consequences

When modeling scenes are being devised, the use of reward to the model for the target behavior might be considered. Research has shown that observation of model reward increases imitation (Thelen & Rennie, 1972), especially when the client expects to perform the modeled behavior (Thelen, Rennie, Fryrear, & McGuire, 1972). Marsten (1966) and Bandura (1965) found that selective model reward and punishment help the observer to discriminate which behaviors to imitate and which to avoid. Model reward and punishment might be especially effective in the treatment of behavior problems that involve a component that needs strengthening and one that needs to be decreased or eliminated. For example, in the treatment of hyperactive children, the model's quiet, on-task behavior might be rewarded, and disruptive behavior might be punished.

6.4. Pretherapy Training

Members of certain populations (e.g., autistic and mentally retarded children) often lack the skills that are necessary for imitative learning. When children have a substantial deficit in the ability to imitate, pretraining efforts may be used to prepare them for modeling treatment. Pretraining programs are typically used to increase the ability to attend to and imitate models. The reader might recall from Section 5.1 that Lovaas and his colleagues (1967) used a pretraining program with autistic children that involved the extinction of bizarre behavior and a reward for appropriate attending behavior and imitation. Most pretherapy training programs consist of giving rewards to the client for imitating simple choices on a task that may be unrelated to the clinical target behavior. As a result, children learn how to imitate other people's behavior, including the target behavior demonstrated during formal treatment. Although some children need to be taught to imitate, others may imitate too much (e.g., echolalia) and may require training in discriminating when imitation is appropriate.

6.5. Strengthening Imitation

Even when clients have the skills to imitate, certain procedures may be used to increase imitation. For example, direct rewards for imitation increase the overall level of imitation (Bandura, 1965). The experimental literature on schedules of reward suggests that continuous rewards be used initially to establish a high rate of imitation and that intermittent rewards be used later in training to maintain imitative behavior (Kerns, 1975).

Research has shown that when clients verbally describe the actions of the model, their level of imitation increases (Bandura, Grusec, & Menlove, 1966). Giving the client direct instructions to imitate also tends to increase imitation (Rennie & Thelen, 1976). Still another strategy for increasing imitation involves the effect of being imitated. Research has demonstrated that when older peers or adults initially imitate children, the children tend to imitate reciprocally and increase their attraction toward that peer or adult (Thelen, Dollinger, & Roberts, 1975; Thelen & Kirkland, 1976). Therefore, treatment agents might initially imitate the client's appropriate behavior on a variety of simple tasks in order to increase the client's imitation later during formal treatment. This approach should be used cautiously, however, depending on the individual client's response to being imitated.

6.6 Conclusion

In this section, we described many aspects and decision points in modeling-program development that need consideration and that may have a substantial bearing on treatment outcome. At present, these guidelines are necessarily speculative, since most of the relevant research has been conducted with nonclinical populations. Therefore, it would be a positive and timely contribution to the modeling field if researchers would assess and identify considerations that are critical with various clinical populations.

7. Discussion

A variety of issues which relate to the use of modeling in treatment will now be discussed in an attempt to inform the reader of general considerations for current application procedures, and suggest topics for future research. In addition, a summary of major findings cited in this review will be offered, and concluding remarks will be made.

7.1. Multiple versus Single Models

Limited research has demonstrated that multiple models elicit stronger treatment effects than single models. For example, Bandura and Menlove (1968) found that children's fear of dogs decreased after exposure to multiple models. As cited earlier, Marburg et al. (1976) found that mentally retarded children who observed three models imitated new skills more than children trained with only one model. Although these two studies suggest that multiple models may be superior to single models, many experiments that used only single models obtained positive behavioral changes (e.g., Bandura, Grusec, & Menlove, 1967; Melamed et al., 1975; Melamed & Siegel, 1975). Other research that used only multiple models obtained positive effects (Lewis, 1974; Thomas, 1974; Vernon, 1973, 1974; Vernon & Bailey, 1974). Therefore, additional research is needed to make a direct comparison of the effects of single and multiple models.

7.2. Live versus Filmed Models

Several studies have shown that live and filmed models are equally effective (Bandura, Ross, & Ross, 1963; Stephan et al., 1973). Bandura, Blanchard, and Ritter (1969) found that live modeling plus guided participation was more effective in the reduction of snake fears than viewing a filmed model without guided participation. Future research might assess the effect of filmed modeling plus guided participation.

A variety of modeling studies have obtained positive treatment effects using only live models (Butterfield & Parson, 1973; Lovaas et al., 1966, 1967; Marburg et al., 1976; Sarason & Ganzer, 1973) or only filmed models (Bandura & Menlove, 1968; Melamed et al., 1975;

O'Connor, 1969, 1972; Vernon, 1973, 1974). Hence, current research with predominantly nonclinical child populations indicates that positive treatment effects may be obtained with either live or filmed models. However, the reader might consider a number of cost–efficiency considerations which support the use of filmed models rather than live models. Automated techniques provide a flexible method for treatment because they accommodate the portrayal of naturalistic modeling sequences that would be difficult to create within institutional settings. In addition, video or filmed scenes provide a convenient way to present multiple models while using a minimum of the models' time, and they can be used repeatedly with a variety of children. Films also afford the consistent presentation of the modeled behavior, which may not always be possible with live modeling. Hence, automated modeling treatment represents an important technological advancement in applied service and provides a tool for creative, flexible programs (Fry & Thelen, 1976).

7.3. Generalization and Maintenance

Modeling-treatment effects are of little value unless they generalize from the clinic to a variety of real-life situations and unless they are maintained over time. Since *in vivo* practice of the modeled behavior may be used to facilitate naturalistic generalization effects (Bandura, 1976; Bandura, Jeffery, & Gajdos, 1975; Bandura, Jeffery, & Wright, 1974), treatment agents might accompany the child to various locations for practice and encourage the child to practice the new skills on a regular basis. Research also shows that treatment with multiple models yields better generalization effects than treatment with single models (Bandura & Menlove, 1968; Marburg *et al.*, 1976; Stokes, Baer, & Jackson, 1974).

Better maintenance of effects might be achieved if treatment agents would gradually increase the amount of time between treatment sessions and continue to see clients on an infrequent basis long after behavioral changes have been achieved. Maintenance might also be increased if parents and teachers were trained to reward the child for the target behavior on an intermittent basis. Future research might carefully evaluate follow-up effects and explore techniques for strengthening generalization and maintenance.

7.4. Future Research

Research has demonstrated that modeling is an effective and efficient treatment method for certain clinical problems. In the future, researchers might apply modeling to treat other clinical problems that have not received attention in the empirical literature. Target problems might include, for example, temper tantrums, enuresis, loss of appetite, attention-seeking behavior, jealousy of siblings, sleep disturbances, shoplifting, drug abuse, and lying. Imaginative researchers might devise modeling scenes to treat a multitude of childhood and adolescent problems, and they might develop viable, efficient alternatives to traditional treatment methods.

More research is needed to assess the efficacy of modeling compared to other treatments, such as systematic and *in vivo* desensitization, role playing, operant shaping, live participation, coaching, prompting, guided practice, and cognitive–emotive imagery. In addition, the effect of combining one or more treatments with modeling might be assessed for whether single or combined approaches are more effective. Researchers might explore whether the organismic and situational variables that have been shown to facilitate modeling are effective with clinical populations either alone or in combination. In addition, the feasibility of using covert modeling approaches, which have been successful in the reduction of adult avoidance-responses (Cautela, Flannery, & Hanley, 1974; Kazdin, 1973), might be assessed with upper-elementary and junior-high-school populations who are cognitively advanced enough to use imagery techniques.

7.5 Summary

We have reviewed a wide variety of documented reports on the treatment of childhood behavioral problems via modeling. Our intent was to inform researchers and practitioners of the current state of knowledge in the use of modeling, to explore adjunctive and remedial treatments, and to describe conditions that facilitate modeling-treatment effects. The following is a summary of the major findings cited in this review:

1. Modeling to treat children with focal fears and phobias (e.g., fear of animals or medical procedures) consistently reduces fear and increases interaction with the feared stimuli. Short-term treatment is usually effective with focal fears, especially when live guided participation is used.

2. The treatment of grossly deficient children is more difficult and time-consuming than the treatment of normal children with focal fears. Autistic and mentally retarded children usually require remedial pretraining in order to acquire imitative skills. However, pretraining plus modeling can be used to train these children in a variety of simple social, motor, and intellectual skills. Limited research suggests that

reward for imitation facilitates the maintenance of imitative responsiveness and that the use of multiple models increases response generalization.

3. Limited anecdotal research suggests that modeling can be useful in training distractible children to focus their attention on tasks.

4. Modeling treatment of children with severe social withdrawal problems has produced generally positive short-term effects. However, research is needed to clarify the conditions under which modeling might bring about long-term increases in social interaction.

5. Social-skills training with juvenile delinquents may be effective on a short-term basis, although more research is needed to establish strategies for enhancing the transfer of training and maintenance effects.

6. In an attempt to assist the reader in the development of individualized treatment programs, we have reviewed a variety of model and observer characteristics that positively enhance treatment effects. In addition, we have described a number of treatment procedures that facilitate imitation.

7.6. Conclusion

We have witnessed a great increase in the clinical application of modeling in recent years, and it holds considerable potential for continued development. Modeling provides a treatment that can be administered alone or as an adjunct to other forms of therapy with a minimum expenditure of time and effort. Automated modeling tapes can be accommodated to group and self-administered treatment and can be used repeatedly. It is our hope that this review has stimulated interest in modeling research and has informed the reader of the potential application of modeling to the treatment of children with behavioral and adjustment problems. For further information on the topic of modeling, the reader might refer to articles and/or books by Gelfand and Hartman (1975), Marlatt and Perry (1975), Rachman (1972), Rimm and Masters (1974), and Rosenthal (1976).

References

Baer, D. M., Peterson, R. F., & Sherman, J. A. The development of imitation by reinforcing behavioral similarity to a model. *Journal of the Experimental Analysis of Behavior*, 1967, 10, 405–416.

Bandura, A. Influence of models' reinforcement contingencies on the acquisition of imitative responses. *Journal of Personality and Social Psychology*, 1965, 1, 589–595.

Bandura, A. *Principles of behavior modification*. New York: Holt, Rinehart and Winston, 1969.

Bandura, A. Effecting change through participant modeling. In J. D. Krumboltz & C. E. Thoresen (Eds.), *Counseling methods*. New York: Holt, Rinehart, and Winston, 1976.

Bandura, A., Blanchard, E. B., & Ritter, B. The relative efficacy of desensitization and modeling approaches for inducing behavioral, affective, and attitudinal changes. *Journal of Personality and Social Psychology, 1969, 13,* 173–199.

Bandura, A., Grusec, J. E., & Menlove, F. L. Observational learning as a function of symbolization and incentive set. *Child Development, 1966, 37,* 499–506.

Bandura, A., Grusec, J. E., & Menlove, F. L. Vicarious extinction of avoidance behavior. *Journal of Personality and Social Psychology, 1967, 5,* 16–23.

Bandura, A., Jeffery, R. W., & Gajdos, E. Generalizing change through self-directed performance. *Behavior Research and Therapy, 1975, 13,* 141–152.

Bandura, A., Jeffery, R. W., & Wright, C. L. Efficacy of participant modeling as a function of response induction aids. *Journal of Abnormal Psychology, 1974, 83,* 56–64.

Bandura, A., & Menlove, F. L. Factors determining vicarious extinction of avoidance behavior through symbolic modeling. *Journal of Personality and Social Psychology, 1968, 8,* 99–108.

Bandura, A., Ross, D., & Ross, S. Imitation of film-mediated aggressive models. *Journal of Abnormal and Social Psychology, 1963, 66,* 3–11.

Butterfield, W. H., & Parson, R. Modeling and shaping by parents to develop chewing behavior in their retarded child. *Journal of Behavior Therapy and Experimental Psychiatry, 1973, 4,* 285–287.

Butz, R. A., & Hasazi, J. E. Developing verbal imitative behavior in a profoundly retarded girl. *Journal of Behavior Therapy and Experimental Psychiatry, 1973, 4,* 389–393.

Cautela, J. R., Flannery, R. B., & Hanley, S. Covert modeling: An experimental test. *Behavior Therapy, 1974, 5,* 494–502.

Chittenden, G. E. An experimental study in measuring and modifying assertive behavior in young children. *Monographs of the Society for Research in Child Development, 1942, 7* (1, Serial No. 31).

Coleman, S. L., & Stedman, J. M. Use of a peer model in language training in an echolalic child. *Journal of Behavior Therapy and Experimental Psychiatry, 1974, 5,* 275–279.

Eaton, P., & Brown, R. I. The training of mealtime behavior in the subnormal. *British Journal of Mental Subnormality, 1974, 20,* 78–85.

Evers, W. L., & Schwarz, J. C. Modifying social withdrawal in preschoolers: The effects of filmed modeling and teacher praise. *Journal of Abnormal Child Psychology, 1973, 1,* 248–256.

Fry, R., & Thelen, M. H. Therapeutic videotape and film modeling: A review. 1976. Unpublished manuscript, University of Missouri.

Fryrear, J. L., & Thelen, M. H. The effect of sex of model and sex of observer on the imitation of affectionate behavior. *Developmental Psychology, 1969, 1,* 298.

Gelfand, D. The influence of self-esteem on rate of verbal conditioning and social matching behavior. *Journal of Abnormal and Social Psychology, 1962, 65,* 259–265.

Gelfand, D. M., & Hartman, D. P. *Child behavior analysis and therapy.* New York: Pergamon Press, 1975.

Gittelman, M. Behavior rehearsal as a technique in child treatment. *Journal of Child Psychology and Psychiatry, 1965, 6,* 251–255.

Grusec, J. E., & Mischel, W. Model's characteristics as determinants of social learning. *Journal of Personality and Social Psychology, 1966, 4,* 211–214.

Hetherington, E. M., & Frankie, G. Effects of parental domination, warmth, and conflict on imitation in children. *Journal of Personality and Social Psychology*, 1967, *6*, 119–125.

Horner, R. D., & Keilitz, I. Training mentally retarded adolescents to brush their teeth. *Journal of Applied Behavior Analysis*, 1975, *8*, 301–309.

Johnson, R., & Machen, J. B. Behavior modification techniques and maternal anxiety. *Journal of Dentistry for Children*, 1973, *40*, 20–24.

Jones, M. C. The elimination of children's fears. *Journal of Experimental Psychology*, 1924a, *7*, 382–390.

Jones, M. C. A laboratory study of fear: The case of Peter. *Pedagogical Seminar*, 1924b, *31*, 308–315.

Kanareff, V. T. & Lanzetta, J. T. Effects of success–failure experiences and probability of reinforcement upon the acquisition and extinction of an imitative response. *Psychological Reports*, 1960, *7*, 151–166.

Kazdin, A. E. Covert modeling and the reduction of avoidance behavior. *Journal of Abnormal Psychology*, 1973, *81*, 87–95.

Keller, M. F., & Carlson, P. M. The use of symbolic modeling to promote social skills in preschool children with low levels of social responsiveness. *Child Development*, 1974, *45*, 912–919.

Kerns, C. D. Effects of schedule and amount of observed reinforcement on response persistence. *Journal of Personality and Social Psychology*, 1975, *31*, 983–991.

Kleibhan, J. M. Effects of goal-setting and modeling on job performance of retarded adolescents. *American Journal of Mental Deficiency*, 1967, *72*, 220–226.

Koegel, R. L., & Rincover, A. Treatment of psychotic children in a classroom environment: I. Learning in a large group. *Journal of Applied Behavior Analysis*, 1974, *7*, 45–59.

Lewis, S. A comparison of behavior therapy tchniques in the reduction of fearful avoidance behavior. *Behavior Therapy*, 1974, *5*, 648–655.

Lovaas, O. I., Berberich, J. P., Perloff, B., & Schaeffer, B. Acquisition of imitative speech by schizophrenic children. *Science*, 1966, *151*, 705–707.

Lovaas, O. I., Freitag, K. N., & Whalen, C. The establishment of imitation and its use for the development of complex behavior in schizophrenic children. *Behavior Research and Therapy*, 1967, *5*, 171–181.

MacFarlane, J. W., Allen, L., & Honzik, M. P. *A developmental study of the behavior problems of normal children between 21 months and 14 years.* Berkeley: University of California Press, 1954.

Machen, J. B., & Johnson, R. Desensitization, model learning, and the dental behavior of children. *Journal of Dental Research*, 1974, *53*, 83–87.

Marburg, C. C., Houston, B. K., & Holmes, D. S. Influence of multiple models on the behavior of institutionalized retarded children: Increased generalization to other models and other behaviors. *Journal of Consulting and Clinical Psychology*, 1976, *44*, 514–519.

Marlatt, G. A., & Perry, M. A. Modeling methods. *In* F. H. Kanfer & A. P. Goldstein (Eds.), *Helping People Change.* 1975, New York: Pergamon Press.

Marshall, N. R., & Hegrenes, J. R. Programmed communication therapy for autistic mentally retarded children. *Journal of Speech and Hearing Disorders*, 1970, *35*, 70–83.

Marsten, A. R. Determinants of the effects of vicarious reinforcement. *Journal of Experimental Psychology*, 1966, *71*, 550–558.

Mausner, B., & Block, B. A study of the additivity of variables affecting social interaction. *Journal of Abnormal and Social Psychology*, 1957, *54*, 250–256.

Melamed, B. G., Hawes, R. R., Heiby, E., & Glick, J. Use of filmed modeling to reduce uncooperative behavior of children during dental treatment. *Journal of Dental Research*, 1975, *54*, 797–801.

Melamed, B. G., & Siegel, L. J. Reduction of anxiety in children facing hospitalization and surgery by use of filmed modeling. *Journal of Consulting and Clinical Psychology*, 1975, *43*, 511–521.

Melamed, B. G., Weinstein, D., Hawes, R., & Katin-Borland, M. Reduction of fear-related dental management problems with use of filmed modeling. *Journal of the American Dental Association*, 1975, *90*, 822–826.

Metz, J. R. Conditioning generalized imitation in autistic children. *Journal of Experimental Child Psychology*, 1965, *2*, 389–399.

Mischel, W., & Grusec, J. Determinants of the rehearsal and transmission of neutral and aversive behaviors. *Journal of Personality and Social Psychology*, 1966, *3*, 197–205.

Nixon, S. B. Increasing task-oriented behavior. *In* J. D. Krumboltz & C. E. Thoresen (Eds.), *Behavioral counseling: Cases and techniques.* New York: Holt, Rinehart and Winston, 1969.

O'Brien, F., & Azrin, N. H. Developing proper mealtime behaviors of the institutionalized retarded. *Journal of Applied Behavior Analysis*, 1972, *5*, 389–399.

O'Connor, R. D. Modification of social withdrawal through symbolic modeling. *Journal of Applied Behavior Analysis*, 1969, *2*, 15–22.

O'Connor, R. D. Relative efficacy of modeling, shaping, and the combined procedures for modification of social withdrawal. *Journal of Abnormal Psychology*, 1972, *79*, 327–344.

Rachman, S. Clinical applications of observational learning, imitation, and modeling. *Behavior Therapy*, 1972, *3*, 379–397.

Rennie, D. L., & Thelen, M. H. Generalized imitation as a function of instructional set and social reinforcement. *JSAS Catalog of Selected Documents in Psychology*, 1976, *6*, 107–108 (manuscript number 1360).

Rimm, D. C., & Masters, J. C. *Behavior therapy: Techniques and empirical findings.* New York: Academic Press, 1974.

Ritter, B. The group desensitization of children's snake phobias using vicarious and contact desensitization procedures. *Behavior Research and Therapy*, 1968, *6*, 1–6.

Ritter, B. The use of contact desensitization, demonstration-plus-participation, and demonstration-alone in the treatment of acrophobia. *Behavior Research and Therapy*, 1969, *7*, 157–164.

Roberts, M. C., Santogrossi, D. A., & Thelen, M. The effects of prior task experience in the modeling situation. *Journal of Experimental Child Psychology*, 1976, *21*, 524–531.

Rosenthal, T. L. Modeling therapies. *In* M. Hersen, R. M. Eisler, & P. M. Miller (Eds.), *Progress in behavior modification*, Vol. 2. New York: Academic Press, 1976.

Ross, D. Relationship between dependency, intentional learning, and incidental learning in preschool children. *Journal of Personality and Social Psychology*, 1966, *4*, 374–381.

Ross, D. M., Ross, S. A., & Evans, T. A. The modification of extreme social withdrawal by modeling with guided participation. *Journal of Behavior Therapy and Experimental Psychiatry*, 1971, *2*, 273–279.

Sarason, I. G., & Ganzer, V. J. Modeling and group discussion in the rehabilitation of juvenile delinquents. *Journal of Counseling Psychology*, 1973, *20*, 442–449.

Schell, R. E., Stark, J., & Giddan, J. Development of language behavior in an autistic child. *Journal of Speech and Hearing Disorders*, 1967, *32*, 51–64.

Stark, J., Giddan, J. J., & Meisel, J. Increasing verbal behavior in an autistic child. *Journal of Speech and Hearing Disorders*, 1968, *33*, 42–47.

Stephan, C., Stephano, S., & Talkington, L. Use of modeling in survival skill training with educable mentally retarded. *Training School Bulletin*, 1973, *70*, 63–68.

Stokes, T., Baer, D., & Jackson, R. Programming the generalization of a greeting response in four retarded children. *Journal of Applied Behavior Analysis*, 1974, *7*, 599–610.

Thelen, M. H., Dollinger, S. J., & Kirkland, K. D. *Imitation as a function of response uncertainty and social influence: A review of the literature.* Unpublished manuscript, University of Missouri at Columbia, 1976.

Thelen, M. H., Dollinger, S. J., & Roberts, M. C. On being imitated: Its effects on attraction and reciprocal imitation. *Journal of Personality and Social Psychology*, 1975, *31*, 467–472.

Thelen, M. H., Fry, R. A., Dollinger, S. J., & Paul, S. C. Use of videotaped models to improve the interpersonal adjustment of delinquents. *Journal of Consulting and Clinical Psychology*, 1976, *44*, 492.

Thelen, M. H., & Kirkland, K. D. On status and being imitated: Effects on reciprocal imitation and attraction. *Journal of Personality and Social Psychology*, 1976, *33*, 691–697.

Thelen, M. H., Paul, S. C., Dollinger, S. J., & Roberts, M. C. *Response uncertainty and imitation: The interactive effects of age and task options.* Unpublished manuscript, University of Missouri, 1975.

Thelen, M. H., & Rennie, D. L. The effect of vicarious reinforcement on limitation: A review of the literature. In B. A. Maher (Ed.), *Progress in experimental personality research: A review of the literature,* Vol. 6. New York: Academic Press, 1972.

Thelen, M. H., Rennie, D. L., Fryrear, J. L., & McGuire, D. Expectancy to perform and vicarious reward: Their effects upon imitation. *Child Development*, 1972, *43*, 699–703.

Thomas, G. M. Using videotaped modeling to increase attending behavior. *Elementary School Guidance and Counseling*, 1974, *9*, 35–40.

Vernon, D. T. Use of modeling to modify children's responses to a natural, potentially stressful situation. *Journal of Applied Psychology*, 1973, *58*, 351–356.

Vernon, D. T. Modeling and birth order in response to painful stimuli. *Journal of Personality and Social Psychology*, 1974, *29*, 794–799.

Vernon, D. T., & Bailey, W. C. The use of motion pictures in the psychological preparation of children for induction of anesthesia. *Anesthesiology*, 1974, *40*, 68–72.

Walters, R. H., & Amoroso, D. M. Cognitive and emotional determinants of the occurrence of imitative behavior. *British Journal of Social and Clinical Psychology*, 1967, *6*, 174–185.

Walters, R. H., Bowen, N. V., & Parke, R. D. Influence of looking behavior of a social model on subsequent looking behavior of observers of the model. *Perceptual and Motor Skills*, 1964, *18*, 469–483.

Weissbrod, C. S., & Bryan, J. H. Filmed treatment as an effective fear reducing technique. *Journal of Abnormal Child Psychology*, 1973, *1*, 196–201.

White, W. C., Jr., & Davis, M. T. Vicarious extinction of phobic behavior in early childhood. *Journal of Abnormal Child Psychology*, 1974, *2*, 25–32.

9   Research on the Education of Autistic Children: Recent Advances and Future Directions

ARNOLD RINCOVER
AND ROBERT L. KOEGEL

1. Introduction

The purpose of this chapter is twofold: first, to report on some recent advances in the treatment of autistic children, and second, to propose some directions for future research with these children. In general, autism has been described as an extreme form of childhood psychopathology, characterized by deficits in language and in social and emotional behavior, as well as a preoccupation with bizarre, stereotyped mannerisms and, in some cases, tantrums or self-injurious behavior. The first application of the principles of behavior modification to the specific problems of autistic children appeared in the literature in 1961. Three papers by Ferster during that year (Ferster, 1961; Ferster & De Myer, 1961a,b) gave a major impetus to subsequent research in the field. During the last 15 years, the developing discipline has begun to establish a useful technology of behavior change for autistic children, including the training of self-help skills (e.g., Marshall, 1966), speech (Hewett, 1965; Metz, 1965; Risley & Wolf, 1967; Lovaas, 1966, 1967), and reading skills (Hewett, 1964); the elimination of self-injurious be-

ARNOLD RINCOVER • Department of Psychology, University of North Carolina at Greensboro and H. W. Kendall Center, Greensboro, North Carolina. ROBERT L. KOEGEL • University of California at Santa Barbara and Camarillo Behavior Development and Learning Center, Santa Barbara, California. Preparation of this manuscript was facilitated by United States Public Health Service Research Grants MH28210 and MH28231 from the National Institute of Mental Health.

havior and other severe behavior excesses (e.g. Wolf, Risley, & Mees, 1964; Lovaas, Freitag, Gold, & Kassorla, 1965a; Tate & Baroff, 1966; Lovaas & Simmons, 1969; Carr, Newsom, & Binkoff, 1976); and the establishment of classroom programs (Kozloff, 1975; Koegel & Rincover, 1974; Rincover & Koegel, 1977) and training regimens for parents (Davison, 1964; Schreibman & Koegel, 1975) and teachers (Koegel, Russo, & Rincover, 1977). Given the previous pessimistic prognoses for autistic children in psychotherapy (Kanner & Eisenberg, 1955; Brown, 1960; Rutter, 1966; Havelkova, 1968), the success and replicability of these behavior-modification procedures have been cause for a new optimism on the part of parents, educators, and researchers alike.

2. Recent Advances

Although we are still in need of considerable research before we can speak of "curing" this disorder (see Section 3), recent research reporting significant developments in the understanding and treatment of autistic children lead us to feel quite optimistic about the future. These developments are summarized in the following sections under the general headings of: "Self-injurious Behavior," "Self-stimulatory Behavior," "Prompting and Prompt Fading," "Generalization and Maintenance of Behavior Change," "Parent and Teacher Training," and "Classroom (group) Instruction."

2.1. Self-Injurious Behavior

We consider self-injurious and self-stimulatory behaviors first because their elimination appears to be a prerequisite to any serious attempt to help autistic children. One variable that has been implicated in the motivation of self-injurious behavior is the attention that such behavior evokes from parents, teachers, institutional staff, etc. That attention can be a reinforcer for this behavior is now common knowledge, and studies are readily available demonstrating that treatment procedures based upon extinction, time out, or differential attention have been successful in eliminating self-injurious behavior in autistic and retarded children (Wolf, Risley, & Mees, 1964; Lovaas, Freitag, Gold, & Kassorla, 1965a; Hamilton, Stephens, & Allen, 1967; Bucher & Lovaas, 1968; Lovaas & Simmons, 1969).

It is notable, however, that differential-attention procedures may not always be the treatment of choice. First, various authors have cautioned their readers that differential-attention procedures may produce an increase in the maladaptive behavior before it decreases and that the suppression of self-injurious behavior may require a pro-longed period of time that includes a large number of potentially harmful, self-injurious acts (Bucher & Lovaas, 1968). Both of these factors pose additional dangers to the child. Second, to further complicate matters, differential-attention procedures may in fact have no effect (Risley, 1968) or even a reinforcing effect (Solnick, Rincover, & Peterson, 1977; Carr, Newsom, & Binkoff, 1976) on self-injurious behavior. In at least some cases, attention is not the prime motivating factor in self-injurious behavior, and as a result, different treatment procedures are required.

An alternative approach to treatment is the contingent application of aversive stimulation (usually electric shock), which has in general produced a more predictable and rapid suppression of self-injurious behavior (Risley, 1968; Tate & Baroff, 1966; Lovaas & Simmons, 1969; Corte, Wolf, & Locke, 1971; Lovaas, Schaeffer, & Simmons, 1965; Lichstein & Schreibman, 1976). A discussion of these data and the sensitive ethical issues involved is presented in Lovaas and Newsom (1976). In brief, the authors note that while electric shock usually produces a rapid and reliable suppression of self-injurious behavior, this procedure has not yet been shown to produce generalized, durable behavior change. In addition, the measurement of possible "side effects" needs to be more thoroughly addressed in future research. Moreover, despite the potential efficacy of this procedure, there is a good deal of controversy in many quarters over the ethical use of electric shock, which in the final analysis may prove to be the most formidable obstacle to the development and refinement of punishment procedures for self-injurious behavior.

A third approach to the treatment of self-injurious behavior has been suggested in two studies that found that self-destructive behavior was maintained by *negative* reinforcement (Carr et al., 1976; Solnick et al., 1977). In each study, self-injurious behavior served an escape function in that it produced the termination of an aversive situation, such as the termination of a demanding learning session. Rather than rearranging only the consequences of self-injurious behavior, in these experiments the authors tried to increase the reinforcing properties of the setting in which the learning sessions were conducted. That is, the learning tasks remained, but the setting was "enriched" by the introduction of a "positive context" (Carr et al., 1976) via storytelling between instructional trials or toys, music, and social interactions (Solnick et al., 1977) between trials. In each case, self-injurious behavior was virtually eliminated, presumably because the enrichment functioned to make the termination of the task a punishing event rather than a negative reinforcer.

These data showing that self-injurious behavior can be maintained by negative reinforcement have important implications for treatment. If self-injurious behavior that is in fact motivated by negative reinforcement is incorrectly assumed to be maintained by positive reinforcement (attention), the therapist may design an extinction or time-out procedure to remove attention from the child. Unfortunately, such differential-attention procedures also include the termination of instructions or demands, and as a result, the therapist or teacher may inadvertently be negatively reinforcing self-injurious behavior. In short, these results illustrate the importance of performing a functional analysis of each individual case and of not simply assuming that all behaviors sharing a similar topography also share a similar set of controlling variables.

2.2 Self-Stimulatory Behavior

One of the most salient characteristics of autistic children is self-stimulatory behavior, typically described as persistent, stereotyped, repetitive behavior. While only a small percentage of autistic children engage in self-injurious acts, a large majority engage in self-stimulation. In fact, many autistics occupy all of their waking hours engaged in various forms of self-stimulation, such as spinning objects, flapping their fingers or arms, and rhythmically rocking back and forth.

Self-stimulation presents one of the most formidable obstacles to the treatment of autistic children. Such behavior seems to produce no external consequences and has been notoriously resistant to extinction. Despite some success with various punishment procedures (e.g., Lovaas, Schaeffer, & Simmons, 1965b; Foxx & Azrin, 1973), the generalized, durable elimination of self-stimulatory behaviors remains difficult. This is particularly unfortunate in that a number of positive "side effects" have been observed when self-stimulation has been even temporarily reduced. Risley (1968) and Lovaas & Newsom (1976) have discussed various prosocial and attentional behaviors that seemed to occur as a by-product of the suppression of self-stimulation. Koegel and Covert (1972) similarly found that the discrimination learning of autistic children may be enhanced if certain self-stimulatory behaviors are reduced, while Epstein, Doke, Sajwaj, Sorrell & Rimmer (1974) and Koegel, Firestone, Kramme, & Dunlap (1974) reported increases in spontaneous appropriate play when self-stimulation was restrained.

Various studies have been conducted recently to investigate the motivational properties of self-stimulation. One study assessed the role of sensory consequences in the maintenance of self-stimulatory behavior (Rincover, Peoples, & Packard, 1976). In this experiment, various types of sensory feedback were masked or removed in an attempt to see if such behavior was operant behavior maintained by its sensory consequences. For each of three children, a sensory event was found that, when made unavailable, reduced the child's rate of self-stimulatory behavior to near zero. To illustrate, one child would incessantly spin objects (a classic type of self-stimulatory behavior) in a stereotyped, repetitive fashion. After various unsuccessful manipulations, we found that blocking the auditory feedback by covering the surface used to spin the objects (e.g., carpeting a table) resulted in a reliable and complete suppression of self-stimulatory behavior that proved durable within and across sessions. Within-subject replications, conducted with each child, clearly demonstrated that these self-stimulatory behaviors were maintained by their sensory consequences and that such behavior could be eliminated via "sensory extinction." Although these results are encouraging, additional research is needed to assess the generality of sensory extinction procedures.

2.3. Prompting and Prompt Fading

Prompt fading is a very common, widely used technique that has in the past been used successfully in the teaching of normal and retarded children (e.g., Touchette, 1968; Sidman & Stoddard, 1967; Moore & Goldiamond, 1964; Storm & Robinson, 1973; Dorry & Zeaman, 1973). In general, a prompt is an extra stimulus (e.g., underlining) that is presented to the student in an attempt to guide correct responding to the target stimulus (e.g., a square). The prompt is then gradually faded until it is entirely removed, so that the learner is responding to the target stimulus alone. Recent research has shown that autistic children often respond selectively to the prompt. They respond correctly throughout fading until the final fading step, when the prompt is removed entirely, at which point they then respond at chance level. That these children typically "hook" on the prompt during prompt fading, and learning nothing about the training stimuli, has been repeatedly demonstrated (e.g., Acker, 1966; Koegel & Rincover, 1976; Schreibman, 1975; Rincover, 1976).

One approach to this problem was suggested by Schreibman (1975) and by Rincover (1976), who have developed procedures for teaching autistic children even when stimulus overselectivity occurs. In this approach, the researchers guided the children to respond correctly by exaggerating a distinctive feature of the correct stimulus during training. For example, in the teaching of a difficult discrimination between two numbers (e.g., 5 and 3), the straight horizontal line atop the 5 might be selected as the prompt, since it is not contained on the incorrect (3) stimulus. That line would be initially exaggerated (in width and length), and then the exaggeration would be gradually reduced during subsequent fading steps. Thus, when fading is completed and the exaggeration has been removed, *that line remains,* but in its normal length. In short, when a cue that is contained in the correct stimulus is selected as a prompt, the child need only respond to that cue during fading in order to continue to respond correctly when fading is completed. Under these conditions, prompt fading facilitates learning in autistic children. Furthermore, Rincover (1976) found that the children learned more about the correct stimulus (e.g., 5) than just the pretrained cue (e.g., the horizontal line).

2.4. Generalization and Maintenance of Behavior Change

Producing generalized durable behavior change is one of the most formidable problems currently facing behavior modification. In most cases, investigators have reported that generalization across settings and over time does not occur without special intervention (cf. Wahler, 1969; Stokes & Baer, 1977). For example, in working specifically with autistic children, Lovaas, Koegel, Simmons, & Long (1973) found that even after prolonged treatment, autistic children would regress during follow-up if the parents were not trained in behavioral techniques.

An important distinction between different deficits in extratherapy responding has become apparent. In many studies, the initial behavior change is acquired in the therapy setting and posttreatment responding is then assessed both in other settings (reflecting generalization) and over a period of time or trials (reflecting maintenance). When no improvement is observed in the posttreatment environment, which is usually the case, one does not know whether the behavior change did not *generalize* or whether it did generalize but was not *maintained* in the extratherapy setting (Rincover & Koegel, 1975; Koegel & Rincover, 1977).

This distinction between the generalization and the maintenance of extratherapy responding is illustrated in Figure 1. The continuous line represents responding in the therapy setting and the broken line represents responding in the extratherapy setting. During training in various receptive language tasks, such as "Touch your nose" or "Clap your hands," the data show that all three children acquired the new behavior in the treatment room and that correct responding was subsequently maintained at a high level in that setting. In addition, all three children showed 0% correct responding in the extratherapy environment by the end of the experiment. There were, however, differences between the children. Two of the children (Child 1 and Child

3) initially responded in the extratherapy environment, and then responding gradually decreased. For these two children, the behavior change acquired in the treatment setting generalized to the extratherapy setting, but this extratherapy responding was not maintained. The other (Child 2) *never* responded correctly in the extratherapy setting. For this child, no generalization to the extratherapy setting occurred.

This distinction becomes quite important if the variables that influence generalization are different from the variables that influence maintenance, and as a result, they may require different treatment procedures. In one study (Rincover & Koegel, 1975), we investigated the problem of generalization. Ten autistic children were taught a new behavior in one setting and their responding was recorded in an extratherapy environment. Four of the children showed no generalization to the posttreatment setting (e.g., Child 2 in Figure 1). For these children, the problem of generalization turned out to be a prob-

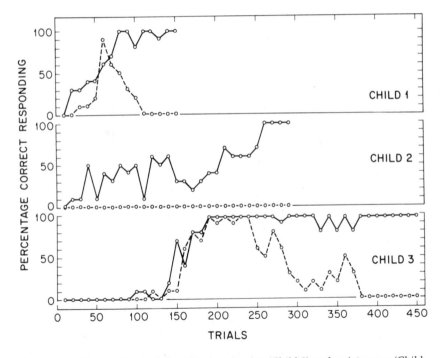

FIGURE 1. Differentiating problems of *generalization* (Child 2) and *maintenance* (Child 1 and Child 3) in extratherapy responding. The percentage of correct responding *during training* is measured concurrently in the therapy and the extratherapy settings. —— Therapy setting, - - - extratherapy setting.

lem of stimulus control. That is, each child was found to be responding to an incidental stimulus during training, such as a hand movement of the teacher that inadvertently coincided with the beginning of
trial. However, once the functional stimulus in the treatment setting
was identified and introduced in the posttreatment setting, correct
responding in the extratherapy environment occurred for each child.
The remaining six children in the study did generalize to the extratherapy setting without any special intervention (e.g., Child 1 and
Child 3 in Figure 1). For these children, the question became: Would
extratherapy responding be maintained over time? In a second study
(Koegel & Rincover, 1977), we investigated some variables influencing
the maintenance of extratherapy responding. The results suggested that
maintenance was a function of the discriminability of reinforcement
schedules in the treatment and posttherapy settings. Thus, the thinner
(less frequent) the schedule of reinforcement in the treatment setting,
the greater the maintenance of extratherapy responding in extratherapy settings. In addition, the presence of noncontingent reinforcers in the extratherapy setting served to increase the maintenance
of extratherapy responding.

In short, these studies distinguish two different kinds of deficits
in extratherapy responding, with each having different implications
for treatment. The data showing no correct responses in the extratherapy setting were labeled a problem of generalization. The data
showing initial correct responding in the extratherapy setting and
then subsequent extinction were labeled a deficit in maintenance. The
results suggest that deficits in generalization and maintenance may
have different treatment implications: Generalization was found to be
a function of stimulus control, and maintenance was influenced by
both reinforcement control and the discriminative stimulus properties
of reinforcers (e.g., noncontingent reinforcers).

The distinction between generalization and maintenance deficits
seems important because the correct diagnosis of the problem may
often be required if one is to design an effective treatment procedure.
For example, the use of multiple therapists during training (e.g.,
Stokes, Baer, & Jackson, 1974) might reduce the probability of a
child's learning a new behavior on the basis of the highly idiosyncratic stimulus of a particular therapist. Thus, increased generalization
would be expected; yet this might have little or no influence on the
durability of the extratherapy responding (cf. Lovaas et al., 1973). On
the other hand, a treatment program using "natural" (Ferster, 1967)
reinforcers (i.e., reinforcers likely to be present in extratherapy settings) on a very thin schedule might have a strong influence on the
maintenance of extratherapy responding. Thus, both dimensions of

extratherapy responding need to be considered in the planning of the *original treatment program.*

2.5. Parent and Teacher Training

In the field of behavior therapy, it has frequently been productive to train parents and teachers in the child's natural environment (e.g., Patterson, 1976; Kazdin & Moyer, 1977; Nordquist & Wahler, 1973; Gardner, 1972; Ringer, 1973), since it may facilitate generalization and maintenance as well as providing ongoing training for the child. Various authors have also encouraged the training of parents and teachers of autistic children (e.g., Risley, 1968; Nordquist & Wahler, 1973; Koegel, Russo, & Rincover, 1977; Schreibman & Koegel, 1975; Lovaas, Koegel, Simmons, & Long, 1973). In fact, Lovaas *et al.* (1973) suggested that parent training is an essential prerequisite for positive follow-up results of autistic children in their treatment program.

Koegel, Russo, and Rincover (1977) designed and assessed procedures for training persons working with autistic children in generalized behavior-modification skills. Initially, observers evaluated the performance of 11 teachers regarding the extent to which they used five essential skills in teaching new behaviors to autistic children. The five skills were (1) clear and consistent presentation of instructions; (2) effective use of prompts and prompt fading; (3) shaping through successive approximations; (4) presentation of immediate and appropriate consequences; and (5) distinctive intertrial intervals. Before training, the teachers generally did not use these procedures correctly more than 50% of the time. Consequently, none of the children showed any improvement in the behaviors being taught. Subsequently, the teachers participated in a one-week training program, which consisted of watching video tapes illustrating the correct and incorrect use of the five procedures, reading literature on these particular skills, direct modeling, and actual practice with feedback. After training, each of the teachers correctly used the five procedures at least 90% of the time, independent of the child or the task involved, and all of the children made progress on the target behaviors assigned during these sessions. This study shows that teachers who are naïve with respect to clinical psychology and behavior theory can be trained in a relatively short period of time if the training deals with generalizable, fundamental skills. Such procedures have also been used successfully in the training of parents of autistic children (Schreibman & Koegel, 1975).

Undoubtedly, there are limits to how far a teacher can take a child without additional training or supervision. For example, recent research in the design of classroom programs shows that training the teacher in behavioral skills alone is not sufficient to facilitate learning in a classroom setting (Koegel & Rincover, 1974; Rincover & Koegel, 1977). Section 2.6 describes some additional training procedures required for a teacher to work effectively with a group of autistic children.

2.6. Classroom Instruction

It is typical for school systems to exclude autistic children from their classroom programs. A commonly reported reason is that it is so difficult to provide the continuous supervision and training required for children with such severe behavior problems. Even when teachers have utilized the most current treatment procedures reported in the research literature, they have been required to rely heavily on a one-to-one teacher–child ratio (Lovaas & Koegel, 1973; Rutter, 1970). Although such procedures can be effective, they cannot be implemented on a wide scale, as the cost of providing one teacher for each autistic child would be prohibitively expensive.

Several investigators have suggested guidelines for the development of classroom programs for autistic children (Elgar, 1966; Halpern, 1970; Hamblin, Buckholdt, Ferritor, Kozloff, & Blackwell, 1971; Martin, England, Kaprowy, Kilgour, & Pilek, 1968; Rabb & Hewett, 1967; Koegel & Rincover, 1974; Rincover & Koegel, 1977). However, one problem that immediately surfaces in a classroom setting is that behaviors acquired in a one-to-one situation often do not generalize to a larger group setting (Bijou, 1972; Koegel & Rincover, 1974; Peterson, Cox, & Bijou, 1972). This problem is illustrated in Figure 2. In this study (Koegel & Rincover, 1974), eight autistic children were individually taught a number of basic classroom skills, such as attending to the teacher, verbal and nonverbal imitation, and simple receptive language skills. Then their performance of these same skills was measured in larger groups of different sizes. The black bar depicts the percentage of correct responding in 1:1, the dark gray bar represents responding in 2:1, and the light gray bar shows responding in 8:1. The data show that the performance of behaviors learned in 1:1 sessions was greatly reduced in a classroom-sized group of eight children with one teacher. Furthermore, this performance was significantly reduced in a group of only two children. In conjunction with these data, additional weekly observations of these children in a group of eight, during which time the teacher attempted to train new behaviors, indicated that no new learning occurred.

In the second phase of this experiment, procedures for gradually increasing the group size were introduced in an attempt to program generalization from 1:1 to 8:1. Initially, children participated in 1:1 sessions in which the schedule of reinforcement was thinned from CRF (continuous reinforcement) to FR2 (a reinforcer after two correct responses). Then, two children were brought together with one teacher and two teacher's aides, and the aides alternately reinforced the children. The aides initially prompted the children to respond when no response occurred, and the prompt was faded on subsequent trials. When these two children were responding correctly on at least 80% of the trials, the schedule of reinforcement was again gradually thinned to FR4. At that point, the two children were brought together with two other children who had gone through similar training to form a group of four. Again, the teacher's aides prompted correct responses when necessary and gradually faded the prompt until all four children were responding at the criterion of 80% correct. The schedule of reinforcement was then faded to variable ratio 8 (a reinforcer after eight correct responses on the average). These four chil-

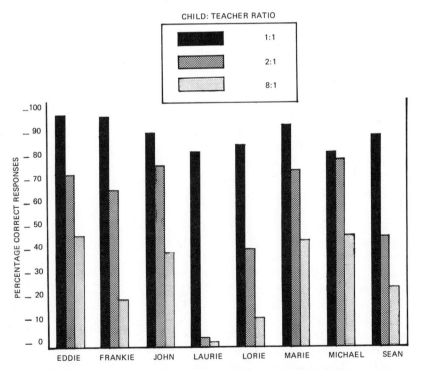

FIGURE 2. Performance of learned behavior in various group sizes. The percentage of correct responses is plotted individually for each child during test sessions in groups of one, two, or eight children with one teacher.

dren were then combined with the remaining four children, who had met the same criterion, to form the final group size of eight children. Both teacher's aides were then removed from the classroom. As a result of this gradual increase in the group size and the simultaneous thinning of the reinforcement schedule, a classroom situation was achieved in which each child would reliably and accurately respond to questions and instructions for infrequent rewards. Furthermore, it is significant that when these basic attention and imitation skills generalized to the group of eight, via this fading procedure, each child then acquired *new* skills in the classroom of eight children with one teacher. That is, the teacher was able to introduce a standard preschool curriculum and teach new behaviors. In a short time, the children were engaged in various activities such as telling time, reading first-grade books, printing letters of the alphabet, and solving simple arithmetic problems.

Additional problems have been encountered, however, even when the teacher–child ratio has been successfully reduced. As the children became more proficient at complex behaviors, their individual differences in ability became increasingly important. When classroom instruction was paced to a particular student, or a few students, the remaining children learned very little. One approach to this problem, suggested in previous research on classrooms for retarded children, would be to supplement the group instruction with individualized programs (Birnbrauer, Kidder, & Tague, 1964; Bijou, Birnbrauer, Kidder, & Tague, 1966).

In a second study (Rincover & Koegel, 1977), we assessed the feasibility of providing individualized instruction for each autistic child without providing one teacher for each child. In order to work individually, the children would have to be taught to engage in long sequences of behavior without continuous supervision from the teacher. For this purpose, an intervention was designed to increase the number of written responses performed after each instruction from the teacher. Initially, for example, a child would be handed a sheet of paper containing lines to be traced, and the teacher would give the instruction, "Trace the lines." When the child traced one line, he would be rewarded with praise and edibles. When the child would reliably perform one response after each instruction, he was then prompted to perform a second response before a reward was given, and then the prompt was gradually faded. When the child was reliably producing two responses after one instruction from the teacher, the criterion was changed to three responses before the reinforcer was presented. By this gradual increase of the response requirement, each child learned to provide at least 12 written responses after each instruction from the teacher. As a result, each child learned to work alone for as long as 15

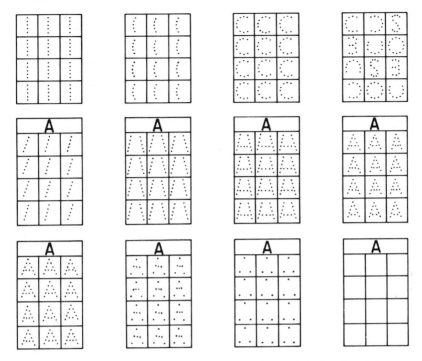

FIGURE 3. Illustrations of programmed instructional materials developed for several target behaviors in the classroom.

or 20 minutes. Thus, the teacher could circulate among the children, providing instructions and reinforcers to each, while the children worked continuously throughout the classroom session. Significantly, sequences of instructional materials were designed for each child, with each new worksheet building on the last, so that each child was learning new behaviors while working alone. Examples of the sequencing of worksheets are provided in Figure 3. The top row illustrates intermediate steps in teaching a child to trace various curved shapes; the second and third rows illustrate some of the worksheets used in teaching a child to print letters of the alphabet. As the children learned more complex skills, similar worksheets were designed to teach simple reading, arithmetic, and conceptual skills (Rincover & Koegel, 1977).

Several benefits resulted from this personalized system of instruction:

1. Each child was able to work at his own rate on those tasks most beneficial to his individual development.

2. Each child was working and learning throughout the school-day, rather than remaining idle or being disruptive while the teacher worked with other children.

3. Only one teacher and one teacher's aide were required in a classroom of 8–10 children.

4. Finally, it is noteworthy that the teachers reported the day-to-day instruction to be much more pleasant and less harried after the introduction of these individualized procedures.

The results of these studies may also have implications for "main-streaming" autistic children into classrooms of nonautistic children, where more appropriate models would be available. Some investigators have suggested that segregating handicapped or emotionally disturbed children into special classes may actually hinder learning (Johnson, 1962; Quay, 1968). If every child in a class is working on his own instructional materials and at his own pace, with minimal supervision from the teacher, it may not be necessary to segregate children according to specific handicaps (cf. Nedelman & Sulzbacher, 1972; Russo & Koegel, 1977), particularly if these procedures are combined with techniques for modifying other classroom behaviors, such as the generalized following of instructions (Craighead, O'Leary, & Allen, 1973), basic classroom skills (Koegel & Rincover, 1974), motivation training (Solnick et al., 1977; Rincover, Newsom, Lovaas & Koegel, 1977), and teacher- and parent-training procedures (Wetzel, Baker, Roney, & Martin, 1966; Nordquist & Wahler, 1973; Koegel, Russo, & Rincover, 1977). The various possible problems and benefits, for *both the autistic and the nonautistic children*, remain to be thoroughly assessed in the integration of classrooms.

These studies illustrate that classroom programs can be and are being used to provide educational experiences for autistic children. However, some previous assumptions regarding classroom education must now be rejected. Neither one-to-one training nor repeated exposure to the classroom group for periods up to six months resulted in any new classroom learning for any autistic child: the transition from one-to-one training to classroom (group) instruction had to be systematically programmed. Similarly, it is not reasonable to assume that a child who behaves appropriately in the presence of a teacher will also behave appropriately in the teacher's absence. Rather, the ability to continue behaving appropriately in the teacher's absence was, itself, a separate target behavior requiring gradual, piecemeal training.

Clearly, in designing classroom programs for autistic children, we are confronted with numerous problems that often do not even exist in classrooms for normal and less severely handicapped children. However, it is just as clear that these problems are gradually being detected and solved.

3. Future Directions: Response Generalization

In comparisons of the results of behavior therapy with those of early psychodynamic (and other) treatments, wherein improvement was unrelated to therapy (Rutter, 1966), behavior therapy appears very promising indeed (Lovaas, Koegel, Simmons, & Long, 1973). At the same time, however, the ultimate evaluation of behavior therapy with autistic children will not be concerned with its effectiveness compared with other techniques but rather will be assessed according to the degree of socialization or normalization it produces in these children. Viewed in this way (i.e., Can behavior therapy modify the behavioral repertoires of autistic children so as to fall into the range of behaviors befitting normal children?), it becomes quickly apparent that much of the technology is still missing. In perhaps the most systematic and comprehensive evaluation of autistic children in behavior therapy to date, Lovaas et al. (1973) reported the limitations as well as the many benefits of treatment: "Our program did not give everything to every child. Sometimes it gave very little to a particular child, but it did give something to each child we saw. The improvement was analogous to making from 10 to 20 steps on a 100 step ladder" (p. 160). As the authors implied, an important question now facing us is how to make progress toward the remaining 80–90 steps.

It seems that we must investigate ways to get more behavior change for a given amount of treatment. Autistic children do not display deficits that are single, isolated, or scattered absences of skills, so that a few applications of effective teaching would solve the presenting problems. Rather, we are confronted with children who show extreme deficits in language, play, and social and intellectual behavior; who are often untestable on standardized intelligence and social maturity scales; and who frequently exhibit excessive inappropriate or harmful behaviors, such as self-stimulation, tantrums, and self-injurious behavior. When we are faced with such extensive behavioral deficits and excesses, it would seem of limited value to pursue one-behavior-at-a-time applications of behavior principles. Instead, we may need to develop treatment procedures that produce multiple behavior changes. Lovaas et al. (1973) were looking for such generalized changes in behavior but did not find them:

> The most significant disappointment was the failure to isolate a "pivotal" response, or, as some might describe it, the failure to effect changes in cer-

tain key intervening variables. This means that in the beginning, we searched for one behavior which, when altered, would produce a profound "personality" change. We could not find it. We had hoped, for example, that when a child was taught his name ("My name is Ricky") that his awareness of himself (or some such thing) would emerge. It did not. Similarly, the child who learned to fixate visually on his therapist's face did not suddenly discover people. (pp. 160–161)

What we seem to be lacking is a technology of response generalization, wherein the application of contingencies for one behavior (target behavior) produces predictable and reliable changes in other behaviors for which no direct contingencies are in effect (nontarget behaviors). While the need for research investigating covariation among responses has been noted by many authors (Baer, Wolf, & Risley, 1968; Bandura, 1969; Wahler, Sperling, Thomas, & Teeter, 1970; Conway & Bucher, 1976), there is very little known about it. Reviews of the literature on the "generalizations" emphasize research on setting generality and generalization over time (maintenance), but they either omit the issue of response generalization or state that we know very little about it (e.g., Conway & Bucher, 1976; Marholin, Siegel, & Phillips, 1976; Wahler, 1975). One notable exception is the literature on generalized imitation (Lovaas, Berberich, Perloff, & Schaeffer, 1966; Baer, Peterson, & Sherman, 1967; Peterson, 1968; Garcia, Baer, & Firestone, 1971; Peterson & Whitehurst, 1971), which has become an integral part of the present technology for teaching language to autistic and retarded children.

There is also a growing body of literature investigating the learning characteristics of autistic children that suggests several promising directions for future research on the programming of multiple behavior changes. Research in each of the areas of stimulus overselectivity, motivation, and observational learning may have important implications for the design of new treatment programs for autistic children.

3.1. Stimulus Overselectivity

There is a growing body of research that indicates that autistic children show a unique "attentional" deficit, which has proved to be a formidable obstacle to the design of treatment. This problem, which has been called *stimulus overselectivity*, is evidenced when a child responds selectively to a very restricted portion of his stimulus environment. Since this extreme overselectivity may parsimoniously account for many of the learning deficits that are characteristic of autistic children (cf. Lovaas, Schreibman, Koegel, & Rehm, 1971b), it may be worthwhile to describe here in some detail the nature of the deficit as well as its detrimental effect on learning.

Lovaas *et al.* (1971b) trained groups of autistic, retarded, and normal children to respond (bar-press) in the presence of a complex stimulus consisting of visual (red floodlight), auditory (white noise), and tactile (blood-pressure cuff) cues. After training, the components of the stimulus complex were presented individually in probe trials so that the investigators could assess the amount of control achieved by each of these cues over the child's behavior. The authors found that the normal children responded uniformly to all three cues; the autistic children primarily responded to only one of the three cues; and the retarded children responded between these extremes. Importantly, the deficit shown by the autistic children in this study was found not to be a sensory deficit since the children learned to respond to the previously nonfunctional cues with additional training. Since the original demonstration by Lovaas *et al.* (1971b), this stimulus overselectivity in autistic children has now been replicated in a two-cue situation (Lovaas & Schreibman, 1972), with all cues visual (Koegel & Wilhelm, 1973) or auditory (Reynolds, Newsom, & Lovaas, 1974).

The most important implication of this overselectivity is that it is likely to retard or prevent learning. Much learning depends on the contiguous or nearly contiguous presentation of stimuli. In classical conditioning paradigms, the CS (conditioned stimulus) is presented temporally close to the UCS (unconditioned stimulus). In operant-conditioning paradigms, contiguous presentation of stimuli occurs when one seeks to achieve a transfer in stimulus control, as when a teacher presents a prompt (an extra stimulus to guide correct responding). In either case, selective responding to a single cue would result in a failure to learn. In sum, the extreme stimulus overselectivity found in autistic children may theoretically account for their retarded social, emotional, and language development (cf. Lovaas *et al.*, 1971b). For example, consider some of the implications of overselective attention for certain kinds of learning.

1. Various authors report that the acquisition of conditioned reinforcers (e.g., verbal praise and smiling) is a necessary prerequisite to the development of most human behavior (e.g., Ferster & De Myer, 1962). If conditioned reinforcers are acquired by association with primary reinforcers, then it is possible that overselective responding would account for the difficulty in training conditioned reinforcers with autistic children (cf. Lovaas, Freitag, Kinder, Rubenstein, Schaeffer, & Simmons, 1966b) and, therefore, for the deficits in subsequent language and intellectual development that may be acquired through such conditioned reinforcers.

2. The lack of appropriate affect in autistic children is also well known (Rimland, 1964). Overselective responding may also be impli-

cated in the deficit in emotional behavior if affect is acquired by the contiguous presentation of a UCS and a CS.

3. Most autistic children are either mute or echolalic (meaninglessly repeating words or phrases immediately or after a delay). Such speech is contextually impoverished. To the extent that contextual speech requires a number of cues, one might expect autistic children to overselect and fail to learn.

4. Stimulus overselectivity might also contribute to failures in the acquisition of new behavioral topographies (e.g., nonverbal imitation) and receptive language. The usual means of teaching new nonverbal behaviors include prompting—which typically consists of the simultaneous presentation of multiple cues—in which case, selective responding would hinder the acquisition of such skills. That is, autistic children may selectively respond to the prompt and learn nothing about the training stimuli.

It is apparent that a child who exhibits such generalized and extreme stimulus overselectivity will not acquire many of the social and intellectual skills typical in the development of normal children. By the same token, however, designing treatment programs to expand stimulus control, such as training autistic children to respond to multiple cues, does not necessarily mean that such children will then acquire those skills. The point here is that given the extensive deficits evidenced in autistic children and the very gradual benefits of one-behavior-at-a-time applications of behavior modification, it certainly seems worthwhile to design treatment programs based on stimulus control or "attention" training in order to assess whether or not widespread behavior changes will occur. The studies reviewed above suggest some very general target behaviors, which may be only the first few steps in a comprehensive "attention"-training program. Various studies show that autistic children respond to *fewer* cues in their immediate environment than do normal children (e.g., Lovaas *et al.*, 1971b). Therefore, one approach might be to make reinforcers contingent upon responding to an increasing number of cues and continuing such treatment until the children show a generalized responding to multiple cues—that is, until they respond to multiple cues on transfer tests without direct training (Koegel & Schreibman, 1977). Another approach might be to teach autistic children to respond to cues that are increasingly separated in space, since Rincover (1976) has found that responding is generally restricted to stimuli in a very small area of their environment. A third approach might emphasize responding to cues in different modalities. For example, Lovaas *et al.* (1971b) found that a child did not imitate the teacher's speech when the teacher covered her mouth. For such children, responding to a large number of cues may not have benefited verbal imitation, while training them to respond to auditory cues may well have proved beneficial.

The point we would like to make here is that there seems to be a basic deficit in overselective responding in autistic children and that there is as yet no research available attempting to remediate it. Given the detrimental effects, and the pervasiveness, of stimulus overselectivity, the possibility of extensive response generalization suggests that this should be one direction of future research.

3.2. Motivation

A major difficulty encountered in the treatment of autistic children is the problem of motivation. Left to themselves, these children show little, if any, motivation to learn new appropriate behaviors. In the past, most treatment programs have attempted to overcome this problem by selecting powerful primary reinforcers, such as food (Risley & Wolf, 1967; Lovaas, Berberich, Perloff, & Schaeffer, 1966a) and pain reduction (Lovaas, Schaeffer, & Simmons, 1965b). However, serious problems often arise in the use of these experimental reinforcers. Such primary reinforcers are "artificial" in the sense that they do not occur contingently in the natural environment (Ferster, 1967). As a result, the child seems to discriminate between training and posttraining settings on the basis of these reinforcers, and responding eventually extinguishes in extratherapy environments (Lovaas, Koegel, Simmons & Long, 1973; Koegel & Rincover, 1977). The behaviors developed with primary reinforcers are generally limited to those environments where such reinforcers are consistently available.

What can we do about this problem? Currently, the most popular solution has been to train parents, institutional staff, teachers, etc., in the use of primary reinforcers. This procedure reduces the discriminability of therapy and extratherapy settings and has proved an effective procedure for maintaining and even increasing the gains of autistic children (Lovaas et al., 1973; Koegel, Russo, & Rincover, 1977). However, this solution is less than ideal. A more ideal treatment would be to normalize the child's motivational system so that he could learn from his natural environment.

3.2.1. Conditioned Reinforcers

The major reason "artificial" reinforcers have been so widely used is that "natural" events—such as a smile or a frown, praise, and the closeness of others—usually do not operate as reinforcers for autistic children (Ferster, 1961; Ferster & De Myer, 1962; Rimland, 1964; Lovaas, Freitag, Kinder, Rubenstein, Schaeffer, & Simmons, 1966b). Furthermore, various authors have attributed many of the deficits of autistic children in social and intellectual development to the paucity of reinforcers in their natural environment (cf. Leff, 1970). Ferster (1961), in the first (behavioral) theoretical treatment of the etiology of autism, presented a compelling argument for the deficit in social reinforcers as a cause of autism. Although the precise relationship between conditioned reinforcement and social and intellectual growth is not at all clear, it is safe to say that acquired reinforcers quickly replace biological reinforcers in the acquisition and maintenance of many behaviors in normal children. While a mother may respond to the needs of an infant by cuddling, feeding, and hugging, eventually she turns primarily to smiles, praise, screaming, etc., to control the older child's behavior. Conversely, it seems just as obvious that if these events do not acquire some value as reinforcers, the child's social and intellectual development will be to some extent retarded.

This notion, that inadequate conditioned reinforcers will result in developmental retardation, is not new. Many authors argue that the establishment of generalized conditioned reinforcers may be a necessary step in the treatment of psychotic children. Lovaas et al. (1966b) emphasized that an integral part of treatment is to render other persons "Meaningful in the sense of becoming rewarding to the child." Baer and Wolf (1970) proposed that we initially modify those behaviors of the subject that will promote his "entry into natural communities of reinforcement." In his discussion of the behavioral literature on autism, Leff (1968) concluded that "an appropriate behavior-modification program, therefore, consists of an arragement of reinforcement contingencies so as to establish conditioned and then generalized reinforcers, many of which are social in nature" (p. 398).

While the importance of establishing generalized social reinforcers in autistic children is not new, the establishment of generalized social reinforcers in autistic children certainly would be. Many authors have used social consequences in addition to primary reinforcers in treatment (e.g., Metz, 1965; Wolf, Risley, & Mees, 1964; Risley & Wolf, 1967). However, considering that these early studies were primarily designed to alleviate severe behavior problems, it is not surprising that the role of social consequences in the success of treatment was not evaluated. In addition, some studies reported that the autistic child exhibited prosocial behaviors and responded for social reinforcers (e.g., Hewett, 1965; Risley & Wolf, 1967). However, in each case this was reported as an unexpected by-product of treatment, without data on the development or reinforcing function of social stimuli.

Two studies are available, however, that did succeed in establishing social stimuli as reinforcers for autistic children. In the first study, a negative-reinforcement paradigm was used, in which the removal of pain (termination of shock) was made contingent on the child's seeking out one of the adults in the room (Lovaas, Schaeffer, & Simmons, 1965b). In a subsequent study, the word *good* was established as a discriminative stimulus by the reinforcement of approach behavior (with edibles) following the word *good* (Lovaas, Freitag, Kinder, Rubenstein, Schaeffer, & Simmons, 1966b). While social reinforcers were clearly established in each study, the authors reported that they were setting-specific and that the procedures were too cumbersome to be of much practical significance.

Since the authors were able to change neutral stimuli into reinforcing stimuli for autistic children—the remaining problems being the generalization (across settings) and the maintenance of those conditioned reinforcers—it is surprising that there has been virtually no follow-up work in this area. Furthermore, Stokes and Baer's (1977) review of the literature on setting generality and maintenance of behavior change, and the various strategies and technologies described therein, have clear and direct applications to the problem of producing generalized, durable conditioned reinforcers. For example, training conducted in multiple settings and by various personnel has in the past been a very effective procedure for increasing generalization and maintenance (Stokes, Baer, & Jackson, 1974). Combining the tools now available for conditioning social stimuli (Lovaas *et al.*, 1965b; Lovaas *et al.*, 1966b) and for producing generalization and maintenance (reviewed by Stokes and Baer, 1977) might help provide a technology for promoting the autistic child's "entry into natural communities of reinforcement." The applied significance of research in this area, however, depends on the extent of changes in nontarget (social and intellectual) behaviors after the target behaviors (i.e., generalized, durable social reinforcers) are developed.

3.2.2. Sensory Stimulation

Autistic children may spend many hours engaged in stereotyped, repetitive motor behavior, such as rhythmic rocking, finger flapping, and spinning objects in their environment (Rimland, 1964; Foxx & Azrin, 1973; Lovaas, 1967). In general, these self-stimulatory behaviors appear to provide no external consequences. Rather, they appear to be maintained primarily by the sensory stimulation they produce (Rincover, Peoples, & Packard, 1976).

Since autistic children spend so much time engaged in self-stimulatory behavior, sensory stimulation may be an extremely powerful reinforcer for these children. Furthermore, a substantial amount of data has accumulated that demonstrates the phenomenon described as *sensory reinforcement,* which refers to the unconditioned property of sensory events to increase the probability of the behaviors they follow (Kish, 1966; Siqueland, 1968; Stevenson & Odom, 1964; Rheingold, Stanley, & Doyle, 1964; Bailey & Meyerson, 1969; Rehagen & Thelen, 1972; Kerr, Myerson, & Michael, 1965; Fineman, 1968). If autistic children are highly motivated by sensory stimulation, then the task at hand may be to develop more normal types of sensory reinforcers, such as play and music. If sensory stimuli in the natural environments assume a reinforcing function, perhaps these settings will then be better able to help (teach) these children.

Two approaches can now be identified in which a child's response to sensory stimulation (target behavior) might be manipulated in an attempt to facilitate other adaptive changes (nontarget behaviors). First, we have attempted to identify and use sensory events as (external) reinforcers to teach these children. Teachers of four autistic children were asked what kind of sensory stimulation was preferred by each child. When these stimuli (strobe, music, etc.) were briefly presented contingent on correct responses, the children were able to learn simple language skills. Subsequently, we investigated how powerful these sensory stimuli were in maintaining behavior by providing 5 sec of each type of sensory stimulation contingent on 5 bar presses (FR5). The results showed, first of all, that the reinforcing effects of these sensory stimuli were idiosyncratic to specific children. For example, one child worked only for the music and another child only for the strobe. In addition, we found that these sensory reinforcers often produced a very high rate of responding (up to 40 responses per minute) that proved quite durable over time (up to 52 sessions). At the same time, however, the response rates varied to a great extent across sessions. Finally, we found that the children did eventually satiate on their initially preferred sensory event. However, only a small change in that sensory event (e.g., changing the frequency of the strobe) resulted in a renewed high rate of responding that was equally durable over time (Rincover, Newsom, Lovaas, & Koegel, 1977).

This study demonstrated that some sensory events occurring in the child's natural environment can have a powerful effect on the behavior of autistic children. These reinforcers also were found to have very low satiation characteristics, which may yield more favorable results in treatment than edible reinforcers. An important question remains however: Will the naturally occurring contingencies of sensory reinforcement teach and support *new* behavior? This question, crucial to an analysis of response generalization, is currently being investigated in our laboratories.

A second approach to programming multiple response changes lies in the direct manipulation of self-stimulatory behavior. For example, research in the area of sensory deprivation illustrates that under various conditions of sensory restriction, organisms will respond to obtain additional sources of sensory stimulation (Zubeck, 1969). Therefore, Newsom and Ferris (1974) conducted a study to investigate the effects of restricting certain types of sensory stimulation by restraining the most persistent self-stimulatory behavior. Interestingly, they found that when one such behavior was suppressed, another self-stimulatory behavior immediately, and dramatically, increased in its place. Koegel, Firestone, Kramme, and Dunlap (1974) then set out to determine the effects of suppressing all of the child's self-stimulatory behavior. Initially, in an attempt to "prime" an adaptive behavior to "replace" self-stimulation, they first trained each child to play appropriately with a variety of toys. After the pretraining with the toys, with no restrictions yet on self-stimulatory behavior, the children spent virtually all of their time engaged in self-stimulation and showed no interest in the toys. When self-stimulation was subsequently suppressed, appropriate play rose to a high level *without external reinforcement*. Similar results have been reported by Epstein, Doke, Sajwaj, Sorrell, and Rimmer (1974). An important problem still remained, as discussed in Koegel *et al.* (1974), in the continued dependence of appropriate play on the suppression of self-stimulation. When the children were returned to baseline conditions (no suppression), in a reversal design, self-stimulation immediately increased to base level and appropriate play decreased or dropped out entirely.

Further research is obviously needed in this area to investigate the extent of behavior change that can be produced by the restriction of self-stimulation, in addition to procedures for maintaining changes in these nontarget behaviors. One such study is currently in progress to investigate the amount of adaptive-behavior change that can be programmed and maintained by the elimination of self-stimulatory behavior through "sensory extinction," a procedure that has produced a durable suppression of self-stimulation. As noted earlier, self-stimulatory behavior was eliminated in two autistic children when a certain sensory consequence of that behavior was masked or removed. For example, a child who initially would spin or twirl objects (e.g., a plate) on a hard surface immediately ceased to engage in that self-stimulatory behavior when the auditory feedback was removed by carpeting the table. In a follow-up study (Rincover, Peoples, & Packard, 1976), we then taught that child to play with a variety of toys producing different kinds of sensory stimulation: a music box was used to provide auditory stimulation, and toy blocks and beads were used to provide kinesthetic stimulation. After training on the toys, the carpet was removed from the table and each of the three toys and the plate were placed on the table within arm's reach of the child. The results showed the following: (1) The child engaged in spontaneous appropriate play; however,he played only with the toy producing auditory feedback; and (2) with no carpeting on the table, self-stimulation was maintained near zero frequency. Significantly, a second child who participated in the sensory-extinction procedure also participated in this follow-up experiment. Child 2 engaged in steroptyped, repetitive finger flapping which we subsequently extinguished by masking the kinesthetic stimulation with a vibrator (placed on the back of his hand). The results for Child 2 were similar to those for Child 1, with the following exception: this child played only with the toys producing kinesthetic stimulation.

3.3. Observational Learning

Most psychologists now assume that normal children learn a great deal simply by observing events in their environment. Bandura (1969) has presented a great amount of data and a compelling discussion of the central role of observational learning in child development. Any child who does not learn by watching others necessarily falls behind children who do.

Autistic children do not appear to learn by observation, at least not in the same manner as normal children. A recent study suggests that stimulus overselectivity may delay or retard the vicarious acquisition of new behaviors (cf. Lovaas & Newsom, 1976). In this experiment, a child sat across the table from two adults, one serving as the model and one as the teacher. Various objects were placed on the table, and the child was to observe the model manipulate an object in response to the teacher's instruction. For example, when the teacher said, "Phone," the model simply picked up the phone and was then rewarded with a piece of candy from the teacher. The purpose of this experiment was to assess whether autistic children would learn how to respond to the teacher's instructions by watching the model. A child's correct performance on probe trials meant that he had learned through observation. The results of this study suggest that the autistic children learned about the model's responses during the observation period but did not discriminate the verbal instructions of the teacher. Lovaas and Newsom (1976) concluded that the children selectively responded to the visual cues of the model's behavior while the auditory cues of the teacher acquired no control.

One possible explanation of this deficit in observational learning might be found in the stimulus overselectivity evidenced in autistic children, in which case multiple-cue training, discussed earlier, might help to some extent to remediate this deficit. The point here is that there seems to be a deficit in observational learning in autistic children, and there is as yet no research available attempting to remediate it. The possibility of extensive response generalization suggests that this be one direction of future research.

4. Conclusions

In this chapter, we have attempted to describe some recent advances in the education of autistic children and to outline some suggestions for future research in the area. In general, it seems that significant advances continue to be made in both our understanding and our ability to remediate the various pathological behaviors characteristic of autistic children. Effective programs are becoming increasingly available for treating various behavioral excesses—such as self-stimulation, tantrums, and self-injurious behavior—as well as for treating the many behavioral deficits, such as those in self-help, speech, receptive, and academic skills. In addition, concern for the generalization and the maintenance of behavior change has stimulated research projects in various community settings, such as public-school instruction and home-based training, which report some encouraging preliminary findings.

In discussing future directions for research on the treatment of autistic children, we have emphasized the notion of *response generalization*—programming changes in behaviors for which contingencies are not directly applied. Our hope is that a better understanding of the variables influencing multiple behavior change will help us design more efficient and productive educational programs in the future. In the past 15 years, there has been a tremendous amount of progress in improving the educational experiences of autistic children. However, it is sobering to note that most of these children are still relegated to locked wards of closed mental institutions. Despite our current capability of treating many of their pathological behaviors, we may need to investigate more *efficient* procedures that produce *multiple* or *widespread* changes in behavior in order to increase the socialization of autistic children.

References

Acker, L. Errorless discrimination training in autistic and normal children. Unpublished doctoral dissertation, University of California at Los Angeles, 1966.

Baer, D., Peterson, R., & Sherman, J. The development of imitation by reinforcing behavioral similarity to a model. *Journal of Experimental Analysis of Behavior*, 1967, 10, 405–416.

Baer, D. M., & Wolf, M. M. The entry into natural communities of reinforcement. *In* R. Ulrich, T. Stachnik, & J. Mabry (Eds.), *Control of human behavior*, Vol. 1. New York: Scott Foresman, 1970, pp. 319–324.

Baer, D. M., Wolf, M. M., & Risley, T. Some current dimensions of applied behavior analysis. *Journal of Applied Behavior Analysis*, 1968, 1, 91–97.

Bailey, J., & Meyerson, L. Vibration as a reinforcer with a profoundly retarded child. *Journal of Applied Behavior Analysis*, 1969, 2, 135–137.

Bandura, A. *Principles of behavior modification*. New York: Holt, 1969.

Bijou, S. W. The technology of teaching handicapped children. *In* S. W. Bijou & E. Ribes-Inesta (Eds.), *Behavior modification: Issues and extensions*. New York: Academic Press, 1972.

Bijou, S. W., Birnbrauer, J. S., Kidder, J. D., & Tague, C. Programmed instruction as an approach to the teaching of reading, writing, and arithmetic, to retarded children. *Psychological Record*, 1966, 16, 505–522.

Birnbrauer, J. S., Kidder, J. D., & Tague, C. Programming reading from the teachers' point of view. *Programmed Instruction*, 1964, 3 (7), 1–2.

Brown, J. L. Prognosis from presenting symptoms of preschool children with atypical development. *American Journal of Orthopsychiatry*, 1960, 33, 382–390.

Bucher, B. B., & Lovaas, O. I. Use of aversive stimulation in behavior modification. *In* M. R. Jones (Ed.), *Miami Symposium on the Prediction of Behavior, 1967: Aversive stimulation*. Coral Gables, Fla.: University of Miami Press, 1968.

Carr, E. G., Newsom, C. D., & Binkoff, J. A. Stimulus control of self-destructive behavior in a psychotic child. *Journal of Abnormal Child Psychology*, 1976, 4, 139–153.

Conway, J. B., & Bucher, B. D. Transfer and maintenance of behavior change in children: A review and suggestions. *In* E. J. Mash, L. A. Hammerlynck, & L. C. Handy (Eds.), *Behavior modification and families*. New York: Brunner/Mazel, 1976.

Corte, H. E., Wolf, M. M., & Locke, B. J. A comparison of procedures for eliminating self-injurious behavior of retarded adolescents. *Journal of Applied Behavior Analysis*, 1971, 4, 201–213.

Craighead, W. D., O'Leary, K. D., & Allen, J. S. Teaching and generalization of instruction—following in an "autistic" child. *Journal of Behavior Therapy and Experimental Psychiatry*, 1973, 4, 171–176.

Davison, G. C. A social learning therapy programme with an autistic child. *Behaviour Research and Therapy*, 1964, 2, 149–159.

Dorry, G. W., & Zeaman, D. The use of a fading technique in paired-associate teaching of a reading vocabulary with retardates. *Mental Retardation*, 1973, 11, 3–6.

Elgar, S. Teaching autistic children. *In* J. K. Wing (Ed.), *Early childhood autism: Clinical, educational, and social aspects*. London: Pergamon Press, 1966.

Epstein, L. H., Doke, L. A., Sajwaj, T. E., Sorrell, S., & Rimmer, B. Generality and side effects of overcorrection. *Journal of Applied Behavior Analysis*, 1974, 7, 385–390.

Ferster, C. B. Positive reinforcement and behavioral deficits of autistic children. *Child Development*, 1961, 32, 437–456.

Ferster, C. B. Arbitrary and natural reinforcement. *Psychological Record*, 1967, 17, 341–347.

Ferster, C. B., & De Myer, M. K. The development of performances in an automatically controlled environment. *Journal of Chronic Diseases*, 1961a, 13, 312–345.

Ferster, C. B., & De Myer, M. K. Increased performances of an autistic child with prochlorperizive administration. *Journal of the Experimental Analysis of Behavior*, 1961b, 4, 84.

Ferster, C. B., & De Myer, M. K. A method for the experimental analysis of the behavior of autistic children. *American Journal of Orthopsychiatry*, 1962, *32*, 89–98.

Fineman, F. R. Shaping and increasing verbalizations in an autistic child in response to visual-color stimulation. *Perceptual and Motor Skills*, 1968, *27*, 1071–1074.

Foxx, R. M., & Azrin, N. The elimination of autistic self-stimulatory behavior by over-correction. *Journal of Applied Behavior Analysis*, 1973, *6*, 1–14.

Garcia, E., Baer, D. M., & Firestone, I. The development of generalized imitation within topographically determined boundaries. *Journal of Applied Behavior Analysis*, 1971, *4*, 101–112.

Gardner, J. M. Teaching behavior modification to nonprofessionals. *Journal of Applied Behavior Analysis*, 1972, *5*, 517–522.

Halpern, W. I. Schooling of autistic children. *American Journal of Orthopsychiatry*, 1970, *40*, 665–671.

Hamblin, R. L., Buckholdt, D., Ferritor, D., Kozloff, M., & Blackwell, L. *The humanization process*. New York: Wiley, 1971.

Hamilton, J., Stephens, L., & Allen, P. Controlling aggressive and destructive behavior in severely retarded institutionalized residents. *American Journal of Mental Deficiency*, 1967, *71*, 852–856.

Havelkova, M. Follow-up study of 71 children diagnosed as psychotic in preschool age. *American Journal of Orthopsychiatry*, 1968, *38*, 846–857.

Hewett, F. M. Teaching reading to an autistic boy through operant conditioning. *American Journal of Orthopsychiatry*, 1964, *17*, 613–618.

Hewett, F. M. Teaching speech to autistic children through operant conditioning. *American Journal of Orthopsychiatry*, 1965, *35*, 927–936.

Johnson, G. O. Special education for the mentally handicapped—A paradox. *Exceptional Children*, 1962, *29*, 62–69.

Kanner, L., & Eisenberg, L. Notes on the follow-up studies of autistic children. *In* P. H. Hock & J. Zubin (Eds.), *Psychopathology of childhood*. New York: Greene & Stratton, 1955.

Kazdin, A., & Moyer, W. Training teachers to use behavior modification. *In* S. Yen & R. McIntire (Eds.), *Teaching behavior modification*. Kalamazoo, Mich.: Behaviordelia, 1977, in press.

Kerr, N., Myerson, L., & Michael, J. A procedure for shaping vocalizations in a mute child. *In* L. P. Ullman & L. Krasner (Ed.), *Case studies in behavior modification*. New York: Holt, Rinehart, & Winston, 1965.

Kish, G. B. Studies of sensory reinforcement. *In* W. K. Honig (Ed.), *Operant behavior: Areas of research and application*. New York: Appleton-Century-Crofts, 1966.

Koegel, R., & Covert, A. The relationship of self-stimulation to learning in autistic children. *Journal of Applied Behavior Analysis*, 1972, *5*, 381–387.

Koegel, R. L., Firestone, P. B., Kramme, K. W., & Dunlap, G. Increasing spontaneous play by suppressing self-stimulation in autistic children. *Journal of Applied Behavior Analysis*, 1974, *7*, 521–528.

Koegel, R. L., & Rincover, A. Treatment of psychotic children in a classroom environment: I. Learning in a large group. *Journal of Applied Behavior Analysis*, 1974, *7*, 45–59.

Koegel, R. L., & Rincover, A. Some detrimental effects of using extra stimuli to guide learning in normal and autistic children. *Journal of Abnormal Child Psychology*, 1976, *4*, 59–71.

Koegel, R. L., & Rincover, A. Research on the difference between generalization and maintenance in extra-therapy responding. *Journal of Applied Behavior Analysis*, 1977, *10*, 1–12.

Koegel, R. L., Russo, D. C., & Rincover, A. Assessing and training teachers in the generalized use of behavior modification with autistic children. *Journal of Applied Behavior Analysis*, 1977, in press.

Koegel, R. L., & Schreibman, L. Teaching autistic children to respond to simultaneous multiple cues. *Journal of Experimental Child Psychology*, 1977, in press.

Koegel, R. L., & Wilhelm, H. Selective responding to the components of multiple visual cues by autistic children. *Journal of Experimental Child Psychology*, 1973, *15*, 442–453.

Kozloff, M. A. *Reaching the autistic child: A parent-training program*. Champaign, Ill.: Research Press, 1973.

Kozloff, M. A. *Educating children with learning and behavior problems*. New York: Wiley, 1975.

Leff, R. Behavior modification and the psychoses of childhood: A review. *Psychological Bulletin*, 1968, *69*, 396–409.

Lichstein, K. L., & Schreibman, L. Employing electric shock with autistic children: A review of the side effects. *Journal of Autism and Childhood Schizophrenia*, 1976, *6*, 163–174.

Lovaas, O. I. Program for establishment of speech in schizophrenic and autistic children. *In* J. K. Wing (Ed.), *Early childhood autism: Clinical, educational, and social aspects*. London: Pergamon Press, 1966.

Lovaas, O. I. Behavior therapy approach to the treatment of childhood schizophrenia. *Minnesota Symposium of Child Development*. Minneapolis: University of Minnesota Press, 1967.

Lovaas, O. I., Berberich, J. P., Perloff, B. F., & Schaeffer, B. Acquisition of imitative speech in schizophrenic children. *Science*, 1966a, *151*, 705–707.

Lovaas, D. I., Freitag, G., Gold, V. J., & Kassorla, I. C. Recording apparatus and procedure for observation of behaviors in free play settings. *Journal of Experimental Child Psychology*, 1965a, *2*, 108–120.

Lovaas, O. I., Freitag, G., Kinder, M. I., Rubenstein, B. D., Schaeffer, B., & Simmons, J. Q. Establishment of social reinforcers in two schizophrenic children on the basis of food. *Journal of Experimental Child Psychology*, 1966b, *4*, 109–125.

Lovaas, O. I., & Koegel, R. L. Behavior therapy with autistic children. *Seventy-second Yearbook of the National Society for the Study of Education*. Chicago: University of Chicago Press, 1973, pp. 230–258.

Lovaas, O. I., Koegel, R. L., Simmons, J. Q., & Long, J. S. Some generalization and follow-up measures on autistic children in behavior therapy. *Journal of Applied Behavior Analysis*, 1973, *6*, 131–165.

Lovaas, O. I., Litrownik, A., & Mann, R. Response latencies to auditory stimuli in autistic children engaged in self-stimulatory behavior. *Behaviour Research and Therapy*, 1971a, *9*, 39–49.

Lovaas, O. I., & Newsom, C. D. Behavior modification with psychotic children. *In* H. Leitenberg (Ed.), *Handbook of behavior modification and behavior therapy*. New York: Appleton-Century-Crofts, 1976.

Lovaas, O. I., Schaeffer, B., & Simmons, J. Q. Experimental studies in childhood schizophrenia: Building social behavior by use of electric shock. *Journal of Experimental Studies in Personality*, 1965b, *1*, 99–109.

Lovaas, O. I., & Schreibman, L. Stimulus overselectivity of autistic children in a two-stimulus situation. *Behaviour Research and Therapy*, 1971, *9*, 305–310.

Lovaas, O. I., Schreibman, L., Koegel, R. L., & Rehm, R. Selective responding by autistic children to multiple sensory input. *Journal of Abnormal Psychology*, 1971b, *77*, 211–222.

Lovaas, O. I., & Simmons, J. Q. Manipulation of self-destruction in three retarded children. *Journal of Applied Behavior Analysis*, 1969, *2*, 143–157.

Marholin, D., Siegel, L., & Phillips, D. Treatment and transfer: A search for empirical procedures. *In* M. Hersen, R. Eisler, & P. Miller (Eds.), *Progress in behavior modification*, Vol. 3. London: Academic Press, 1976.

Marshall, G. R. Toilet training of an autistic eight year old through operant conditioning therapy: A case report. *Behaviour Research and Therapy*, 1966, *4*, 242–245.

Martin, G. L., England, G., Kaprowy, E., Kilgour, K., & Pilek, V. Operant conditioning of kindergarten classroom behavior in autistic children. *Behaviour Research and Therapy*, 1968, *6*, 281–294.

Metz, J. R. Conditioned generalized imitation in autistic children. *Journal of Experimental Child Psychology*, 1965, *2*, 389–399.

Moore, R., & Goldiamond, I. Errorless establishment of visual discrimination using fading procedures. *Journal of the Experimental Analysis of Behavior*, 1964, *7*, 269–272.

Nedelman, D., & Sulzbacher, S. I. Dicky at 13 years of age: A long term success following early application of operant conditioning procedures. *In* G. Semb (Ed.), *Behavior analysis and education*. Lawrence, Kan.: University of Kansas Press, 1972, pp. 3–10.

Newsom, C. D., Carr, E. G., & Lovaas, O. I. The experimental analysis and modification of autistic behavior. In R. S. Davidson (Ed.), *Modification of behavior pathology*. New York: Gardner Press, 1977, in press.

Newsom, C., & Ferris, C. Self-stimulation and symptom substitution. Paper presented at annual meeting of the Western Psychological Association, San Francisco, 1974.

Nordquist, V. M., & Wahler, R. G. Naturalistic treatment of an autistic child. *Journal of Applied Behavior Analysis*, 1973, *6*, 79–87.

Patterson, G. The aggressive child: Victim and architect of a coercive system. *In* E. J. Mash, L. A. Hamerlynck, & L. C. Handy (Eds.), *Behavior modification and families*. New York: Brunner/Mazel, 1976.

Peterson, R. F. Some experiments on the organization of a class of imitative behavior. *Journal of Applied Behavior Analysis*, 1968, *1*, 225–235.

Peterson, R. F., Cox, M. A., & Bijou, S. W. Training children to work productively in classroom groups. *Exceptional Children*, 1971, *37*, 491–500.

Peterson, R. F., & Whitehurst, G. J. A variable influencing the performance of generalized imitative behaviors. *Journal of Applied Behavior Analysis*, 1971, *4*, 1–9.

Quay, H. C. The facets of educational exceptionality: A conceptual framework for assessment, grouping, and instruction. *Exceptional Children*, 1968, *35*, 25–32.

Rabb, E., & Hewett, F. M. Development of appropriate classroom behaviors in a severely disturbed group of institutionalized children with a behavior modification model. *American Journal of Orthopsychiatry*, 1967, *37*, 313–314.

Rehagen, N. J., & Thelen, M. H. Vibration as a positive reinforcer for retarded children. *Journal of Abnormal Psychology*, 1972, *80*, 162–167.

Reynolds, B. S., Newsom, C. D., & Lovaas, O. I. Auditory overselectivity in autistic children. *Journal of Abnormal Child Psychology*, 1974, *2*, 253–263.

Rheingold, H. L., Stanley, W. C., & Doyle, G. A. Visual and auditory reinforcement of a manipulatory response in the young child. *Journal of Experimental Child Psychology*, 1964, *1*, 316–326.

Rimland, B. *Infantile autism*. New York: Appleton-Century-Crofts, 1964.

Rincover, A. Variables in stimulus-fading influencing discrimination learning in autistic children. Unpublished doctoral dissertation, University of California at Santa Barbara, 1976.

Rincover, A., & Koegel, R. L. Setting generality and stimulus control in autistic children. *Journal of Applied Behavior Analysis*, 1975, *3*, 235–246.

Rincover, A., & Koegel, R. L. Treatment of psychotic children in a classroom environment: II. Individualized instruction in a group. *Journal of Abnormal Child Psychology*, 1977, *5*, 123–136.

Rincover, A., Newsom, C. D., Lovaas, O. I., & Koegel, R. L. Some motivational properties of sensory reinforcement in psychotic children. *Journal of Experimental Child Psychology*, 1977, in press.

Rincover, A., Peoples, A., & Packard, D. Sensory extinction and sensory reinforcement in psychotic children. Paper presented at annual meeting of the American Psychological Association, Washington, D.C., 1976.

Ringer, V. M. The use of a "token helper" in the management of classroom behavior problems and in teacher training. *Journal of Applied Behavior Analysis*, 1973, 6, 671–678.

Risley, T. R. The effects and side effects of punishing the autistic behaviors of a deviant child. *Journal of Applied Behavior Analysis*, 1968, 1, 21–34.

Risley, T. R., & Wolf, M. M. Establishing functional speech in echolalic children. *Behaviour Research and Therapy*, 1967, 5, 73–88.

Russo, D. C., & Koegel, R. L. A method for integrating an autistic child into a normal public school classroom. *Journal of Applied Behavior Analysis*, 1977, in press.

Rutter, M. Prognosis: psychotic children in adolescence and early adult life. *In* J. K. Wing (Ed.), *Early childhood autism.* London: Pergamon Press, 1966.

Rutter, M. Autism: Educational issues. *Special Education*, 1970, 59, 6–10.

Schreibman, L. Effects of within-stimulus and extra-stimulus prompting on discrimination learning in autistic children. *Journal of Applied Behavior Analysis*, 1975, 8, 91–112.

Schreibman, L., & Koegel, R. L. Autism: A defeatable horror. *Psychology Today*, 1975, 8, 61–67.

Sidman, M., & Stoddard, L. T. The effectiveness of fading in programming a simultaneous form discrimination for retarded children. *Journal of the Experimental Analysis of Behavior*, 1967, 10, 3–15.

Siqueland, E. R. Reinforcement patterns and extinction in human newborns. *Journal of Experimental Child Psychology*, 1968, 6, 431–442.

Solnick, J. V., Rincover, A., & Peterson, C. R. Determinants of the reinforcing and punishing effects of time-out. *Journal of Applied Behavior Analysis*, 1977, in press.

Stevenson, H. W., & Odom, R. D. Visual reinforcement with children. *Journal of Experimental Child Psychology*, 1964, 1, 248–255.

Stokes, T. F., & Baer, D. M. An implicit technology of generalization. *Journal of Applied Behavior Analysis*, 1977, in press.

Stokes, T. F., Baer, D. M., & Jackson, R. L. Programming the generalization of a greeting response in four retarded children. *Journal of Applied Behavior Analysis*, 1974, 7, 599–610.

Storm, R. H., & Robinson, P. W. Application of a graded choice procedure to obtain errorless learning in children. *Journal of the Experimental Analysis of Behavior*, 1973, 20, 405–410.

Tate, B. G., & Baroff, G. S. Aversive control of self-injurious behavior in a psychotic boy. *Behavior Research and Therapy*, 1966, 4, 281–287.

Touchette, P. E. The effects of graduated stimulus change on the acquisition of a simple discrimination in severely retarded boys. *Journal of the Experimental Analysis of Behavior*, 1968, 11, 39–48.

Wahler, R. G. Setting generality: Some specific and general effects of child behavior therapy. *Journal of Applied Behavior Analysis*, 1969, 2, 239–246.

Wahler, R. G. Some structural aspects of deviant child behavior. *Journal of Applied Behavior Analysis*, 1975, 8, 27–42.

Wahler, R. G., Sperling, K. A., Thomas, M. R. & Teeter, N. C. The modification of childhood stuttering: Some response–response relationships. *Journal of Experimental Child Psychology*, 1970, 9, 411–428.

Wetzel, R., Baker, I., Roney, M., & Martin, M. Outpatient treatment of autistic behavior. *Behavior Research and Therapy*, 1966, *4*, 166–177.

Wolf, M. M., Risley, T. R., & Mees, H. Application of operant conditioning procedures to the behavior problems of an autistic child. *Behaviour Research and Therapy*, 1964, *1*, 305–312.

Zubek, J. P. *Sensory deprivation: Fifteen years of research.* New York: Appleton-Century-Crofts, 1969.

10 The Prevention of Childhood Behavior Disorders

Donna M. Gelfand
and Donald P. Hartmann

The idea of preventing behavioral disorders has great intuitive appeal. In addition to sparing children and their families needless suffering, the prevention of behavioral problems would ease the service burden on overextended educational and community treatment services and would constitute a social and an economic blessing. There are many different types of potential preventive measures, and prevention programs can be aimed at various points in the development of a behavioral disorder. Caplan (1964) has suggested distinguishing among prevention efforts in terms of their temporal focus. The term *primary prevention* is used for programs intended to reduce the incidence of new cases of various types of disorders. Two other types of intervention occur after individuals have been identified as exhibiting problems. Programs aimed at reducing the duration or severity of a problem are termed *secondary prevention* efforts; and *tertiary prevention* consists of attempts to reduce long-term disability such as that leading to chronic institutionalization. While useful, Caplan's scheme does not entirely resolve classification problems, since variations in definitions of target behavior and stated program goals can result in differing category placement for essentially identical programs. For example, a project dealing with children who have committed criminal acts might be conceived as a secondary prevention effort to see that an existing problem does not worsen. Alternatively, the project could be termed a treatment effort, or even a primary prevention program designed to

Donna M. Gelfand and Donald P. Hartmann • Department of Psychology, the University of Utah, Salt Lake City, Utah.

lessen the probability that the youths do not evolve into adult criminal offenders.

Because intervention efforts are often complex and multifaceted and incorporate several types of treatment and prevention measures, most programs do not lend themselves to such straightforward classification as Caplan's system suggests. For the most part, the present review will focus on the primary prevention of behavioral disorders in high-risk groups of children. Inevitably, however, many of the projects described contain elements of treatment of already-existing problem behaviors (secondary prevention). This characteristic is not surprising, since families with no self-perceived problems are understandably reluctant to engage in time-consuming and effortful education and prevention programs. Later sections of this paper deal more fully with this and other obstacles to prevention. First, we describe some programs in operation.

1. Person-Oriented Programs

There are many possible routes in the implementing of intervention programs. The physical environment might be altered to increase opportunities for the emergence of desirable behavior, and to discourage problem behaviors such as antisocial aggression or isolation. Alternatively, one could focus on the social rather than the physical environment. In these latter programs, some attempt is made to increase the coping skills of high-risk children directly or to educate their caretakers in working with the children to reduce the probability of the occurrence of future problems. Such programs may be directed at selected, specific behaviors or may aim to change the children's general functioning, such as their beliefs about the causation of human behavior. Similarly, caretakers can be instructed in specific childrearing practices such as the use of praise rather than punishment, or an attempt may be made to alter their attitudes so that they perceive the children as more competent and appealing. Usually, though, the prevention team is so eager to effect some positive change that every technique that could conceivably be of help is included in the program. If such an intervention proves effective, it is virtually impossible to discover the active ingredients, and further investigation is required to do so.

Moreover, rather than being based on empirical evidence, many manipulations are based on hunches or clinical intuitions regarding the causes of and the appropriate treatment for behavior disorders. This intuitive approach often results in failure, as will be seen. In contrast, intervention tactics derived from demonstrably powerful techniques such as modeling and shaping have been relatively more effective.

Person-oriented prevention programs have most frequently been directed toward three groups: (1) the family, including prospective parents, parents of children of varying ages, and the target children themselves; (2) teachers, principals, and other school personnel; and (3) medical, nursing, and dental personnel, such as pediatricians, pediatric dentists, and school nurses. We first consider those programs directed toward all or some portion of the family unit.

1.1. The Family as Focus

1.1.1. Primary Prevention

1.1.1.1. Programs for New Parents. At least until adolescence, children receive most of their social training from members of their own families, particularly their parents. Consequently, preventive programs are very often directed at the family constellation. Inexperienced mothers of first-born babies have viewed a series of three half-hour educational videotapes in a program described by Broussard (1976). The programs were designed to increase the new mother's understanding and acceptance of her baby and so to produce a more positive and beneficial climate for the child's development. The tapes have been shown to a group of mothers of normal babies soon after delivery and while mother and baby were still at the hospital. The tapes dealt with possible feelings of postpartum depression, the customary delay in onset of motherly feelings toward the baby, and normal variations in newborn babies' behavior and also provided demonstrations of techniques for infant care. Compared with a matched control group, mothers who viewed at least two of the three tapes developed significantly more positive perceptions of their babies. Broussard felt that the mothers' greater acceptance of their babies may have acted to optimize the child's social development. Whether this is the case remains to be seen. Tavormina (1974) has reviewed parent-counseling studies and conluded that, in itself, the altering of parent attitudes may have little or no effect on child behavior. If parents cannot translate their improved attitudes into superior child-rearing practices, there is little reason to expect that the more positive attitudes will even persist, much less produce desirable changes in the children's behavior.

Instructional videotapes need not be addressed solely to attitude change, however. Tapes can be devised to present appropriate role models, to teach child-training and disciplinary skills, and to provide other information helpful to parents. Videotapes seem a promising educational vehicle because they can be used repeatedly and flexibly, for example, in combination with discussion sessions and with guided rehearsal of the skills portrayed. Brief videotape cassettes demonstrating optimal child-management practices could be run continuously in obstetricians' or pediatricians' waiting rooms or in well-baby clinics. This service could provide parents with new skills to promote their children's social development. Because the demand for instruction is so widespread, and our resources so limited, the use of videotapes and of the mass media makes good economic sense (O'Dell, 1974).

1.1.1.2. Programs for Low-Income Groups. Low-income and welfare-supported mothers and their children are frequently offered preventive services. These children are raised in poverty with attendant limitations in medical, educational, recreational, and vocational opportunities, and they experience many problems. Predictably the poor have poorer physical health than do more economically advantaged groups, and they exhibit higher rates of psychological disorders as well (Hollingshead & Redlich, 1958; Srole, Langer, Michael, Opler, & Rennie, 1962). Thus, they could benefit greatly from effective preventive measures.

Several groups of investigators have attempted to foster the cognitive and language development of high-risk, poverty-family infants through home visits and maternal instruction. These programs have been ably reviewed by Horowitz and Paden (1973) and by Chilman (1973). Consequently, only a few examples of such programs are discussed here. Although these approaches aim mostly at preventing academic failure, similar strategies could be employed to reduce the possibility of social adjustment problems among high-risk groups, such as children of drug-addicted, physically abusive, or actively psychotic parents.

One group of investigators (Karnes, Teska, Hodgins, & Badger, 1970) provided lower-income mothers of 13-month-old to 27-month-old infants with over a year of group instruction in the use of stimulating toys, positive reinforcement and shaping procedures, and the importance of parent–child respect. Home visits were used to help the mothers apply the prescribed teaching program. Their children displayed significantly higher IQ scores and better language skills following the mothers' training than did either (1) a group of control children matched with the experimental group on a *post hoc* basis, or (2) the experimental group's older siblings, who had been tested earlier when they were the same age as the experimental children.

Despite the fact that the mothers were paid for attending the groups, 25% of them failed to complete the training program. The remaining mothers may have represented a self-selected group of highly motivated and enthusiastic parents. The remainers may have been the more capable mothers, whose children would have flourished in any case. In the Karnes group's study, the test scores for the target children's siblings provide at least some indication that it was the program rather than the mothers' characteristics that produced the positive results. In many other experimental programs, no such comparison group is included, and differential dropout rates may be at least partially responsible for any positive results obtained. It is distressing that those most in need of help may be the least likely to seek it or to persist in participating when help has been offered.

Toddlers who are from impoverished families and who display slight developmental lags have been treated in a program developed by Jason and his colleagues (Jason, 1975; Jason, Clarfield, & Cowen, 1973; Jason, Gersten, & Yock, 1976; Specter & Cowen, 1971). The toddlers were provided a verbally, visually, and socially stimulating environment in a special center-based relational program. Weekly parent-group meetings designed to promote educational and personal growth were conducted by the professional staff. Following treatment, the children enrolled in the relational program were functioning within normal limits on the Bayley Scales of Infant Development, while comparable, untreated children retained their initial developmental lags.

In a recent study (Jason *et al.*, 1976), the relational program was compared with a home-based behavior modification program conducted largely by undergraduate students. A student visited each toddler's home twice weekly to shape child skills such as attending and verbal imitation through the contingent use of both social and nonsocial reinforcers. Family members were encouraged to watch and to participate in the training. Both the relational and the behavioral treatments produced improvements in the toddler's functioning, and the behavioral treatment produced significant increases in Bayley Mental Subscale scores. If, in further comparisons, both interventions continue to produce nearly equivalent performance gains not only on test performance, but on everyday behavior as well, the less costly of the two would appear to be the method of choice. Of course, followup evaluations will also be necessary to assess the enduring value of such brief, early intervention with these high-risk children.

Even if such studies were successfully conducted, it would be virtually impossible to characterize the interventions, which were extremely complex and were used in a flexible fashion which may have varied considerably among families and therapists. This problem is nearly universal among prevention and treatment studies and makes replication attempts particularly difficult. Documentation of a program's nature through film or videotape archives and through objective ratings of program staff members' behavior during treatment will probably prove necessary. The work of Stallings (1975) in evaluating the effectiveness of the various Follow Through classroom-intervention models is exemplary with respect to the use of procedural-reliability assessments to ensure that the various intervention programs actually did operate as they were supposed to. Other preventive and therapeutic research projects should be encouraged to emulate this model.

A less costly and demanding parental instruction system has been devised by Levenstein (Levenstein, Kochman, & Roth, 1973). Nonprofessional workers are trained as "toy demonstrators" and conduct home visits to demonstrate the use of specially selected gift toys in active verbal play with toddlers. As soon as possible, the demonstrator transfers the training role to the mother, who then initiates verbal exchanges with her toddler. Such interactions presumably stimulate the child's language and cognitive development. Although the program aims to promote the child's conceptual growth, the emphasis in the home visits is on fun and play, and the visitor is described to the parents as a demonstrator rather than as a teacher or a mental-health expert. Although the group that has received the program is small at present, results are promising. An average IQ gain of 16.2 points was reported for 37 preschool children in four such home-visit programs. More research will be required to identify the factors responsible for the children's gains and to assess the generality and the durability of behavior changes.

An attractive feature of Levenstein's program is the relatively modest reported cost of less than $400 per child for each of two years of home visits. Because expense is a major consideration in the evaluation of prevention projects, it is important that investigators begin to record and report the cost of their programs per child and family served. There are not yet any guidelines for the computation of cost–benefit ratios in service programs, although there is a recent movement to include such analyses in program evaluations. As many investigators begin to test various methods of computing both costs and benefits, there will be a better basis for judging the appropriateness of different approaches to this very difficult evaluation problem. At present, even the best projects include only a very primitive assessment of both the expenses incurred and the benefits derived.

It is not yet clear what advantage there is for the child who exhibits an increased IQ score, although children with higher preschool IQs do typically perform better academically in their early school years. Raising the child's IQ through special educational opportunities for parent and child may only temporarily improve the child's prospects of school success. Some of the most effective intellectual-enrichment programs treat children and families over an extended time span (e.g., Klaus & Gray, 1968). A number of social critics have contended that only major and enduring changes in educational and economic structures will improve the lot of the poor (e.g., Chilman, 1973).

In a promising new trend, some investigators are seeking to demonstrate that their interventions actually do alter the mother–child interactions that are thought to produce academically handicapping child behavior patterns (see, for example, Lasater, Briggs, Malone, Gilliom, & Weisburg, 1975). In their Milwaukee Project, Falender and Heber (1975) studied the behavioral impact of a longitudinal intervention program that combined the child's enrollment in a full-day, cognitively oriented child-care center with social-skills and employment training for the low-income, low-IQ mothers. These mothers have been shown to produce a disproportionate number of retarded children, and the program aimed to prevent child retardation. Children were enrolled in the program from the ages of 6 months to 6 years, so the investment of time and funds was considerable. As compared with matched controls, the trained mothers used more positive and less negative feedback in teaching their 4-year-old to 5-year-old youngsters. The treated children engaged in more verbal and less physical demonstrations and requests than did their control-group counterparts. In addition, the treated children actually seemed to stimulate positive verbal interchanges with their mothers. They also exhibited a 20-point to 30-point IQ score advantage over the control group and continued to do so for several years after the treatment terminated (Trotter, 1976). If these promising results prove replicable, prevention of familial retardation will have become truly possible.

Intervention programs for impoverished and culturally different populations have been criticized for their implied assumption that deviations from the majority-group norms constitute some sort of deficit or inferiority (e.g., Ginsburg, 1972). At the very least, such programs, if conducted by Caucasian, middle-class investigators, may inadvertently undermine traditional minority-group cultural values and behavioral traditions. In an effort to promote participants' awareness of and pride in their cultural heritage, Garcia and his associates (Garcia, Trujillo, & Batista, in press) have established a bilingual–bicultural nursery school for Chicano children. With consultation from psychologists, educators, and psycholinguists, the mothers determine the school curriculum and also teach the classes. Preliminary results indicate (1) that the mothers use both Spanish and English, although primarily English, in their instruction; (2) that they gain confidence in their own teaching skills; and (3) that the children do master the material presented in each instructional unit. This program is in its beginning phases, so many questions about its utility remain unanswered. But this bicultural program, unlike most others, does strive to preserve cherished elements of the family's cultural background while preparing the child for entry into conventional public schools.

1.1.2. Secondary Prevention Programs

1.1.2.1. Parental Instruction. Most efforts at parent and child counseling take place after the child has exhibited some form of problem behavior and thus constitute secondary rather than primary prevention programs. The parents often lack and are seeking very specific child-training skills and consequently find training in child-behavior modification both appealing and helpful. Sometimes very brief, limited professional guidance suffices to ameliorate the problem. Herbert and Baer (1972) found that with less than 10 minutes of instruction in a self-recording procedure, two mothers could successfully modify the behavior of their 5-year-olds, who had been excluded from kindergarten classes because of their unacceptable behavior. The mothers were simply instructed to increase the amount of attention they gave to their children's appropriate behavior and were issued wrist counters to help them monitor their behavior. This extremely simple instructional program successfully changed both the mothers' and the children's performances. Because only two mother–child pairs were studied, the general applicability of this technique is not yet known. Unfortunately, most parents do not seem to be this easy to influence.

Two other, more extensive parent-training programs are in widespread use. Both are experimentally based and employ applied behavior-analysis methods of the type developed by Bijou and Baer and their associates (Baer, Wolf, & Risley, 1968; Hawkins, Peterson, Schweid, & Bijou, 1966), and by Lindsley (1966), in which the current environmental causes of the child's problem behavior are identified and modified. Parents are taught to make accurate, objective records of their child's behavior, are trained in reinforcement-contingency management and other behavioral techniques, and are given the responsibility for modifying their child's behavior. Such parent-conducted projects often include reinforcement-contingency reversals or multiple-baseline designs in which various child behaviors are successively manipulated to provide a check on the treatment method's efficacy and on the utility of this parent-education approach. The relative success of such modification programs is revealed in the behavioral records for each child, and observer reliability checks are often used to minimize the possibility that positive results are due to therapeutic expectations and consequent bias in the parents' observations. These reliability checks are an important feature of this system because data collected by Eyberg and Johnson (1974) have indicated that parents may well overestimate their child's therapeutic improvement relative to the amount of improvement detected in home visits conducted by trained observers. Thus, sole reliance on unchecked parental observations is likely to yield overestimates of treatment potency.

There are a number of behavioral self-help manuals for parents (see Bushell's, 1973 annotated bibliography of these books). Although the methods advocated have their basis in controlled laboratory and field demonstrations of effectiveness, there is no evidence yet available that parents can improve their handling of their children simply by studying a parenting manual. Typically, these materials are used in conjunction with supervised practice in record keeping and in the use of the behavioral techniques.

A number of behavioral parent-instruction programs are in operation (e.g., Karoly & Rosenthal, in press; Miller, 1975; Rinn, Vernon, & Wise, 1975; Tharp & Wetzel, 1969; Watson & Bassinger, 1974). One project, the Regional Intervention Project, gives the parents an unusual degree of responsibility and autonomy in selecting and implementing the goals of modification efforts with their own behavior disordered preschool children (Ora & Reisinger, 1971). This intervention model, which is currently in use in at least two states (Reisinger, Frangia, & Hoffman, 1977), typically employs one Ph.D.-level program director and a small number of master's-level staff members representing disciplines such as special education, psychology, and speech therapy. Parents of children enrolled in the program constitute at least 50% of an advisory committee, which meets monthly to provide binding opinions regarding the program's direction and the adequacy of program results. Daily charting of each child's behavior makes results public and the program accountable to its consumers. The industrial engineering department at the University of Tennessee has conducted a cost–benefit analysis and reported that the program returned to the state of Tennessee at least 66 cents of monetary benefits beyond each dollar expended during the first three years of operation (Snider, Sullivan, & Manning, 1974).

In return for services, each mother repays five hours of time in instructing incoming families for each hour of training that she has received. The mothers also train the fathers so that the program can be carried out consistently in the home. Parents routinely introduce newcomers to the program, instruct them in objective behavior observation of their children, and offer training in teaching their children skills such as toileting, imitation, object naming, and cooperation. A special preschool is available, and the child's transition from the project's preschool to regular nursery schools or kindergartens is carefully planned and supervised by project staff.

The originators of this system, Ora and Reisinger (1971), believe that parents are the persons most aware of their child's needs and progress, are the most dedicated and continuously available therapists, and are best able to provide encouragement and support to other parents of handicapped youngsters. Parent training is often thought to be efficient in that parents are in a good position to oversee the application of the child's individual instructional program in a variety of natural settings. Prior to the Ora and Reisinger project, there was very little evidence to support this belief (O'Dell, 1974; Reisinger, Ora, & Frangia, 1976). The parents' use of improved techniques, such as prompting and reinforcing, has been found to generalize only minimally to new settings in which parent training has not occurred (Miller & Sloane, 1976). In fact, long-term follow-up observations of treated families by Patterson and his associates (Patterson, 1974, 1976) have indicated that parents may cease to implement burdensome child-treatment programs after the termination of regular contacts with professional staff. In Patterson's method, brief and periodic retraining seems to be necessary but may be relatively inexpensive to conduct, as Patterson's experience indicates.

Recently conducted observations of parents enrolled in the Regional Intervention Project, however, have indicated that the parents generalized the use of training procedures across environments (Reisinger & Ora, in press) and continued to utilize the techniques they had been taught for at least a year after the training was completed (Reisinger, Frangia, & Hoffman, in press). The emphasis on parental autonomy in the Regional Intervention Project model may have been responsible for the parents' persistent use of the behavioral techniques. Alternatively, the extensive participation requirements for parents could have discouraged the involvement of those parents who were less committed to their child's improvement, leaving only the highly motivated parents who would be most likely to implement the program prescribed for their child. A functional analysis of each participating child's behavior change as a result of treatment cannot, in itself, reveal the role of parental enthusiasm in effecting the child's improvement.

A second applied operant-training program in large-scale use is the Responsive Teaching system formulated by Hall, Copeland, and their colleagues (Hall & Copeland, 1972; Hall, Copeland, & Clark, 1975). Adult-education classes on behavioral child-management procedures are offered in lectures, films, and discussion groups. Following the lecture presentations, small discussion groups meet with trained leaders who administer quizzes to ensure that the participants master the material on objective child-behavior observation and on reinforcement principles and their application. The participants' progress is closely monitored as they plan and carry out a behavioral-training program with a child. To maximize consistency in adults' responses to the child in various settings, parents, teachers, and school principals are all trained in the responsive teaching methods. In a refreshing contrast to the usual aloof, disciplinary role played by the school principal, for example, a principal trained in responsive teaching is reported to have students sent to his office to receive special commendations for good work, rather than to receive punishment for misdeeds (Hall, Copeland, & Clark, 1975). A visit to the principal thus becomes a treat rather than a dreaded punishment. This principal also autographs good student papers, and teachers in his school frequently send home notes detailing children's academic accomplishments. Although this program seems exceptionally promising, no group-comparison data are available to evaluate its preventive or treatment accomplishments.

Christophersen and his associates (Christophersen, Barnard, Ford, & Wolf, 1976) have employed their behavioral family-training program in a comparison with conventional clinic-outpatient treatment for groups of matched, then randomly assigned children. The Family Training Program resembles the treatments described by Bernal (Bernal, Delfini, North, & Kreutzer, 1976) and by Stuart (1971) in which therapists originally demonstrated behavioral child management techniques such as the use of praise and attention, to reinforce children's appropriate behavior. Parents and children were also trained to negotiate contracts specifying the reinforcers that the children would receive for engaging in desirable behavior. Ultimately, the parents assumed the major responsibility for the child's treatment. Parents reported a greater decrease in the daily occurrence of problem behaviors for the Family Training group children than for the clinic-treated children, but the former program required somewhat more therapist time (an average of 30 hours) than did the clinic treatment (an average of 25 hours). Further outcome evaluations utilizing child-behavior ratings by experimentally naïve observers will be required before the relative utility of each of these two treatment methods can be assessed. Such comparisons among treatments are extremely difficult to conduct, as is indicated by their relative infrequency in the literature.

Over the course of the past 10 years, Patterson and his colleagues have developed a family-treatment program for aggressive boys and

have evaluated its immediate and long-term impact. The adult-adjust-
ment prognosis is extremely poor for children with antisocial, acting-
out behavior problems, so a secondary prevention program for these
high-risk youngsters would represent a major contribution. In the
Oregon Social Learning Project, parents are taught child-management
skills such as (1) observing family members' behavior and keeping
records; (2) using effective punishment (e.g., withdrawal of reinforcers) for their son's undesirable coercive behaviors; and (3) using more
effective social and nonsocial reinforcers for the boy's prosocial behaviors.

This project has contributed valuable information on the coercive
nature of social systems within the families of aggressive youngsters,
and has demonstrated how such systems can operate to promote and
maintain undesirable, aggressive behavior (Patterson, 1976; Patterson
& Reid, 1970). Early detection of a coercive social system within a family might well allow preventive intervention in the form of parenting-
skills training before serious child-behavior problems emerge. The
family-intervention approach appears to be effective in disrupting coercive interchanges and promoting mutually satisfying ones, even
among the untreated siblings of the target child (Arnold, Levine, &
Patterson, 1975). Moreover, the social-learning treatment has been
shown to be superior to a placebo treatment (Walter & Gilmore, 1973)
and to a waiting list control condition (Wiltz & Patterson, 1974). Although an early replication attempt by independent investigators
proved relatively unsuccessful (Ferber, Keeley, & Shemberg, 1974), a
more recent effort appears to have replicated Patterson's (1974) earlier
impressive outcome effects in both home and school settings (Fleishman, 1976). In an attempt to enhance the replicability of their procedures, the Oregon group has issued a very detailed treatment description (Patterson, Reid, Jones, & Conger, 1975) and has made a set of
videotapes for the training of therapists.

If effective parenting skills can be widely taught, perhaps in the
public schools, and if the skills can be actually applied in child rearing, many child-behavior disorders could be prevented. At present,
research findings indicate that parents of behavior-disordered youngsters can be taught new and more effective child-management skills
(see review papers by Johnson & Katz, 1973; O'Dell, 1974; Tavormina,
1974; Wahler, 1976). Whether such skills training can be used as a
primary prevention measure is a crucial, as yet unanswered research
question.

1.1.2.2. Surrogate Families for Antisocial Youths. The Achievement
Place program is an extremely ambitious attempt to prevent institutionalization and further trouble with the law for court-adjudicated

adolescent boys. In this intervention model, a trained child-care couple, the teaching parents, live with and treat a small group of about six youths who have been in repeated contact with juvenile authorities and who are threatened with institutionalization. The treatment takes place in a group home in the community and teaches the boys social and academic skills, such as controlled rather than aggressive responding to criticism and direction, conversation and appropriate use of language, completing schoolwork assignments, job-interview and job-performance techniques, and self-government of the boys' group. Other skills taught include room-cleaning, grooming, promptness, and the appropriate handling of money (Phillips, Phillips, Fixsen, & Wolf, 1971).

This program is currently in operation in about 100 locations in eight states, and careful evaluations have indicated that the positive results obtained from the original program (e.g., lowered recidivism rates) can be replicated (Braukmann, Kirigin, & Wolf, 1976). Independent investigators have also been able to replicate most portions of the program (Lieberman, Ferris, Salgado, & Salgado, 1975). The key to successful replication seems to be the careful, year-long, in-service training of new teaching couples in the application of the techniques used in the program. Each group home is run on a token-economy system in which each boy receives points for desired behavior and is fined points for rule violations. The points can be exchanged for spending money, for television-viewing time, for outings, and for other attractive items and activities. Reliance on the points is gradually reduced and is finally eliminated. Training parents learn how to apply these teaching techniques, as well as how to interact with community agencies and neighbors. Their ability to work effectively in the community is particularly emphasized. The training parents are formally evaluated on their success in dealing with the community board of directors, the courts, the police, the schools, other social-service agencies, and the youths and their parents. Training parents are expected to build positive relationships with the boys and to use reasoning in convincing the boys of the desirability of behavior change. In preparation for their return to their own homes, the youths and their parents are trained to negotiate conflict situations, and there is evidence that this training generalizes to the solution of actual conflict situations in the home (Kifer, Lewis, Green, & Phillips, 1974).

This program is particularly notable for the investigators' taking care to conduct a rigorous experimental analysis of each treatment component, a feature not found in most such interventions. In addition, an independent evaluator has been asked to assess the effectiveness of the Teaching Family model (Jones, 1976). The results to date indicate that the Teaching Family approach is considerably less expensive, and is somewhat more effective in reducing offenses and posttreatment institutionalization, than are alternative programs, such as institutional treatment (Braukmann, Kirigin, & Wolf, 1976). This project has demonstrated the feasibility of nationwide dissemination of intervention programs, even those of a complex nature.

1.1.2.3. Children of Psychotic Parents. Psychotic parents, especially schizophrenic mothers, produce children who exhibit excessive rates of behavior problems in adulthood (see review by Rolf & Harig, 1974). Some 15–17% of these children later develop psychotic behaviors, and still others exhibit different but also serious behavior disorders (Anthony, 1972). For as yet unidentified reasons, these children appear to be at high risk. A number of investigators are attempting to study the development of children of schizophrenic and other behaviorally deviant parents (e.g., Garmezy & Streitman, 1974; Mednick & Schulsinger, 1968; Neale & Weintraub, 1975; Ragins, Schachter, Elmer, Preisman, Bowers, & Harway, 1975; Rolf, 1976). Such efforts are expensive, and time-consuming and are plagued by problems such as the unreliability of psychiatric diagnosis. Even should researchers determine why children of psychotic parents are particularly vulnerable to behavioral problems, prevention may prove extremely difficult, perhaps impossible. Because they are experiencing grave problems themselves, the parents may well be unable to profit from parenting skill-training programs. Moreover, such parents provide seriously deviant social models for their children. As Bandura (1969) has suggested, these deviant parental models may be primarily responsible for the bizarre behavior displayed by some children of psychotic parents.

Anthony (1972) has concluded that the school-aged children of psychotic parents must be trained to help themselves, particularly during the parent's seriously psychotic episodes. Treatment-center staff members provide the children with crisis counseling and emotional support at sensitive times and may prescribe tranquilizing drugs for upset children. The therapists try to interpret the parent's psychotic behavior for the child and to set a standard of reality for children who themselves report experiencing delusions or hallucinations. During the intervals between the parent's psychotic episodes, the child is provided with group and individual nondirective therapy, with special recreational programs and with whatever other form of individual instruction and support is judged necessary. This program is very clinically oriented, so it may be difficult to assess the program's results relative to no treatment or to alternative treatments. At the very least, this approach offers sanctuary and guidance to seriously troubled children.

1.2. School-Based Prevention Programs

The public school presents an attractive location for prevention programs because nearly all children attend school, so could be reached (Zax & Specter, 1974). Moreover, children with seriously disturbed, neglectful, or violent parents could be served regardless of whether their parents could or would participate actively, so long as they would consent to their child's participation. Thus, the unfortunate effects of parental deviance might be counteracted to some degree. In any case, schools undoubtedly do affect children's social as well as their academic development. As Madden (1972) and Zax and Specter (1974) have noted, it would surely be advantageous to acknowledge that this social-influence process exists and to evaluate its effect on children rather than to allow it to proceed in a haphazard, unevaluated, and possibly harmful manner.

1.2.1. Primary Prevention in the Schools

Caplan (1964) has long advocated the use of preventive programs based on mental health consultation to caregivers such as teachers. Mental-health consultation services have proliferated in recent years, yet there is rather scant empirical evidence of their effectiveness (see Mannino & Shore, 1975, for a review of this research). Consultation does seem to build rapport between teachers and consultants (Iscoe, Pierce-Jones, Friedman, & McGehearty, 1967; Mariner, Brandt, Stone, & Mirmow, 1961; Tyler, 1971) and to increase teachers' self-confidence in dealing with children's behavior problems (Teitelbaum, 1961). But consultation services to teachers have not had the expected impact on student behavior. For example, consultation has not been found to decrease students' anxiety (Thurlow, 1971), nor to improve their sociometric and adjustment status (Kellman & Schiff, 1967; Lewis, 1969), nor to increase their acceptance of self nor improve their attitudes toward school, nor to enhance their classroom group interactions (Schmuck, 1968; but see Keutzer, Fosmire, Diller, & Smith, 1971, for an exception). The available research evidence thus seems to indicate that, as now employed, the teacher-consultation model fails to serve its stated purpose of positively affecting children's social adjustment.

1.2.2. Secondary Prevention in the Schools

1.2.2.1. The Rochester Model. Like many of the family-oriented preventive efforts, school programs have often been directed toward children who have already begun to experience behavior problems. In the well-known Rochester Project (Cowen, Trost, Lorion, Dorr, Izzo, & Isaacson, 1975; Cowen, Zax, Izzo, & Trost, 1966; Zax & Cowen, 1967), first-grade children were identified as having problems or potential problems in social adjustment. Then, a preventive mental health program was set up in these children's school, and the results were compared with those obtained on tests and observations conducted at comparison schools. The preventive program was applied successively in the first three grades in school and consisted of (1) teacher conferences with mental-health consultants; (2) psychiatric consultant services and after-school group meetings for the disturbed children; (3) in-service mental-health education for teachers; and (4) parents' discussion groups dealing with child-rearing practices. These investigators are able methodologists who have dealt knowledgeably with many difficult problems typical of this type of longitudinal, preventive research, for example, differential subject attrition among groups. The program itself, however, was loosely structured and intuitively based. The results were somewhat encouraging in that children at the experimental school were rated as better adjusted by their teachers (who were aware of the treatment), and treated children had higher achievement-test scores in the third grade than did children at control schools. The advantage for the treated children in teacher ratings and in arithmetic-reasoning scores was maintained even at a follow-up evaluation four years after the program was terminated (Zax & Cowen, 1967). Nevertheless, the children who were identified as having problems as first-graders continued to have them throughout the course of the study. By the time they had reached third-grade, these children were performing significantly less well than their classmates on achievement, peer relationships, anxiety level, and classroom adjustment (Zax & Cowen, 1967). It appears that the program primarily benefited the better-adjusted children but that the target children did not improve relative to their classmates. These latter results were disappointing, and in their more recent work, the Rochester group has pursued a different intervention tactic. The program now relies heavily on paraprofessional workers (housewives and students) in individual-classroom and after-school interactions with disturbed schoolchildren. The nonprofessional workers establish warm, supportive relationships with the children and provide them with appropriate adult models (Zax & Cowen, 1967). As yet, there is little information on the efficacy of this secondary prevention approach. Certainly the child-therapy outcome studies (e.g. Waldron, 1976) provide little basis for optimism regarding the results to be obtained from relationship-based therapeutic interventions.

1.2.3. Social- and Academic-Skills Training

The relatively slim returns for the great expenditure of effort in the original Rochester School Project and in many other such programs (see the review by Levine & Graziano, 1972) indicate that some alternative approach should probably be pursued. Many investigators (e.g., Kelley, Snowden, & Muñoz, 1977) are now advocating a less global, more directive skills-training approach in which an attempt is made to teach children and specific skills they need to succeed in academic and social situations. General personality changes are not attempted, but rather children are taught particular competencies. As Kelly *et al.* have suggested, social-learning research has produced a number of techniques for skill training that could be used in prevention programs. Academic-survival-skills training provides a good example of this new treatment direction. Many young children exhibit patterns of social behavior that interfere with their academic functioning and result in low achievement. During work periods, the child may be roaming around the room, or he may be seated but not looking at the work materials, or he may be failing to listen while the teacher is giving directions. Such a child will probably begin to fall behind the others in academic achievement and may be singled out for criticism by teachers and peers. Behaviors such as attending to the teacher, working, volunteering answers, and looking at one's work rather than elsewhere have been termed academic-survival skills (Greenwood, Hops, Delquadri, & Guild, 1974; Hops & Cobb, 1973). These skills are correlated with achievement-test scores in the elementary-school years, and classroom training in these behaviors has been demonstrated to improve first graders' reading scores (Cobb & Hops, 1973; Hops & Cobb, 1974). These investigators have developed a Program for Academic Survival Skills (PASS) to train teachers to use group-reinforcement contingencies employing both tangible and social consequences for appropriate classroom behavior. Teachers specify rules of classroom conduct (e.g., "Look at the teacher when (s)he talks or is giving directions."), then operate a clock to time the duration of intervals when all children are behaving appropriately. The children then receive a reinforcer of their choice, such as extra recess time, for meeting or exceeding their goal as measured by the duration of the group's study behavior. It should be emphasized that this procedure is placed in effect only during portions of the schoolday such as during reading- or arithmetic-instruction periods and that these highly structured periods can be easily and flexibly interspersed with art, recreation, and group-oriented activities. Teachers can operate the PASS system effectively but may not transfer the techniques to appropriate instructional settings other than the one in which they received training. Generalization to other class settings has been slight and inconsistent among teachers (Greenwood & Hops, 1976) unless generalization training has been included. Providing teachers with visible reminders to use the techniques (prompts) and with feedback on their performance has produced a more consistent teacher use of the behavioral techniques in a variety of settings (Hops, Greenwood, & Guild, 1975). When treatment components, such as the use of the clock, were eliminated gradually over a period of two weeks, or when teachers continued to use the PASS program following the consultants' departure, the children were able to maintain their performance gains over a six-week follow-up period (Greenwood, Hops, & Walker, 1975). Thus, this program shows considerable promise for the prevention of academic underachievement.

The teacher is the central figure in the school setting, and most prevention and therapeutic interventions have been administered in classrooms by teachers. Teachers' use of praise has been found to be highly and positively related to children's appropriate classroom behaviors. Moreover, the teacher's praise and criticism of student performance seems to be causally related to disruptive-behavior rates. In an important demonstration study, Thomas, Becker, and Armstrong (1968) found that when a teacher's disapproval statements were briefly experimentally increased, the children's rates of disruptive behavior rose markedly, then decreased again when the teacher resumed her accustomed practice of praising good student efforts. It appears that even minor alterations in teacher behavior can have profound effects on students' conduct, especially in the elementary grades.

In carefully conducted research studies, teachers have been taught a variety of behavior-management techniques, such as the systematic use of publicly stated rules, praise for appropriate behavior, and ignoring inappropriate behavior so as to avoid reinforcing it with attention (e.g., Hall & Copeland, 1972; Madsen, Becker, & Thomas, 1968). When social consequences have not proved sufficiently powerful to motivate children to increase their rates of desirable social and academic behavior, then token reinforcement programs have been introduced (see, for example, Barrish, Saunders & Wolf, 1969; Harris & Sherman 1973, O'Leary & O'Leary, 1976). In these latter programs, children earn tokens (points) for appropriate responding and may lose accumulated tokens for misbehavior (see reviews by Kazdin & Bootzin, 1972; Kazdin, 1975; O'Leary & Drabman, 1971). Tokens can be turned in for whatever back-up reinforcers are convenient and attractive. In some instances, entire schools are operated on token systems (e.g., Boegli & Wasik, 1976) or on individualized contingency contracts specifying a child's reward for engaging in appropriate behavior (Arnett, Spates, & Ulrich, 1974). As is the case in teacher training, care must be taken to ensure that children's behavioral improvements become general and permanent (Walker & Buckley, 1972). A persistent problem associated with nearly all types of prevention and therapy programs is that any behavioral change achieved often does not transfer to other settings, for example, from the school to the home (Bernal, Delfini, North, & Kreutzer, 1976; Patterson, 1974; Wahler, 1976). Researchers are now more frequently examining indirect as well as direct effects of interventions and are devising methods to promote more general and persistent behavior change (see the review of such techniques by Gelfand & Hartmann, 1975, Chapter 9).

1.2.4. Problems in Implementation

There are many obstacles to the introduction of preventive programs in the schools. In schools, as in any established institutions, traditions are cherished and customary practices are difficult to alter. For example, retaining poorly performing students in a grade rather than promoting them with their age mates has been shown nearly uniformly to be counterproductive, yet schools continue their nonpromotion policies (Levine & Graziano, 1972). Levine and Graziano have further described how political considerations can determine the fate of a program regardless of the empirical data. Often, objective evaluations are neither sought nor employed if available, and programs are retained or discontinued on the basis of the vested interests of the decision makers.

Preventionists must become effective politicians and public-relations experts if they are to work in school systems. In order to operate, a program must be endorsed by groups as diverse as school boards, principals, individual teachers and teachers' unions, parents, and children. To further complicate matters, any one of the preceding groups can be composed of two or more warring factions with differing opinions on the appropriate role of preventive programs in the schools. And an active, vocal minority can sabotage any program, no matter how effective or generally desirable the program would appear to be.

There are a number of ways to gain acceptance for new programs. One method of approach would be to begin a project in stages, with the most broadly accepted, least threatening components instituted first. Zax and Specter (1974) suggest that as participants' confidence in the program staff is built and as demand for the service develops, the more ambitious and potentially controversial features can be introduced. Another alternative that is feasible only in large school districts is to provide many different programs either within individual schools or in various schools and to allow families and school personnel to be associated with the programs they prefer. Then, if one approach proves particularly effective and appealing, more teachers and students should prefer that model, and the model should proliferate.

To succeed with either method of gaining acceptance, the prevention team must be persuasive and socially sensitive.

1.3. Intervention by Health Professionals

New parents are most likely to seek child-rearing advice from their pediatricians. Indeed, as much as 85% of a pediatrician's time may be spent in counseling and guidance about children's psychological or developmental problems (Brazelton, 1975). Recognition of the pediatrician's central role in the prevention of behavior disorders and in the early detection of behavioral problems has led to the development of a new specialty, behavioral pediatrics. An effort is now being made to provide pediatricians with better preparation for such activities (e.g., see Friedman, 1975). Brazelton (1975) has recommended that pediatricians make themselves available to parents in times of stress and that physicians attempt to alleviate parents' anxiety about their responsibility for problems that their child develops. Pediatricians can also provide parents with information about normal variations in behavioral and physical development and so reassure them about the status of their infant. Unfortunately, we have no controlled studies to demonstrate that such counseling reduces the incidence of problem behaviors, but the pediatrician's advice and reassurance must be welcomed by worried parents.

1.3.1. Desensitization

The physician can, however, prevent the development of children's extreme fears of and avoidance of medical treatment. Brazelton has recommended that prior to a physical examination, the frightened child should make brief visits to the medical office to receive treats and to play with attractive toys. He has suggested further that the parent accompany the child to provide an additional source of reassurance and emotional security. This gradual introduction to the examination and treatment process bears an obvious resemblance to the systematic desensitization treatment which has been found to be effective in eliminating a variety of children's fears (see the review by Gelfand, 1977). Desensitization, consisting of a graded introduction to dental or surgical equipment and procedures, has been found to be an effective technique for reducing children's fears of and resistance to treatment (e.g., Johnson & Machen, 1973; Machen & Johnson, 1974).

1.3.2. Modeling

Another behavioral technique, symbolic (film) modeling is also an effective prevention technique. A series of well-executed experimental studies by Melamed and her associates has demonstrated that brief films or videotapes showing a child overcoming his initial apprehension and receiving treats and commendations for his cooperation are extremely effective in increasing children's cooperation during painful dental treatment (Melamed, Hawes, Heiby, & Glick, 1975). In this study, control-group children who had seen a film unrelated to dentistry increased their resistive behavior (e.g., crying, complaining, kicking, refusing to open mouth) 256% from the initial exam to observations made during a restorative treatment session. After viewing the modeling film, the experimental-group children showed a remarkable 23% *decrease* in their resistive behavior during the restorative treatment session. These results have been replicated with other groups of children (Melamed, Weinstein, Hawes, & Katin-Borland, 1975). Moreover, a similar filmed modeling sequence has been shown to reduce pre- and postoperative fear arousal in children who are surgical patients beyond the reduction levels associated with the customary preparatory explanations of surgical procedures (Melamed & Siegel, 1975). It appears that we now have a reliable, effective, and inexpensive technology for the prevention of unduly negative reactions to necessary health-care practices. Within the next few years, modeling techniques should be widely field-tested. If their initial promise is fulfilled, such procedures will probably be used in medical and dental facilities throughout the country.

1.3.3. Stimulus Preexposure as a Preventive Measure

Poser (1970; Poser & King, 1975) has advocated using behavior therapy techniques such as desensitization and modeling to prevent the occurrence of many different types of fears, for example, fears of snakes and other animals, of school entry and separation from parents, of speaking before groups, and of other common stressors. Poser believes that children can be psychologically innoculated against developing maladaptive avoidance reactions by gradual preexposure of the children to the aversive stimuli. He maintains that it is the sudden and novel encounter with the stress stimulus that produces negative emotional reactions but that such unexpected encounters need not produce maladaptive behavior patterns if children have had prior exposure to the stimulus. According to Poser, "It may turn out that primary prevention in the mental health field is better served by the deliberate exposure of susceptible individuals to learning experiences spontaneously encountered by more normal individuals than by providing them with sheltered or protective environments" (1970, p. 42). This interesting proposal warrants pursuit in future prevention research.

2. The Physical Environment

2.1. The Geography of the Community

The programs described thus far require continued educational contacts over extended time periods. Sagacious design of children's physical environments could be a powerful and economical alternative method for preventing problems. Certainly, the isolation, impersonality, and danger of physical attack associated with life in high-rise, low-cost city-apartment complexes has convinced many observers that architectural features can produce adjustment problems (e.g., Gump, 1975). Stumphauzer and his colleagues (Stumphauzer, Aiken, & Veloz, 1976) have analyzed the environmental factors presumed to support the high rate of juvenile crime in a particular area of Los Angeles. They concluded that one such factor was the community's isolated location, being bounded by freeways that physically obstructed interaction with nearby lower-crime neighborhoods. A hillside location and limited access by road enabled youthful lawbreakers to detect the approach of the police and to elude them. Nor was there any haven within this area for children who wished to avoid associating with the outlaw gangs that terrorized the community. The research investigators concluded that, combined with social pressures, the physical design of the area effectively forced children to become delinquents.

Like the Stumphauzer *et al.* study just described, much of the currently available information is observational and correlational in nature. Consequently, it is difficult to trace the sources of any child-behavior disorders that might develop in various housing arrangements. It may be unsafe to conclude that providing environments similar to those of the best-adjusted children will necessarily alleviate children's behavioral problems. Barker and Gump (1964), in careful observational studies, have found that small schools required the social participation of less able students who were similar to those excluded from extracurricular activities in larger schools. It would be tempting to infer that school size should be decreased in order to encourage social activity for marginal students, but although this may prove to be the case, other factors may be at work. It is admittedly hazardous to base social prescriptions on the purely observational data that are currently available. But in sensitive issues such as the assignment of children to schools, it may be impossible to conduct decisive experimental studies, and we may ultimately be forced to rely on the results of naturalistic observation and laboratory analogue research in formulating social policies. At least this would represent an advance over basing vital decisions on emotion, prejudice, and political considerations.

2.2. Design of Child Care Facilities

One group of investigators is experimentally analyzing the effects of environmental designs on the behavior of infants and toddlers in day-care centers (see Cataldo & Risley, 1974, for an overview of this research). This promising line of investigation has thus far established that an open environment enabled caretakers to observe the children more frequently, did not disturb the sleep of the children, and was as conducive to small-group activities as a floor plan divided into smaller rooms (Twardosz, Cataldo, & Risley, 1974b). The open plan is cheaper and more convenient than the customary divided space and appears to be preferable. In a related set of experiments, these investigators have found that children's participation in play activities was as great in required activities as in optional ones, given a sufficient supply of play materials (Doke & Risley, 1972). Also, having teaching staff assigned to a particular area and activity produced greater group participation and less inactivity among the children than did having teachers accompany the same group of children as they passed from one activity to another (LeLaurin & Risley, 1972). Given the large and increasing number of children receiving group care, the behavioral effects of the physical plant and the activity schedule obviously merit more such research investigation.

2.3. Design of Play Materials

Toys can greatly affect children's play interactions which serve a major socialization function. Many years ago, Van Alstyne (1932) established that play materials determine children's rates of cooperation, their conversation, and their attention span. Recently, researchers have once again begun to investigate the impact of toys on children's behavior. Twardosz, Cataldo, and Risley (1974a) have found that crib toys in fact occupy a considerable portion of infants' waking time. Further, the crib toys did not adversely affect the infants' sleep patterns, so seemed to have generally beneficial effects.

The social behavior of older children can be modified to some extent by the types of toys available. Not surprisingly, it has been established that aggressive toys such as play guns reliably increase children's rates of aggressive interaction (Turner & Goldsmith, 1976). It would seem unwise, then, to provide aggressive playthings for children who frequently interact aggressively, lest their behavior become problematic.

Toys could be used in a preventive fashion with shy, withdrawn children, also. Quilitch and Risley (1973) have found that social play occurred 78% of the time when children were provided with toys that could be used jointly, whereas social play occurred only 16% of the time when the children were given toys that required individual use. It is also likely that the latter toys would stimulate more selfish and demanding behavior among the children, although this possibility has not yet been examined.

The use of toys in programs designed to aid in children's cognitive development has been discussed earlier. In that domain, also, toys have proved extremely useful, for example, in optimizing encounters between parent and child. Although it is unlikely that we can rely solely on play equipment and environmental design to alter behavior in desirable ways, these aspects of children's everyday life could prove to be important contributors to prevention programs.

3. Implementing Prevention Programs

The general consensus is that we should prevent rather than treat behavioral disorders. Berlin (1975) has argued that the right to prevention of emotional, neurological, and learning disturbances should be recognized as one of the most fundamental of children's rights. Other writers, such as Glidewell (1971), have suggested that the prevention of disorders in childhood should be the highest priority in mental-health services to communities. Yet, in his 1973 review of community interventions, Cowen found that only 2–3% of the references in the community mental-health literature dealt with prevention, and many such references were to philosophical essays rather than to evaluations of preventive services. In the preparation of the present review, we have found only a slight recent increase in the number of preventive-research reports. Notable and encouraging exceptions, however, are to be found in the areas of prevention of specific fears and in social-skills training. In these latter areas, effective preventive interventions have been based on procedures developed in laboratory analogue research, rather than on traditional, but unproven, clinical techniques. We return to this more optimistic theme a bit later. First, let us consider the forces arrayed against the preventionist.

3.1. Obstacles to Prevention

Mental-health professionals themselves represent a formidable barrier to the development of preventive mental-health programs. The social workers, nurses, psychiatrists, psychologists, and others employed in community mental health centers have nearly all been trained to diagnose and to treat psychological disorders rather than to prevent them. Because the demand for services to the behaviorally disabled continues to be extremely high, it is hardly surprising that community mental-health workers have nearly no time left to devote to challenging and unfamiliar preventive efforts (Broskowski & Baker, 1974). Moreover, prevention does not afford immediate gratification in the form of the thanks of grateful clients sometimes experienced by therapists. The personal rewards associated with the practice of therapy are absent in prevention efforts, in which the preventionist and the beneficiary may never meet.

Worse still, professional status and monetary considerations dissuade mental-health workers from attempting prevention. Chu and Trotter (1974) have charged that community mental-health-center facilities have often been diverted for the appealing and profitable private-practice treatment of middle-class patients, while the poor have been neglected and prevention has not been attempted. It appears that professionals' training, interests, and economic and professional status all work toward the concentration of attention on the treatment of middle-class adults rather than on the prevention of problems among children.

Broskowski and Baker (1974) have asserted that the most serious barrier to prevention programs is the lack of demand for such services by a powerful constituency. There is simply no great public outcry for prevention activities as there is for protection from and adequate services to the behaviorally deviant. If there were a demand for preventive services, we would undoubtedly have them, despite the personal proclivities of many mental-health workers. As Broskowski and Baker have stated, "health and peace have in common the fact that it is difficult to organize a constituency that defines its need as the maintenance of a positive state of affairs" (p. 716).

Until recently, there seemed little possibility of building such a constituency. The initial preventive attempts were costly and mostly fruitless, as the preceding review has indicated. Few people are likely to demand expensive but ineffective services. Public awareness of some of the more recent, demonstrably beneficial prevention programs should alleviate this problem, but there is a history of past failures to overcome, and the unwarranted optimism characteristic of past prevention programs has increased public skepticism. It is very probably impossible to treat children so optimally as to ward off the occurrence of all behavioral problems, and to suggest that we can do so strains credulity.

3.2. Ethics of Intervention

It should be noted that even effective prevention programs can meet with considerable public resistance. To be of genuine social value, interventions must involve the identification of high-risk children, and the detection process may be interpreted as an invasion of privacy. High-risk populations, such as the urban poor and particularly ethnic minority groups, have come to view all intervention tactics with suspicion, believing that these programs are exploiting the target groups while economically benefiting the project staff. No matter how well intended or how effective a program might actually be, consumer resistance may remain high enough to defeat it. An obvious solution, and one utilized in many projects (e.g., Ball & Bogatz, 1972; Garcia et al., in press; Reisinger, Ora & Frangia, 1976), is to involve representatives of the consumer group in all phases of planning, implementation, and evaluation of the service-delivery system.

Then there is the question of the choice of goals. In a pluralistic society such as ours, it is extremely difficult to achieve public consensus on any issue, even on such a seemingly obvious one as providing adequate nutrition for poor children. Consider how difficult it will be to reach agreement on desirable child and adult behavioral attributes. Sanford (1972) believes that certain ideals such as "competence" and "wholeness" are probably acceptable positive mental-health objectives for everyone. But disagreement would doubtless arise when ideals were translated into actual behaviors to be fostered or eliminated.

The more modest aim of offering services to receptive families, schools, and neighborhoods appears to be more feasible and palatable than the grand public mental-health designs of the past. The current programs meeting with the greatest success and the best acceptance are those that offer training in behavior-management skills to parents, teachers, and children and that allow the recipients to select their own goals. This solution is not foolproof, however. Winett and Winkler (1972) have charged that interventionists often unquestioningly fulfill teachers' requests to produce less noise, more work, and more obedience in the classroom. Such behaviors may be neither necessary nor ultimately desirable if children are to become active, curious, and socially oriented problem-solvers. In a reply to Winett and Winkler, O'Leary (1972) demonstrated that behavioral treatments have been aimed at groups of children whose extraordinarily high rates of socially inappropriate behavior have impeded their own and their classmates' learning, rather than representing an attempt to transform children into docile automata. In addition, treatments have often been designed to increase children's social participation, their initiative, and their creativity, as well as to deal with unacceptably high rates of disruptive behavior. Nevertheless, it appears obvious that transferring the major role in the selection of goals to caretakers or to the children themselves will not relieve professionals from ethical responsibility. Decisions regarding goals must be shared, not dictated by the consumer or, as in the past, determined largely by the therapist or the educator.

Yet another major question is whether we have sufficient information to make a wise selection of intervention goals. Forrester (1971) and Broskowski and Baker (1974) have observed that most social systems are so complex that intuitively based interventions may have a number of unanticipated consequences. In working within inadequately understood causal networks, change agents may too often select the results rather than the causes of disorder as the targets for treatment. Or the changes effected may prove detrimental. Certainly, our past record in introducing technological intrusions into natural physical environments has been far from reassuring. The dangers to life posed by such chemical agents as pesticides and herbicides, by substances in general use such as asbestos, and by food additives such as some dyes became apparent only after many years of use. As a result of such experiences, we have become much more wary of possible unintended effects of technological developments in the natural sciences. Willems (1974) has made a strong case for exercising similar caution in introducing new behavior modification systems, especially on a large scale. He has observed that, "we have become fairly conservative and sophisticated about introducing new biotic elements and new chemicals into our ecological systems, but we display almost childish irresponsibility in our attitudes toward behavioral and behavioral–environmental systems" (pp. 154–155). There is some supporting evidence that behavioral-treatment interventions may have complex and unpredicted effects. Wahler (1976) has found that introducing a therapeutic program to alter the rate of occurrence of one behavior affected a host of behaviors displayed by the treated child in a variety of settings. Not all of the changes were socially desirable ones, so it is no longer possible to assume that all correlates of therapeutic behavior changes are themselves positive. As Baer (1974) has suggested, however, it may ultimately prove impossible to predict the entire range of behavioral impacts of any particular intervention. And failure to intervene poses problems, too. To do nothing while an identified problem continues may be neither judicious nor professionally satisfying. Nevertheless, those who choose to intervene in either a therapeutic or a preventive context must evaluate the effect of their manipulations on a variety of client behaviors in various everyday situations over a meaningful period of time. Only then can we determine the worth of social programs.

3.3. Present Status and Future Prospects

Despite these many practical and ethical constraints, progress has been made toward preventing several types of childhood disabilities. Specific fears are being prevented by means of modeling and by desensitization through gradual preexposure to fear-provoking stimuli. Although these programs have been small, experimental demonstrations, larger-scale application of the procedures is likely in the near future. Developmental lags and progressive retardation in high-risk toddlers can be detected and considerably reduced, although the present methods are expensive and time-consuming. Play materials and physical environments can be designed to reduce the incidence of troublesome social withdrawal or aggressive behavior. Finally, children's caretakers can be taught to identify and alleviate precursors to problem behaviors and to promote desirable academic and social behaviors. Although there is as yet no panacea, we are rapidly developing the means to prevent as well as to treat the behavioral disorders of childhood.

References

Anthony, E. J. Primary prevention with school children. In H. H. Barten & L. Bellak (Eds.), Progress in community mental health, Vol. 2. New York, Grune & Stratton, 1972, pp. 131–158.

Arnett, M. S., Spates, C. R., & Ulrich, R. E. Learning Village: Positive control in a group situation. In A. Jacobs & W. W. Spradlin (Eds.), The group as agent of change. New York: Behavioral Publications, 1974.

Arnold, J. A., Levine, A., & Patterson, G. R. Changes in sibling behavior following family intervention. Journal of Consulting and Clinical Psychology, 1975, 43, 683–688.

Baer, D. M. A note on the absence of a Santa Claus in any known ecosystem: A rejoinder to Willems. Journal of Applied Behavior Analysis, 1974, 7, 167–170.

Baer, D. M., Wolf, M. M., & Risley, T. R. Some current dimensions of applied behavior analysis. Journal of Applied Behavior Analysis, 1968, 1, 91–97.

Ball, S., & Bogatz, G. A. Summative research of Sesame Street: Implications for the study of preschool children. *In* A. D. Pick (Ed.), *Minnesota Symposia on Child Psychology*, Vol. 6. Minneapolis: University of Minnesota Press, 1972.

Bandura, A. *Principles of behavior modification.* New York: Holt, Rinehart, and Winston, 1969.

Barker, R. G., & Gump, P. V. *Big school, small school.* Stanford, Calif.: Stanford University Press, 1964.

Barrish, H., Saunders, M., & Wolf, M. M. Good behavior game: Effects of individual contingencies for group consequences on disruptive behavior in a classroom. *Journal of Applied Behavior Analysis*, 1969, *2*, 119–124.

Berlin, I. N. Some models for reversing the myth of child treatment in community mental health centers. *Journal of the American Academy of Child Psychiatry*, 1975, *14*, 76–94.

Bernal, M. E., Delfini, L. F., North, J. A., & Kreutzer, S. L. Comparison of boys' behaviors in homes and classrooms. *In* E. J. Mash, L. C. Handy, & L. A. Hamerlynck (Eds.), *Behavior modification approaches to parenting.* New York: Brunner/Mazel, 1976.

Boegli, R. G., & Wasik, B. H. *Use of the token economy system to intervene on a schoolwide level.* Unpublished manuscript, University of North Carolina, 1976.

Braukmann, C. J., Kirigin, K. A., & Wolf, M. M. *Achievement Place: The researchers' perspective.* Paper presented at the American Psychological Association meeting, Washington, D.C., September 1976.

Brazelton, T. B. Symposium on behavioral pediatrics: Anticipatory guidance. *Pediatric Clinics of North America*, 1975, *22*, 533–544.

Broskowski, A., & Baker, F. Professional, organizational, and social barriers to primary prevention. *American Journal of Orthopsychiatry*, 1974, *44*, 707–719.

Broussard, E. R. Evaluation of televised anticipatory guidance to primiparae. *Community Mental Health Journal*, 1976, *12*, 203–210.

Bushell, D. *Classroom behavior.* Englewood Cliffs, N.J.: Prentice-Hall, 1973.

Caplan, G. *Principles of preventive psychiatry.* New York: Basic Books, 1964.

Cataldo, M. F., & Risley, T. R. Infant day care. *In* R. Ulrich, T. Stachnik, & J. Mabry (Eds.), *Control of human behavior*, Vol. 3. Glenview, Ill.: Scott, Foresman, 1974.

Chilman, C. S. Programs for disadvantaged parents. *In* B. M. Caldwell & H. N. Ricciuti (Eds.), *Review of child development research*, Vol. 3. Chicago: University of Chicago Press, 1973.

Christophersen, E. R., Barnard, J. D., Ford, D., & Wolf, M. M. The family training program: Improving parent-child interaction patterns. *In* E. J. Mash, L. C. Handy, & L. A. Hamerlynck (Eds.), *Behavior modification approaches to parenting.* New York: Brunner/Mazel, 1976.

Chu, F., & Trotter, S. *The madness establishment.* New York: Grossman, 1974.

Cobb, J. A., & Hops, H. Effects of academic survival skill training on low achieving first graders. *Journal of Educational Research*, 1973, *67*, 108–113.

Cowen, E. L., Trost, M. A., Lorion, R. P., Dorr, D., Izzo, L. D., & Isaacson, R. V. *New ways in school mental health: Early detection and prevention of school maladaptation.* New York: Behavioral Publications, 1975.

Cowen, E. L., Zax, M., Izzo, L. D., & Trost, M. Prevention of emotional disorders in the school setting. *Journal of Consulting Psychology*, 1966, *30*, 381–387.

Doke, L. A., & Risley, T. R. The organization of day-care environments: Required vs. optional activities. *Journal of Applied Behavior Analysis*, 1972, *5*, 405–420.

Eyberg, S. M., & Johnson, S. M. Multiple assessment of behavior modification with families: Effects of contingency contracting and order of treated problems. *Journal of Consulting and Clinical Psychology*, 1974, *42*, 594–606.

Falender, C. A., & Heber, R. Mother–child interaction and participation in a longitudinal intervention program. *Developmental Psychology*, 1975, *11*, 830–836.

Ferber, H., Keeley, S. M., & Shemberg, K. M. Training parents in behavior modification: Outcome of and problems encountered in a program after Patterson's work. *Behavior Therapy*, 1974, *5*, 415–419.

Fleishman, M. J. Controlled metamorphosis—Taking social learning from laboratory to field. Paper presented at the meeting of the American Psychological Association, Washington, D.C., September 1976.

Forrester, J. Counterintuitive behavior of social systems. *Technology Review*, 1971, *73*, 1–16.

Friedman, S. B. (Ed.). *The pediatric clinics of North America: Symposium on behavioral pediatrics*, Vol. 22, No. 3. Philadelphia: W. B. Saunders, 1975.

Garcia, E. E., Trujillo, A., & Batista, M. An early childhood parent–child centered bilingual–bicultural program. *Young Children*, in press.

Garmezy, N., & Streitman, S. Children at risk: The search for the antecedents of schizophrenia. *Schizophrenia Bulletin*, 1974, No. 8, 14–90.

Gelfand, D. M. Social withdrawal and negative emotional states: Behavior therapy. In B. B. Wolman, A. O. Ross, & J. Egan (Eds.), *Handbook of treatment of mental disorders in childhood and adolescence*. Englewood Cliffs, N.J.: Prentice-Hall, 1977.

Gelfand, D. M., & Hartmann, D. P. *Child behavior analysis and therapy*. New York: Pergamon Press, 1975.

Ginsburg, H. *The myth of the deprived child: poor children's intellect and education*. Englewood Cliffs, N.J.: Prentice-Hall, 1972.

Glidewell, J. C. Priorities for psychologists in community mental Health. In J. C. Glidewell (Ed.), *Issues in community psychology and preventive mental health*. New York: Behavioral Publications, 1971.

Greenwood, C. R., & Hops, H. *Generalization of teacher praising skills over time and setting: What you teach is what you get*. Paper presented at the meeting of the Council for Exceptional Children, Chicago, April, 1976.

Greenwood, C. R., Hops, H., Delquadri, J., & Guild, J. Group contingencies for group consequences in classroom management: A further analysis. *Journal of Applied Behavior Analysis*, 1974, *7*, 413–425.

Greenwood, C. R., Hops, H., & Walker, H. M. *The program for academic survival skills (PASS): Maintenance of changes in student behavior within the same school year*. (Tech. Rep. No. 18). Eugene, Ore.: Center at Oregon for Research in the Behavioral Education of the Handicapped, Center on Human Development, July 1975.

Gump, P. V. Ecological psychology and children. In E. M. Hetherington (Ed.), *Review of child development research*, Vol. 5. Chicago: University of Chicago Press, 1975.

Hall, R. V., & Copeland, R. E. The responsive teaching model: A first step in shaping school personnel as behavior modification specialists. In F. W. Clark, D. R. Evans, & L. A. Hamerlynck (Eds.), *Implementing behavioral programs for schools and clinics*. Champaign, Ill.: Research Press, 1972.

Hall, R. V., Copeland, R., & Clark, M. Management strategies for teachers and parents: Responsive teaching. In N. Haring & R. L. Schiefelbusch (Eds.), *Teaching special children*. New York: McGraw-Hill, 1975.

Harris, V. W., & Sherman, J. A. Use and analysis of the "Good Behavior Game" to reduce disruptive classroom behavior. *Journal of Applied Behavior Analysis*, 1973, *6*, 405–417.

Hawkins, R. P., Peterson, R. F., Schweid, E., & Bijou, S. W. Behavior therapy in the home: Amelioration of problem parent-child relations with the parent in a therapeutic role. *Journal of Experimental Child Psychology*, 1966, *4*, 99–107.

Herbert, E. W., & Baer, D. M. Training parents as behavior modifiers: Self-recording of contingent attention. *Journal of Applied Behavior Analysis*, 1972, 5, 139–149.

Hollingshead, A. B., & Redlich, F. C. *Social class and mental illness.* New York: Wiley, 1958.

Hops, H., & Cobb, J. A. Survival behaviors in the educational setting: Their implications for research and intervention. *In* L. A. Hamerlynck, L. C. Handy, & E. J. Mash (Eds.), *Behavior change: Methodology, concepts, and practice.* Champaign, Ill.: Research Press, 1973.

Hops, H., & Cobb, J. A. Initial investigations into academic survival-skill training, direct instruction, and first-grade achievement. *Journal of Educational Psychology*, 1974, 66, 548–553.

Hops, H., Greenwood, C. R., & Guild, J. J. *Programming generalization of teacher praising skills: How easy is it?* Paper presented at the meeting of the Association for the Advancement of Behavior Therapy, San Francisco, December 1975.

Horowitz, F. D., & Paden, L. Y. The effectiveness of environmental intervention programs. *In* B. M. Caldwell & H. N. Ricciuti (Eds.), *Review of child development research*, Vol. 3. Chicago: University of Chicago Press, 1973.

Iscoe, I., Pierce-Jones, J., Friedman, S. T., & McGehearty, L. Some strategies in mental health consultation: A brief description of a project and some preliminary results. *In* E. L. Cowen, E. A. Gardner, & M. Zax (Eds.), *Emergent approaches to mental health problems.* New York: Appleton-Century-Crofts, 1967.

Jason, L. Early secondary prevention with disadvantaged children. *American Journal of Community Psychology*, 1975, 3, 33–46.

Jason, L., Clarfield, S., & Cowen, E. Preventive intervention with young disadvantaged children. *American Journal of Community Psychology*, 1973, 1, 50–61.

Jason, L. A., Gersten, E., & Yock, T. Relational and behavioral interventions with economically disadvantaged toddlers. *American Journal of Orthopsychiatry*, 1976, 46, 270–278.

Johnson, C. A., & Katz, R. C. Using parents as change agents for their children: A review. *Journal of Child Psychology and Psychiatry*, 1973, 14, 181–200.

Johnson, R., & Machen, J. B. Behavior modification techniques and maternal anxiety. *Journal of Dentistry for Children*, 1973, 40, 272–276.

Jones, R. R. *Achievement Place: The independent evaluator's perspective.* Paper presented at the American Psychological Association meeting, Washington, D.C., September 1976.

Karnes, M. B., Teska, J. A., Hodgins, A. S., & Badger, I. D. Educational intervention at home by mothers of disadvantaged infants. *Child Development*, 1970, 41, 925–935.

Karoly, P., & Rosenthal, M. Training parents in behavior modification: Effects on perceptions of family interaction and deviant child behavior. *Behavior Therapy*, 1977, 8, 406–410.

Kazdin, A. E. Recent advances in token economy research. *In* M. Hersen, R. M. Eisler, & P. M. Miller (Eds.), *Progress in behavior modification*, Vol. 1. New York: Academic Press, 1975.

Kazdin, A. E., & Bootzin, R. R. The token economy: An evaluative review. *Journal of Applied Behavior Analysis*, 1972, 5, 343–372.

Kellman, S. G., & Schiff, S. K. Adaptation and mental illness in the first-grade classrooms of an urban community. Washington, D.C.: American Psychiatric Association, *Psychiatric research report 21: Poverty and mental health*, 1967.

Kelley, J. G., Snowden, L. R., & Muñoz, R. F. Social and community interventions. *In* M. R. Rosenzweig & L. W. Porter (Eds.), *Annual review of psychology*, Vol. 28, Palo Alto, Calif.: Annual Reviews, 1977.

Keutzer, C. S., Fosmire, F. R., Diller, R., & Smith, M. D. Laboratory training in a new social system: Evaluation of a consulting relationship with a high school faculty. *Journal of Applied Behavioral Science*, 1971,*7*, 493–501.

Kifer, R. E., Lewis, M. A., Green, D. R., & Phillips, E. L. Training predelinquent youths and their parents to negotiate conflict situations. *Journal of Applied Behavior Analysis*, 1974, *7*, 357–364.

Klaus, R. A., & Gray, S. W. The early training project for disadvantaged children: A report after five years. *Monographs of the Society for Research in Child Development*, 1968, *33*, (Serial No. 120, Whole No. 4).

Lasater, T. M., Briggs, J., Malone, P., Gilliom, C. F., & Weisburg, P. *The Birmingham model for parent education.* Paper presented at the meeting of the Society for Research in Child Development, Denver, April 1975.

LeLaurin, K., & Risley, T. R. The organization of day-care environments: "Zone" versus "man-to-man" staff assignments. *Journal of Applied Behavior Analysis*, 1972, *5*, 225–232.

Levenstein, P., Kochman, A., & Roth, H. A. From laboratory to real world: Service delivery of the Mother–Child Home Program. *American Journal of Orthopsychiatry*, 1973, *43*, 72–78.

Levine, M., & Graziano, A. M. Intervention programs in elementary schools. *In* S. E. Golann & C. Eisdorfer (Eds.), *Handbook of community mental health.* New York: Appleton-Century-Crofts, 1972.

Lewis, M. D. A study of the relative effects of counseling and consultation upon personal and social adjustment, sociometric status, and achievement oriented behavior of third-grade children. (Doctoral dissertation, University of Michigan, 1969) *Dissertation Abstracts International*, 1970, *31*, 609A. (University Microfilm No. 70-14, #581).

Lieberman, R. P., Ferris, C., Salgado, P., & Salgado, J. Replication of the Achievement Place model in California. *Journal of Applied Behavior Analysis*, 1975, *8*, 287–299.

Lindsley, O. R. Experimental analysis of cooperation and competition. *In* T. Verhave (Ed.), *The experimental analysis of behavior: Selected readings.* New York: Appleton-Century-Crofts, 1966.

Machen, J. B., & Johnson, R. Desensitization, model learning, and the dental behavior of children. *Journal of Dental Research*, 1974, *53*, 83–87.

Madden, P. C. Skinner and the open classroom. *School Review*, 1972, *81*, 100–107.

Madsen, C., Jr., Becker, W., & Thomas, D. Rules, praise, and ignoring: Elements of elementary classroom control. *Journal of Applied Behavior Analysis*, 1968, *1*, 139–150.

Mannino, F. V., & Shore, M. F. The effects of consultation. A review of empirical studies. *American Journal of Community Psychology*, 1975, *3*, 1–21.

Mariner, A. S., Brandt, E., Stone, E. C., & Mirmow, E. L. Group psychiatric consultation with public school personnel. A two-year study. *Personnel and Guidance Journal*, 1961, *40*, 254–258.

McCord, W., McCord, J., & Zola, I. K. *Origins of crime: A new evaluation of the Cambridge-Somerville youth study.* New York: Columbia University Press, 1959.

McPheeters, H. L. Primary prevention and health promotion in mental health. *Preventive Medicine*, 1976, *5*, 187–198.

Mednick, S. A., & Schulsinger, F. Some premorbid characteristics related to breakdown in children with schizophrenic mothers. *In* D. Rosenthal & S. S. Kety (Eds.), *The transmission of schizophrenia.* Oxford: Pergamon Press, 1968.

Melamed, B. G., Hawes, R. R., Heiby, E., & Glick, J. The use of filmed modeling to reduce uncooperative behavior of children during dental treatment. *Journal of Dental Research*, 1975, *54*, 797–801.

Melamed, B. G., & Siegel, L. J. Reduction of anxiety in children facing hospitalization and surgery by use of filmed modeling. *Journal of Consulting and Clinical Psychology,* 1975, *43,* 511–521.

Melamed, B. G., Weinstein, D., Hawes, R., & Katin-Borland, M. Reduction of fear-related dental management problems with use of filmed modeling. *Journal of the American Dental Association,* 1975, *90,* 822–826.

Meyers, A. W., Craighead, W. E., & Meyers, H. H. A behavioral–preventive approach to community mental health. *American Journal of Community Psychology,* 1974, *2,* 275–285.

Miller, W. H. *Systematic parent training: Procedures, cases, and issues.* Champagne, Ill.: Research Press, 1975.

Miller, S. J., & Sloane, H. N. *The generalization effects of parent training across stimulus settings.* Unpublished manuscript, University of Utah, 1976.

Neale, J. M., & Weintraub, S. Children vulnerable to psychopathology: The Stony Brook High-Risk Project. *Journal of Abnormal Child Psychology,* 1975, *3,* 95–113.

Newton, M. R., & Brown, R. D. A preventive approach to developmental problems in school children. *In* E. M. Bower & W. G. Hollister (Eds.), *Behavioral science frontiers in education.* New York: Wiley, 1967.

O'Dell, S. Training parents in behavior modification: A review. *Psychological Bulletin,* 1974, *81,* 418–433.

O'Leary, K. D. Behavior modification in the classroom: A rejoinder to Winett and Winkler. *Journal of Applied Behavior Analysis,* 1972, *5,* 505–511.

O'Leary, K. D., & Drabman, R. S. Token reinforcement programs in the classroom: A review. *Psychological Bulletin,* 1971, *75,* 379–398.

O'Leary, S. G., & O'Leary, K. D. Behavior modification in the school. *In* H. Leitenberg (Ed.), *Handbook of behavior modification and behavior therapy.* Englewood Cliffs, N.J.: Prentice-Hall, 1976.

Ora, J. P., & Reisinger, J. J. Preschool intervention: A behavior service delivery system. Paper presented at the American Psychological Association meeting, Washington, D.C., September 1971.

Patterson, G. R. Intervention for boys with conduct problems: Multiple settings, treatments, and criteria. *Journal of Consulting and Clinical Psychology,* 1974, *42,* 471–481.

Patterson, G. R. The aggressive child: Victim and architect of a coercive system. *In* L. A. Hamerlynck, L. C. Handy, & E. J. Mash (Eds.), *Behavior modification and families: Vol. 1. Theory and research.* New York: Brunner/Mazel, 1976.

Patterson, G. R., & Reid, J. B. Reciprocity and coercion: Two facets of social systems. *In* C. Neuringer & J. Michael (Eds.), *Behavior modification in clinical psychology.* New York: Appleton-Century-Crofts, 1970.

Patterson, G. R., Reid, J. B., Jones, R. R., & Conger, R. E. *A social learning approach to family intervention,* Vol. 1. Eugene, Ore.: Castalia Publishing Co., 1975.

Phillips, E. L., Phillips, E. A., Fixsen, D. L., & Wolf, M. M. Achievement Place: Modification of the behaviors of pre-delinquent boys within a token economy. *Journal of Applied Behavior Analysis,* 1971, *4,* 45–59.

Poser, E. G. Toward a theory of "behavioral prophylaxis." *Journal of Behavior Therapy and Experimental Psychiatry,* 1970, *1,* 39–43.

Poser, E. G., & King, M. C. *Primary prevention of fear: An experimental approach.* Unpublished manuscript, McGill University, Montreal, 1975.

Quilitch, H. R., & Risley, T. R. The effects of play materials on social play. *Journal of Applied Behavior Analysis,* 1973, *6,* 573–578.

Ragins, N., Schachter, J., Elmer, E., Preisman, R., Bowers, A. E., & Harway, V. Infants and children at risk for schizophrenia. *Journal of the American Academy of Child Psychiatry,* 1975, *14,* 150–177.

Reisinger, J. J., Frangia, G. W., & Hoffman, E. H. Toddler Management training: Generalization and marital status. *Journal of Behavior Therapy and Experimental Psychiatry,* in press.

Reisinger, J. J., & Ora, J. P. Parent–child clinic and home interaction during Toddler Management training. *Behavior therapy,* in press.

Reisinger, J. J., Ora, J. P., & Frangia, G. W. Parents as change agents for their children: A review. *American Journal of Community Psychology,* 1976, *4,* 103–123.

Rinn, R. C., Vernon, J. C., & Wise, M. J. Training parents of behaviorally disordered children in groups: A three years' program evaluation. *Behavior Therapy,* 1975, *6,* 378–387.

Rolf, J. E. Peer status and the directionality of symptomatic behavior: Prime social competence predictors of outcome for vulnerable children. *American Journal of Orthopsychiatry,* 1976, *46,* 74–88.

Rolf, J. E., & Harig, P. T. Etiological research in schizophrenia and the rationale for primary intervention. *American Journal of Orthopsychiatry,* 1974,*44,* 538–554.

Sanford, N. Is the concept of prevention necessary or useful? *In* S. Golman & C. Eisdorfer (Eds.), *Handbook of Community Mental Health,* New York: Appleton-Century-Crofts, 1972.

Schmuck, R. A. Helping teachers improve classroom group processes. *Journal of Applied Behavioral Science,* 1968, *4,* 401–435.

Snider, J., Sullivan, W., & Manning, D. Industrial engineering participation in a special education program. *Tennessee Engineer,* 1974, *1,* 367–373.

Specter, G., & Cowen, E. A pilot study in stimulation of culturally deprived infants. *Child Psychiatry and Human Development,* 1971, *1,* 168–177.

Srole, L., Langer, T. S., Michael, S. T., Opler, M. K., & Rennie, T. A. C. *Mental health in the metropolis: Midtown Manhattan study.* Vol. 1. New York: McGraw-Hill, 1962.

Stallings, J. Implementation and child effects of teaching practices in Follow Through classrooms. *Monographs of the Society for Research in Child Development,* 1975, *40* (7–8, Serial No. 163).

Stuart, R. B. Behavioral contracting within the families of delinquents. *Journal of Behavior Therapy and Experimental Psychiatry,* 1971, *2,* 1–11.

Stumphauzer, J. S., Aiken, T. W., & Veloz, E. V. East side story: Behavioral analysis of a high juvenile crime community: Alternative to incarceration? Unpublished manuscript, University of Southern California Medical Center; Los Angeles, 1976.

Surwit, R. *The anticipatory modification of the conditioning of a fear response in humans.* Unpublished doctoral dissertation, McGill University, 1972.

Tavormina, J. B. Basic models of parent counseling: A critical review. *Psychological Bulletin,* 1974, *81,* 827–835.

Teitelbaum, D. I. An evaluation of an experimental program of assistance for newly appointed teachers in certain elementary schools of New York City. (Doctoral dissertation, New York University, 1961). *Dissertation Abstracts International,* 1962, *23,* 159. (University Microfilm No. 62-1457).

Tharp, P. G., & Wetzel, R. J. *Behavior modification in the natural environment.* New York: Academic Press, 1969.

Thomas, D. R., Becker, W. C., & Armstrong, M. Production and elimination of disruptive classroom behavior by systematically varying teachers' behavior. *Journal of Applied Behavior Analysis,* 1968, *1,* 35–45.

Thurlow, B. H. A comparative analysis of the elementary counseling role and the elementary consulant role with selected anxious fifth grade students. (Doctoral dissertation, University of Maine, 1971). *Dissertation Abstracts International,* 1972, *32,* 4362A. (University Microfilm No. 72-5629).

Trotter, R. Environment and behavior: Intensive intervention program prevents retardation. *APA Monitor*, September/October 1976, pp. 4–5; 19; 46.

Turner, C. W., & Goldsmith, D. Effects of toy guns and airplanes on children's antisocial free play behavior. *Journal of Experimental Child Psychology*, 1976, *21*, 303–315.

Twardosz, S., Cataldo, M. F., & Risley, T. R. Infants' use of crib toys. *Young Children*, 1974a, *29*, 271–276.

Twardosz, S., Cataldo, M. F., & Risley, T. R. Open environment design for infant and toddler day care. *Journal of Applied Behavior Analysis*, 1974b, *7*, 529–546.

Tyler, M. M. A study of some selected parameters of school psychologist–teacher consultation. (Doctoral dissertation, University of Kansas, 1971.) *Dissertation Abstracts International*, 1972, *32*, 5626 A. (University Microfilm No. 72-11, #721).

Ullmann, L. P., & Krasner, L. *A psychological approach to abnormal behavior*, 2nd ed. Englewood Cliffs, N.J.: Prentice-Hall, 1975.

Van Alstyne, D. *Play behavior and choice of play materials of pre-school children*. Chicago: University of Chicago Press, 1932.

Wahler, R. G. Deviant child behavior within the family: Development speculations and behavior change strategies. *In* H. Leitenberg (Ed.), *Handbook of behavior modification*. New York: Appleton-Century-Crofts, 1976.

Waldron, S., Jr. The significance of childhood neurosis for adult mental health: A follow-up study. *American Journal of Psychiatry*, 1976, *133*, 532–538.

Walker, H. M., & Buckley, N. K. Programming generalization and maintenance of treatment effects across time and across settings. *Journal of Applied Behavior Analysis*, 1972, *5*, 209–224.

Walter, H. I., & Gilmore, S. K. Placebo versus social learning effects in parent training procedures designed to alter the behaviors of aggressive boys. *Behavior Therapy*, 1973, *4*, 366–377.

Watson, L. S., & Bassinger, J. F. Parent training technology: A potential service delivery system. *Mental Retardation*, 1974, *12*, 3–10.

Willems, E. P. Behavioral technology and behavioral ecology. *Journal of Applied Behavior Analysis*, 1974, *7*, 151–165.

Wiltz, N. A., & Patterson, G. R. An evaluation of parent training procedures designed to alter inappropriate aggressive behaviors of boys. *Behavior Therapy*, 1974, *5*, 215–221.

Winett, R. A., & Winkler, R. C. Current behavior modification in the classroom: Be still, be quiet, be docile. *Journal of Applied Behavior Analysis*, 1972, *5*, 499–504.

Zax, M., & Cowen, E. L. Early identification and prevention of emotional disturbance in a public school. *In* E. L. Cowen, E. A. Gardner, & M. Zax (Eds.), *Emergent approaches to mental health problems*. New York: Appleton-Century-Crofts, 1967.

Name Index

Subject Index

A B experimental design, 49
ABA experimental design, 205
ABAB or reversal design, 7
A=B=C model of behavioral assessment, 49
academic performance, reinforcement of, in controlling classroom misbehavior and remediating academic deficits, 88-89, 102-106, 113
  school-based prevention programs, 376-379
accountability of psychological services to children, 3
achievement place model of treatment for delinquency, 372-374
achievement tests, role in behavioral assessment, 48, 66-68
aggression, 164, 175, 313-314
  in hypermasculine boys, 267
  indirect aggression and popularity, 168
  provoked physical aggression and popularity, 168
altruism, 162
amphetamines, 236
analogue treatment studies, 12
assertiveness training, 191-194
autism, 329-330
  classroom instruction, 338-343
  generalization and maintenance of behavior change, 334-337
  modeling in treatment, 315-316
  parent and teacher training, 337-338
  perinatal factors, 134

autism (*cont'd*)
  response generalization, 343-344; self-injurious behavior, 330; self-stimulatory behavior, 332-333, 349-352
  stimulus overselectivity, 333-334, 344-347

BASIC—ID model of behavioral assessment, 49
behavioral assessment, 47
  A=B=C model, 49
  BASIC—ID model, 49
  behavior rating scales, 56-60
  classification, 50-54
  and diagnosis, 50
  direct observation, 60-65
  ecological assessment, 53
  educational prescription, 73-75
  factor and cluster analysis, 51
  functional analysis of behavior, 49
  interviews, 54-56
  multifaceted model, 68
  the psychological evaluation, 69-76
  psychophysiological assessment, 65-66
  response channels, 48
  role of intelligence and achievement tests, 48
  self-recording, 64
  S=O=R=K=C model, 49
behavior rating scales, 56-60
  factor analysis, 5
  reliability and validity, 57-60
bias, sources in treatment studies, 22-23

409